**Studia Fennica**
Litteraria 11

The Finnish Literature Society (SKS) was founded in 1831 and has, from the very beginning, engaged in publishing operations. It nowadays publishes literature in the fields of ethnology and folkloristics, linguistics, literary research and cultural history.

The first volume of the Studia Fennica series appeared in 1933. Since 1992, the series has been divided into three thematic subseries: Ethnologica, Folkloristica and Linguistica. Two additional subseries were formed in 2002, Historica and Litteraria. The subseries Anthropologica was formed in 2007.

In addition to its publishing activities, the Finnish Literature Society maintains research activities and infrastructures, an archive containing folklore and literary collections, a research library and promotes Finnish literature abroad.

Studia Fennica Editorial Board

Editors-in-chief
Pasi Ihalainen, Professor, University of Jyväskylä, Finland
Timo Kallinen, University Lecturer, University of Helsinki, Finland
Taru Nordlund, Professor, University of Helsinki, Finland
Riikka Rossi, Title of Docent, University Researcher, University of Helsinki, Finland
Katriina Siivonen, Title of Docent, University Teacher, University of Turku, Finland
Lotte Tarkka, Professor, University of Helsinki, Finland

Deputy editors-in-chief
Anne Heimo, Title of Docent, University of Turku, Finland
Saija Isomaa, Professor, University of Tampere, Finland
Sari Katajala-Peltomaa, Title of Docent, Researcher, University of Tampere, Finland
Eerika Koskinen-Koivisto, Postdoctoral Researcher, Dr. Phil., University of Helsinki, Finland
Kenneth Sillander, University Lecturer, University of Helsinki, Finland
Laura Visapää, Title of Docent, University Lecturer, University of Helsinki, Finland

Tuomas M. S. Lehtonen, Secretary General, Dr. Phil., Finnish Literature Society, Finland
Tero Norkola, Publishing Director, Finnish Literature Society, Finland
Anu Miller, Secretary of the Board, Finnish Literature Society, Finland

oa.finlit.fi

Editorial Office
SKS
P.O. Box 259
FI-00171 Helsinki
www.finlit.fi

# Migrants and Literature in Finland and Sweden

Edited by Satu Gröndahl and Eila Rantonen

Finnish Literature Society · SKS · Helsinki · 2018

**STUDIA FENNICA LITTERARIA 11**

The publication has undergone a peer review.

© 2018 Satu Gröndahl, Eila Rantonen and SKS
License CC-BY-NC-ND 4.0 International

A digital edition of a printed book first published in 2018 by the Finnish Literature Society.

Cover Design: Timo Numminen
EPUB: Tero Salmén

ISBN 978-952-222-992-2 (Print)
ISBN 978-951-858-035-8 (PDF)
ISBN 978-951-858-034-1 (EPUB)

ISSN 0085-6835 (Studia Fennica)
ISSN 1458-5278 (Studia Fennica Litteraria)

DOI: http://dx.doi.org/10.21435/sflit.11

This work is licensed under a Creative Commons CC-BY-NC-ND 4.0 International License.
To view a copy of the license, please visit http://creativecommons.org/licenses/by-nc-nd/4.0/

 A free open access version of the book is available at http://dx.doi.org/10.21435/sflit.11 or by scanning this QR code with your mobile device.

BoD – Books on Demand, Norderstedt, Germany 2018

# Contents

RANTONEN, EILA & GRÖNDAHL, SATU
Acknowledgements 7

## I Cartography of the Field

ANNE HEITH, SATU GRÖNDAHL & EILA RANTONEN
Introduction: 'The Minoritarian Condition'. Studies in Finnish
and Swedish Literatures after World War II 11

## II Generational Shifts

SATU GRÖNDAHL
Sweden-Finnish Literature: Generational and Cultural Changes 37

MARJA SORVARI
Native, Foreign, Translated? 'Russian' Migrant Literature between Finland
and Russia 57

## III Reception and Multicultural Perspectives

KUKKU MELKAS
Literature and Children in-between – the Entangled History of Finland
and Sweden in *Svinalängorna*, *Mother of Mine* and *Ingenbarnsland* 83

JOHANNA DOMOKOS
The Multicultural Dynamics and the Finnish Literary Field 97

HANNA-LEENA NISSILÄ
Women Writers with Im/migrant Backgrounds: Transnationalizing Finnish
Literature – Perspectives on the Reception of Debut Novels by Lindén,
ElRamly, Abu-Hanna and Salmela 113

## IV Writing Migrant Identities

ANNE HEITH
The African Diaspora, Migration and Writing: Johannes Anyuru's *En civilisation utan båtar*  141

PIRJO AHOKAS
Is Love Thicker Than Blood? A Bi-cultural Identity Process in Astrid Trotzig's *Blod är tjockare än vatten*  166

MARTA RONNE
Narratives of Exile, Gender and Disability in Swedish-Latvian Zenta Mauriņas Autobiographical Writings  187

EILA RANTONEN
Writing Biography by E-mail – Postcolonial and Postmodern Rewriting of Biographical and Epistolary Modes in Jonas Hassen Khemiri's *Montecore*  204

List of Contributors  225
Abstract  229
Index of Names  231

# Acknowledgements

The quest of writing this book arose at the colloquium 'The Contemporary Migrant Novel in Quebec and Scandinavia: Performativity, Meaningful Conflicts and Creolization', which was held in Turku in September 2011. There we discussed that there was a specific need for a comparative study dealing with migrant issues in Finnish and Swedish literature. At that time, only a few Nordic scholars were specialized in this research area. Since 2011 the interest in these issues has significantly increased. We can mention, for example, the organization DINO (Diversity in Nordic literature), which has been an important forum for the researchers, who study migration and minority issues in literature. Further IASS (International Association of Scandinavian Studies) has organized important conferences including migrant issues.

When this volume was in process in 2015, there was a rapid increase in the number of asylum seekers to Europe. Over 1.3 million people sought asylum in Europe because of the conflicts in Syria, Iraq and Afghanistan. This made the account of displaced people the highest level since World War II. To Sweden fled circa 163 000 asylum seekers via various parts of Europe. This led to the restoring of border controls. Over 32 000 asylum seekers, mostly Iraqis and Afghans, entered Finland over the land border of Sweden and Russia. The reaction of Finnish Red Cross was efficient to this unexpected situation. New reception centers for the asylum seekers were grounded rapidly all over Finland. This resulted in Arabic becoming quite unexpectedly the third largest foreign language spoken in Finland.

The process of editing the volume has not been without its hardships. In the past years, due to various reasons, the project has been delayed. We greatly thank and acknowledge the contribution of the Kordelin Foundation and the Finnish Literature Society for funding this volume. We also want to thank Associate Professor Anne Heath for joining us in the making of the introduction of the volume and translator Judith Crawford for the careful checking of the language of most of the articles. Heith's contribution is the outcome of the research project 'Other Places in Literature: Sápmi, Meänmaa and Migrant Cartographies' funded by Umeå University. We are especially grateful to the Finnish Literature Society for including our book in the Studia Fennica Litteraria publication series. Moreover, we want to express our gratitude to our two anonymous peer reviewers whose careful comments on our manuscript helped us greatly in the revision of the volume.

Finally, we owe our greatest debt of gratitude to the editor-in-chief of the Studia Fennica Litteraria series Docent, Ph.D. Riikka Rossi for her invaluable assistance and patience with the volume.

We want to dedicate this book to our friend Ph.D. Matti Savolainen, who was devoted to the studies of a range of minorities.

Tampere and Uppsala, January 2018
*Eila Rantonen and Satu Gröndahl*

# Cartography of the Field

Anne Heith
https://orcid.org/0000-0002-0682-2668

Satu Gröndahl
https://orcid.org/0000-0002-7471-6306

Eila Rantonen
https://orcid.org/0000-0002-1807-4361

# Introduction: 'The Minoritarian Condition'. Studies in Finnish and Swedish Literatures after World War II

When people are in motion, it changes nations, national and ethnic identities, cultures, people and peoples. *Migrants and Literature in Finland and Sweden* presents new comparative perspectives on cultural transformations and depiction of migration in Finnish and Swedish literature. The volume provides a contribution to the production of new narratives of the nation during recent decades synthesising and comparing Finnish and Swedish literatures. The volume, thus, offers a unique comparative perspective to the study of Nordic literature, since Finnish literature, especially, is often separated from the Nordic literary studies and literary contexts.

*Migrants and Literature in Finland and Sweden* explores the ways in which intersectional identities and transcultural connections have affected the national self-understanding in the Nordic context and how they relate to concepts and conditions of marginal situations including race, gender, class and disability. Many articles of the volume tackle the issues of reception and classification and ask how experiences of migration have resulted in new modes of writing and generic innovations. Narratives of migration depict Finland and Sweden being lived not only transnationally but also transculturally. The latter signifies how individuals and social groups are no longer cultures but people. It is a question of what individuals and social groups do with culture in an increasingly globalized world (Schulze-Engler 2009, 93). In this volume, studies of fiction and autobiographies lucidly show how migrational processes, cultural transformations and transcultural connections are experienced on an individual level.

The volume demonstrates the complexity of grouping literatures according to nation and ethnicity producing such categories such as 'Finnish literature', 'Swedish literature' or 'immigrant literature', which recently been under discussion. For instance, in 2007, the Karelian Finnish writer Arvi Perttu strongly asserted that the missing pages of migrants living in Finland should be written. He also insisted that Finnish literary institutions should be more open to writers who have a migrant background. Another author, Somali-Swedish Mohamed Hassan, who works at the Scansom publishing house in Stockholm, defiantly proclaimed in 2008, 'We are here, whether you like it or not!' at the 'Kielten kudos [Tissue of Language] – textum linguarum' seminar in Helsinki dealing with multicultural writing in Finland and Sweden. Perttu's and Hassan's proposals exemplify a call for more visibility of authors with a minority background. However, migrants are not a homogeneous category and the obstacles to being acknowledged by the dominant national literary field which the major literary institutions are part of vary. When considering issues of presence and visibility in relation to literary fields, it is important to have in mind the target groups of the works of authors with a minority background. To claim that migrants *per se* are marginalised is a simplification. It is obvious that there are barriers when it comes to language. Authors writing in minority languages such as Karelian and Somali, for example, are often not acknowledged by the dominant national literary field simply because they will not reach out to readers in the majority population, including those actors in the literary field, such as publishers, academics and critics, who may contribute to the visibility and success of a writer.

The fact that migration and minority status are diverse and multifaceted phenomena is illustrated by the authors mentioned above. Minority groups may be seen as more or less 'strange' and 'alien' compared to the ethnic majority. This is certainly the case in Finland and Sweden where black Muslim migrants from Africa often are seen as more different than white European immigrants. For immigrants themselves who have been violently uprooted, the contexts of upheaval vary. They may have been subjected to displacement due to shifting national borders as in the case of the Karelians, or as an effect of conflicts on geographically distant continents such as Africa.

The studies in part II, III and IV of this volume relate to different geographical and historical contexts, which are interconnected with the various forms of migration that have led to the arrival of people who have found themselves struggling to cope with Finnish and Swedish society, respectively. Experiences of encounters with the new country, which by and by may become the new homeland, are reflected in imaginative writing by authors with experiences of migration. The migration of Finnish labourers to Sweden is reflected in Satu Gröndahl's and Kukku Melkas's contributions to this volume, the latter also discusses material related to the placing of Finnish war children ('krigsbarn') in Sweden during World War II. Migration between Russia and Finland is discussed by Marja Sorvari, while Johanna Domokos attempts at mapping the Finnish literary field and offering a model for literary analysis. Transformations of the Finnish literary field are also the focus of Hanna-Leena Nissilä's article discussing the reception of novels by a selection of women authors with an im/migrant background.

The African diaspora and the arrival of refugees to Europe from African countries due to wars and political conflicts in the 1970s is the backdrop of Anne Heith's analysis of migration and literature, while Pirjo Ahokas deals with literature related to the experiences of a Korean adoptee in Sweden. Migration from Africa to Sweden also forms the setting of Eila Rantonen's article about a novel by a successful, Swedish author with roots in Tunisia. Exile, gender and disability are central, intertwined themes of Marta Ronne's article, which discusses the work of a Swedish-Latvian author who arrived

*Helena Laukkanen's collages Jag ('I') 1999–2009. Each spiral includes all 'I-words' cut out from one novel and can be seen as an illustration for the fragility of the modern subject. Photo: Jouni Suomalainen / Liekki ruotsinsuomalainen kulttuurilehti.*

in Sweden in connection to World War II. As this brief survey indicates, migration is a heterogeneous phenomenon, and migrants do not share a common history or cultural background. However, there are experiences which migrants share, namely the encounter with a new country, a new language and new traditions. These encounters may be described as frustrating, but also as transformative when ideas of home and belonging change. It is not rare that authors describe feelings of multiple belongings and the shaping of new hybrid identities and cultural forms that emerge when the baggage from the past is intertwined or replaced with experiences of living in a new country, which gradually becomes more and more familiar.

The Finnish literary institutions mentioned by Arvi Perttu above are part of a literary field where mechanisms of exclusion and inclusion operate. In Bourdieu's influential description of the literary field, the concept of 'cultural capital' plays an important role for analysing issues of power, inclusion and exclusion (Bourdieu 1996). People with the appropriate cultural capital have the power to make statements about literary value, which an author's success or failure is based upon. If we accept Bourdieu's model, it is hardly correct to claim that all authors with a minority background are marginalised. On the contrary, it is a significant feature of the contemporary literary scene both in Finland and Sweden that there are authors with a minority background who have been very successful when it comes to getting positive attention in major national newspapers, as well as other media. This means that they have been successful on the dominant literary field. To some extent, alternative literary flora has emerged in connection to possibilities for getting subsidies for publishing literature in minority languages. This development is related to political decisions aiming at supporting publishing in minority languages.

In Sweden, The Swedish Arts Council has granted support for literature published in immigrant languages since the 1970s, the decade when immigrant policy in general was reformulated by the Swedish government. When it comes to authors with an immigrant background, there are both commercially successful authors published by the major commercial publishers in Finland and Sweden, as well as writers published by small publishing houses with a specific ethnic, cultural or ideological profile. The status of these publishers varies. In a study of 'immigrant' and 'minority' literature in Sweden between 1970–2000, Lars Wendelius suggests that Swedish publishers of fiction form a hierarchy with four levels. The old, well-established, Stockholm publishers Bonniers and Norstedts are found on the most prestigious top level, while publishers with an ethnic profile are found at the bottom (Wendelius 2002, 25).

There are also transnational publishing houses engaged in publishing for diasporic groups. Scansom Publishers, mentioned above, describes itself as 'the leading publisher and distributor in Somali language materials' on its website. Considering the marginal status of Somali languages in Finland and Sweden, it is hardly surprising that literature in Somali languages receives little attention in the Finnish and Swedish literary fields, respectively. The target group of literature in Somali languages is a transnational, diasporic group of readers. As a rule, this type of literature does not get any attention on the dominant national literary field in Finland or Sweden. However, if an author of African descent writes in Finnish or Swedish in Finland and Sweden respectively, there is the possibility that s/he may be appreciated for providing new perspectives on the new homeland when depicting it from the vantage point of a stranger. This is the case, for example, in Swedish Sami Said's successful first novel *Väldigt sällan fin* from 2012 (Heith 2016). Said, who was born in Eritrea, came to Sweden at the age of ten. The reception of Said's novel shows that being black and a Muslim, and writing fiction about it in a predominantly white society, may prove to be positive assets when critics with a cultural capital that qualifies them as literary judges applaud the work as interesting and important. If an author with a migrant background and roots in a culture traditionally seen as alien to white European culture, such as African cultures, successfully writes about the particular experiences of being black Muslim and Swedish, there is nothing to indicate that this author will be marginalised on the literary field (Heith 2016).

However, there are different responses to how to deal with issues such as ethnicity and background. While Arvi Perttu and Mohamed Hassan seem to wish for more visibility of the authors with a minority and migrant background, there are also those who wish to dismiss the category of ethnicity altogether. In an essay from 2005, the Swedish writer Astrid Trotzig critically examines categorisations such as 'suburban novel' ('förortsroman') and 'immigrant literature' ('invandrarlitteratur', Trotzig 2005). The essay is included in a volume about Orientalism in Sweden and it is presented as an example of how authors with an immigrant background are exotified and othered in Swedish mainstream culture (Matthis ed. 2005).[1] But, there are also diametrically different responses to terms such as 'immigrant writer'. Finnish Zinaida Lindén, for example, who has been described in reviews as an immigrant author, does not perceive this label negatively, declaring that 'I'm definitely an immigrant author' (Hämäläinen 2005).

There are many examples of successful author's with a minority background, and experiences of migration, who extensively use themes related to migration and minority status in their work (Heith 2004, Heith 2012, Heith 2014). In fact, this forms a body of literature which transforms national literatures in both Finland and Sweden by introducing new perspectives, themes and modes of writing. It is obvious that themes like ethnicity, race, cultural – and not least religious – diversity, cultural encounters, as well as issues of transforming identities, home and belonging are explored in contemporary Finnish and Swedish literature related to experiences of minority status and migration. Backdrop of this volume is the fact that nations are transformed and that this calls for new modes of writing. The volume brings together researchers from various countries doing research on intersections between cultural transformations, transnationalism and migration in Finland and Sweden.

The focus of the contributions is contemporary fiction relating to experiences of transnational migration and changing borders as in the case of the Karelian migration to Finland. Other central themes are cultural transformations related to the displacement of groups of people and the emergence of new cultural forms. Migratory flows are discussed below in the section 'Migration to Sweden and Finland: Refugees and labour immigrants'. Migration and cultural diversity are central themes of this volume, but it must be kept in mind that neither migration, nor cultural diversity, are new phenomena. A study of multicultural Sweden claims that Sweden, historically, has never been as cosmopolitan as it was in the 17$^{th}$ century, when political debates were held in Low German, Dutch and Swedish (Svanberg & Runblom 1990, 9).

The development of a body of literature by authors with experiences of transnational migration has been different in Sweden and Finland. In Sweden, this kind of literature has been part of the literary field since World War II, while in Finland this cultural phenomenon has become visible only during the last decades. As mentioned above, the aim of this volume is to offer perspectives on transformations of the nation, which occur when the Finnish and Swedish society and culture are narrated by transnational migrants, or citizens with an immigrant background.

---

1   Also see Magnus Nilsson's study *Den föreställda mångkulturen. Klass och etnicitet i svensk samtidsprosa* (Nilsson 2010). Nilsson dismisses studies of ethnicity while proposing that class is a more relevant category to investigate. This perspective is not relevant for this volume, although Satu Gröndahl discusses ethnicity *and* class as relevant categories for analysing literature relating to the migration of Finnish labourers to Sweden.

## Some Reflections upon Terminology

The time span in focus for this volume is the period after World War II. Naturally, the terminology for categorising and analysing literature related to migration has changed during the decades. Today there are a number of concepts and theories for analysing this literature. Concepts such as 'multicultural literature', 'postcolonialism', 'transculturalism', 'transnationalism', 'migrant writer', 'migration literature' and 'migratory aesthetics' are problematized in contemporary literary theory. The abundance of terms demonstrates that the concepts connected with immigration are socially and politically charged. For instance, the concept of 'immigrant literature' has been contested and new terms have been proposed. As the diametrically opposite views of the authors Astrid Trotzig and Zinaida Lindén concerning the terms 'immigrant literature' and 'immigrant author' mentioned above show, there are different responses to terminology and there is no consensus that terms like 'immigrant literature' or 'migrant literature/s' *per se* are essentialising or marginalising.

In some of the case-studies the term 'migrant literature' is used. However, the term ought to be used with caution. Merolla and Ponzanesi highlight problematic aspects of the term, such as the issue of when an individual ceases to be a migrant (Ponzanesi & Merolla 2005, 25). Still, Merolla and Ponzanesi themselves use the term 'migrant literatures'. Another potential problem with the term is its vagueness when used in an extended fashion for designating migration in a symbolic sense. If everybody experiencing flux and transformation is seen as a migrant, the term is no longer useful for categorisations of specific forms of literature. The articles of this volume deal with various forms of migration in a literal sense; thus, when considering the thematics, the terms 'migrant literature' or 'migration literature' are relevant. The term 'migration literature' has been proposed in order to define imaginative writing by *textual, thematic* and *stylistic* criteria (Gebauer & Schwartz Lausten 2010, 4).

In social and literary theory, new concepts that attempt to describe the migratory phenomenon, at the same time avoiding the concepts of 'immigrant', 'migrant' or 'migration', are constantly being proposed. For example, Simon Harel, among others, prefers the term *'postexilic writing'* instead of migrant writing (see Lindberg 2013, 16.). This resembles an older term, *exile literature*, which describes the mental, political and social process of migration and writing literature in exile. Furthermore, Anders Olsson has underlined that modern 'exile literature' is intimately connected to a wide and sophisticated understanding of 'world literature', written by trans-border authors who do not 'have a specific national foothold' (Olsson 2011, 186).

Migrants oscillate between nations, cultures and languages, their presence can thus be seen as a questioning of the supposedly homogeneous nature of nations, cultures and languages. This view has gained ground in the discussions of postcolonial theory concerning alternative spaces, a third space, and contact zones. In the essay 'The Commitment to Theory', Homi K. Bhabha discusses 'the Third Space' as a 'contradictory and ambivalent space of enunciation', which destabilises the 'the narrative of the Western nation'

*What does the world and literature look like without 'I' as a subject? Are our Western literary institutions falling apart? Helena Laukkanen's work of installation art* Jag. Bokskåpet *('I. The Book Case', 1999–2009) consists of books, cut up, without the word 'I'. Photo: Jouni Suomalainen / Liekki ruotsinsuomalainen kulttuurilehti.*

(Bhabha 2008, 54–55). The concept of the 'contact zone' was developed by Pratt to describe social spaces where 'disparate cultures meet, clash and grapple with each other, often in highly asymmetrical relations of dominance and subordination – like colonialism, slavery, or their aftermaths as they are lived out across the globe today' (Pratt 1992, 4). Both the idea of the third space and that of the contact zone has been used in analyses of fiction about encounters between migrants and their new places of residence in order to describe new hybrid cultural forms. For example, Søren Frank characterises the in-between-state of migrants and migration literature as a vibrant and hybrid space that challenges the dualisms with which we categorize the world; migration literature occupies a middle ground where the exclusive either-or can be transformed into an inclusive both-and (Frank 2010, 40–41).

In the present discussion about problematizing nation-building in Finland, the concepts 'transnational literatures' and 'entangled literatures' have been proposed (Pollari et al. 2015, 2–29). This reflects the fact that deficiencies have been observed in the terms 'post-colonial literature' and 'diasporic literature' in referring to cross-cultural literary writing (Ashcroft, Griffiths & Tiffin 2009, 214). The concept 'entangled literatures' has been gaining ground, not least in Estonian studies of national literature.[2] Transnational writing can take place both inside and outside the nation. It presents literature as a travelling phenomenon that changes the cultures of the spaces it enters and is itself changed by them in return. Transnational literature may free literature from the ideological baggage of national concerns as Azaze Seyhan (2010, 13) suggests. The broad definition of 'migration literature' covers the studying of transcultural, transnational and translingual aspects.

Another term that is relevant when considering literature related to the dispersal and displacement of various groups of people is that of 'diaspora literature'. As mentioned above, some prefer the term 'transnational writing' or 'entangled literatures' when focusing upon cross-cultural writing. The term 'diaspora literature' has in particular been used in analyses of the dispersal of black people with roots in Africa (Beezmohun ed. 2016), but also in connection to other groups that have been violently up-rooted from their countries of origin. When discussing the emergence of black cultures in locations where people with African roots have settled, Stuart Hall proposes the term 'diaspora aesthetics' (Hall 1997; Heith 2014).

Recently more attention has been paid to the aesthetic distinctiveness of 'migration literature'. For example, the 'migrant novel' has been defined as *a specific genre* that has its own formal criteria and historical range. Frank (2010, 47–48) emphasizes that through its form, the migrant novel expresses the experiences of cultural relations and globalization. For example, Seyhan (2010, 18) notes that national belonging appears as a trope, in the form of an allegory or metonymy, in the work of many writers situated within and outside a nation. This trope may take, for example, the form of a melancholy longing for a specific city as a metonymy of the old homeland.

## *Theoretical Vantage Points: Postcolonialism, the Minoritarian Condition and New Literatures*

A central theme of postcolonial theory is how minorities and migrants contribute to alternative narratives of the nation, which deconstruct cultural homogenisation based on the notion that the majority has the preferential right of interpretation and that the ethnic majority constitutes a norm, which other groups ought to conform to (Bhabha ed. 2008). These themes have been highlighted in discussions of postcolonialism in the Nordic Region; the role of minorities in changing ideas of the nation is emphasised, including both domestic minorities and groups with an immigrant background (Rantonen

---

2   The aim of the Estonian project 'Entangled Literatures: Discursive History of Literary Culture in Estonia' which runs between 2014–2019 is to rewrite homogenising narratives of Estonian literary history by drawing attention to input from different cultural traditions and linguistic spaces.

& Savolainen 2002). In particular, ideas of Nordic exceptionalism have been challenged as well as implicit notions of Nordic superiority (Keskinen et al eds. 2009; Loftsdóttir & Jensen eds. 2012). When discussing this theme in *Complying with Colonialism: Gender, Race and Ethnicity in the Nordic Region*, Keskinen et al. appropriate Spivak's concept of 'colonial complicity', claiming that colonising structures and practices which have marginalised and racialised minorities and immigrants have prevailed in the Nordic countries, as they have elsewhere (Keskinen et al. 2009).

This is also the major theme of the volume *Whiteness and Postcolonialism in the Nordic Region: Exceptionalism, Migrant Others and National Identities*, which aims at problematizing notions of Nordic exceptionalism, the idea that the Nordic nation-states are more democratic, egalitarian, and modern than the rest of the world (Loftsdóttir & Jensen 2012, 1–11). The notion of Nordic exceptionalism is connected with the shaping of national self-images based on the idea that 'we' are more progressive, modern and enlightened than 'them'. This mode of thinking is presently being problematized in critical whiteness studies, which emphasise that whiteness is socially constructed and that there are various forms of whiteness. In the context of Swedish race biology, for example, which flourished in the 1930s, the so called 'Nordic racial character' was constructed as the superior racial category, while other groups, such as the Sámi and the Tornedalians were seen as 'not quite white' (Lundborg & Linders 1926; Heith 2012b; Heith 2015).

In the preface of the Routledge Classics Edition of *The Location of Culture*, Bhabha discusses a 'minoritarian condition', which he claims is a kind of global citizenship (Bhabha 2008, xxi). Bhabha's discussion is related to migration in the last two or three decades characterised by 'more people living across or between national borders than ever before' (ibid.). The reasons and backgrounds to the minoritarian condition vary. Bhabha makes connections to the transnational migration of labour and refugees, and internally displaced peoples, respectively. As a response to these new minoritarian conditions connected with migration, Bhabha proposes remapping, against the backdrop that unassimilated minorities historically have been seen as a threat to national unity (Bhabha 2008, xxii). In this context, Bhabha dwells upon the minorities' right to narrate (Bhabha 2008, xxv).

Remapping is also a central theme of the study *Migrant Cartographies: New Cultural and Literary Spaces in Post-Colonial Europe* (Ponzanesi & Merolla 2005). The main conclusion of the volume is that new migrant cartographies are emerging in imaginative writing, and that these transform notions of home, belonging, space and identity.[3] The cultural production of these emerging migrant cartographies are characterised by hybridity and blending, central traits of post-colonial literatures (Ashcroft, Griffiths

---

3   Ponzanesi and Merolla refer to the debate in France about the term 'migrant literature', which has been connected with marginalisation. There has also been a discussion about whether the concept of the 'migrant' is used metaphorically or not (Ponzanesi & Merolla 2005, 25). Against the backdrop of this discussion, some researchers have chosen not to use the term 'migrant literature' (Heith 2016).

& Tiffin 2009, 108–111). In order to emphasise the emerging and diverse character of post-colonial literature, the term 'New Literatures' has been proposed. '– "New Literatures" stressed the emergent nature of work from post-colonised societies and connoted freshness and difference' (Ashcroft, Griffiths & Tiffin 2009, 150). This definition suggests that 'freshness and difference' are characteristics of new postcolonial literatures – both are qualities that may be positive assets contributing to success in the literary field, where innovation and newness traditionally have been prerequisites for visibility and praise. These new literatures are connected with a 'minoritarian condition', to paraphrase Bhabha, and to themes related to migration. Being a part of Europe and the globalised world, Finland and Sweden are of course affected by transnational migratory flows, which transform the nation, and by how it is narrated in fiction.

One effect of migration from the African continent is that the issue of skin colour has become a prominent theme in European literature. This is reflected in the volume *Continental Shifts, Shifts in Perception: Black Cultures and Identities in Europe* (Beezmohun ed. 2016). This volume is part of the growing research field of African-European Studies, which focuses upon how experiences of the African diasporas are expressed in imaginative writing. In Sweden, this theme is explored for example by the successful writer Johannes Anyuru (Heith 2012; Heith 2014; Heith 2016). Prominent themes of this kind of writing is the racialisation of black (brown, or non-white) bodies, and bordering practices, which traditionally have defined the nation as white, Christian (or secular) and non-Muslim.

## Migration to Sweden and Finland: Refugees and labour immigrants

Over the past decades, the Nordic capital cities have become increasingly multicultural. After World War II, Sweden especially has been a destination for labour immigrants and refugees from around the world. Its industry grew rapidly and required an expansion of the labour force. From the 1970s onwards, an increasing number of refugees from different continents have ended up in Sweden. Today Sweden receives more refugees than any other country in Europe per capita. Finnish immigration to Sweden has also been extensive since the World War II and especially in the 1970s (Reinans 1996, 69–71).

During the period of 1945–1980, roughly 400,000 individuals moved from Finland to Sweden as labour force immigrants. Thousands of political refugees sought asylum in Sweden during the 1970s, due to the activities and persecution of intellectuals by dictatorial regimes. A large number of Greeks also migrated to Sweden during the period of Greek military dictatorship, 1967–1974. After the military coup in Chile in 1973, a large number of Chileans came to Sweden as refugees. In Swedish immigrant history, the 1980s has nevertheless been characterized as the 'decade of asylum seekers' when refugees from many war-torn countries such as Iran, Iraq, Lebanon, Syria, Turkey, Eritrea and Somalia tried to come to Sweden. Also refugees from Kosovo and the former Communist Bloc joined the queues of asylum seekers (cf. Svanberg & Runblom 1988). During the 1990s, ethnic cleansing connected with the collapse of Yugoslavia sent many people into exile. Sweden became a host country for more than 100,000 former Yugoslavians, mainly Bosnians. Many of the ethnic groups referred to above, such as Estonians, Sweden-Finns, Latin Americans, Kurds and Iranians, started to organize publishing activities collectively, even their own publishing houses and distribution channels, soon after arrival. The literature produced by these ethnic groups mirrors their specific political and cultural background, but also their socio-economic situation in Sweden.

An understanding of multiculturalism, as well as of ethnicity in general, in the 1970s was in the Swedish official policy connected to social movements and progress in terms of the liberal welfare state's ambitions to guarantee freedom of choice and equal conditions to all citizens, including immigrants. During this period, the Swedish government declared that immigrants and other ethnic groups required affirmative action in order to be integrated, in order to enrich the Swedish culture and finally, in order to promote cultural exchange with the former home countries (Lundström 1996, 45). What distinguishes Sweden from Finland and most other European countries is that the cultural and linguistic rights of ethnic minorities in Sweden were initially formulated from the perspective of immigrants' needs, alongside the need to define practices in what was generally understood as being a new 'multicultural' society. The introduction of what was termed 'home language tuition' in 1964 (called 'mother-tongue tuition' from 1996 onwards) at school level initially referred to immigrant languages, but the historical languages Finnish and Sámi were nevertheless included in the practice. These domestic languages were also included as recipients of public subsidies for literature published in other languages than Swedish, introduced in 1978 and managed by The Swedish Arts Council.[4]

Today, 18,5 % of the population in Sweden was born abroad (ca 1,9 million people) and every fifth child born in Sweden has at least one foreign-born parent. According to the demography statistics from 2017, the most common countries of origin for foreign-born people in Sweden are Syrien (172,000), Finland (ca 151,000), Iraq (140,100), Poland (92,000), the former Yugoslavia and Somalia (66,000), Iran (74,000), Bosnia-Hercegovina (59,000) and Germany (51,000). Next come countries such as Afghanistan and Turkey (44,000–48,000); and Eritrea and Thailand (38,000–41,000). (SCB 2018) During the last years, the number of Syrians has increased and

---

4 From 1999, when Sweden ratified the European Charter for Regional or Minority languages and the Framework Convention for the Protection on National Minorities, there has been an official separation between integration policy and minority policy, the latter directed to national minorities. National minorities and minority languages in Sweden are Jews/Yiddish, Roma/Romani Chib with all varieties, Sámi/Sámi with all varieties, Sweden-Finns/Finnish, Tornedalians/Meänkieli. Even though Finnish is officially defined as a national minority language in Sweden, Sweden-Finnish literature can also be understood as migration literature since the contemporary Sweden-Finnish population consists of first, second and third generation immigrants.

the number of asylum seekers from the war-torn Syria was, during 2015 until November, ca 149,000 (FORES 2016).

Migration has not been as widespread a phenomenon in Finland as in Sweden. Still, migration is not a new phenomenon in Finland either. Historically, the largest group of people immigrating to Finland consisted of the evacuated Karelians from the Karelian Isthmus, Ladoga Karelia and East Karelia, areas that Finland lost to the Soviet Union after World War II. The estimated number of evacuated Karelians was around 400,000 and the total number of evacuees constituted 11 % of the entire Finnish population in 1944. Finland has even been considered the most multicultural country in Scandinavia in the beginning of the twentieth century. In the first decades of the twentieth century, most migratory waves came to Finland from Russia and the Soviet Union, as well as from the Baltic countries. Then numerous immigrants and refugees from the neighbouring regions, such as Ingrians, Karelians, Russians, Estonians, Latvians and Lithuanians moved or escaped to Finland. Many of them already belonged to different groups of minorities when still living in Russia or the Soviet Union.

Later on, the largest immigrant groups in Finland have been the refugees from Chile and Vietnam in the 1970s and from the 1990s onwards especially from Somalia, Iran, Iraq and from the regions of the former Yugoslavia, in particular from Bosnia-Herzegovina. Due to the collapse of the Soviet Union, most contemporary immigrants in Finland originate from Russia or the Baltic countries. Consequently, Russian and Estonian are the most spoken languages among immigrants in Finland, followed by Arabic, Somali and English. As Russians in Finland constitute an old minority group and Russian has been spoken in Finland for a long time, it is not surprising that Finnish-Russian literature today seems to constitute the largest 'migration' literature in the country. Regarding the country of origin, the largest immigrant groups in Finland at the end of 2017 were those born in the former Soviet Union / Russia (approximately 75,000), Estonia (50,000), and immigrants born in Iraqi (20,000), Somalia (19,000) and former Yugoslavia (12,000) (TI 2018). During recent decades, immigrant groups from India and China, in particular, have found work in the information technological companies.

At the end of 2017, about 385,000 persons of foreign origin, were living in Finland. This makes up ca 7 % of the whole population (TI 2018).

## *Short survey: Research on Migration and Literature in Finland and Sweden*

After the end of the war, there was a flow of refugees to Sweden from countries such as Germany and the Baltic States, comprising considerable numbers of intellectuals and cultural workers. Even though we tend today to understand the 1970s as a constitutional decade when migrant and ethnic writing started in Sweden, such literature was in fact already under way after World War II. The existence of this literature has been discussed by critics in Sweden at least since the late 1940s, when Nelly Sachs (1981–1970) published her first volume of poetry in Sweden, *In den Wohnungen des Todes* (1947, [In the Houses of Death]). Sachs was of Jewish origin and was born in Berlin. She arrived to Sweden as a refugee in 1940 and was awarded prestigious prizes in Sweden and Germany, the most famous of which is The Nobel Prize in Literature 1966. To a certain extent, one can say that Sweden has offered significant political support to many exile authors – as well as 'migrant' authors – and Sweden has also afforded support and residence to them. Another example is Latvian Zenta Mauriņa (1897–1978), discussed below in chapter IV.

Literature written by refugees from war-torn Europe and the Baltic States does nonetheless exhibit a difference in character compared with what was later often to be known as multicultural, ethnic, migrant or migration writing. These earlier authors were already well acquainted with European literature and possessed a fair amount of cultural capital, which could immediately be adjusted and used under Nordic circumstances. As the debate on multicultural society started on a larger scale during the 1970s, the writing of authors with their roots in other countries became more visible during this period and from then on. After the end of the World War II, there was a shortage of labour in Sweden and many immigrants of working age found jobs in an expanding market. Immigrants came chiefly from neighbouring Nordic countries, plus Italy, Greece, the former Yugoslavia and Turkey. During several decades, the most famous author of foreign origin in Sweden has been Greek-born Theodor Kallifatides (b. 1938). He writes in Swedish, made his debut as early as 1969, and has published more than 30 works. Kallifatides' extensive production has without doubt contributed to the concept of the (im)migrant author in Sweden – it has been said that he indeed embodies 'the immigrant author' – and he has contributed to the growth of this concept in scholarly debate relatively early on. During the late 1990s, the anachronous term 'second generation immigrant author' was launched and Jonas Hassen Khemiri's novel *Ett öga rött* (2003), in particular, generated a widespread discussion about the authenticity and representation of 'immigrant literature' (cf. Boije 2010).

The contribution of migrants to Finnish and Swedish society has been large and its effects on culture, as well as literature, have not yet been properly estimated. 'Migration literature' has been studied increasingly in Sweden since the 1970s. The earliest works and studies of immigrant and ethnic minority authors published in Sweden consist of general mappings and presentations of the works and authors, such as Helmer Lång's *Svenska europeer. Essäer om invandrarförfattarna Martin Allwood, Karl H. Bolay, Jörgen Nash, Alexander Weiss* (1976, [Swedish Europeans. Essays on the Immigrant Authors Martin Allwood, Karl H. Bolay, Jörgen Nash, Alexander Weiss]). Since the 1980s, the mapping of the various immigrant literatures continued, such as Anneli Eriksson's *Grekisk invandrarlitteratur i Sverige* [Greek Immigrant Literature in Sweden, 1982] and Mana Aghaee's *Lexikon över iranska författare i Sverige* (Aghaee 2002a, [Lexicon of Iranian Authors in Sweden, 2002]). Surveys have also been made of Kurdish, Estonian, and Polish exile or migration literatures in Sweden.

When it comes to general presentations of diasporic literatures as autonomous literary fields, the scholars often seem to fetch their descriptive models from the traditional, canonized literary histories of their home lands, based on the idea of a relatively homogenous nation. These literatures – such as the Estonian, Persian and Kurdish literature in Sweden – are connected to the old homeland and native language; literature written in Swedish by the descendants of these groups is understood as a special category. Because the implicit model for these presentations derives from the concept of national literary history, the exile or diaspora literature described can rarely be thought of as complete, sufficiently aesthetically attractive, or viable in the long term. Estonian first-generation exile literature in Sweden has, for example, been characterized as an offshoot of Estonian national literature, written in Estonian and related to the political situation of Estonia itself. In Sweden, some overviews that focus on Estonian writing in a Swedish national context have been published and included in anthologies concerning larger mappings of ethnic groups in Sweden (Nõu 1988; Warfvinge 2002).[5] After the independence of Estonia 1991, the exile Estonian publishing activities of the first generation came to an end in Sweden (Warfvinge 2002, 257). The production of Estonian authors has been characterized as of high quality and modern, this reflects the fact that the group of refugees from Estonia included one third of the members of the Estonian Writers Union.

Furthermore, Mana Aghaee's (2002b) presentation of Persian writing in Sweden locates this particular literature in an Iranian and international context, rather than a Swedish one. Therefore, in Aghaee's article 'Den persiska litteraturen i Sverige' as in some other overviews, there is an inbuilt contradiction when it describes exile literature of today as an incomplete literary form, defined through deprivation. This description is motivated with comments on the varying literary quality, lack of certain genres such as children's literature, lack of continuity etc. On the other hand, Aghaee also pays attention to the rich and varied flora of magazines published in Sweden, with, for example, a focus on gender related issues. It is also emphasized that publishing in Sweden offers opportunities for freedom of speech in a way that is not possible in Iran.

Kurdish literature, especially literature written in North Kurdish, Kurmanji, attracted particular attention in Sweden during the 1990s and 2000s. As opportunities for the development of Kurmanji and writing in the language have been greatly limited even criminalized in Turkey, Sweden with its subsidy system for literature in immigrant languages became an important residence for authors and scholars from North Kurdistan (Tayfun 1998). M. Tayfun's (1998) analysis of literature production in Kurmanji can be seen as a typical example of research produced outside the academic world. The point of departure is clearly the politics of identity and the Kurds' situation in their homeland. Tayfun considers Kurdish literature published in Sweden to be part of the ethnic and national movement of the Kurds.

---

5   The Eesti Kirjanike Kooperatiiv, Sweden-Estonian cooperative publishing house in Lund, has also published overviews on Estonian literature (for example, Kangro 1989).

The anthology *Litteraturens gränsland: Invandrar- och minoritetslitteratur i nordiskt perspektiv* (2002, [The Borderlands of Literature: Immigrant and Minority literatures from the Nordic Perspective]), edited by Satu Gröndahl, includes several surveys of migration literatures in the Nordic countries. Even though studies on this type of literature have never occurred on a larger scale in Sweden, it is obvious that the interest has grown considerably over the years.

The earliest works and studies of immigrant and ethnic-minority authors published in Sweden before the 1980s were practically and pragmatically orientated, rather than theoretically. During the 1990s, the surveys of such literatures written in other languages than Swedish were more often than not included in diverse anthologies, frequently in historical or interdisciplinary volumes. Alternatively, they were products of individual cultural workers outside of academic circles, and were published by small publishing houses with an ethnic profile. These surveys endeavoured to situate and analyse immigrant and ethnic literatures as relatively autonomous fields, taking account of the specific group's history, culture and socio-political circumstances.

The monolingual paradigm prevails in Swedish literary histories, and one can say that literature written in 'other languages' are still waiting for surveys and more comprehensive expositions in Sweden. However, literary anthologies such as *Den osynliga litteraturskatten* (2010, [The invisible treasure of literature]) offer valuable insights into exile and migration literature written in Sweden today. Interestingly, the editors Anna Franklin and Reza Rezvani have used relatively strict criteria when choosing the authorships – the authors should be members of The Swedish Writers' Union, preferably use an established publisher, and use their mother tongue as their literary tool (Franklin & Rezvani 2010, 9). The carefully edited anthology includes, in addition to translated texts, comprehensive interviews with Leonardo Rossiello (Uruguay), Farhad Shakely (Iraq), Helga Nõu (Estonia), Morteza Rezvan (Iran), Rafik Saber (Iraq), Kostas Koukoulis (Greece) and Ak Welsapar (Turkmenistan).

Comprehensive studies of migration literature have not yet been published in Finland although many journals and anthologies contain discussions and surveys on migration literature as well as research on specific authors. One of the earliest theoretical discussions of migration literature in Finland is Kai Mikkonen's article 'Muukalaisten kielellä. Maahanmuuttajien kirjallisuus ja monikulttuurisuuden merkitys' (2001, [In the Language of Strangers. Migrant literature and the Meaning of Multiculturality] in the journal *Kanava*. In his article, Mikkonen discusses the applicability of the concepts 'migrant author' and 'migrant literature' to the Finnish literary field. He emphasises the shifting multi-ethnic and multilingual contexts of the ethnicity and nationality of authors with migrant background. Mikkonen also points out that their texts should not be read only as an expression of cultural identity. Moreover, Eila Rantonen (2006, 2010) has written overviews of migration literature in Finland, and co-written with Hanna-Leena Nissilä a survey of international writers in Finland as well as the representation of migrants in Finnish literature in *Suomen nykykirjallisuus*

(2013a, [Contemporary Literature in Finland]). Furthermore, *Rethinking National Literatures and Literary Canon in Scandinavia* (2015) includes Olli Löytty's critical discussion on the use of the concept of 'immigrant literature' in Finnish literary studies. He prefers, instead of 'immigrant literature', the term 'transnational literature' (see also Nilsson 2010; Löytty 2013).

Hanna-Leena Nissilä's dissertation '*Sanassa maahanmuuttaja on vähän kitkerä jälkimaku'. Kirjallisen elämän ylirajaistuminen 2000-luvun alun Suomessa* (2016, ['The word migrant has a somewhat bitter aftertaste'. The transnationalization of literary life in Finland at the beginning of the 2000's]) focuses on four female migrant authors' novels and how transnational and cross-border writers are situated in the literary field in Finland. So far, Nissiläs' work is the most extensive study on migrant or transnational literature in Finland.

Only a few mappings of specific migrant literary groups and their historical developments exist in Finland. Sorvari's chapter in this volume, for example, presents a cartography of works by writers with a Russian background in Finland. Eila Rantonen (2009) and Anna Rastas (2014) have written about writers of African descent in Finland. Rastas has also edited a book dealing with multicultural issues in children's literature *Kaikille lapsille: lastenkirjallisuus liikkuvassa monikulttuurisessa maailmassa* (2013, [To All Children: Children's Literature in a Moving Multicultural World]).

*Suomen nykykirjallisuus* I and II (2013, [Contemporary Literature of Finland]) includes chapters that discuss contemporary writers with a migrant background, as well as multicultural themes in Finnish literature such as children's literature, detective novels and science fiction. Anthologies, for example *Både och, sekä että: Om flerspråkighet – Monikielisyydestä* (2011, [A bit of both: About multilingualism]) edited by Heidi Grönstrand and Kristina Malmio, also discuss the new multilingual and multicultural conception of 'Finnish literature'. The most fruitful and multifaceted studies about 'migration literature' in Finland and Sweden of today seem to be produced in the intersection between contemporary, multilingual literature and the extended concept of a national literature.

During recent years, studies on what is called the 'monolingual paradigm' have been introduced both in Sweden and Finland, with inspiration from amongst others, Yasemin Yildiz' critical study *Beyond the Mother Tongue: The Postmonolingual Condition* (2012). According to Yildiz, the appearance of the monolingual paradigm around 1800 and its continuing impact have changed the meaning of multilingual practises. In his thesis, Markus Huss studies Peter Weiss' (1916–1982) bilingual authorship in Sweden as a literary reflection on how human language 'might be imagined, what it means to "possess" a language, but also the existential as well as aesthetic consequences of having one's language "taken away" from you' (Huss 2014, 217). Julia Tidigs underlines in her study of multilingualism in the prose of two Finnish-Swedish authors, Jac Ahrenberg (1847–1914) and Elmer Diktonius (1896–1961) respectively, that the author's multilingual background is often used as an explanation for textual strategies (Tidigs 2014, 315). Tidigs argues for recognition 'of the diversity and variety' of the effect of multilingualism as a literary phenomenon (Tidigs 2014, 320).⁶ The language situation and discourses of multiculturalism are also topicalized in *Literature, Language, and Multiculturalism in Scandinavia and the Low Countries* (Behschnitt et al 2013).

Since the mid-1990s, there has been a renewed interest among the literary readership and within scholarly studies in what is termed 'working class literature' in Sweden (cf. Furuland & Svedjedal 2006, 372). In many respects, Swedish working-class literature had withdrawn from the literary scene, i.e. media and research, during the period characterised by liberal market ideologies during the 80s, which undermined the significance of this traditionally important genre in the Nordic countries. The renewed interest in 'working class literature' and class-related theory construction might, on the one hand, be seen as an attempt to find analytical tools for the social critical novels of a group of authors who started publishing their works from about the mid-1990s. These authors, such as Sweden-Finnish Susanna Alakoski (b. 1962) and Eija Hetekivi Olsson (b.1973), deal with the experiences of growing up in the Swedish welfare state during the 1980s, when the proud national social engineering project, 'folkhemmet', was already beginning to show signs of cracking, inequality in society grew and segregation became more apparent. On the other hand, this interest might also be linked to the critical view of the concept of multiculturalism and influences from intersectional approaches, launched mostly within gender studies during this very period.

The institutionalizing processes within the field of migration literature are different in Finland and Sweden. While there in Sweden have been literary magazines, publishing houses and authors' organizations for several migrant groups ever since the Estonian refugees and asylum seekers found their way to Sweden during the 1940s, it seems that in Finland, authors of specifically Russian origin have organized themselves into a literary group. The cross-cultural literary journal *LiteraruS – literaturnoe slovo* was founded in 2003 and it publishes works and texts by writers living in Russia and Russian-Finnish writers. One reason for the discrepancy between authors' organizations in Finland and Sweden is without doubt the considerably higher number of migrants in Sweden. One has also to bear in mind that since the 1970s, the Swedish Arts Council has administered a special allowance for literature written in languages other than Swedish. This in turn, has encouraged the organization of migrant authors and publishing houses. The Immigrant Institute, a non-governmental organization, was founded in 1973 in Borås⁷ and The Institute of Migration in Turku was founded in 1974. These

---

6   Moreover, the project 'Multilingualism in contemporary literature in Finland' (2014–2016) is likely to influence the description of Finnish literature; the project analyses multilingual elements of Finnish literature within a relatively broad scope. The project is funded by Kone Foundation and the project leader is PhD Heidi Grönstrand.
7   During the 1970s, the Immigrant Institute started to publish bibliographies of immigrant and exile authors in Sweden. While the first volume *Lexikon över invandrarförfattare i Sverige* ['Lexicon of Immigrant authors in Sweden', Diehl & Strömberg 1977] deals with authors of different ethnic backgrounds, the following

institutes have also documented the works of immigrant writers in Sweden and Finland.

The migrant experience as an impetus to writing and creativity is frequently featured in migration and transnational literature. (Kongslien 2013, 133.) This volume explores multicultural writing and the position of a writer between cultures. It also discusses less studied contemporary literary groups from a historical perspective. Further, it presents comparative aspects on the reception of literary works and explores theoretically the intersectional perspectives of identities (e.g. class, gender, ethnicity, 'race' and disability).

*Outline of the volume*

Besides the introductory chapter, this four-part anthology consists of a selection of articles representing diverse theoretical, historical, thematic and analytical approaches to the study of contemporary Finnish and Swedish fiction related to the emergence of new literatures concerning migration and 'a minoritarian condition'. The case-studies are divided into three chapters: II 'Generational Shifts', III 'Reception and Multicultural Perspectives' and IV 'Writing Migrant Identities'.

The first article of chapter II, 'Generational Shifts', is 'Sweden-Finnish Literature: Generational and Cultural Changes' by Satu Gröndahl. The article presents a general, historical survey of selected works by different generations of Sweden-Finnish authors. Gröndahl's conclusion suggests that a gradual shift has occurred away from narratives of language loss and conflicts with the Swedish society among Finnish migrant workers. This involves a move from an emphasis on Finnish ethnicity towards a hybridized understanding of Sweden-Finnishness, which in turn reflects a gradual integration into Swedish society. Furthermore, the article discusses a growing focus upon social class in later works by Sweden-Finnish authors, as opposed to questions of ethnicity, which predominated previously.

As suggested by the title of the second article of chapter II, Marja Sorvari's 'Native, Foreign, Translated? 'Russian' Migrant Literature between Finland and Russia', the author examines literary representations of 'in-between spaces'. These spaces are described as locations where migrants are caught up between languages, cultures and 'homes'. Sorvari discusses how the works by Zinaida Lindén, Liudmila Kol', Arvi Perttu, Inna Latysheva and Inna Patrakova may be related to the concepts *transculturation*, *contact zone* and *diaspora*, all known from postcolonial theory. The conclusion of the article is that the authors discussed can be subsumed under the concepts of 'migrant or transnational literature in Finland'. Their work contributes to changing the

> volumes were based on presentations by a group of authors. These lexicons, published from the 70s to mid-90s, dealt with Estonian, Finnish, Latin American and Polish immigrant authors in Sweden. Later on, the Immigrant Institute started to publish biographical data on immigrant authors on their website. http://www.immi.se/ Quoted 24.3. 2015.

understanding of cultural identities, when these are constructed in a 'contact zone' where different cultures, languages and spaces operate.

The first article of part III is 'Literature and Children In-Between – The Entangled History of Finland and Sweden in *Svinalängorna*, *Mother of Mine* and *Ingenbarnsland*' by Kukku Melkas. The article discusses the reception of works by Susanna Alakoski, Eija Hetekivi Olsson and Klaus Härö with perspectives from trauma theory and research on transnational literature. Melkas proposes that Sweden-Finnish literature exists in a no man's land, 'in between two literary canons'. Further, the theme of an in-between status is reflected thematically in the story told by children in between childhood and adolescence.

The second article of part III, Johanna Domokos's 'Multicultural Dynamics and the Finnish Literary Field' has a two-fold aim: 1) to discuss transformations of the Finnish literary field from the vantage point of constructions of 'the multicultural', and 2) to explore a theory and methodology of an *écriture multiculturelle*. Domokos aims to develop a structuralist methodology for the narrative analysis of texts categorised as multicultural. The article includes a close reading of ElRamly in the light of the proposed concept *écriture multiculturelle*.

The final article of part III is Hanna-Leena Nissilä's 'Transnationalizing Finnish Literature – Perspectives on the Reception of Debut Novels by Zinaida Lindén, Ranya ElRamly, Umayya Abu-Hanna and Alexandra Salmela. Nissilä discusses the reception of the debut novels of four female authors with an immigrant background, highlighting the role gender plays for the public reception of the novels. The article concludes that the discussed novels represent transnationalism and that they contribute to changing the Finnish literary institution.

The final section, 'Writing Migrant Identities', begins with Anne Heith's article 'The African Diaspora, Migration and Writing: Johannes Anyuru's *En civilisation utan båtar*'. The article examines Johannes Anyuru's autobiographical text from 2011. *En civilisation utan båtar* is analysed against the backdrop of Paul Gilroy's discussion of the Black Atlantic, hybrid identity formations and literary aesthetics of the diaspora as formulated by Stuart Hall. The article concludes that Anyuru's multifaceted text contributes newness to the Swedish literary field by exploring the identity-formation of a black Swedish Muslim, as well as exploring new modes of writing based on the blending of elements from different cultural and literary traditions.

This analysis is followed by Pirjo Ahokas's contribution 'Is Love Thicker Than Blood? A Bi-Cultural Identity Process in Astrid Trotzig's *Blod är tjockare än vatten*'. Ahokas's article deals with the themes of migration in relation to transnational adoption, the identity formation of a Korean adoptee in Sweden and a criticism of Sweden's colour-blind multiculturalist ideology. The discussion is based on an analysis of Astrid Trotzig's autobiographical novel *Blod är tjockare än vatten*. 'Identity' and 'trauma' are key concepts in Ahokas's exploration of racialization in Trotzig's novel.

The next article, Marta Ronne's 'Narratives of Exile, Gender and Disability in Swedish-Latvian Zenta Mauriņa's Autobiographical Writings', focuses upon the interconnectedness between the themes of exile, gender and disability in the writings of Zenta Mauriņa. The article explores the theme of exile from various theoretical vantage points. It also introduces perspectives from disability studies. Ronne proposes that Mauriņa's exile in Sweden was negatively inflected, that disability is conceptualised as exclusion, and that melancholy and sorrow are ever-present in her exile writings.

The final article of the volume is Eila Rantonen's 'Writing Biography by E-Mail – Postcolonial and Postmodern Rewriting of Biographical and Epistolary Modes in Jonas Hassen Khemiri's *Montecore*'. Using perspectives from postcolonial theory and aesthetics, Rantonen performs a close reading of the epistolary mode in the novel *Montecore*. The article focuses on generic renewal, proposing that there are connections between migration literature and new modes of writing.

# References

Aghaee, Mana 2002a: *Lexikon över iranska författare i Sverige.* Uppsala.
Aghaee, Mana 2002b: Den persiska litteraturen i Sverige. *Litteraturens gränsland: Invandrar- och minoritetslitteratur i nordiskt perspektiv.* Uppsala Multiethnic Papers 45. Uppsala: Centrum för multietnisk forskning. 315–332.
Ashcroft, Bill, Gareth, Griffiths & Tiffin, Helen 2009: *Post-Colonial Studies: The Key Concepts*, 2nd ed. London & New York: Routledge.
Behschnitt, Wolfgang, De Mul, Sarah & Minnaard, Liesbeth (eds.) 2013: *Literature, Language, and Multiculturalism in Scandinavia and the Low Countries.* Textet. Studies in Comparative Literature 71. Amsterdam & New York: Rodopi.
Beezmohun, Sharmilla (ed.) 2016: *Continental Shifts, Shifts in Perception: Black Cultures and Identities in Europe.* Newcastle upon Tyne: Cambridge Scholars Publishing.
Bhabha, Homi K. 2008: *The Location of Culture.* London & New York: Routledge.
Boije, Ronja 2010: *Äktast möjliga? Jonas Hassen Khemiris Ett öga rött och föreställningar om autenticitet.* Avhandling pro gradu i nordisk litteratur. Vårterminen 2010. Finska, finskugriska och nordiska institutionen. Helsingfors: Helsingfors universitet.
Bromley, Roger 2000: *Narratives for a New Belonging. Diasporic Cultural Fictions.* Edinburgh: Edinburgh University Press.
Diehl, Barbro & Strömberg, Gabriella 1977: *Lexikon över invandrarförfattare i Sverige.* Borås: Immigrant-institutet.
ElRamly, Ranya 2002: Egyptiläisen isän tyttärenä. *Helsingin Ylioppilaslehti* 16.
Eriksson, Anneli 1982: *Grekisk invandrarlitteratur I Sverige.* Borås: Invandrarförlaget.
FORES. Forskning och statistik om integration och migration i Sverige. Migrationsinfo. se. http://www.migrationsinfo.se/migration/sverige/ [Quoted: 5.1.2016].
Frank, Søren 2010: Four Theses on Migration and Literature. *Migration and Literature in Contemporary Europe.* Ed. by Mirjam Gebauer and Pia Schwarz Lausten. München: Martin Meidenbauer. 39–57.
Franklin, Anna & Rezvani, Reza 2010: *Den osynliga litteraturskatten.* Stockholm: Bokförlaget Tranan.
Furuland, Lars & Svedjedal Johan 2006: *Svensk arbetarlitteratur* [Swedish working-class literature]. Årsbok för Arbetarnas Kulturhistoriska Sällskap 2006. Skrifter utgivna av Avdelningen för litteratursociologi vid Litteraturvetenskapliga institutionen i Uppsala, nr 49, Jubileumsskrift Brunnsvik 100 år. Stockholm: Atlas.
Gebauer, Mirjam & Schwarz Lausten, Pia 2010: Migration Literature: Europe in

Transition. *Migration and Literature in Contemporary Europe*. Ed. by Mirjam Gebauer and Pia Schwarz Lausten. München: Martin Meidenbauer. 1–8.

Gröndahl, Satu (ed.) 2002: *Litteraturens gränsland: Invandrar- och minoritetslitteratur i nordiskt perspektiv*. Uppsala Multiethnic Papers 45. Uppsala: Centrum för multietnisk forskning: Uppsala.

Grönstrand, Heidi & Malmio, Kristina (eds.) 2011: *Både och, sekä että: Om flerspråkighet / Monikielisyydestä*. Helsinki: Schildts.

Hall, Stuart 1997: Cultural Identity and Diaspora. *Identity and Difference*. Ed. by Katherine Woodward. London, Thousand Oaks & New Delhi: Sage Publications. 51–59.

Heith, Anne 2004: Postkolonialism och poetik. Alejandro Leiva Wengers *Till vår ära*. *Kulturella perspektiv* 2 (13). 2–11.

Heith, Anne 2012: Beyond Hegel and Normative Whiteness: Minorities, Migration and New Swedish Literatures. *Multiethnica* (34). 18–19.

Heith, Anne 2012b: Ethnicity, Cultural Identity and Bordering: A Tornedalian Negro. *Folklore* 52. 85–108.

Heith, Anne 2014: Blackness, Religion, Aesthetics: Johannes Anyuru's Literary Explorations of Migration and Diaspora. *Nordlit* 1 (31). 59–70.

Heith, Anne 2015: Indigeneity, Cultural Transformations and Rethinking the Nation: Performative Aspects of Sámi Elements in Umeå 2014. *Culture and Growth: Magical Companions or Mutually Exckusive Counterparts?* UNEECC FORUM VOLUME 7. Ed. by Britta Lundgren & Ovidiu Matiu. Sibiu: Lucian Blaga University of Sibiu Press. 110–126.

Heith, Anne 2016: Displacement and Regeneration: Minorities, Migration and Postcolonial Literature. *Continental Shifts, Shifts in Perception: Black Cultures and Identities in Europe*. Ed. by Sharmilla Beezmohun. Newcastle upon Tyne: Cambridge Scholars Publishing. 49–71.

Huss, Markus 2014: *Motståndets akustik. Språk och (o)ljud hos Peter Weiss 1946-1960*. Lund: Ellerströms.

Huttunen, Laura 2013: Improvisointi, kitka ja kulttuurin käsitteellistäminen. *Liikkuva maailma. Liike, raja, tieto*. Ed. by Mikko Lehtonen. Tampere: Vastapaino. 245–260.

Hämäläinen, Timo 2005: Zinaida Lindén palkittiin kahdesti Runebergin päivänä. *Helsingin Sanomat*. 6.2.2005.

Kangro, Bernard 1989: *Eesti kirjakuulutaja eksiilis. Biblio- ja biograafiline teatmik aastaist 1944-1986*. Eesti Kirjanike Kooperativ. Lund.

Keskinen, Suvi et al. (eds.) 2009: *Complying with Colonialism: Gender, Race and Ethnicity in the Nordic Region*. Farnham & Burlington: Ashgate.

Kivimäki, Sanna 2012: *Kuinka tämän tuntisi omaksi maakseen. Suomalaisuuden kulttuurisia järjestyksiä*. Viestinnän, median ja teatterin yksikkö. Tampere: Tampereen yliopisto.

Komulainen, Sirkka 2013: A Chick Cosmopolitan Migrant Condition: *Tulkki* by Inna Patrakova. *Le roman migrant au Québec et en Scandinavie. The Migrant Novel in Quebec and Scandinavia*. Ed. by Svante Lindberg. Frankfurt am Main et al.: Peter Lang. 161–179.

Kongslien, Ingeborg 2013: The Scandinavian Migrant Novel – A New National Narrative and a Cosmopolitical Tale. *Le roman migrant au Québec et en Scandinavie. The Migrant Novel in Quebec and Scandinavia*. Ed. by Svante Lindberg. Frankfurt am Main et al.: Peter Lang. 125–139.

Lindberg, Svante 2013: Introduction. *Le roman migrant au Québec et en Scandinavie. The Migrant Novel in Quebec and Scandinavia*. Ed. by Svante Lindberg. Frankfurt am Main et al.: Peter Lang. 15–21.

Loftsdóttir, Kristín & Jensen, Lars 2012: Introduction: Nordic Exceptionalism and the Nordic 'Others'. *Whiteness and Postcolonialism in the Nordic Region: Exceptionalism,*

*Migrant Others and National Identities.* Ed. by Kristín Loftsdóttir & Lars Jensen. Farnham & Burlington: Ashgate. 1–11.

Lundborg, Herman & Linders, F. J. 1926: *The Racial Characters of the Swedish Nation.* Stockholm: Anthropologica Suecica MCMXXVI.

Lundström, Stig 1996: Invandrarpolitikens framväxt och svenskt-finskt migrationssamarbete. *Finnarnas historia i Sverige 3. tiden efter 1945.* Ed. by Jarmo Lainio. Helsinki: Finska Historiska Samfundet; Stockholm: Nordiska museet. 185–228.

Löytty, Olli 2013: Kun rajat eivät pidä, eli mihin maahanmuuttajakirjallisuutta tarvitaan. *Liikkuva maailma. Liike, raja, tieto.* Ed. by Mikko Lehtonen. Tampere: Vastapaino. 261–279.

Matthis, Moa (ed.) 2005: *Orientalism på svenska.* Stockholm: Ordfront förlag.

Mikkonen, Kai 2001: Muukalaisten kielellä. Maahanmuuttajien kirjallisuus ja monikulttuurisuuden merkitys. *Kanava.* N:o 8. 553–559.

Nilsson, Magnus 2010: *Den föreställda mångkulturen. Klass och etnicitet i Svensk samtidsprosa.* Hedemöra, Möklinta: Gidlund.

Nissilä, Hanna-Leena 2016: *'Sanassa maahanmuuttaja on vähän kitkerä jälkimaku' Kirjallisen elämän ylirajaistuminen 2000-luvun alun Suomessa.* Acta Universitatis Ouluensis B Humaniora 136. Oulu: Oulun yliopisto.

Nissilä, Hanna-Leena ja Rantonen, Eila 2013: Kansainvälistyvä kirjailijakunta. *Suomen nykykirjallisuus 2.* Ed. by Mika Hallila, Yrjö Hosiaisluoma, Sanna Karkulehto, Leena Kirstinä ja Jussi Ojajärvi. Helsinki: SKS. 55–71.

Nõu, Enn 2009: *Helga Nõu bibliograafia.* http://dspace.utlib.ee Quoted 2012-08-13

Olsson, Anders 2011: *Ordens asyl. En inledning till den moderna exillitteraturen.* Stockholm: Albert Bonniers förlag.

Perttu 2007: Uussuomalainen ja muita rooleja. Venäläiset maahanmuuttajat: suurin ja hiljaisin siirtolaisryhmä. Puheenvuoro SKS:n seminaarissa 8.11.2007. http://arviperttu.vuodatus.net/page/Ven_l_iset_maahanmuuttajat

Pollari, Mikko et al. 2015: National, Transnational and Entangled Literatures: Methodological Considerations Focusing on the Case of Finland. *Rethinking National Literatures and the Literary Canon in Scandinavia.* Ed. by Ann-Sofie Lönngren, Heidi Grönstrand, Dag Heede & Anne Heith. Newcastle upon Tyne: Cambridge Scholars Publishing. 2–29.

Ponzanesi, Sandra & Merolla, Daniela 2005: Introduction: Cultural Travelers and New Literatures. *Migrant Cartographies: New Cultural and Literary Spaces in Post-Colonial Europe.* Lanham, Boulder, New York, Toronto & Oxford: Lexington Books. 1–52.

Pratt, Mary Louise 1992: *Imperial Eyes: Travel Writing and Transculturation.* London: Routledge.

Rantonen, Eila 2006: Kirjallisia tuliaisia. Maahanmuuttaja-kirjallisuus kulttuurien välissä. *Fiktiota! Levottomat genret ja kirjaston arki.* Toim. Kaisa Hypén. Helsinki: BTJ Kirjastopalvelu. 121–135

Rantonen, Eila 2009: African Voices in Finland and Sweden. *Transcultural Modernities. Narrating Africa in Europe.* Ed. by Elisabeth Bekers, Sissy Helff and Daniela Merolla. *Matatu. Journal for African Culture and Society.* Amsterdam, New York: Rodopi. 71–83.

Rantonen, Eila 2010: Maahanmuuttajien kirjallisuus Suomessa ja Ruotsissa. *Vähemmistöt ja monikulttuurisuus kirjallisuudessa.* Ed. by Eila Rantonen. Tampere: Tampere University Press.163–191.

Rantonen, Eila & Savolainen, Matti 2002: Postcolonial and ethnic studies in the context of Nordic minority literatures. *Litteraturens gränsland: Invandrar- och minoritetslitteratur i nordiskt perspektiv.* Uppsala Multiethnic Papers 45. Uppsala: Centrum för multietnisk forskning. 71–94.

Rantonen, Eila & Nissilä, Hanna-Leena 2013: 'Pelottavia muukalaisia ja arkisempia maahanmuuttajia.' *Suomen nykykirjallisuus 2*. Toim. Mika Hallila, Yrjö Hosiaisluoma, Sanna Karkulehto, Leena Kirstinä ja Jussi Ojajärvi. Helsinki: SKS. 76–91.

Rastas, Anna 2013: *Kaikille lapsille. Lastenkirjallisuus liikkuvassa, monikulttuurisessa maailmassa*. Helsinki: SKS.

Reinans, Sven Alur 1996: Den finländska befolkningen i Sverige – en statistisk-demografisk beskrivning. *Finnarnas historia i Sverige 3. tiden efter 1945*. Ed. by Jarmo Lainio. Helsinki: Finska Historiska Samfundet; Stockholm: Nordiska museet. 63–106.

SCB. Statistiska centralbyrån – Statistics Sweden. http://www.scb.se/sv_/hitta-statistik/artiklar/fortsatt-okning-av-utrikes-fodda-i-sverige/ [Quoted: 13.9.2018].

Seyhan, Azade 2001: *Writing Outside the Nation*. Princeton: Princeton University Press.

Schulze-Engler, Frank 2009. Transcultural Modernities and Anglophone African Literature. *Transcultural Modernities. Narrating Africa in Europe*. Ed. by Elisabeth Bekers, Sissy Helff and Daniela Merolla. *Matatu. Journal for African Culture and Society*. Amsterdam, New York: Rodopi. 87–101.

Seyhan, Azade 2010: Unfinished Modernism. European Destinations of Transnational Writing. *Migration and Literature in Contemporary Europe*. Ed. by Mirjam Gebauer and Pia Schwarz Lausten. München: Martin Meidenbauer. 11–21.

SVT Suomen virallinen tilasto: Väestörakenne [verkkojulkaisu]. ISSN=1797-5379. 2013. Helsinki: Tilastokeskus [Quoted: 8.3.2015]. http://tilastokeskus.fi/til/vaerak/2013/vaerak_2013_2014-03-21_tie_001_fi.html

Svanberg, Invar & Runblom, Harald 1990: *Det mångkulturella Sverige. Det mångkulturella Sverige. En handbok om etniska grupper och minoriteter*. Stockholm: Gidlunds. 9–11.

Szigeti, László 2002: A multikulturalizmus esztétikája. *Helikon* 4. 395–421.

Tayfun, Mehmet 1998: *Kurdiskt författarskap och kurdisk bokutgivning. Bakgrund, villkor, betydelse*. Spånga: Apec.

TI Tilastokeskus. Helsinki [Quoted: 14.9.2018]. https://www.stat.fi/tup/maahanmuutto/maahanmuuttajat-vaestossa/ulkomaalaistaustaiset.html.

Tidigs, Julia 2014: *Att skriva sig över språkgränserna. Flerspråkighet i Jac. Ahrenbergs och Elmer Diktonius prosa*. Åbo: Åbo Akademis förlag.

Trotzig, Astrid 2005: Makten över prefixen. *Orientalism på svenska*. Ed. by Moa Matthis. Stockholm: Ordfront förlag. 104–127.

Warfvinge, Katarina 2002: Från flyktingslitteratur till sverigeestnisk litteratur. En immigrantlitteratur under femtio år. *Litteraturens gränsland. Invandrar- och minoritetslitteratur i nordiskt perspektiv*. Ed. by Satu Gröndahl. Uppsala: Centrum för multietnisk forskning. 257–272.

Wendelius, Lars 2002: *Den dubbla identiteten. Immigrant och minoritetslitteratur på svenska 1970–2000*. Uppsala: Centrum för multietnisk forskning.

Yildiz, Yasemin 2012: *Beyond the Mother Tongue: The Postmonolingual Condition*. New York: Fordham University Press.

# Generational Shifts  II

Satu Gröndahl
https://orcid.org/0000-0002-7471-6306

# Sweden-Finnish Literature: Generational and Cultural Changes

In the beginning of 2012, Eija Hetekivi Olsson's (born 1973) newly-published novel *Ingenbarnsland* (2012, [No Place for Children]) caused dissension on the Sweden-Finnish mailing list *Ruosulista*. Eija Hetekivi Olsson's debut novel is about Miira, a Finnish-born girl, and her experiences in Swedish school during the 1980s. As Miira's first language is Finnish, she is placed in a so-called 'home-language class', instead of an ordinary class where the tuition language is Swedish. In practice, this means that tuition is of low standard, that there is no continuity of teachers and that the pupils from the home-language class obtain lower marks in their final grade than their schoolmates do from ordinary Swedish classes. Miira's mother works as a cleaning woman and her father as a building caretaker. The young girl is surrounded by teenagers involved in petty crime, by drugs and abusers, and her future prospects do not look promising.

The Swedish critics were overwhelmed by the novel's strong pathos, concern for human rights and the description of segregation and obviously very different conditions for children in the Swedish social welfare state, 'folkhemmet', during the 1980s. The Sweden-Finnish public, on the other hand, became irritated.[1] Eija Hetekivi Olsson's *Ingenbarnsland* was described in one of the leading Swedish daily newspapers, Dagens Nyheter, as 'a penetrating contemporary description about the extreme vulnerability which exposed children are living under'. The author of the article, literary critic Malin Ullgren, also stated that the novel calls for well needed and actual political debate on poverty in today's Sweden (Ullgren 2012).

Since the 1990s, so called 'working-class literature' has been more visible on the Swedish book market, even though this genre has been recognized as an integral part of Swedish literature since the 1930s. During the past years, there has been a renewed and intensive debate among Swedish literary critics concerning how the categories 'class' and 'ethnicity'/'race' relate to each other when analysing working-class literature. Magnus Nilsson argues that ethnifying tendencies occur when interpreting literature that deals

---

1 'Folkhemmet' means literally 'the people's home'. It is a political concept and often refers to the period between 1932–1976 when the Social Democrats were in power, but it is also used as a poetic description of Swedish welfare state.

with experiences of class related themes; that is, class is regarded as 'culture', in a '(multi)cultural' discourse that denies or derogates the importance of social injustices (cf. Nilsson 2010, 58). However, there have hardly been any reflections on how language as a category relates to class and ethnicity. The vantage point of this chapter is the understanding of Sweden-Finnish literature as part of Swedish working-class literature, focusing on changes in themes and language-related identity markers. As Sweden has, since 2000, formulated official language policies, which is the first time in the nation's history, my hypothesis is that the significance of language as a category has changed during the last decades. Since the turn of the millennium, 'language' has become an officially politicised category; the Swedish language has been defined as the main language in the country.

The Sweden-Finnish minority group on the other hand, has been defined as a national minority and the Swedish government is obliged to support and maintain the Sweden-Finnish culture and the Finnish language. Sweden ratified the Council of Europe's Framework Convention for the Protection of National Minorities and the European Charter for Regional or Minority languages in 2000. This political development has defined Sweden-Finns, previously regarded as an immigrant group, as part of the national history; and has even changed the understanding of what the multicultural Swedish society of today is.

The acknowledgment of Sweden Finns as a national minority seems to have led to increased Sweden-Finnish cultural activities, such as the founding of new local literary associations and an increased production of books in Finnish (cf. Tikkanen-Rósza 2015). In 2005, a national Sweden-Finnish literature prize, the Kaisa Vilhuinen Prize, was established. Because of the radically changed minority political situation, it seems likely that the concept of 'Sweden-Finnishness' has undergone changes after the turn of the millennium.

For Sweden-Finns, *Ingenbarnsland* was nevertheless primarily seen as yet another novel about this group's shortcomings, about their failures to advance in society, and about Finns' alcohol consumption, all these characteristics are part of the stereotypical images occurring in Sweden of the Sweden-Finnish minority, even of the Finns. However, the main focus in the debate on Ruosulista concerned the negative picture of Finnish as the language of tuition. Could the Swedish politicians use Hetekivi Olsson's novel as an argument against Sweden-Finnish schools, which have been struggling for a long time for their survival, or as an argument against other linguistic or minority rights?[2] The discussion on Ruosulista seems to implicate that language has become an even more important identity marker when discussing 'Sweden-Finnishness'.

The image of Sweden-Finns as labour immigrants was formed during the 1960s and 1970s, when the major part of the immigrant movement

---

2   There were about 250 members on the Sweden-Finnish mail-list during 2012. Many of the members are cultural workers, teachers and minority activists. (*Ruosulista* 2012)

from Finland to Sweden took place. The official estimation of the number of Sweden-Finns is 450 000 of which about 220 000 are estimated to speak Finnish. According to a survey from 2009, carried out by Statistiska Centralbyrån SCB, Statistics Sweden, the number of Sweden-Finns amounts to approximately 675 000 individuals when taking into account the first, second and third generation (Björklund 2010, 36). While the first generation of Sweden-Finns found their place of work on a large scale within industry, agriculture, the service industry and other unqualified jobs, the second and third generation is generally seen as better integrated. One has also to bear in mind that there has been continuous influx of well-educated Finns who have found jobs on the professional labour market for several decades.

Nevertheless, one can ask why the representation of the Sweden-Finnish group seems to be so homogeneous on the Swedish book market since the turn of the millennium. Even Susanna Alakoski (1962), a celebrated winner of the Swedish August prize 2006, described in her *Svinalängorna* (2006, [The Pigsties]), a tragic childhood story about siblings living with parents suffering from alcoholism. However, in Swedish magazines and newspapers, the central themes of these authors' production appear to have been perceived mainly as rather stereotypical descriptions of the impact of class on individuals, although the main characters belong to the Sweden-Finnish group (Ullgren 2012; Johansson Rissén 2008, 9–11). One must also bear in mind that the definition of 'working class literature' has changed. As Magnus Nilsson and John Lennon have underlined, this concept is always historically and geographically situated, thus assuming divergent shapes in different times and locations. 'We argue that working-class literature as a phenomenon is, therefore, always in a process of new formations. In doing so, we move away from narrow nationalistic views of working-class literature as a defined term and, using a comparative approach, allow for new vantage points in the analysis of the relationship between class and culture' (Nilsson & Lennon 2016:39). Therefore, it is also interesting to scrutiny how literature focusing on a specific ethnic group such as Sweden-Finns, relates to the understanding of (Swedish) 'working class literature'.

One interesting question is how Eija Hetekivi Olsson's and Susanna Alakoski's production can be conceptualized when analysing their works in a wider Sweden-Finnish context and when relating them to other Sweden-Finnish novels. In which way are the categories 'class', 'ethnicity' and 'language' understood in Sweden-Finnish literature? What are the intersections between class and ethnicity, and how do they relate to the question of language through which the institutional power relations between majority and minority often are expressed? (cf. Bourdieu 1991/2007, 44–46) How are themes about integration and identity described in general? Is it possible to see generational changes when it comes to topical themes and markers for 'Sweden-Finnishness'? Does an authorship written in Swedish, indicate more stereotypical representation of this minority?

## Sweden-Finnish literature: Short overview

The definition of (im)migrant, migrancy or minority literature has varied significantly, not least because scholars have wanted to avoid essentialist and even stigmatizing labels on this literature. One way to relate to the terminological question is to contextualize the actual term in relation to how this literature positions itself in multicultural and minority discourses (cf. Behschnitt 2010, 81; Gröndahl 2014). In this way, it is also possible to avoid ethnification of the author – as we know, many authors with their roots in other countries have emphasized that they do *not* wish to be seen as '(im)migrant' authors. Here, using the term Sweden-Finnish literature, I mean literature that addresses themes about migrancy, language, identity and belonging, and deals with experiences of the Sweden-Finnish group. Sweden-Finnish literature can also be regarded as part of Swedish working-class literature, as it connects thematically to class-related themes and phenomena related to working-class life. (cf. Nilsson & Lennon 2016, 39.)

Sweden-Finnish literature came into being already during the 1970s when the first generation of Finnish emigrants started to write novels and poems on a larger scale. During that decade, several Sweden-Finnish organizations and publishing houses were founded, such as Sverigefinska Riksförbundet ('National Association of Sweden-Finns'), Sverigefinska språknämnden ('Sweden-Finnish Language Board'), Föreningen för Sverigefinska Skribenter ('Association for Sweden-Finnish Writers'), and the publishing house Finn-Kirja etc. As an immigrant or minority group, Sweden-Finns have – from their very arrival to Sweden – been known as a well-organized and politically active group. The fact that many Sweden-Finns were active in party-politics also intensified their ethnic organizing.

Establishment of one's own organizations has been an important tool when settling in the new country. Literary events and writing groups were popular leisure activities among Sweden-Finns; they were regarded as important activities to maintain and develop their language. For the most part, Finnish was the language used for this early production. As has been the case for many other immigrant literatures, writing was a collective phenomenon; clubs of writers and authors published collective anthologies, arranged literary contests etc. It has been pointed out in literary criticism, as well as by many scholars, that there are plenty of writers among the Sweden-Finns, but few of them can be classified as qualified authors (Vallenius 1998, 41).

When it comes to earlier scholarly studies, one can especially mention Marja-Liisa Pynnönen's fundamental mapping of the field in *Siirtolaisuuden vanavedessä. Tutkimus ruotsinsuomalaisen kirjallisuuden kentästä vuosina 1956–1988* (1991, [In the Wake of Migration. A Study of the Sweden-Finnish Literary Field during 1956–1988]), and in Erkki Vallenius' work on modernization and Sweden-Finnish migration *Kansankodin kuokkavieraat. II maailmansodan jälkeen Ruotsiin muuttaneet suomalaiset kaunokirjallisuuden kuvaamina* (1998, [Uninvited Guests of Folkhemmet. Finnish immigrants in Sweden after World War II in fiction]). Pynnönen's work covering more than 30 years, deals with a large amount of material, including

*Sweden-Finnish book fair at Finland's Institute (Finlandsinstitutet, Stockholm) is an annual meeting forum for authors and artists. Conversation between visual artist Markku Huovila and editor-in-chief Jaana Johansson in 2016. Photo: Jouni Suomalainen / Liekki, ruotsinsuomalainen kulttuurilehti.*

Sweden-Finnish magazines, correspondence and interviews with several authors. Vallenius' study also covers the most central authors in the field, even though he especially concentrates on two male authors, Hannu Ylitalo and Antti Jalava, and their works.

Both Pynnönen and Vallenius also summarize main themes and topicalized motifs in Sweden-Finnish literature. According to Pynnönen, the central themes during the 1956–1988 period consist of the move (i.e. migration) to Sweden, work environment, relations between the Finns and other groups, alignment, segregation and relation to Finland (Pynnönen 1991, 192–193). One central ambition in Sweden-Finnish literature is also to expose the linguistic situation of this minority group, and shed light on the question of minority rights as regards the status of the language, tuition in one's mother tongue, bilingual services etc (Pynnönen 1991, 213). Vallenius, on the other hand, is of the opinion that work (i.e. labour, working life) is thematized as the most significant issue in Sweden-Finnish literature. Work does not only determine the migrants' life situation, working hours as well as leisure time, but in an urbanized and modern world, it also gives individuals the possibility to control their own life situation (Vallenius 1998, 232). More generalizing literary-historical overviews, such as Maijaliisa Jokinen's article 'Sverigefinska kulturssträvanden' (1996, [Sweden-Finnish Cultural Endeavours]) have underlined that Sweden-Finnish literature, like immigrant literatures in general, deals with existential questions of migrancy on a very concrete level and with a fundamental tone of sorrow and homelessness (Jokinen 1996, 381).

For my overview, I will examine some representative and well known Sweden-Finnish novels published during the 1970s and 2010s. When selecting the novels, I have tried to find works that deal with experiences of different Finnish migrant generations. As further clarified in the following presentations, they describe experiences of both the first and second generation of Sweden-Finns and also different types of immigration waves to Sweden. While the 'first generation' refers to Finns who migrated to Sweden during the 1970s as labour immigrants, the 'second generation' refers to those who are born in Sweden or who migrated to Sweden at a very young age. The article also includes one novel that focuses on well-educated Finnish middle-class people, settling down in Sweden in order to elaborate a professional career.

Most of the authors – Martta Matinlompolo, Hannu Ylitalo, Antti Jalava, Susanna Alakoski, Eija Hetekivi Olsson and Henriikka Leppäniemi – have also been noticed in scholarly studies as well as literary histories, which is of interest when analysing their works as part of a discursively constructed 'Sweden-Finnishness' and its different markers. All these authors have an immigrant background themselves. My intention has not been to choose novels on the basis of a particular group of authors or ethnic background, but the novels I could find when looking for narratives of Sweden-Finns all turned out to be written by authors with roots in Finland. Below, I will give a short presentation of the chosen authors and their works.

Both Martta Matinlompolo (1934–2008) and Hannu Ylitalo (1934–2007) belong to the first generation of Sweden-Finnish labour immigrants that moved to Sweden during the 1970s, and they published their novels during the same decade. They both have a working-class background. Martta Matinlompolo's educational background was limited to courses at a residential college for adult education but she was active in local politics and as a social commentator. Hannu Ylitalo was a qualified elementary school teacher. In Sweden, he worked as a teacher for Finnish children. Matinlompolo and Ylitalo were, and still are, often referred to as the founding authors for Sweden-Finnish literature. They both write in Finnish and focus on the experiences of the first generation of Sweden-Finnish immigrants, especially their initial years after settling down in Sweden. Martta Matinlompolo wrote short stories and polemic articles, but her main literary work is *Ken tietäis huomisen* (1976, [Who knows about tomorrow]). Hannu Ylitalo is best known for the trilogy *Saatanan suomalainen* (1971, [Fucking Finn]), *Ruotsalaisten maa* (1972, [The land of Swedes]) and *Raukat menköhöt merten taa* (1974, translated into Swedish as *Hemma bäst*, [Home Sweet Home]).

Antti Jalava (1949), on the other hand, moved to Sweden with his family when he was ten years old. He was born in a working-class family and grew up in Eastern Finland. He has mentioned that breaking up from his childhood milieu was a traumatic experience. In Finland he was a well-adapted, successful pupil with a stable circle of friends; in Sweden he became isolated and had problems in school, becoming an underachiever. He stopped speaking his mother tongue at the age of 13 and only learned it again as an adult (Jokinen 1996, 391). Antti Jalava started his literary career in the mid-1970s with a book for juveniles *Jag har inte bett att få komma* (1976, [I did not ask to come]), but his main works were published during the

1980s and 1990s, namely *Asfaltblomman* (1980, [Asphalt Flower]), *Sprickan* (1993, [The Flaw]) and *Känslan* (1996, [Emotion]). Jalava's psychological novels concentrate in particular on describing such experiences of second-generation Sweden-Finns that were marked by identity crisis, language loss and marginalization. Antti Jalava's educational background consists of elementary school and high school. He writes in Swedish and he has also translated qualified contemporary works from Finnish into Swedish.

Susanna Alakoski (1962) was born in Finland, while Eija Hetekivi Olsson (1973) was born in Sweden. Their novels represent the second generation's production published after the turn of the millennium and they deal with the theme of Sweden-Finnish youngsters and teenagers and their living conditions during the 1980s. Susanna Alakoski's *Svinalängorna* (2006) was followed by *Håpas du trifs bra i fengelset* (2010, [Ope yo like it in jail] a story about Anni and Sami, sister and brother whose adult life is deeply influenced and traumatized by experiences of growing up in a home where both parents were heavily alcoholised. Eija Hetekivi Olsson with her *Ingenbarnsland* (2012) can be seen as a sort of continuation of Alakoski's authorship. Neither of them has focused on identity-related problems in terms of language loss, as Jalava did. Instead, their protagonists are followed by class-related markers and are described through these.

Both Susanna Alakoski and Eija Hetekivi Olsson have their background in working-class immigrant families. Alakoski is a social worker by profession. She has pursued a career as a debater and lecturer concerning social issues, recently especially about child poverty issues. Eija Hetekivi Olsson, too, has a university education and she works as teacher. Hetekivi Olsson graduated from high school in adulthood, through adult education.

Henriikka Leppäniemi (1974) moved to Sweden in 1997 to study, and she now works at the University of Lund as a teacher of Swedish as a foreign language. Leppäniemi writes both in Finnish and Swedish. In 2008, she won a writing competition in Finland, organized to honour Mika Waltari's hundredth anniversary. Leppäniemi's humorous novel *syntymäpaikka: naimaton* (2009, [birth place: unmarried]) is about a young Finnish woman, Tuovi, who works as a translator at a Swedish advertising agency. Her novel moves the focus from a working-class milieu to middle-class office work, which requires higher education. In this sense, Leppäniemi's novel opens up for a deepened and widened representation of the living conditions of Sweden-Finns and their encounters with the Swedish society.

## Concerning class and ethnicity during the 1970s

Hannu Ylitalo's trilogy, *Saatanan suomalainen* (1971, [Fucking Finn]), *Ruotsalaisten maa* (1971, [The land of Swedes]) and *Raukat menköhöt merten taa* (1974, [Home Sweet Home]), was received as typical working-class literature, since it deals with the theme of immigration as a class-bound phenomenon. The contents of the trilogy connect to a wider literary trend with focus on critical review of working conditions in the labour market. Ylitalo's production was published during a period when working-class literature in general was topical and a noticed literary genre. During the 1960s and 1970s, cultural life in Sweden, as in many other parts of the Western world, was marked by radicalizing and left-wing influences that also led to greater interest in social realist literature (Furuland & Svedjedal 2006, 316-318). In Sweden, authors like Göran Palm, Sara Lidman and Maja Ekelöf, published documentary report books that contributed to highlighting deficient workplace environments.

The trilogy was translated into Swedish and it received attention in the Swedish press, even in the prestigious *BLM* (Bonniers Litterära Magasin), which was characterised by left-wing literary criticism during the 1970s, with an interest in social realist literature in contemporary settings (Wendelius 2002, 78). The trilogy begins with a description of Finland towards the end of the 1960s, where the main character Raimo Kujala ends his military service and finds himself in a hopeless labour market, without any chance of getting permanent employment. As his family in Finland need money for their subsistence, he leaves for Sweden where he finds work in the motor industry in Borås. Initially, Raimo Kujala lives in miserable simple housing for the male workers at the factory. The life of the Finnish men in these barracks is monotonous and poor, dominated by their hard and inhuman work that reduces them to tiny cogs in the industrial machinery. Raimo's rescue proves to be, on the one hand, his fiancée Anja who represents forward-looking, positive energy and vitality, and on the other his intellectual interests and love of reading.

Later on, Raimo's mother and two siblings immigrate to Sweden as the mother is unable to care for the family in Finland. The trilogy ends with Raimo's marriage and the birth of his son. However, Raimo's story is far from a positive and affirmative narrative about any successful view of integration. After the death of Raimo's mother, by that time grandmother, Raimo decides to return to Finland, because he does not have any faith in a harmonious future as a Finnish immigrant in Sweden.

Within the Swedish literary field, Ylitalo's trilogy was at the time characterized as the best documentary and most penetrating description of Swedish working life, written from an immigrant's point of view (Wendelius 2002, 78). Work is the central factor that dominates and determines the life of the main characters, their place of residence and living conditions in general, their possibilities to develop as individuals, and even their leisure time. In Ylitalo's trilogy, which deals with the workplace environment at the factories owned by Volvo and Algots (sewing industry where most part of the seamstresses were Finnish female workers), the question of class is intimately interwoven with the question of ethnicity. As Saarela, one of Raimo's friends mentions ironically about Volvo's car factory: '[it is] the biggest car factory in Finland' (Ylitalo 1971, 142).[3]

In Ylitalo's trilogy, 'class' or the working class is defined in quite a complex way. On the one hand, there is a general understanding of the unity of all workers – or proletarians – while on the other hand, the foreign labour force seems to signify a more authentic representation of class. Ylitalo's narrator

---

3  All translations from Swedish and Finnish are made by Satu Gröndahl.

is aware of the variation of the status hierarchy between the different ethnic groups as well as the hierarchy between these groups and native Swedes. Different ethnic groups are described through their cultural background, even their appearance, but also through their 'other', marked languages. What especially distinguishes the Finnish workers from their Swedish colleagues is their marginalized situation as a non-Swedish-speaking population. Their possibilities of gaining political influence in trade unions are limited and they feel that the Swedish foremen disfavour them. It is also typical for the Sweden-Finnish literature in general, as is for Ylitalo's trilogy, that the Finnish workers are described as more radical – or fundamental – in their political orientation than the Swedes. For example, the Finns advocate a wildcat strike at Volvo's factory, while the Swedes tend to follow what is decreed by the trade union. Episodes like this can express the fact that the extreme left wing at the time had more support in Finland, but it can also be seen as a minority's attempt to emphasize their capability. In Sweden-Finnish literature, there are plenty of cherished descriptions about the working capacity of the Finnish immigrants, for example, how they pushed the piece rates by working very fast, to the vexation of their Swedish colleagues.

Stereotypes of ethnic minorities are also made fun of in accounts of encounters and coexistence with the majority. In his study, Erkki Vallenius has noticed that even though Hannu Ylitalo's narrator expresses pride about Finnish workers' efforts at the Volvo factory, the narrator also speaks ironically about the stereotypes of them. *Ruotsalaisten maa* reproduces a story that obviously had circulated among the immigrants, focusing on the hierarchy between different ethnic groups on the labour market (Vallenius 1998, 167). A discussion takes place between Swedish directors who want to maximize production. One director mentions that if he made the decisions, he would only employ Finns, as they are 'the best workers north of the equator'. The next director was of the opinion that since Finns are related to the peoples of the East, they already have slavery in their blood. The conclusion of the discussion was that the optimal proportions of different ethnic groups on the labour market in Sweden should be the following: 'if only we could develop Sweden in the direction that industrial work were done by Finns, the service profession were undertaken by southern immigrants and Swedes could be educated to become professional consumers. They could be paid for running from one store to another when buying things' (Ylitalo 1971, 94).

In Ylitalo's trilogy the whole of Swedish society, its social engineering machinery, officials and even native work force tend to represent an antipode or even antagonist to the 'real', authentic working class, the core consisting of Finns and other immigrants. Lack of language proficiency is an ever-present cause of misunderstandings and it shuts the immigrants inside a vacuum. From this point of view, Ylitalo's trilogy problematizes the subject and image of the traditional social realist novel or working-class literature, since it (already during the 1970s) problematized the intersection between class, ethnicity and 'other' languages. Ethnicity and marked language are in Ylitalo's production intimately bound with the definition of class; as a matter of fact, they are postulations to it. Generally, one could say that Swedish working-class literature more often than not has been described as 'literature about labourers, by labourers and for labourers' referring first and foremost to persons of Swedish origin within a monolingual Swedish body of literature (cf. Furudal & Svedjedal 2006, 24). Therefore, Ylitalo's novels widen a traditional, essentialist and ethnically homogeneous understanding of 'working class literature' in the Nordic countries.

The protagonist in Martta Matinlompolo's *Ken tietäis huomisen* (1976) is the teenager Liisa who comes to Sweden with her mother Alma in the early 1970s. The novel describes the life of Liisa during the period of about a year. The psychological relation between mother and daughter is described with a sure hand and the novel is permeated by a positive and humorous tone. Both mother and daughter seem to be strong individuals with clear goals for their lives. There is a contradiction between Alma's and Liisa's approach to life; while Alma is more of a practical person and her interests concern securing the future in material terms, Liisa is obviously an intellectual person, thoughtfully trying to understand the world and persons that surround her. Matinlompolo's novel also documents the perceived injustices and the dualistic hierarchy that divides individuals into groups of different status. Even while she was still in Finland, Liisa understood (listening to Sweden-Finns on holiday) that despite their prosperity on the Swedish labour market, they felt that they were not accepted as equals in society (Matinlompolo 1976, 24). Later on, Liisa herself experiences how her background and Finnish language gives rise to prejudices.

What is striking, nevertheless, is that Matinlompolo's novel expresses belief in the future; both Alma and Liisa are persons with integrity and ambitions. Even though Alma has problems with the Swedish language, it seems neither to bother her nor cause problems when planning for the future. *Ken tietäis huomisen* is primarily an optimistic story, and migration is seen as an opportunity for an individual to get a better life and determine one's own life conditions. The novel also connects to the description of strong women or mothers in working-class literature, a feature that has been characterized as a typical – but also idealized – feature in Swedish working-class literature (Johansson Rissén 2008, 14).

When comparing the productions of Hannu Ylitalo and Martta Matinlompolo, one could say that the attitude and approach to migration differs. While Ylitalo analyses immigration and the labour movement primarily from an ideological point of view, as a product of global capitalism, even describing the development of the protagonist becoming a class conscious citizen, Matinlompolo's narrative focuses on the individual level and emphasizes the individual's possibilities to form his/her own future. Even though Liisa criticizes Alma for her biased interest in providing them with material things and welfare, Alma also represents the female archetype who is actively taking part in the construction of the 'folkhemmet' and the future of the nation. From this angle, Alma can be seen as a representative for the progress of modernity as it (more often than not) is understood in the Nordic countries where women's contribution and equality between the sexes are seen as fundamental parts. For Alma there is only one way and direction, to the future and better prospects. Attributes connected to minority existence, such as marginalization, class-belonging and shame of one's origin or language, do not exist for her. In earlier Sweden-Finnish literature, there are plenty of novels with male protagonists, not only in Hannu Ylitalo's and Antti Jalava's works, and in this sense, Martta Matinlompolo's female characters Alma and her daughter Liisa are unique.

## Language, identity and class of the second generation

The main theme in the whole of Antti Jalava's authorship is identity and language-related issues of the second generation of Finnish-born immigrants in Sweden. One could say that Antti Jalava continues the generational storytelling after Hannu Ylitalo, who mainly focused on the experiences of the first generation, since Jalava gives voice to the growing generation and their life conditions. Nevertheless, one has to bear in mind that Jalava's production especially deals with the lives of those second generation Sweden-Finns who experienced their move to Sweden as traumatic and who were not able to build up a coherent identity after settling down in the new country.

Even the title of Jalava's early novel from the 1970s is indicative for his production and central aspects in his authorship, *Jag har inte bett att få komma* ('I did not ask to come', 1976). One often-quoted line, which can be found in the blurb on the cover of Antti Jalava's *Asfaltblomman* is his comment on his choice of literary language: 'Due to unfortunate circumstances, I write my novels in Swedish'. The narrator of *Jag har inte bett att få komma*, fourteen-year-old Markku begins his seventh grade in Swedish school. He does not understand Swedish, he is beaten and bullied, and finally starts to use his fists to defend himself. His family try to help him and his father suggests that they should switch languages at home and only speak Swedish. The attempt fails as the children and the mother feel uncomfortable with this, even humiliated. Swedish is still a forced language for them, without emotional content. Markku's opinion of the matter is that 'it is ridiculous when he tries to force us to say a lot of empty and cold words. Haven't we the right to speak the language we have learnt. At least we can do it at home' (Jalava 1976/1984, 144).

*Asfaltblomman* (1980, [Asphalt Flower]) was Jalava's breakthrough as an author and it was even seen as the first immigrant novel of high literary quality within Sweden-Finnish literature (cf Jokinen 1996). The main character, Erkki, works at a car wash in Stockholm, but like Ylitalo's Raimo Kujala, he has intellectual ambitions. He is writing an autobiographical novel about an immigrant boy called Hannu. In this projection of his own life, Erkki describes Hannu's shortcomings and his marginalization, which lead to feelings of shame and self-hatred. Hannu is not able to speak idiomatic Swedish. His Finnish background is a burden to him. He is looked down on and despised by others, and this turns into self-loathing. The only possibility is to repress and deny one's own background. As Erkki writes:

Piece after piece is drawn out and broken into bits; memories that he desperately had been holding on to, are set on fire and turned into ashes. Words are exploded and trodden upon; those that run away are hunted down and beaten up until they are unrecognizable. Contempt sows self-loathing now; hate sows self-hatred, deprecation inhibition and shame. [...] While his identity and language are destroyed he learns the others' way of reacting and talking. Sometimes he pronounces words the wrong way and then they sneer.' (Jalava 1980, 43)

In Hannu Ylitalo's trilogy, there is a similar description of Raimo's younger brother Teuvo, a boy who also became isolated and silent, finally almost mute, when moving to Sweden and starting in a Swedish class at school. The picture of the second generation's language situation is nevertheless, as we have seen, more nuanced in Martta Matinlompolo's *Ken tietäis huomisen*, which does not thematize language loss or multilingualism as a significant issue. Matinlompolo's narrator describes the challenges of learning a new language but she also stresses different strategies and possibilities of communicating even with insufficient knowledge of the majority language.

While the Finns in Ylitalo's trilogy assert themselves and retain their self-confidence by emphasizing their working capacity, Erkki's weapons in *Asfaltblomman* are more sofisticated. Erkki is fully aware of the fact that language is the ultimate ground for power relations. He has stubbornly been learning Swedish as fully and idiomatically as possible; he has literary ambitions and he exceeds his colleagues when it comes to expressions in their own mother tongue. 'The Finn', as he is called, has his revenge. While Erkki has plans for the future, his girlfriend Sirkka stands out as a lost and self-destructive person. She is attracted to drugs and prostitution and, finally, she attempts suicide. She can be seen as an ultimate representative of rootlessness and self-hatred, living for long periods in a mental 'hole' as she herself puts it, a vegetative and apathetic condition when she just lies in bed and drinks wine.

In his novels *Sprickan* (1993) and *Känslan* (1996), Jalava continues his story of the destiny of the second generation. Now, the protagonists are older, in *Sprickan* about 35 years old, but it seems that their lives have stagnated and the longing for a coherent narrative in life is still present. In *Sprickan*, the main character Hannu meets the young kitchen assistant Päivi at a Finnish parish summer house; she evokes unconscious memories from his childhood. Päivi, like many other female characters in Jalava's novels, serves as a mirror for the main character's emotions. Sirkka in *Asfaltblomman* symbolizes the destructive sides of the narrator, while Päivi with her perfect Finnish language and bright essence reminds him of Karelian nature, life in the countryside and connectedness (Jalava 1993, 142–144).

Jalava also uses other common symbols with a genderalized aspect when describing migrancy and belonging. In *Känslan*, the narrator refers to the dream of starting a family but he states that migrancy per se is an infertile state of condition. He refers to the notion of woman or the female body as a cornfield or sown field, and says bitterly to his Sweden-Finnish girlfriend: 'You will never be a mother and wife because you do not have a home land, a field.' (Jalava 1996, 90).

In *Jag har inte bett att få komma*, school and home form central spatial locations and the description of workplaces remains in the background. In Jalava's later authorship, too, it is obvious that the significant spatialities are different to those in Ylitalo's production. Urban environments and even metropolitans are prominent, as well as the restless searching for identity. In Hannu Ylitalo's and Martta Matinlompolo's novels, the Sweden-Finnish families still went to Finland, referred to as their 'home land', for holidays, while Antti Jalava's protagonists, travel both to Europe and to Finland, exploring their roots and attitude to life, trying to form a coherent narrative of their own life history. As several scholars have emphasized, cultural identities are under continuous negotiation and they can be seen as different ways of positioning oneself in the mirror of stories from the past (cf. Hall 1990/1999, 233). In Jalava's later novels from the 1990s, *Känslan* and *Sprickan*, the essence of Finnishness or Sweden-Finnishness changes and is broadened, including traits of urban nomadism. The problematic understanding of the connection between nationality and geographical belonging is clearly demonstrated, and loss of homeland and identity is also intertwined with the loss of one's first language. This in-between position amidst different nations, cultures and languages of the second generation is a universal and well-documented feature in many (im)migrant literatures. As Meyda Yegenoglu has put it, concerning the Turkish German author Emine Sevgi Özdamar's writing, the loss of native language is a 'dramatic way of demonstrating the detachment or alienation from cultural "origins" or home' (Yegenoglu 2005, 145).

## *Demanding equality in 'folkhemmet'*

Topics frequently focused on by Swedish critics in the 2000s and 2010s when analyzing Susanna Alakoski's and Elsa Hetekivi Olsson's novels concern the situation of children and young people, and child poverty in families. Their works have been seen as descriptions of the failure of the Swedish social engineering project, folkhemmet, to secure equality and safe life conditions for everyone, and, as such, they have been analyzed as part of working-class literature. It has been questioned whether the term 'working-class literature' is still adequate, and if alternative terms such as 'modern' or 'contemporary working-class literature' should be used, not least because the labour market as well as the working class have been through considerable changes since the 1920s when the term was established (Johansson Rissén 2008, 9–11).

Generally, one could say that Swedish working-class literature in many respects vanished from the official literary scene during the 1980s. While literature focusing on the lower classes and labourers was still a flourishing literary genre during the 1970s, the following decades with their dominating liberal market ideologies, undermined the significance of this literature in the public sphere. It is nevertheless obvious that since the middle of the 1990s and especially after the turn of the millennium, there has been a greater focus on class both in literary criticism and in public debate (Furuland & Svedjedal 2006, 372). Ann-Christine Johansson Rissén concludes in her reception study that younger Swedish authors like Susanna

Alakoski (b. 1962), Lena Andersson (b. 1970), Torbjörn Flygt (b. 1964), Åsa Linderborg (b. 1968) and Tony Samuelsson (b. 1961) have in interviews and reviews in leading daily newspapers clearly been associated with working-class literature. Nevertheless, all of these authors have been of the opinion that the traditional term 'working-class literature' is antiquated and that it could have an obstructive and negative effect on their authorship. Each of them emphasizes, however, that their literary production belongs to the social critical tradition. 'Class author' has also been used as an alternative term to 'working-class author' for these authors (Johansson Rissén 2008, 68). Moreover, Eija Hetekivi Olsson's *Ingenbarnsland*, published in 2012, has subsequently been characterized with similar attributes, as 'a flaming protest against social injustices in Sweden' (Littorin 2012, 12).

Both Susanna Alakoski's and Eija Hetekivi Olsson's novels have been criticized in Sweden-Finnish social groups, as well as in Sweden-Finnish media in reviews, due to the negative picture these novels convey of this minority (cf. Gröndahl 2012). When it comes to alcohol abuse, as Johansson Rissén has mentioned, several of the Swedish 'class authors' in her study deal with this problem in their novels; especially in Åsa Linderborg's *Mig äger ingen* (2007) and Susanna Alakoski's *Svinalängorna*, it is handled as a pervasive and pregnant theme. The reception of Linderborg and Alakoski has also underlined the primary role of alcohol abuse as a central theme in their works (Johansson Rissén 2008, 47–48). Thus, this (by Sweden-Finns criticized) theme in Alakoski's novel can be seen as a typical feature for the genre, rather than a specific attribute just for the Finns.

It has also been questioned whether Alakoski and Hetekivi Olsson can adequately represent Sweden-Finns' experiences, since their Finnish language is not complete enough for writing in the language. 'Is there nobody in our 'club of a half million [Sweden-Finns]' who could write about us in a somewhat positive tone!' writes pseudonym 'En helt vanlig finne' [An ordinary Finn] in the broadcast of Sisuradio's talk column (Sisuradio, 2012). Nevertheless, as was the case for Hannu Ylitalo, the novels of Alakoski's and Hetekivi Olsson are highly topical and fit in with the times in the Swedish literary field. The gallery of characters, the themes and the aspects of the narrators or focalizers in *Svinalängorna* and *Ingenbarnsland*, respectively, seem to fit well with the renewed Swedish concept of 'class literature'.

One more reason why the Sweden-Finnish literary and cultural field has criticized *Svinalängorna* and *Ingenbarnsland* is that the most important marker for Finnishness, the Finnish language, is not thematized as an identity marker in these novels. In Alakoski's novel Liisa does not seem to have problems with her two languages and her mother can at least speak passable Swedish. Language is topicalized in Hetekivi Olsson's *Ingenbarnsland* primarily as a category that produces social inequality between children with Finnish as a native language and 'Swedish' children. The main character Miira knows that her possibilities to advance in higher studies and a professional career will be limited with a final grade from home-language class tuition. She is nevertheless able to use the Swedish language and it seems that she does not have essential problems when communicating with Swedish-speaking friends. In *Svinalängorna* and *Ingenbarnsland*, a Finnish background or Finnish ethnicity does not seem to play such an important – or problematic – role as in previously presented Sweden-Finnish novels. In this way, the limits of the former, more essentialist definition of Sweden-Finnishness are questioned by Alakoski and Hetekivi Olsson and one could say that 'Finnishness' is drawn closer to what is understood as lower Swedish working class.

On the other hand, during the past years Magnus Nilsson has paid attention to what he calls 'ethnifying' of Swedish working-class literature. According to Nilsson, there has been a strong tendency to interpret social conditions in ethnic terms in Swedish literary criticism (Nilsson 2010, 58). As there is an exaggerated focus on the category of ethnicity, this has led to a discursively produced understanding where all so-called multicultural literature is primarily understood through an 'ethnic filter'. In his analysis of contemporary Swedish literature, Magnus Nilsson discusses what he calls the imaginary notion of multiculturalism that makes class invisible and culturalizes it. In Nilsson's opinion, the ultimate consequence is that exploitation of the working class is 'made invisible, or exploitation is combated by counterproductive measures' (Nilsson 2010, 79). Nilsson's critique connects to a larger discussion of multiculturalism that tries theoretically to deconstruct essentialist categories within literary criticism. However, some (im)migrant and minority literatures like early Sweden-Finnish literature and Sámi literature, are clearly connected to identity-political themes and focus especially on group-specific attributes like language. For these literatures, 'class' seems to be intimately interwoven with 'ethnicity' as a category, as well as with language, forming the core value for group identity. With reference to Nilsson's critique, Åsa Arping has also pointed out that an intersectional approach with focus on several power mechanisms – class, ethnicity, gender – produces a broader and more multifaceted analysis than when concentrating only on one aspect, such as class (Arping 2011, 196).

In his analysis of Alakoski's *Svinalängorna*, Magnus Nilsson underlines that for Alakoski, class is more important as an explanatory category than nationality or ethnicity. He points out that 'Finnishness' is not represented as a stable and homogenous category; the characters show a great variety of difference when defining their Finnish ethnicity. Thus, 'Finnishness' cannot be seen as the fundamental code for interpretation. According to Nilsson, ethnicity appears in *Svinalängorna* to be a contradictory and solely constructed category, and the novel therefore results in criticism of the notion of multiculturalism (Nilsson 2010, 159–160.) Nilsson's strong emphasis on the class aspect seems to exclude ethnicity even as an intersectional category interwoven with other factors that produce marginalization and otherness. Nevertheless, one can say that the construction of 'Finnishness' changes and is broadened in the novels of the second generation authors such as Alakoski and Hetekivi Olsson. From this point of view, Nilsson's argumentation fits into the renewed debate on multiculturalism and identity politics in today's Sweden.

The significant time for the young protagonists of Alakoski and Hetekivi Olsson is the present; the children are not thinking about the past in terms of longing for Finland or their 'home land' – for them home is Sweden, even though they have Finnish roots. Miira sometimes even refuses to accompany her parents to Finland during holidays and sees this as a release. Both Alakoski's Liisa and maybe especially Hetekivi Olssons' Miira, are proud of their Finnish background, but the reality is in Sweden, and everyday life takes place in Sweden. The school environment is one of the important spatial locations in both Alakoski's *Svinalängorna* and Hetekivi Olsson's *Ingenbarnsland*. For Liisa, the elder sister in Alakoski's family, school is the place where she can feel safe, meet functional adults and get food – and even take some home with her – when the refrigerator is empty at home. Other focused locations are the multicultural suburbs and also home settings. As Sanna Kivimäki and Eila Rantonen have pointed out, the spatial borders for movement for Alakoski's Moilanen family are most limited (Kivimäki & Rantonen 2010, 142-144). A classic example of child poverty is of course when families cannot afford holiday trips or school trips. Even though Miira's mother borrows money for her language-study visit to England, the trip is spoiled by Miira herself who refuses to participate in language training as she dislikes the dominating and authoritative English teacher. Instead, she spends her time in uncongenial slums, hiding from her host family and school mates. On a symbolic level, one could say that Miira is bound to her unfavourable background, not capable of making use of opportunities that could open up her world.

Relations to Swedes are not topicalized in terms of contradictions, as is the case in Ylitalo's or even Jalava's production, but both Alakoski and Hetekivi Olsson reproduce episodes where native Swedes represent the higher classes and those who are in practice included in the welfare state's attention. In school, both Liisa and Miira try to compensate their inferiority through sporting achievements. It is of course well known that such activities as sports can offer opportunities to segregated groups to advance in society. The inferior social position of the families is noticeable even when describing housing standard, eating habits and leisure activities. The families' possibilities to buy clothes for the children are also limited. While Liisa's mother, during the worst times, gets furniture and clothes from charity organizations, Miira herself starts to steal fashion clothes. In many respects, Alakoski and Hetekivi Olsson describe typical life conditions for poor families, without cultural and material capital and education. The Sweden-Finnish families are nevertheless seen as a part of Swedish society, and the indignant tone is directed toward social injustices, not to migration policy or treatment of immigrants.

## Renewed concept of 'Sweden-Finnishness'?

Sweden-Finnish literature has largely been defined as social-realist literature with themes of working life and harsh conditions for immigrants, characterized by power constructions and societal practices that marginalize minority languages. There has furthermore been a clear tendency in literary studies to exclude works that deal with descriptions of the Finnish-Swedish middle class, in general, educated and even well integrated Sweden-Finns.

Therefore, it is not surprising that Henriikka Leppäniemi's *syntymäpaikka: naimaton* (2009) does not seem to have left any deeper traces in the debate about Sweden-Finnish literature. The novel is about Tuovi, a thirty-year-old Finnish woman who is employed as a translator at an advertising agency in Southern Sweden, in the city of Kalmar. The novel connects to the genre of chick-lit, and it deals with Tuovi's life situation and her troubles about being unmarried. The narrator, Tuovi, ably uses the discursive stereotypes and imaginations of Swedes and Finns respectively; cultural 'differences' are described in a humorous way. At a workplace interview, Tuovi's attitude is positive and she thinks: 'There will hardly be any cultural clashes here' (Leppäniemi 2010, 11). She is filled with optimism and sees employment in Sweden as a way of advancing her career and as an exciting adventure.

After a while, Tuovi nevertheless starts to register differences in cultural behaviour. When a Swede says 'maybe' or 'we'll see', it means 'no'; the meetings at the office are extremely protracted and inefficient, and it is difficult to understand underlying messages, since the communication is too fair-spoken and indirect (Leppäniemi 2010, 32–33). These stereotypes about polite but inefficient Swedes at workplaces are well known and documented, as well as the perception of a specific Swedish 'meeting culture', characterized by consensus-thinking rather than purposefulness (Kangasharju 2007, 346). There are still no deeper conflicts and Tuovi is, despite her concerns and observations, capable of mastering her life situation and integrating into society. She moves in different environments and socialises with Finns as well as Swedes, with different class backgrounds. Leppäniemi's novel was praised by some Sweden-Finnish critics for her renewed concept when describing Finnish migrancy; certainly, for the humorous and self-ironical tone too. Furthermore, the play with cultural stereotypes reveals the conscious distance of the narrator to the subject (Niemi 2012). In this respect, one could say that Leppäniemi uses the discursive construction of 'Sweden-Finnishness' as a framing notion for her novel, and her attempt even carries traces of the carnivalization of the prevailing concept of 'Sweden-Finnishness' and 'Swedishness', respectively. Leppäniemi's novel widens the thematic areas of Sweden-Finnish literature but, more importantly, it presents a new approach when playfully using a large register of mental-historical reminiscences embedded in the common history of these groups.

As (im)migrant literature is often connected to the representativeness of certain groups or minorities, the works are understood within an 'ethnic' context that is liable to exclude wider interpretations. Interestingly, there are hardly any comparisons between Sweden-Finnish and Swedish literature in existing scholarly studies, or attempts to analyze Sweden-Finnish literature as part of two (national) literatures. In earlier scholarly studies, there has been a tendency to define Sweden-Finnish literature as a literary form that first and foremost connects to and mirrors the migrant movement during the 1970s, and as such it has been characterized as a stagnated expression belonging to the past rather than the present. As postcolonial and minority studies have pinpointed, there is an immanent paradox when positioning minorities, women and in general, 'the others', in the continuum of time. Different kinds of minorities and minority cultures are temporally often

*Finnish Book Store in Stockholm is an important venue for Sweden-Finnish authors. Photo: Jouni Suomalainen / Liekki, ruotsinsuomalainen kulttuurilehti.*

positioned in an immutable and unchangeable vacuum, as separate entities of 'our' valid time, or they are also described as non-modern, traditional and patriarchal. Demands of linguistic and grammatical purity and the use of Finnish as a literary tool belong to this 'authentic' and ethnifying definition of Sweden-Finnish literature.

On the other hand, the recent and contemporary development of Sweden-Finnish literature shows that different generations of authors deal with similar themes from different aspects, mostly depending on which time period their production concerns. It is also likely that the changed minority policy has affected the aspects of and views concerning the situation of Sweden-Finns. While Hannu Ylitalo and Antti Jalava refer to the second generation's experiences of assimilation and stigmatizing in school during the 1970s, Susanna Alakoski's and Eija Hetekivi Olsson's novels were published after 2000 when Sweden recognized Sweden-Finns as a national minority and Finnish as a minority language. Since then, this group has been assigned certain cultural and linguistic rights, and the Swedish state is obligated to support Sweden-Finnish culture as well as guarantee that the language will in the long term survive in the country. As Sweden-Finns are defined as a part of the Swedish nation and Swedish history since 2000, it is not surprising that this group might also be posed as a representative for the folkhemmet, People's Home. While 'Finnishness' is drawn closer to 'Swedishness', the Finnish language as a universal criterion for Sweden-Finns is loosening its hold. At the same time, previous contradictions between the Swedes and the Finns are losing significance and other, class-bound conflicts become more visible.

# References

Alakoski, Susanna 2006: *Svinalängorna*. Stockholm: Albert Bonniers Förlag.
Alakoski, Susanna 2010: *Håpas du trifs bra i fängelset*. Stockholm: Albert Bonniers Förlag.
Arping, Åsa 2011: Att göra skillnad. Klass, kön och etnicitet i några av det nya seklets svenska uppväxtskildringar. *Från Nexø till Alakoski. Aspekter på nordisk arbetarlitteratur*. Eds. Bibi Jonsson et al. Lund: Lunds universitet. 189–198.
Behschnitt, Wolfgang 2010: The Voice of 'Real Migrant': Contemporary Migration Literature in Sweden. *Migration and Literature in Contemporary Europe*. Ed. by Mirjam Gebauer and Pia Schwarz Lausten. München: Martin Meidenbauer Verlagbuchhandlung. 77–98.
Björklund, Krister 2010: Sverigefinländarnas långa väg från invandrare till minoritet. *Siirtolaisuus-Migration*. Turku: Siirtolaisuusinstituutti, Institute of Migration.
Bourdieu, Pierre 1991/2007: *Language & Symbolic Power*. Ed. by John B. Thompson. Transl. by Gino Raymond and Matthew Adamson. Cambridge & Malden: Polity Press.
Furuland, Lars & Svedjedal Johan 2006: *Svensk arbetarlitteratur*. Årsbok för Arbetarnas Kulturhistoriska Sällskap. Skrifter utgivna av Avdelningen för litteratursociologi vid Litteraturvetenskapliga institutionen i Uppsala, nr 49. Jubileumsskrift Brunnsvik 100 år. Stockholm: Atlas.
Gröndahl, Satu 2012: Missä viipyy suomalaisten menestystarina? *Liekki* 2012/1. Stockholm.
Gröndahl, Satu 2014: Different Directions in Analyzing Migration and Minority Literatures in the Nordic Countries. *Globalization in Literature*. Ed. Per Thomas Andersen. Acta Nordica: Studier i språk- og litteraturvitenskap. Bergen: Fagbokforlaget. 93–110.
Hall, Stuart 1990/1991: Kulturell identitet och diaspora. [orig. Cultural Identity and Diaspora]. *Globaliseringens kulturer. Den postkoloniala paradoxen, rasismen och det mångkulturella samhället*. Ed. by Catharina Eriksson, Maria Eriksson Baaz & Håkan Thörn. Nora, Nya Doxa. 1–8.
Hetekivi Olsson, Eija 2012: *Ingenbarnsland*. Stockholm: Norstedts.
Jalava, Antti 1976/1984: *Jag har inte bett att få komma*. Stockholm: Litteraturfrämjandet.
Jalava, Antti 1980: *Asfaltblomman*. Stockholm: Askild & Kärnekull.
Jalava, Antti 1993: *Sprickan*. Stockholm: Norstedts.
Jalava, Antti 1996: *Känslan*. Stockholm: Norstedts.
Johansson Rissén, Ann-Christine 2008: *Arbetarlitteraturens återkomst. En diskursinriktad analys kring föreställningar om den samtida arbetarlitteraturen i Sverige 1999-2007*. Magisteruppsats i Biblioteks- och informationsvetenskap vid Institutionen biblioteks- och informationsvetenskap / Bibliotekshögskolan 86. Borås: Högskolan i Borås.
Jokinen, Maijaliisa 1996: Sverigefinska kulturstvärvanden. *Finnarnas historia i Sverige 3*. Ed. by Jarmo Lainio. Helsinki & Stockholm: Finska Historiska Samfundet & Nordiska museet. 379-424.
Kangasharju, Helena 2007: Interaktion och inflytande. Finländare och svenskar vid mötesbordet. *Ordens makt och maktens ord. Svenskt i Finland – Finskt i Sverige IV*.

Eds. Olli Kangas & Helena Kangasharju. Helsingfors: Svenska litteratursällskapet i Finland. 341–377.
Kivimäki, Sanna & Rantonen, Eila 2010: Koti ja yhteisöt ruotsinsuomalaisten Susanna Alakosken Sikaloissa ja Arja Uusitalon Meren sylissä. *Vähemmistöt ja monikulttuurisuus kirjallisuudessa*. Ed. by Eila Rantonen. Tampere: Tampere University Press. 132–162.
Leppäniemi, Henriikka 2009: *syntymäpaikka: naimaton*. Stockholm: Finn-Kirja.
Littorin, Jens 2012: Flammande debut mot segregationen. *Dagens Nyheter* 14.1.2012.
Matinlompolo, Martta 1976: *Ken tietäis huomisen*. Stockholm: Finn-Kirja.
Niemi, Riitta 2012: Henriikka Leppäniemi: syntymäpaikka: naimaton. http://sverigesradio.se/sida/artikel.aspx?programid=1003&artikel=2765492. Quoted in 16.7.2012.
Nilsson, Magnus 2010: *Den föreställda mångkulturen. Klass och etnicitet i svensk samtidsprosa*. Hedemora: Gidlunds förlag.
Nilsson, Magnus & Lennon, John 2016: Defining Working-Class Literature(s): A Comparative Approach Between U.S. Working-Class Studies and Swedish Literary History. *New Proposals: Journal of Marxism and Interdisciplary Inquiry*. Vol. 8, No. 2 (April 2016). 39–61.
Pynnönen, Marjaliisa 1991: *Siirtolaisuuden vanavedessä. Tutkimus ruotsinsuomalaisen kirjallisuuden kentästä vuosina 1956-1988*. Helsinki: Suomalaisen Kirjallisuuden Seura, Finnish Literature Society.
Ruosulista 2012: http://groups.yahoo.com/group/ruosulista/message/12291. Quoted in 30.4.2012.
Sisuradio 2012: https://sverigesradio.se/sida/artikel.aspx?programid=185&artikel=4916182 Quoted in 17.7.2012.
Tikkanen-Rósza, Anneli 2015: *Ruotsinsuomalaisia kynäniekkoja II*. Stockholm: Finn-Kirja.
Ullgren, Malin 2012: Eija Hetekivi Olsson: Ingenbarnsland. *Dagens Nyheter* 31.1.
Vallenius, Erkki 1998: *Kansankodin kuokkavieraat. II maailmansodan jälkeen Ruotsiin muuttaneet suomalaiset kaunokirjallisuuden kuvaamina*. Helsinki: Suomalaisen Kirjallisuuden Seura, Finnish Literature Society.
Wendelius, Lars 2002: *Den dubbla identiteten. Immigrant- och minoritetslitteratur på svenska 1970-2000*. Uppsala: Centrum för multietnisk forskning, Centre for Multiethnic Research.
Yegenoglu, Meyda 2005: From Guest Worker to Hybrid Immigrant. *Migrant Cartographies. New Cultural and Literary Spaces in Post-Colonial Europe*. Ed. by Sandra Ponzanesi and Daniela Merolla. Lanham: Lexington Books. 137–149.
Ylitalo, Hannu 1971: *Saatanan suomalainen*. Helsinki: Kirjayhtymä.
Ylitalo, Hannu 1972: *Ruotsalaisten maa*. Helsinki: Kirjayhtymä.
Ylitalo, Hannu 1974: *Raukat menköhöt merten taa*. Helsinki: Kirjayhtymä.

Marja Sorvari
https://orcid.org/0000-0002-3311-726X

# Native, Foreign, Translated? 'Russian' Migrant Literature between Finland and Russia

*Introduction*

This article discusses Russian migrant literature in today's Finland with a focus on the literary representations of 'in-between' spaces, where migrants are caught up between languages, cultures and 'homes'.[1] The concepts of *transculturation, contact zone* and *diaspora* figure as theoretical concepts framing the analysis and interpretation of this literary phenomenon. Texts written by such authors as Zinaida Lindén, Liudmila Kol', Arvi Perttu, Inna Latysheva and Inna Patrakova are contemplated in the context of recent discussions on migrant literature in Finland and elsewhere. Translation, translingualism and bilingualism are at the core of their literary texts, and in fact, they are inevitable for the meaning making in the 'contact zone' between Finland and Russia.

Recognizable phenomena connected with globalization – such as migration, global communication networks, as well as the spread of ideas and people across the globe – have contributed to the construction of identities 'in-between' places and spaces. This, in turn, has brought up the question concerning the '*location* of culture', to refer to Homi Bhabha's much quoted work (cf. Bus 2002, 59). In other words due to the compression of time-space dimensions in societies, globalization has brought changes in the way we conceptualize geographical space and place (Massey 2003, 55; Massey 1991). More importantly, it has also brought changes to our perceptions of how space and place influence the construction of identities within a certain geographically-defined place (Massey 2003, 63). In postcolonial literary studies and studies on migrant literatures, the meaning of place (home, region, city, country) as a self-evident constituent of (cultural) identities has been problematized. Mobility (of people and ideas) evokes a process of hybridization or transculturation which takes place in the contact zone of different cultures, previously separate, but now interactive: they come to be in contact with each other (Hall 2003, 106–107).

---

1  I am indebted to Natalia Baschmakoff, Kirsti Ekonen, Julie Hansen, Tintti Klapuri, and Maija Könönen for reading and criticizing the earlier versions of this article.

The concepts of transculturation and contact zone were coined by Mary Louise Pratt (1992) in her study on travel writing about Africa and South America in relation to European imperial ideology. While Pratt's main focus is on colonialism and Europe's subordinated others, in my article I find these concepts extremely useful in relation to contemporary migrant literature because they raise questions concerning how migrant writers select and invent from the majority's culture as well as what they absorb into their own and what they use it for (Pratt 1992, 6). The concept of contact zone is borrowed from linguistics, where 'contact language' means the improvised language of communication where speakers of different native languages consistently interact with each other, most commonly in the context of trade (ibid.). I use the term of contact zone to refer to those literary representations where the 'spatial and temporal co-presence of subjects previously separated' is invoked (ibid., 7). More specifically, this means drawing attention to the local aspects of the phenomenon of Russian migrant literature in Finland, the *location* where the writers construct their cultural identities, and what meanings this location bears for them and the literary representations in their texts.

The concept of *diaspora* is frequently used in migrant studies to describe how the connections between ethnicity, culture, identity and place have become blurred. Stuart Hall distinguishes two ways to conceptualize 'diaspora': first, it has been used to describe a dispersed nation's striving to return to the home of their real culture, which they have kept intact. Second, it can be used to refer to a dispersed nation which will never return back to its home, but which has to come to some kind of 'agreement' with the new culture. These people belong to more than one world, they speak more than one language, and they have more than one identity and home[2]; they have learned to cope with this situation and *translate* from one culture to another; they have learned to live with differences. (Hall 2003, 121; see also Pyykkönen 2007, 50–52.) The latter definition of diaspora as translation from one culture to another comes close to how I perceive contemporary migrant writing and its location in-between or on the border of cultures. The question is not of translation in any traditional sense, or not *only* in traditional sense. According to Bhabha, '[t]he migrant culture of the "in-between", the minority position, dramatizes the activity of culture's untranslatability' (1994, 224). The 'untranslatability' of migrant culture highlights the fact that culture is 'always mixed with other cultures, because culture always overflows the artificial borders that nations set up to contain it' (Robinson 1997, 27). On the other hand, translation is at the core of migrant everyday culture; it is a 'mundane fact of life' (Robinson 1997, 27) for many migrants. Many of the writers discussed in this article have themselves translated literary texts (from Russian to Finnish, Finnish to Russian, and Swedish to Russian). Translation in the context of migrant cultures is thus not (only) a semantic

---

2  Cf. also R. Radhakrishnan (1997, xiii–xiv) according to whom diasporic subjectivity consists of the duality of an earlier home 'elsewhere' and the present home in the new country of residence; thus 'home' is a place in-between more than just one location.

transfer of meaning from one language (and culture) to another, but a basis of day-to-day existence and communication 'in-between' homes, languages, and cultures.

## Why 'Russian'?

The focus of this article is on 'Russian' migrant writers in the 2000s and 2010s, and as the quotation marks indicate, the use of this word is problematic for various reasons. It evokes the false idea that the writers and their writing form a homogeneous, unified group and mind-set, thus enforcing stereotypical assumptions about 'Russians'. The authors I shall discuss are not all Russian by nationality (one of them is a Karelian Finn), but what is common to them is their background as citizens of Russia or the former Soviet Union. A criterion for discussing them in the framework of migrant literature in Finland is that they have lived in Finland for several years and their published works discuss migrant experiences in Finland. As to the language they write their works in, it is not only Russian, but also Finnish and Swedish (the official languages in Finland) and English. This avoidance of conventional national definitions is, I think, characteristic of migrant literature all over the world. How to define this writing in academic terms is symptomatic of the phenomenon, as there are many 'names' given to this kind of literature: migrant, multicultural, translingual[3], and transnational literature. In reference to literature and writing I use the term migrant, which has connotations of mobile, nomad, and traveling, that is, shifting in-between spaces, places, languages, cultures.

It is important to note that my approach to the phenomenon of migrant literature in Finland and specifically writers with a 'Russian' background in Finland is not aimed at making Russian migrant writers in Finland a fixed category but perhaps at showing how complicated it is to put them under just one category (cf. also Löytty 2013). What *unites* the writers I discuss in this article is how their texts represent the experience of an outsider in Finnish society, and that the experience of being an outsider is linked with representations of Russia and Russianness. The writers and works I shall discuss in this article are not entirely unknown to the Finnish public and they have gained at least some space in the Finnish media (in the form of reviews, interviews etc.). The concept of the field of cultural production proposed by Pierre Bourdieu (1993) may be useful in conceptualizing and acknowledging the writers' position in Finland. The concept takes into account the position of the subject (artist, writer) not only within symbolic systems (language, myth) but also within social relations linked to the symbolic systems (Bourdieu 1993, 32). Bourdieu argues that 'it is not possible […] to make the cultural order […] a sort of autonomous, transcendent sphere, capable of developing in accordance with its own laws' (ibid., 33). In the field of cultural production, a field of positions, social agents act and deploy a possible

---

3   Translingual authors, according to Steven G. Kellman (2000) write in more than one language or in a language other than their primary one.

strategy in order to come into being within that field, to manifest, and to prevail within that field (ibid., 32, 34). Thus, the understanding of literature as part of the field of cultural production, which is not only symbolic but also social, may contribute to understanding the meaning of the phenomenon of migrant literature in contemporary culture and society and the *change* in power relations within that field. To see these writers in the context of the field of cultural production as actors helps to connect their texts with their activities, for example as participants in the competition for symbolic meanings, on the one hand, and in the construction of new contexts, for instance, in the understanding of Russianness in Finland (or Finnishness in Russia), on the other. Most of the writers mentioned in this article take part in such activities as translators (Russian to Finnish and/or Finnish to Russian), teachers (of Russian), and writers of essays, columns, etc. in Finnish and Russian periodicals, newspapers and so on. That the writers are active in the field of cultural production not just as producers of fiction but also in other ways linked to literature contributing to the mutual understanding between Finnish and Russian culture justifies discussing them in the context of this volume as migrant writers from Russia (despite their nationality).

The discussion is limited mainly to prose texts, although poetry is a popular genre in Russian migrant writing. Among poetry publications could be mentioned, for instance, *Struktura sna. Stikhi i prozaicheskie miniatiury molodykh avtorov Finliandii* (2008, [Structure of dream. Poems and prosaic miniatures by young authors in Finland], edited by Liudmila Kol') featuring texts by Polina Kopylova, Tatiana Pertseva and Anna Anokhina.[4] These authors are regularly published also in, for example, *LiteraruS* and other periodicals. In addition, *Volga-antologia,* an anthology of prose and poetry by Finno-Ugrian writers in Russia, was published in Finnish in 2010, including works by Udmurt, Mordva and Mari writers, e.g. Sergei Zavialov.

## Russians in Finland

Russia and Russians have had a historical presence in Finland at least since the early 18$^{th}$ century (Liebkind et al. 2004, 20). Although the proportion of the Russian population in Finland was very small in the early stages, in the 19$^{th}$ century Russia's influence on administrative, economic and cultural affairs was noticeable in the later formation of the Finnish state, then the Grand Duchy of Finland.[5] Historically Russian émigré writers (in the first half of the 20$^{th}$ century) have occupied marginal positions in the Finnish literary field. They wrote in Russian, not known to Finns, they were representatives of the former 'occupier', the Russian empire, and they were thus unwelcome to Finland (Pachmuss 1992, 147–172; Nevalainen 1999, 253–257). The Russian

---

4   Russian words and names have been transliterated according to the Library of Congress style.
5   On the history of Russia and Russians in Finland see, among others, Kurkinen (1985); Baschmakoff & Leinonen (2001); Pachmuss (1992); Protasova (2004); Shenshin (2008); Vihavainen (2004).

minority in Finland can be divided into the 'old' Russian minority, that is, those émigrés and their children, who were already living in Finland before 1917 or moved there after 1917 and the 'new' Russian minority, consisting of people who moved to Finland after 1960 and also those Ingrian Finns who gained the status of repatriates in 1990 when President Mauno Koivisto called them Finns. (Ierman 2006, 166, fn 1.)

Attitudes to Russia and Russians have been ambiguous and there have been many changes, which have been the focus of studies in Finnish history.[6] After the disintegration of the Soviet Union, also sociological, psychological and anthropological research on the growing proportion of immigrants from the territory of the former Soviet Union (mainly the Russian Federation and Estonia) has been published.[7] Today the Russian-speaking population is the third largest language minority group living in Finland; about 75 000 people (1.36 per cent of the population).[8] Many of them have come in hope of a better future or as repatriates to Finland.[9] However, the question of migrants and migration goes beyond statistics and classifications, as Natalia Baschmakoff (2004, 6) has pointed out. Besides the statistics and the social and economic factors, there are also feelings of, for example belonging or not belonging, nostalgia, and misunderstanding which the migrant encounters on an everyday basis (ibid., 7). There are two things at stake in migration, states Baschmakoff, referring to Edward Said's understanding of the intellectual in the world: the actual experience of migration and the *metaphorical* experience. The *metaphorical* experience of migration, displacement and alienation may occur also without the actual experience of migration, as is shown so well in the case of dissidents in the Soviet Union. The feeling of alienation is experienced also by second-generation immigrants. It is apparent that the reality immigrants experience after crossing the border has not always quite met their expectations – the Russian-speaking population is often treated with prejudice in Finland (Jasinskaja-Lahti 2007, 55; Pyykkönen 2007). In previous studies on the Russian minority in Finland, it has been noted that this group strives to become 'invisible', and to hide and assimilate themselves into the majority, because of the anti-Russian

---

6   After the 1917 October revolution and the subsequent declaration of independence of Finland, the attitudes to Russia and the Bolshevik Soviet Union changed rapidly. In the construction of the new independent Finnish national identity — especially in the 1920s and 1930s — the Soviet Union epitomized what was evil; for the communists in Finland, the Soviet Union was a source of enthusiasm (Immonen 1987, 16, 311; also Karemaa 2004). In the 1950s revisionist interpretations on Russian/Soviet-Finnish relations slowly got under way, and in the 1970s and 80s the Soviet Union was perceived as 'the Eastern neighbor', at least in the official discourses (Vihavainen 2004). The situation changed again when the Soviet empire collapsed in 1991.
7   Jasinskaja-Lahti 2000; Jasinskaja-Lahti, Liebkind & Vesala 2002; Liebkind et al. 2004.
8   Population register centre, http://www.tilastokeskus.fi/til/vaerak/2016/vaerak_ 2016_ 2017-03-29/tie_001en.html [downloaded April 7, 2017]
9   For studies on Ingrian Finns in Finland see, e.g., Davydova 2009 and numerous publications by Inga Jasinskaja-Lahti (see http://blogs.helsinki.fi/jasinska/); see also *Studia Slavica* 19/2002.

attitudes of Finns (Ierman 2006, 149). In the last few years, however, Russian writers of emigrant background have given voice to their experiences and critical perceptions of Finnish society and culture. This is where the concept of 'diaspora' as translation and coping between two cultures comes to the fore, and new kind of literature is being created, giving voice to the migrant experiences. It is these writers this article aims to discuss.

Russian diaspora literature has a relatively long history. In the history of Russian literature the term 'emigration' is linked to Russian writers, poets and philosophers who emigrated after the revolution of 1917. The so-called first wave of emigration included such prominent writers as Ivan Bunin, Zinaida Gippius, Marina Tsvetaeva, and Vladimir Nabokov, who became a prominent writer in English, as well as in Russian literature (cf. Beaujour 1989). The second wave of emigration took place after the Second World War and the third wave during the years of stagnation from the 1960s to the 1980s. During the third wave many prominent writers emigrated again, among them Aleksandr Solzhenitsyn, Joseph Brodsky, Sergei Dovlatov and Vasili Aksionov, to name a few. Although during the Soviet period émigré literature was forbidden in the Soviet Union, among the émigré writers and scholars there was a tendency to look at émigré literature as part of the whole, that is, part of Russian literature. The terms 'Russian literature abroad' (*russkaia zarubezhnaia literatura*) or 'Russian literature in exile' (*russkaia literatura v izgnanii*) were used by the prominent literary scholar Gleb Struve (1996) in his study on Russian émigré literature of the twentieth century. These concepts reflected the idea that émigré literature and exiled writers epitomized Russian literature just as well as or even more genuinely than Soviet Russian writers (Struve 1996, 22). Since the years of perestroika in the late 1980s and 1990s the situation changed so that those who emigrated no longer did so for political reasons. Moreover, the writers could return to or visit their home country if they wanted. Thus, Russian emigrant literature since the 1990s seems free to move across borders – hence it no longer is considered as 'emigrant' literature but as transcultural or transnational literature. (Klapuri 2012, 369.)

In his history of Russian émigré literature, Struve lists prominent Russian writers who emigrated for political reasons mostly to Paris, Berlin, Prague, Belgrade and Sofia, which were considered centers of Russian migration in Europe. Finland was not among the most attractive places where the first flow of émigrés headed because of its isolated location (Struve 1996, 27–28), and because they were '[u]nwelcome in Finland' as Temira Pachmuss writes (1992, 147). Finland, the former grand duchy of Russia, had suffered from repression during the last years of Nicholas II's reign, which reinforced the hostility towards Russia.

Some émigré writers, who came to Finland, however, had to stay in Finland because they lacked the means to travel further. Some of them had dachas and other familiar places there. These writers organized their own associations, literary journals and newspapers '[...] in order to endure, through this camaraderie, a new life in an alien and hostile land' (Pachmuss 1992, 147). It was also typical, that Russian émigrés and Finnish refugees (Ingrians and Carelians) formed their own, separate organizations. Russian émigré organizations held quite lively 'high culture' activites – concerts, plays, art exhibitions, literary-philosophical circles etc. – since most of the émigrés were former residents of big cities like St. Petersburg and Moscow, whereas Finnish refugees were organized around, e.g., sports clubs, youth organizations, and amateur clubs (Nevalainen 1999, 258–261).

In Finland the émigrés from Russia formed a quite heterogeneous group: they were Russians or russified citizens, refugees who had Finnish roots (so-called *heimopakolaiset*) (Nevalainen 1999). Although the Russian minority was small and scattered in Finland, their cultural life and activities were in the 1920s and 1930s surprisingly lively, as the historian Pekka Nevalainen points out. They were also subjected to criticism and prejudice, which was expressed in public opinion and the Finnish press. (Nevalainen 1999, 246–247.) Temira Pachmuss brings out quite poignantly in her study that Russian émigré writers and poets in the first half of the 20$^{th}$ century in Finland depicted in their works the hostility of Finns towards Russia and Russians and the alienation that they experienced.[10] However, some of them found solace in the Finnish landscape and nature, like for instance the poet Vera Bulich (cf. Bashmakoff 2005).

## Russian Writers in Finland Today

Russian migrant writers in Finland today continue publishing in their 'own' Russian-language literary journals and almanacs, but they have also sought other routes for publication that make their texts accessible to the readers of their new home country, such as writing texts in Finnish or in Swedish or publishing them as Finnish translations. Today there are several Russian migrant writers who publish their texts in Finnish or Swedish. A notable difference in relation to the situation of the 1920s and 1930s is that today Russian-speaking authors publish their works also in Russia in Russian publishing houses and literary journals. The writers thus actively maintain the connection with the motherland, which was not possible for the émigrés after the 1917 revolution who were separated from their homeland concretely and metaphorically. For many of the émigrés of that time Russia 'ceased to exist' after the 1917 revolution (Figes 2002, 532). They perceived their exile as temporary, and deemed it necessary to preserve their cultural heritage, which formed for them the locus of national identity (ibid., 537–539). In their isolated condition Russian culture became for the émigré communities a substitute for the motherland.[11] Today, Russian migrant writers may aim their works at the many millions of Russian speakers living abroad, and also at the inhabitants of Russia. Besides literary journals and publishing houses, many Russian-language authors publish their works themselves either in print versions or in the Internet. The creation of organizations and

---

10 The viewpoint in Pachmuss's work is sympathetic to the Russian émigrés residing in Finland, and at times her observations are emotional and even biased towards Finns.
11 I thank Natalia Baschmakoff for helping me to formulate this.

associations as well as the publication of print media and literature is an enduring feature of Russian-speaking authors abroad. Their specific goal during the 20th century and in the 21st century is to cultivate Russian language and culture among the émigré communities. A new form of transnational networks is created through the World Wide Web: numerous professional and amateur organizations and communities can be found in the Internet. Web sources create yet another form of transnational cultural 'flow' across national boundaries (Sapienza 1999, 44).

A major group of ethnic Russian 'emigrants' that was formed after the break-up of the Soviet Union without moving anywhere were those who lived in the 'border states' of the Soviet Union: the Baltic countries, Ukraine, Belorussia, Kazakhstan etc. They number about 25 million. Taisia Laukkonen (2012) has investigated Russian authors in Baltic countries and argues that Russian writers who lived in Latvia, Estonia, and Lithuania during the Soviet period experienced a notable change in their status after the break-up of the Soviet Union. Previously they represented the privileged national majority in the state and culture. After the break-up they turned into a peripheral cultural minority. Moreover, they no longer received any support from Russia, and had to search for new parameters of their literary identity. (Laukkonen 2012, 25.) However, the structure of the Russian population in the Baltic countries differs from that of Finland: the potential reading audience is notably larger there than in Finland. Needless to say, the experiences and strategies of this 'Russian diaspora' are quite heterogeneous, so there is no uniform practice in tackling the question of 'Russian identity' (Kolstø 1996, 612).

What is common for the Russian-speaking minority in Finland today and émigré writers from the 1920s and 1930s is their heterogeneity as a group and their literary and civic activity. In Finland today there are numerous associations organized by the Russian-speaking population (see Shenshin 2008, 118–122). There are various clubs, associations and publications. Russian journalists and writers have gained a reputation in the Finnish media; one example is Eilina Gusatinsky, editor-in-chief of the newspaper *Spektr*, which is a Russian-language newspaper about Finland targeted at Russian businesspeople and tourists. Many local clubs and associations have their own publications where also local authors, writers and journalists publish their texts. One of the main publications in the Russian language in Finland is the journal *LiteraruS*.

The journal *LiteraruS – literaturnoe slovo* is not only an example of how the Russian-speaking minority in Finland strives to cultivate the Russian language and culture, but also an indication of the cultural and intellectual capital that they often have. The journal, which is characterized as a historical, cultural and literary journal in Russian in Finland, a 'thick journal', was founded in 2003. The editor-in-chief, Liudmila Kol', argues that such a journal is needed in Finland to foster the process of integration of immigrants into the society and culture of their new homeland: first, the journal is intended to give a possibility for Russian-speaking inhabitants in Finland to contribute to their own culture; and second, to encourage them to participate in the Finnish cultural life by way of enriching it with their own culture and vice versa (Kol' 2004, 212). Furthermore, the journal engages

*The cross-cultural journal* LiteraruS – literaturnoe slovo *publishes texts by writers living in Russia, Russian-Finnish writers and Finnish writers.* LiteraruS *also assists in the publishing in Finland of other literature relating to Russia. The picture shows the front cover of the anthology* Missä hongat humisevat *(2006, 'Where the wind sings in the Pines'). Photo: Ljudmila Kol / LiteraruS.*

not only Russian-speaking writers in Finland, but publishes works and texts by writers living in Russia and Finnish writers with a command of Russian. It publishes translations of works of Finnish literature and essays on Finnish writers. Thus, the journal functions, in a way, as a 'contact zone' facilitating intercultural exchange in matters of literature, culture and history in Finland and in Russia. The journal's main goal is thus the *integration* of Russian speaking inhabitants into Finnish society and culture, not assimilation nor separation. The journal is published quarterly, and it publishes additionally one issue per year in Finnish (since 2008) and one in Swedish (since 2009). The journal is funded by, among others, the Ministry of Education in Finland and the Russkii Mir Foundation. Writers publishing in the journal *LiteraruS*, include Russians who have gained Finnish citizenship and live permanently in Finland, Russians who write and live in Russia, as well as Finns who write in Russian or whose texts have been translated into Russian. This is a cross-cultural publication whose writers are united by the Russian language and their engagement with Russian language and culture. Its aim to further integration through involvement with the immigrants' own native language and culture as well as its endeavor to publish in Finnish and Swedish adhere to the official policy in facilitating immigrants' integration into Finnish society.

What is common to the works discussed in this article is their focus on Finnish society and culture from the perspective of 'Russians' who are no longer silent – their texts talk to us about 'Russian' migrants' strategies of giving voice to their experiences in-between two (or several) homes, languages, cultures and identities.

### *Ljudmila Kol'*

Ljudmila Kol' (pseudonym) has lived in Finland since the early 1990s. Before that Kol' resided in many countries and taught Russian as a foreign language. Kol is the editor-in-chief of the journal *LiteraruS-Literaturnoe slovo*. She began her literary career in Finland. Her first book *Gala-kontsert* (1995) included plays and stories written in Russian, and was published in Finland. Since then Kol has published several books of prose in Russian both in Finland and in Russia, as well as many articles, columns and essays. She writes in Russian and maintains an active connection to the Russian literary field, as she publishes regularly in Russian literary journals such as *Druzhba narodov, Zvezda, Neva, Sever, Carelia, Literaturnaia ucheba* etc. Her prose works can be characterized as psychological prose, focusing on the everyday experiences of their characters. In her novel *Ania, Kiska, Nelivanna, ili istoriia moego seksa* (2002) Kol' deals with the controversial issue of female sexuality in Soviet Russia.

Kol' deals with the immigrant experience in a number of her short stories. Her collection of stories *Roman s zagranitsei* (2009) includes many already previously published stories on the subject. As in her activity as the editor-in-chief of the journal *LiteraruS*, in her prose texts Kol represents the experience of a Russian in Finland who is keen to get to know the country, its inhabitants and its culture, but at the same time remains who she is, a Russian, with a Russian worldview.[12] As has been mentioned, as a writer Liudmila Kol' is

---

12 Symptomatically, a Russian review of *Roman s zagranitsei* concludes that Ljudmila Kol' has done a lot already in order to be entitled to be 'allowed' in Russian literature. (Tul'chinskii 2009, www.)

drawn to the Russian literary field – hence her emphasis on the concept of Russian culture in *diaspora*. Kol writes in her story 'Finnlandiia':

> According to unofficial statistics, more than 10 million Russian-speaking people live outside the borders of the former USSR. Now, when millions of refugees and repatriates move from one place to another and there are no borders, the theme of 'home' is important for many. [...] Finland has its own specialness from the perspective of a [Russian] immigrant. When you move far away from Russia, your own country is at an extreme distance. But here everything is so nearby: it takes three hours by train to the [Finnish-Russian] border, and whether you want it or not, every day you return in your mind back to the Russian reality [*realii*]. (Kol' 2009, 239–240.) [13]

For some Russians the theme of home is indeed part of the nostalgic 'diasporic' identity for those living outside the borders of Russia. Liudmila Kol's activity as an editor and author within the Russian-speaking diaspora in Finland contributing to Finnish-Russian cultural exchange and facilitating the contribution of Russian and Finnish writers mutually to each other's cultures as well as her writing on her own position in Finnish cultural society can be seen as the activity of a cultural mediator, or a cultural translator, who translates for herself the realities and meanings of the foreign culture, and *vice versa*, translates her own culture for the foreigner. For the narrator of Kol's stories in *Roman s zagranitsei*, Finnish culture, mentality and people delve into her Russianness, Russian language and culture. This accentuates her location in-between homes, languages, and cultures, and the formation of her identity as a Russian writer in Finland. The main protagonist of her short stories, the I-narrator, sometimes looks for contact among the 'aboriginals', though sometimes she just does not understand what they mean, as in the following quotation:

> My neighbour looks at the bushes here and there and finally says philosophically:
> – Kastelet... [= you're watering... - MS]
> – Excuse me? I ask.
> – Kastelet! [You're watering! – MS]
> Good God! What is he talking about? Bushes are in Finnish 'pensaat', that I know for sure! And 'castle' is English!
> – What are you saying? I don't understand, what does 'kastelet' mean? (Kol' 2009, 44)

This is one of the humorous encounters that the I-narrator of the opening story 'Tam gde zveniat sosny' from the publication *Roman s zagranitsei* experiences. These cultural meetings or collisions often have to do with language and cultural differences between Finns and Russians. In the above quoted passage it is important how words sound. 'Kastelet' is in a way 'untranslatable' in this case, because the whole incident is based on the sound of the Finnish word and its similarity with the English word 'castle'. This code-switching, the use of foreign words and concepts in the text, is

---

13 All translations from Russian or Finnish are mine – MS.

a feature of a multilingual society as such (Devarenne 2013, 71), but it is also a sign of the 'untranslatability' of the culturally-specific practices and meanings. The presence of the foreign words also indicates the migrant, multilingual style, where the co-presence of several languages is an everyday occurrence. This passage resembles translingual wordplay, as outlined by Julie Hansen, according to whom translingual wordplay '[...] transcend[s] the semantic boundaries of individual languages, remind[ing] the reader that words are not always what they seem, and that they are not always limited to a particular context' (Hansen 2012, 548). Kol', however, is not a translingual writer, because she writes in Russian, her mother tongue, and not in a foreign, acquired language as, for example, Zinaida Lindén, whom I will discuss in the following, does. Yet Kol's text, as the passage above shows, implies the assumption that the reader knows many languages (Finnish, Russian, English) and plays with the interaction/misunderstandings between languages and cultures.[14]

## Zinaida Lindén

As mentioned above Zinaida Lindén, so far perhaps the best-known among contemporary writers with a Russian background in Finland, can be considered as a translingual writer. She was born in Leningrad 1963 and graduated from the University of Leningrad in 1986 with Swedish language and literature as her major. She moved to Finland in the beginning of the 1990s after marrying a Finn. In contrast to many Russian-speaking writers in Finland, Lindén is an exception because she writes her works in Swedish, which is the other official language and the biggest minority language in Finland. Like other writers who emigrated in the late 1980s and early 1990s from Russia, such as Andreï Makine in France and Wladimir Kaminer in Germany, Lindén chose to write fiction in the language of her new home country (Klapuri 2012, 409). According to Adrian Wanner, choosing a foreign language as a literary expression 'involves a radical act of assimilation to the culture of the host society' and is not without risks. It is difficult to master a foreign language so well as to choose it as an artistic medium; and by choosing it one can be accused of abandoning one's native tongue (Wanner 2011, 5–6). The difference in Lindén's case compared to the internationally known writers Makine and Kaminer is that in Finland Swedish is a minority language, which in a way makes her a representative of not only one but two minorities in Finland (Klapuri 2012, 409). Lindén's debut novel was awarded the Runeberg-prize in 2005, so it can be said, that her language choice has proven quite successful.[15]

14 The above quoted story has been translated into Finnish in the anthology *Missä hongat humisevat* (2006) and the translingual aspect has been preserved.
15 Lindén's case forms an interesting analogue with the nineteenth-century writer Marie Linder (1840–1870). Linder was one of the first women authors in late 19th century Finland. She wrote her works in Swedish (which was at the time the official language in the Grand Duchy of Finland). The main character of Linder's novel *En qvinna af vår tid* (1867) represented an exceptional female character in

*Zinaida Lindén. Photo: Katri Lehtola / Schildts & Söderströms.*

The debut novel *I väntan på en jordbävning* (2004, [Before the earthquake]) and its 'sequel' *Takakirves-Tokyo* (2007) describe the experiences of a generation that was born in the 1960s and emigrated from the Soviet Union/Russia – thus adding an autobiographical flavor to the narrative, which is not unusual for emigrant writers (Klapuri 2012, 409; Rantonen 2010, 168).[16] These novels have similar main characters – a Russian woman writer living in Finland and a Russian sportsman living in Japan – and the novels narrate their life stories. The first novel *I väntan på en jordbävning* focuses on the life story of Ivan Demidov, a Russian fireman-cum-Sumo wrestler, narrated from his point of view as an I-narrator. Demidov's story is a *mise en abyme* – a story within a story. The frame story is built around an encounter with a Russian woman, a writer living in Finland, in the

---

the Finnish literary landscape and of the early Finnish women's movement with its cosmopolitanism and liberal views (Launis 2005, 245–246; 292–293). Both novelists address questions that go beyond the strictly national theme, but they nevertheless participate in the discussion of the most heated questions of their own time: the women's movement in late 19th century Finland and the mobility of people, ideologies and values in 21st century Finland.

16 Lindén's publications also include *Överstinnan och syntetisatorn* (1996), *Scheherazades sanna historier* (2000), *Lindanserskan* (2009), *För många länder sedan* (2013) and *Valenciana* (2016).

Tolstoy-train from Moscow to Helsinki. The anonymous woman writer and Demidov start talking. During the long sleepless night in the moving train, 'the space of the foreigner'[17], Demidov tells his story to the woman writer: how he became an elite sportsman and a fireman in Leningrad, and ended up in Japan as a Sumo-wrestler, married to a Japanese woman, and with a daughter. This story of the foreigner/immigrant told overnight in the moving train epitomizes the not only geographical but also psychological, cultural and emotional journey from the previous home to the new home, to another space and time, which, in the transitional/intermediary space of the moving train, become a linear story.

During the conversation with Demidov, the woman writer recalls her own past in the Soviet Union, and her own youth there, and how she found herself uprooted from her Soviet/Russian life and moved into 'another epoch, another dimension, another language'.[18] The narrator experiences strong feelings of nostalgia towards that Soviet/Russian life, which is lost not only because it is past and she has a new life in Finland, but because the Soviet Union ceased to exist: she can never return to her native land and native city, Leningrad. The feeling of nostalgia is connected to everyday 'trifles', tastes, smells, sounds and everyday surroundings, which the narrating I remembers. The recollection of the Soviet life style and commodities forms a parallel with the phenomenon of *Ostalgie* which took place in Germany in the 1990s in the form of remembering the former East Germany (Heinämäki-Sepponen 2010, 397). The nostalgic recollection of socialist childhood and youth is detected also in the works of the Russian-German writer Wladimir Kaminer (Mäkikalli 2010, 387). Lindén's novels contribute to this 'transnational trend' of Soviet nostalgia.[19]

The second novel *Takakirves-Tokyo* consists of the email correspondence between Ivan and Iraida (the woman writer, who is no longer anonymous) (See Sorvari 2016). Both novels thus use literary spaces which construct the metaphorical experience of being 'in-between' cultures – traveling, train, correspondence – which stand as a metaphor for the emigrant's situation when after having left her home country she is not feeling at home in the new country.

Lindén can be considered as a translingual writer, because she writes in the language of her new home country. However, she represents an exception among contemporary Russian translingual diaspora (Wanner 2011) because she translates her Swedish texts into Russian herself, or, as she puts it, she

---

17 'The space of the foreigner is a moving train, a plane in flight, the very transition that preludes stopping' (Kristeva 1991, 7–8).
18 'Då, i augusti åttioåtta, kunde jag ju inte veta att jag bara två år senare skulle bli uttryckt med rötterna ur mitt vanliga, ryska, sovjetiska liv, för att i ett huj, såsom med en tidsmaskin, förflyttas till en annan epok, en annan dimension, ett annat språk' (Lindén 2004). Here, the Swedish word 'huj' has a phonetic resemblance with a well-known Russian swear word, which is recognizable to those readers who know Russian.
19 Lindén's 2013 novel *För många ländar sedan* continues to delve into the Soviet past. The novel – as the title suggests – also discusses the theme of the 'global' lifestyle of modern people, whose lives are not bound to one geographical or national location.

has two working languages at once: Swedish and Russian.[20] Her novels, discussed briefly here, could also be called transcultural, since they move between several cultures: Soviet/Russian, Finnish/Swedish and Japanese. A closer look at her novels might suggest that her texts are translingual, that is, that there is a presence of more than one language, and also a movement *between and beyond* them (Hansen 2012, 543). This is an interesting case for future investigation, and it makes also an interesting parallel with Liudmila Kol's texts which, as I mentioned earlier, presuppose knowledge of several languages.

## *Arvi Perttu*

In contrast to the previous writers, the next writer has a background in Russia, but his mother tongue is Finnish. Arvi Perttu (b. 1961) moved to Finland from Russian Karelia, Petrozavodsk, in 2000, after having lived almost forty years in Russia (and the USSR). Perttu, himself a Karelian, started writing before moving to Finland (e.g. the novels *Nuotio Hirvenkivellä*, 1989 and *Petroskoin symposium*, 2001) in Finnish. However, in the Finnish literary field Perttu's works have not made a break-through as yet, although one of his latest novels *Skumbria* (2011), which I will discuss in this article, would seem to fit the demand for migrant literature perfectly: the experience of a Russian immigrant in Finland. Perttu's first language in Russia was Finnish, as he says in an interview, *Kalevala* Finnish, because he comes from the area where the *Kalevala* (the national epic of Finland) is set. Perttu states that he feels like a stranger both in Russia and in Finland, but that his otherness is not the same as for example someone who comes from Africa to Europe. His otherness is that of being a stranger in one's homeland – belonging to minority, to the margins. (*LiteraruS* 2009: 2.) Writing his works in Finnish while still living in Russia, in the Republic of Karelia, Perttu was not easy to categorize either: was he a Finnish or a Russian writer? In any case, he was a provincial (*provintsial'nyi*) writer, as he states in his essay 'Mol'chanie immigrantov' (2017, [The silence of immigrants]). Perttu also proposes, that one reason for his marginality – in Russia and in Finland – is that he does not belong entirely to *other* people or *own* people.

Perttu's literary identity in its early stages in Petrozavodsk formed in the aftermath of the breakup of the Soviet literary institution, the decline of (socialist) realism, and the advance of modernist tradition and postmodernist (or alternative) literary aesthetics (Kolomainen 1998). Perttu's early works published in the literary journal *Carelia* described openly sexual scenes and alcohol consumption, which caused a shock to the readers of the journal, who were not used to such descriptions in fiction (ibid.). In the reviews on Perttu's works published in Finland, the writer's status as an immigrant writer is a key in the discussion (Waarala 2006, Virkkunen 2006, Kukkola 2008, Mäkelä 2012).

20 This was expressed by Lindén in an e-mail interview with the author of this article in 2014. The discussion of Lindén's work in the context of self-translation is a topic of another paper (Sorvari 2014).

Perttu's first novel published in Finland *Papaninin retkikunta. Romaani Neuvosto-Karjalasta* (2006) describes the dramatic 1930s in Petrozavodsk from the viewpoint of Finns already living in, or returning to Karelia from USA and Canada. The main protagonist and I-narrator, Jarkko Pettersson, is an ambitious journalist and writer who aims to write a novel, but he – like many others at that time – is caught in the middle of the Stalinist purges. The novel epitomizes the fate of many Finns in the Soviet Karelia in the 1930s and touches upon Perttu's own family history (Kukkola 2008). The novel's style shifts between realistic and postmodernist writing: the narrative engages in real historical events but describes them from the subjective perception of the main protagonist with his fantasies, dreams, nightmares and desires, which often carry a distorted understanding of the surrounding reality.

In the second novel published in Finland, *Skumbria* – a word also referring to smoked mackerel in Russia – the narrative is constructed between two characters' perspectives: that of Pauli, a Karelian living in Petrozavodsk with his sister in their late mother's apartment[21] and that of Katri, a Finn who comes to Russian Karelia to participate in a seminar. Both are at a crossroads in their lives. Pauli is tired of instability in his life: he has no apartment, no safe haven in his life, except perhaps for his sister, who is his only remaining close relative. Katri has recently lost her job, ended a relationship and finds herself in a difficult economic situation. For Katri, the trip to Russia offers an escape from her current life and problems; she falls in love with Pauli and apparently with Russia. Pauli also falls in love with Katri, who gives him warmth and love. At first their relationship consists only of robust sex described almost naturalistically, but it ends up with Katri moving to Petrozavodsk to live with Pauli and them getting married. Through this constellation – a Finnish woman and a Russian man – the narrative turns the stereotypical situation upside down (a Russian woman marrying a Finn). Stereotypes and national differences are at the core of the novel: the reality in Russia that Katri sees is bleak, but people look and are happy nevertheless; Katri comes from the rich west but it is Pauli who pays for her because she is penniless; Pauli and other Russians seem poor, but somehow they also seem to have money, to which their attitude is glaringly nonchalant. In this narrative even sex positions portray cultural and social differences: Katri realizes that Pauli's keenness to have anal intercourse is a method of contraception.

Differences between Finland and Russia become more apparent when Pauli and Katri move to live in Finland. Everything seems to work the other way round: Finland is the land of freedom, but paradoxically it is full of prohibitions, regulations and rules, even in their own home. Pauli feels like he is in prison (177). Nevertheless, for him Finland is 'Skumbria' – secure, predictable and a safe haven (179).

---

21 Skumbria is intertextually linked with Perttu's earlier novel *Papaninin retkikunta* continuing Pettersson's story (Pauli is his grandson) and with the cycle of stories with a main character called Lesonen (Pauli's family name is Lesojev). Perttu's latest novel entitled *Kipu* (2014, [Pain]) deals with Vienan Karjala, Northwestern part of Russia, and its history. In 2016 Perttu published a novel *Kuningattaren vuosi* [The year of the queen].

Language is the key issue for Perttu and many other immigrant writers; in other words, if a writer with an immigrant background is able to write a novel in the language of his/her new home country, the chances of getting a publisher and an audience for it increase dramatically. In Perttu's view the reason for the silence of Russian-speaking writers in Finland is language, and that is why the story of a Russian immigrant is needed in Finnish: it is both necessary for the sake of the Finnish audience (most of whom do not know Russian) and the Russian-speaking immigrants themselves (Perttu 2007). Texts by immigrant writers who write in a foreign language often address a double audience – the mainstream readers and members of the ethnic minority (Rantonen 2010, 175). One way of breaking that silence of the immigrants is to publish translations. That there is a demand for Russian-speaking immigrants' stories in Finland was demonstrated by the publicity surrounding two works (an autobiography and a novel) on the Russian immigrant's experience published in Finnish translation by Inna Latysheva and Inna Patrakova in 2010.

## Inna Latysheva and Inna Patrakova

If it is important to consider, beyond classifications, statistics, numbers and calculations, also the *feelings* related to migration, an example *par excellence* is the autobiography by Inna Latysheva (b. 1955) *Ryssänä Suomessa. Vieras väärästä maasta* (Latiševa 2010). However, whereas Baschmakoff points to the feelings of displacement and alienation as *metaphorical* and common to migrants irrespective of place or nationality, Latysheva's work concentrates solely on the (negative) feelings and experiences of a Russian woman in Finland. The book received wide publicity in the media (TV, print media, Internet) with its disheartening description of the prejudice and intolerance of the Finnish people toward the I-narrator. The same year, another book was published, also describing the experiences of a Russian woman in Finland, and with a revealing title – *Tulkki* [The Interpreter] by Inna Patrakova (b. 1970). Whilst Latysheva's autobiographical account describes the immigrant's experience as traumatic, Patrakova's text tells a more optimistic story and is lighter in tone.

These books crossed the linguistic border between Finns and Russians as they were published in Finnish translations (from English and Russian) and were hence addressed to Finnish readers and immigrants who know Finnish. Both describe the difficulties of immigrant single-mothers in adapting to new cultural norms and their experience of being treated as second-class citizens. This immigrant women's writing on their lives in-between cultures and languages can be interpreted not only as a re-definition and re-location of the migrant writers' own identities in the hybrid, 'third' space, but also as an inscription of their voice into Finnish culture, and a re-evaluation of the norms of Russian culture.

For a foreigner, where he or she comes from and where he or she is moving to are of crucial significance. How the hopes and attitudes of those who arrive and those who receive can drastically differ is portrayed in Inna

Latysheva's book. The author describes vividly how she came to Finland as a bright, well-to-do young Russian woman to live in the country of her dreams with the love of her life. However, after only a few months she felt like a second-class citizen in Finland – unemployed, without social networks, dependent on her husband and lonely, because of where she comes from. She continued to feel ashamed of her nationality, although she 'made it', and became a successful businesswoman and manager. Her children were ashamed of their own Russianness and of her. Her son asked her not to speak to him in Russian in public and not in Finnish either because from her accent it could be heard that she was Russian. This feeling of being ashamed of one's language was also noticeable within the 'old' Russian minority in Finland (Baschmakoff & Leinonen 2001). Hence the Russian minority has been called the 'hidden' minority; Russian migrants strived to be 'unseen' for the majority because of the prejudice they experienced (Ierman 2006, 149). The reasons for this prejudice stem from the historical and political situation in Finland, as described at the beginning of this article. This local context and perspective is central in arguing for the specificity of Russian diasporic literature in Finland – all of the writers discussed in this article in one way or another discuss their identity as Russians in Finland. A notable difference, for instance, to Russian migrant literature in the USA is that when Russian-American writers tend to make a brand of their Russianness, (Wanner 2011, 188), or more specifically, of constructed 'Russianness' for foreign readership (ibid., 3), for writers discussed in this article their 'Russianness' bears traumatic experiences and memories in Finland for them as well as for Finns.

This is also the experience of many others in other countries, who 'come from the wrong country', as Latysheva puts it. Latysheva's memoirs bring to mind literary accounts by migrant women writers in other national settings. An especially noted example is Joan Riley's novel *Unbelonging* (1985), which is a fictional account of a young Jamaican woman's experience in London, where she feels herself a second-class citizen without a possibility to escape from her situation. The gloominess of Riley's novel (Fischer 2004) is comparable to that of Latysheva's autobiographical account, which, however, presents the narrator's escape from her desperate situation in Finland to a much brighter and happier setting in Spain. Riley's and Latysheva's accounts – as remote they are from each other geographically, culturally and temporally – indicate the 'pattern' of displacement of migrants, and especially women, who are often emotionally and economically bound to their family, namely their husband and children. Thus, when she then moved to live in Spain, she and her family had a completely different experience as immigrants, and they were each accepted as a 'first-class' citizen, 'one of us' there. According to Latysheva this was because the Spanish society as a whole did not treat immigrants from Russia or Finland with prejudice; on the contrary, they were treated in a very friendly manner (Latiševa 2010, 226, 234).

The voicing of the experience of discrimination, humiliation and displacement is of great importance not only to the immigrant her/himself, or to the fellow immigrants who have experienced the same, but also to those who belong to the majority. The intentional voice of the narrator is quite clear in Latysheva's book: her main goal is to help others who have experienced the same, to overcome the feeling of being second-class, and to inform the majority of how it feels to be rejected, discriminated against and overlooked on the basis of what your nationality/ethnicity is. As in Perttu's novel *Skumbria*, the I-narrator in Latysheva's autobiography wants to find security, that is, a safe haven where she can live in peace and prosperity, and that place for her is Finland. However, that is the place she has imagined before setting foot there. The I-narrator has set in her mind Finland as an *imagined* place that exists only in her dreams, and as soon as she crosses the border her dreams come crashing down. Finland proves to be a cold, unfriendly place, where Russians are 'the enemy'.

Actually Latysheva came to Finland from the Soviet Union in the 1980s, when Finland is quite isolated from outside influences. The flow of immigrants began more actively only in the 1990s. The experience of Inna Patrakova who moved to Finland in the 1990s is already quite different, but there is a difference also in the attitude to the experience of immigration itself in Patrakova's text. The text is 'autobiographical', but it differs quite a lot from Latysheva's autobiography. Patrakova constructs a fictional character, Olga, who works as an interpreter and business consultant in Helsinki. The title is both literal and metaphorical: an interpreter is a specialist in intercultural communication, thus having a command of cultural knowledge of the two language areas she works with. The aim of the novel is apparently to enhance and facilitate the growth of intercultural communication between Russians and Finns.

The story starts 'as if' dramatically: while she is on her way to a business meeting, the heel of Olga's shoe gets stuck in the middle of the road when she's crossing the road in the city of Helsinki. She tries to pull the shoe out and feels like an idiot:

> The passers-by didn't laugh or point fingers at me as they would have done in Russia. Nobody came to my rescue either, but instead looked like nothing had happened, as usual. A driver of one car made a delicate gesture with his hand, as if he was letting me cross the road. Well thanks a lot! (Latysheva 2010, 6.)

Finally a construction worker from a nearby construction place comes and helps Olga to pull out the shoe from the street. Olga hugs and kisses her rescuer, leaving him in the middle of the road shocked by her kiss.

Olga's 'adventures' in Finland take her golfing and sailing, and she moves back to Russia and back to Finland again. Her 12-year-old daughter, Liza, brings a pony to their house. Olga is keen on shopping and her weakness is shoes. Beneath the humorous, light narrative there is a fragile fibre evoking the problematic issues of discrimination and prejudice towards immigrants. Particularly the stereotypical assumption that immigrant women, especially from Eastern Europe, are prostitutes comes up in the text, for instance in the following small scene:

> The drunkard sitting on the bench ([in Finland] every apartment house has at least one) woke up from his deep sleep and greeted me in his usual way:
> – Hello, Estonian whore!
> – Russian, I corrected him with a slight reproach. (Patrakova 2010, 22.)

*Tulkki* could be described as a satire of Finnish society, its immigration policy and its attitude to foreigners. The narrative constructs a different story of the negative experiences of the immigrant than Latysheva's narrative, which revolves around the position of the discriminated immigrant and her images of what Finland and Finns should be like. This situation causes such a strong opposition to everything Finnish that she decides she will never become Finnish (Latiševa 2010, 64). The metaphor for living in Finland as a Russian given in Latysheva's autobiography is like being in a wheelchair after having been able to 'walk, dance and travel' (Latiševa 2010, 82). *Affect and emotions* are the key narrative element, the 'engine' in Latysheva's autobiography: shame caused by her poor circumstances in Finland compared to that in Russia; fear and sorrow caused by her former husband's attitude to his family; anger caused by Finns and their impoliteness and coldness towards other, especially foreign, people. The effect on the reader also evokes affect: shame, anger and sadness, but also laughter caused by the description of how Finns behave seen from the perspective of a foreigner.

The perspective in Patrakova's novel is more ambiguous: the satirical depiction is not limited to Finns and their stereotypical attitudes and perceptions of foreigners and Russians, but expands also to include Russians and contemporary Russian society. Olga happens to meet a rich Russian businessman; they start a relationship and Olga plans to move to Moscow with him. Life in Moscow is at first a relief, but gradually Olga notices that Russia has changed and she herself has changed – she views the Russian way of living through different glasses, perhaps Finnish glasses? At least, she is reluctant to take on the role of a wife, who lives on her husband and spends his money, and whose role is just that – to be his wife. Olga rejects that opportunity and moves back to Finland, where she finds her previous apartment, her friends and her previous worries and problems, but where she is independent.

In her study on the global city and women migrants, Susan Alice Fischer notes that 'women's migration brought about by the pressures of capitalism and postcolonialism [...] calls into question the very definitions of home, belonging, nation, and identity' (Fischer 2004, 107). How is home or landscape viewed from this 'dislocated' view? How does the new status as migrant merge with the historical ways of understanding and interpreting spaces crossed through by 'difference and privilege' (ibid.). Latysheva's home in Finland was not the place of security and peace she had dreamed of, but instead a place of deprivation and loneliness, being the opposite of the place she had left in Russia. Patrakova's Olga did go back to Russia, but found out that home there meant dependence and discrimination of another kind than in Finland, where she at least was allowed to be independent despite being poor and alien.

The success of Patrakova's first published novel prompted her to write more novels on the theme of Russians and Finns, namely *Naapurit* (2011, [Neighbours]) and *Kultahammas* (2012, [Golden tooth]). The title of *Naapurit* is both concrete and metaphorical: the novel describes the relations between two families – one Russian, one Finnish – who have bought neighbouring summer cottages, but it also describes the stereotypical perceptions of Finns and Russians about the neighbouring nation. The plot is similar to Perttu's *Skumbria* but the other way around: a Russian *nouveau riche* couple comes to Finland to find a place to relax after a hectic life in St Petersburg. This is not a story about immigrants in Finland, but rather about the stereotypes that Finns and the Finnish media have about the 'new Russians' who come and buy Finnish summer cottages. As in her debut novel and as in *Skumbria*, the narration plays with both Finnish and Russian gender roles, representing them from an estranged perspective.

## Conclusion

The writers discussed in this article can be associated with the modern concept of migrant or transnational literature in Finland and their works contribute to the change in the understanding of cultural identities as constructed in the contact zone of different cultures, languages and spaces. It can be said that their literary texts construct the experiences of immigrants from Russia in Finland, and this construction has a lot in common with translation as communication between two cultures, languages and countries. While economic, cultural and ethnic boundaries drawn according to nation-states have become more porous, more attention has been called for the 'location' where these boundaries are re-negotiated and challenged. Translation, translingualism and bilingualism are at the core of these literary texts, and in fact, they are inevitable for the meaning making in the 'contact zone' between Finland and Russia. The writers 'translate' the experiences of migrants from Russia for the Finnish readers, as well as Finnish cultural practices and realities for themselves, whether in Finnish, Swedish, or Russian. One thing is sure: these writers and their texts participate in the struggle over meanings of 'Finnishness', 'Russianness', migration, and identity in the field of the cultural production of literature.

# References

Baschmakoff, Natalia & Marja Leinonen 2001: *Russian Life in Finland 1917–1939. A Local and Oral History. Studia Slavica Finlandensia XVIII*. Helsinki: IREES.
Baschmakoff, Natalia 2004: The Émigré and the Question of Otherness: Refugees, Immigrants, Repatriates on their Way Towards Social Participation. *Studia Slavica Finlandensia. Tomus XXI. Russian-speaking immigrant population in Finland*. Ed. by Petra Sinisalo-Katajisto, Katja Hirvasaho & Edvard Hämäläinen. Helsinki: Institute for Russian and East European Studies. 5–15.
Baschmakoff, Natalia 2005: Vera, ritual i otkrovenii: konfessional'nyi obraz V.S. Bulich, russkogo poeta v Finliandii. *Baltiiskie perekrestki. Etnos. Konfessiia. Mif. Tekst*. Ed. by T.V.Tsiv'ian et al.. Sankt-Peterburg. 181–196.
Beaujour, Elisabeth Klosty 1989: *Alien Tongues: Bilingual Russian Writers of the "First" Emigration*. Ithaca: Cornell University Press.
Bhabha, Homi K. 1994: How Newness Enters the World: Postmodern Space, Postcolonial Times and the Trials of Cultural Translation. *The Location of Culture*. Ed. by Homi K. Bhabha. London & New York: Routledge. 212–235.

Bourdieu, Pierre 1993: *The Field of Cultural Production: Essays on Art and Literature.* Ed. and intr. by Randal Johnson. Cambridge: Polity Press.

Bus, Heiner 2002: 'Home as Found'. Homelands in German Turkish Migrant Literature and in U.S. Ethnic and Immigrant Literatures. *Literature on the Move. Comparing Diasporic Ethnicities in Europe and the America.* Ed. by Dominique Marçais, Mark Niedermeyer, Berhard Vincent, Cathy Waegner. Heidelberg: Universitätsverlag C. Winter. 59–69.

Davydova, Olga 2009: *Suomalaisena, venäläisenä, kolmantena: etnisyysdiskursseja transnationaalissa tilassa.* Joensuu: Joensuun yliopisto.

Devarenne, Nicole. 2013: Complicity, Entanglement, and Translation: Three English/Afrikaans Texts. *Journal of Commonwealth Literature* 48:1. 61–76.

Figes, Orlando 2002: *Natasha's Dance. A Cultural History of Russia.* London, New York et al.: Penguin Books.

Fischer, Susan Alice 2004: Women Writers, Global Migration, and the City: Joan Riley's "Waiting in the Twilight" and Hanan Al-Shaykh's "Only in London". *Tulsa Studies in Women's Literature*, 23:1. 107–120.

Hall, Stuart 2003: Kulttuuri, paikka, identiteetti. *Erilaisuus.* Ed. by Mikko Lehtonen & Olli Löytty. Tampere: Vastapaino, 85–128. [Orig. New cultures for the old. *A Place in the World.* Doreen Massey & Pat Jess (eds.). The Open University 1995].

Hansen, Julie 2012: Making Sense of the Translingual Text: Russian Wordplay, Names and Cultural Allusions in Olga Grushin's *The Dream Life of Sukhanov. Modern Language Review* 107. April. 540–558.

Heinämäki-Sepponen, Riina 2010: Jana Hensel ja kadotettu lapsuus. *Muistijälkiä. Esseitä saksankielisestä nykykirjallisuudesta.* Ed. by Lotta Kähkönen & Hanna Meretoja. Helsinki: BTJ. 393–401.

Ierman, Elena [Jerman Helena] 2006: Opyt dialogicheskogo izucheniia identichnosti russkogo menshistva v Finliandii. *Diaspory* 1. 148–170.

Immonen, Kari 1987: *Ryssästä saa puhua... Neuvostoliitto suomalaisessa julkisuudessa ja kirjat julkisuuden muotona 1918–39.* Helsinki: Otava.

Jasinskaja-Lahti, Inga 2000: *Psychological acculturalion and adaptation among Russian-speaking immigrant adolescents in Finland.* Helsinki: Edita.

Jasinskaja-Lahti, Inga 2007: Venäläiset maahanmuuttajat Suomessa. *Venäläiset perheet ja seksuaalisuus murroksessa.* Ed. by Elina Korhonen. Helsinki: Väestöliitto. 46–59.

Jasinskaja-Lahti, Inga, Karmela Liebkind & Tiina Vesala (eds.) 2002: *Rasisimi ja syrjintä Suomessa. Maahanmuuttajien kokemuksia.* Helsinki: Gaudeamus.

Karemaa, Outi 2004: Moraalisesta närkästyksestä kansalliseksi ohjelmaksi. *Venäjän kahdet kasvot. Venäjä-kuva suomalaisen identiteetin rakennuskivenä.* Ed. by Timo Vihavainen. Helsinki: Edita. 226–254.

Kellman, Steven G. 2000: *The Translingual Imagination.* Lincoln, NE, USA: University of Nebraska Press.

Klapuri, Tintti 2012a: Kolmannesta aallosta neljänteen. *Kenen aika. Esseitä venäläisestä nykykirjallisuudesta.* Ed. by Tomi Huttunen & Tintti Klapuri. Helsinki: BTJ. 369–377.

Klapuri, Tintti 2012b: Matkalla ei-kenenkään maassa: Zinaida Lindén. *Kenen aika. Esseitä venäläisestä nykykirjallisuudesta.* Ed. by Tomi Huttunen & Tintti Klapuri. Helsinki: BTJ. 401–410.

Klapuri, Tintti 2016: Literary St. Petersburg in Contemporary Russian Transnational Writing: Anya Ulinich, Gary Shteyngart, and Zinaida Lindén. *Scando-Slavica* 62(2). 235–248.

Kol', Liudmila 2004: Gumanitarnyi faktor kak odin iz osnovnykh v protsesse kulturnoi integratsii. Zhurnal "LiteraruS-Literaturnoe slovo" kak primer integratsionnogo sotrudnichestva. *Studia Slavica Finlandensia. Tomus XXI.* Russian-speaking immigrant population in Finland. Ed. by Petra Sinisalo-Katajisto, Katja Hirvasaho

& Edvard Hämäläinen. Helsinki: Institute for Russian and East European Studies. 209–217.

Kol', Liudmila 2009: *Roman s zagranitsei*. Sankt-Peterburg: Aletheia.

Kolomainen, Robert 1998: Arvi Perttu – Karjalan kirjallisuuden "puuttuva rengas". *Carelia* 12, 89–93. [Accessed via Internet: http://www.locallit.net/lehdet1/kolomainen1998.html, 7.1.2016]

Kolstø, Pål 1996: The new Russian diaspora – an identity of its own? Possible identity trajectories for Russians in the former Soviet republic. *Ethnic and Racial Studies* 19(3). 609–639.

Kristeva, Julia 1991: *Strangers to ourselves*. Transl. by Leon S. Roudiez. New York et al.: Harvester Wheatsheaf (orig. 1988).

Kukkola, Liisa 2008: Tavallisten ihmisten sankariton sota. *Etelä-Saimaa* 15.3. 2008.

Kurkinen, Pauli (ed.) 1985: Venäläiset Suomessa 1809–1917. *Historiallinen arkisto 83*. Helsinki: Societas Historica Finlandiae.

Latiševa, Inna 2010: *Ryssänä Suomessa. Vieras väärästä maasta*. Helsinki: Otava.

Laukkonen, Taisija 2012: "Baltic Russian Literature: Writing from Nowhere?", *Baltic worlds*, 2. http://balticworlds.com/wp-content/uploads/2012/06/tema-uppslag.pdf (17.12.2015)

Launis, Kati 2005: *Kerrotut naiset. Suomen ensimmäiset naisten kirjoittamat romaanit naiseuden määrittelijöinä*. Helsinki: SKS.

Liebkind, Karmela, Simo Mannila, Inga Jasinskaja-Lahti, Magdalena Jaakkola, Eve Kyntäjä & Anni Reuter (eds.) 2004: *Venäläinen, virolainen, suomalainen. Kolmen maahanmuuttajaryhmän kotoutuminen Suomeen*. Helsinki: Gaudeamus.

Lindén, Zinaida 2004: *I väntan på en jordbävning*. Helsingfors: Söderströms.

Lindén, Zinaida 2007: *Takakirves-Tokyo*. Helsingfors: Söderströms.

*LiteraruS* 2009/2: Arvi Perttu. Beseda s glazu na glaz. Besedu vedet Liudmila Kol'. [accessed through the Internet: http://www.literarus.org/arkiv/rus2009/rus2b_2009.php, 7.1.2016]

Löytty, Olli 2013: Kun rajat eivät pidä, eli mihin maahanmuuttajakirjallisuutta tarvitaan. *Liikkuva maailma. Liike, raja, tieto*. Ed. by Mikko Lehtonen. Tampere: Vastapaino. 261–279.

Mäkelä, Matti 2012: Venäläisestä tuli Suomessa kädetön kulmilla seisoskelija. Arvi Perttu: *Skumbria*. *Helsingin Sanomat* 3.1.2012.

Mäkikalli, Aino 2010: Wladimir Kaminerin ja muiden berliiniläisten monikulttuuriset sattumukset. *Muistijälkiä. Esseitä saksankielisestä nykykirjallisuudesta*. Ed. by Lotta Kähkönen & Hanna Meretoja. Helsinki: BTJ. 381–391.

Massey, Doreen 1991: A Global Sense of Place. *Marxism Today*, June. 24–29.

Massey, Doreen 2003: Paikan käsitteellistäminen. *Erilaisuus*. Ed. by Mikko Lehtonen & Olli Löytty. Tampere: Vastapaino, 51–83. [The conceptualization of space. *A Place in the World*. Doreen Massey & Pat Jess (eds.), The Open University 1995.]

Nevalainen, Pekka 1999: *Viskoi kuin Luoja kerjäläistä. Venäjän pakolaiset Suomessa 1917–1939*. Helsinki: SKS.

Pachmuss, Temira 1992: *A Moving River of Tears: Russia's Experience in Finland*. American university studies. Series XII, Slavic languages and literature, vol. 15. New York: Peter Lang.

Patrakova, Inna 2010: *Tulkki*. Helsinki: Ajatus.

Patrakova, Inna 2011: *Naapurit*. Helsinki: Helsinki-kirjat.

Perttu, Arvi 2006: *Papaninin retkikunta. Romaani Neuvosto-Karjalasta*. Helsinki: Minerva.

Perttu, Arvi 2011: *Skumbria*. Helsinki: Like.

Pratt, Marie Louise 1992: *Imperial Eyes. Travel Writing and Transculturation*. London and New York: Routledge.

Protasova, Ekaterina 2004: *Fennorossy: zhizn' i upotreblenie jazyka*. Sankt-Petergurg: Zlatoust.

Pyykkönen, Miikka 2007: *Järjestäytyvät diasporat. Etnisyys, kansalaisuus, integraatio ja hallinta maahanmuuttajien yhdistystoiminnassa.* Jyväskylä Studies on Education, Psychology and Social Research 306. Jyväskylä: Jyväskylän yliopisto.
Radhakrishnan, R. 1997: *Diasporic Mediations. Between Home and Location.* Minneapolis & London: University of Minneapolis Press. (Second printing, first printing 1996.)
Rantonen, Eila 2010: Maahanmuuttajat ja kirjallisuus Suomessa ja Ruotsissa. *Vähemmistöt ja monikulttuurisuus kirjallisuudessa.* Ed. by Eila Rantonen. Tampere: Tampere University Press. 163–191.
Robinson, Douglas 1997: *Translation and Empire. Postcolonial Theories Explained.* Manchester, UK: St Jerome Publishing.
Sapienza, Filipp A. 1999: Communal Ethos on a Russian Émigré Web Site. *The Public* 6(4). 39–52.
Shenshin, Veronica 2008: *Venäläiset ja venäläinen kulttuuri Suomessa. Kulttuurihistoriallinen katsaus Suomen venäläisväestön vaiheista autonomian ajoilta nykypäiviin.* Helsinki: Helsingin yliopisto, Aleksanteri-instituutti.
Sorvari, Marja 2014: Translating between cultures: Zinaida Lindén's translingual novels. Paper presented at the international conference *Translation in Russian Contexts.* 3.–7.6.2014, Uppsala University.
Sorvari, Marja 2016: 'On Both Sides': Translingualism, Translation and Border-Crossing in Zinaida Lindén's *Takakirves-Tokyo. Scando-Slavica* 62(2). 141–159.
Struve, Gleb 1996: *Russkaia literatura v izgnanii.* Third edition. Paris, Moscow: YMCA-press, Russkii put'. (Orig. 1956.)
Vihavainen, Timo 2004: Muuttuva menneisyys – purkaantuva viholliskuva ja historiankirjoitus. *Venäjän kahdet kasvot. Venäjä-kuva suomalaisen identiteetin rakennuskivenä.* Ed. by Timo Vihavainen. Helsinki: Edita. 394–410.
Virkkunen, Juha 2006: Musta Buick Petroskoin yössä. *Parnasso* 3.
Waarala, Hannu 2006: Isä Aurinkoisen synkissä varjostoissa. *Keskisuomalainen* 29.3.2006.
Wanner, Adrian 2011: *Out of Russia: Fictions of a New Translingual Diaspora,* Evanston, Illinois: Northwestern University Press.
Zaionchkovskaia, Zhanna A. 2004: Postsovetskaia emigratsiia iz Rossii v zapadnye strany. *Studia Slavica Finlandensia. Tomus XXI.* Russian-speaking immigrant population in Finland. Ed. by Petra Sinisalo-Katajisto, Katja Hirvasaho & Edvard Hämäläinen. Helsinki: Institute for Russian and East European Studies. 16–38.

WWW pages

Perttu, Arvi 2007: Mol'chanie immigrantov. Proza ru, http://www.proza.ru/2007/09/27/256 (7.1.2016)
Perttu, Arvi. Ulkosuomalainen ja muita rooleja, http://uussuomalainenjamuitarooleja.blogspot.fi/ (7.1.2016)
Tul'chinskii, Grigorii 2009: Ljudmila Kol'. Roman s zagranitsei. *Znamia* 10. http://magazines.russ.ru/znamia/2009/10/tu28.html (7.1.2016)

# Reception and Multicultural Perspectives   III

Kukku Melkas

# Children in-between – the Entangled History of Finland and Sweden in *Svinalängorna, Mother of Mine* and *Ingenbarnsland*

The Sweden-Finnish author Eija Hetekivi Olsson's (b. 1973) debut *Ingenbarnsland* [No Land for Children] was the topic of the day in Sweden in spring 2012. The novel won the Stig Sjödin-prize – a prize for working class literature in Sweden since 1997 – and was also nominated for the prestigious August prize in the autumn of 2012. Before its translation, the novel was noticed and discussed in the Finnish media.[1] The title of the novel – *Ingenbarnsland*[2] – associates with the term No man's land which is a term for land that is unoccupied or is under dispute between parties that leave it unoccupied due to fear or uncertainty. The term was originally used to define a contested territory or a dumping ground.[3]

The title of the novel rounds up all the different layers of contemporary Sweden-Finnish literature. The first layer is institutional; the tradition of Sweden-Finnish literature could be defined as existing in a contested territory – in between two literary canons. The second layer is thematic concerning questions of in-betweenness such as identities, language or belonging. The third layer is symbolic, referring both to the threats of losing one's subjectivity and at the same time to the fruitful possibilities and promises for new openings in literature and in constructing identities. I will analyse all these layers through three works – Susanna Alakoski's *Svinalängorna* (2006), Klaus Härö's *Mother of mine* (2005) and *Ingenbarnsland* – all with a child as their main protagonist, telling stories of different kinds of traumatic history.

*Ingenbarnsland* begins with a violent episode at school where the protagonist – young Miira – beats up a boy who has sexually harassed her and

---

1 In *Helsingin Sanomat* 12.3.2012 journalist Oscar Rossi wrote an extended review 'Olen ulkopuolinen. Eija Hetekivi Olssonin romaani kertoo, miksi ruotsinsuomalaiset ajautuivat ja ajettiin syrjään' ['I am an outsider. Eija Hetekivi Olsson's novel tells why the Sweden-Finnish were drifting and driven aside.'] and in *Aamulehti* 25.11.2012 Simopekka Virkkula's article 'Eija Hetekivi nappaa Ruotsin Finlandian?' ['Eija Hetekivi recieves the Finlandia-prize of Sweden?'].
2 The Finnish translation *Tämä ei ole lasten maa* (2013, [This is not children's land/place]) loses these implications.
3 The term is most commonly associated with the First World War to describe the area of land between two enemy trenches to which neither side wished to move openly or to seize due to fear of being attacked by the enemy in the process.

the other girls at school. Miira's Finnishness and her position as a working class girl automatically makes her an object for stigmatisation as well as for violence and harassment. The school (the teachers) do not pay attention to these violent mechanisms but instead punish the girl reacting on them. This can be seen as allegoric – the school representing the Swedish society – and the indifferent attitude is epitomized in Miira's thought, 'Det var okej att heta hora och skitskalle och att bli tafsad på, men det var inte okej att reagera mot det' (I 16.) [It was all right to be called a whore and be harassed, but it was not all right to react against it]. *Ingenbarnsland* indeed becomes a place in the novel where one is constantly under threat and on uncertain and disputed territory. Hetekivi Olsson's novel is an analysis of the social discrimination that is interwoven in social class, ethnicity and gender in the contemporary Sweden-Finnish literature (see also Gröndahl 2012).

*Ingenbarnsland* largely met with a glowing reception. The novel's social criticism and the analysis of the mechanisms of discrimination in the Swedish society were the most often mentioned issues – in a very laudatory tone – in the reviews.[4] Further, the protagonist Miira was seen as a rebellious and courageous character, an example of a clever survivor (the connection between the author and the protagonist was made in most of the reviews). Almost in every review Hetekivi Olsson was compared with another Sweden-Finnish author, namely Susanna Alakoski (b. 1962) and her debut novel *Svinalängorna* (2006, Finnish translation *Sikalat*, 2007). Alakoski's novel was a huge success when published in Sweden in 2006. The novel was overwhelmingly praised in the Swedish reception and aroused an extensive debate about immigration and poverty, but also about the ideal of Folkhemmet[5] [People's Home] by revealing the sharply outlined class structures existing in the Swedish society. Alakoski's novel won the August prize in 2007 and was filmed by the Swedish director Pernilla August in 2010.[6]

Both novels deal with a kind of social and collective trauma (cf. Leydesdorff et. al. 1999, 2) – the oppressed history of the second generation of the Sweden-Finnish migrants[7]. The reception of the novels can also be

---

4 *Svenska Dagbladet* 30.1.2012: 'Kreativt ordstök', Eva Johansson. *Dagens Nyheter* 6.4.2012: 'Medelklassens skräck – hotet från de förtryckta' [The Anxiety of the Middle Class – the threat of the oppressed], Aase Berg. *Ny tid* 23.9.2012: 'De befläckade i det svenska folkhemmet' [The blemished in the Swedish People's home], Mia Näslund. *Post Scriptum* 8.2.2012: 'En brännande berättelse', Jonna Fries. http://www.tidningenkulturen.se/tk2/index.php/kategorier/litteratur/13-litteratur-kritik/11329-litteratur-eija-hetekivi-olsson-ingenbarnsland (22.1.2013).
5 'Folkhemmet' is a fundamental concept in the history of the Swedish social democracy and has been part of its visions in the national political agenda. It underlines the necessity of the idea of the welfare state.
6 The actors of the film were from both Finland and Sweden. The film was given the Swedish Guldbagge prize in 2011 as well as the prize for the best Nordic film.
7 During the 1960s and 1970s over 400 000 people migrated from Finland to Sweden partly because of the unemployment situation in Finland and partly seeking a better standard of living. This migration has been considered one of the greatest mass migrations in Scandinavia. About the special characteristics of the migration see Vallenius 1998, 16–21.

*Eija Hetekivi-Olsson.*
*Photo: Jerker Andersson /*
*Norstedts.*

analysed within the frame of a social trauma. The reactions in the reviews of Alakoski reveal how most of the critics had a reading experience of a hidden history in their own nation and they were surprised. There was a glow and enchantment (feeling of something new in the literature), but there was also shock caused by the unpleasant subjects (child abuse, violence, subordination, poverty, alcoholism, feelings of unworthiness and rootlessness). The critical view the novel posed on the ideal of the People's Home and the so called miljonprogrammet[8] were at the centre of the reviewers attention – in Hetekivi Olsson's case, too. I will analyse more specifically the reception of Alakoski's novel because it seems to situate the work in a contested territory – between two literary canons (cf. Kivimäki & Rantonen 2011, 135–136; 138–139). It can thus be seen as one example of a transnational work highlighting the varied – context dependent – reception. How was the novel framed in Sweden and in Finland and what kind of discussions did the reception refer to?

Collective trauma in the shared history of Finland and Sweden is also present in the work by the Finnish-Swedish director, Klaus Härö (b. 1971) – the film trilogy: *Näkymätön Elina* (2002, [*Elina: As If I Wasn't there*]), *Äideistä parhain* (2005, [*Mother of Mine*]) and *Uusi ihminen* (2007, [*The New Man*]). The film *Mother of Mine* had its premiere in 2005 and tells the story of a Finnish so-called war child, Eero, who was evacuated to Sweden during WWII. During the war, over 70,000 children were sent temporarily from Finland to the other Nordic countries. Not only does the film describe the situation of a child in a transnational context, (in)between two linguistic

---

8   Miljonprogrammet was a name given to a massive housing production in Sweden during 1965–1975. The goal of the miljonprogrammet was to build a million flats and at the same time improve living standards.

and social settings, but the reception of the film in the two countries also underlines this theme.

This article examines literary transnationalism (all Härö's films are based loosely on novels) within the framework of the entangled histories of Finnish and Swedish political and cultural life. The trauma of a transnational experience and history becomes nested in both personal and collective histories, which are shared and entangled, crossing national borders. Why did these kinds of stories get their 'voice' in the twenty-first century Sweden? In cross-border studies, it is clear that social boundaries of societies, cultures and civilizations are permeable and mutually constitutive (cf. Amelina et. al. 2012, 6). I also ask why in the contemporary scene of Sweden-Finnish literature and film, the voice is given to the children. Why is a child's point of view an efficient way to analyze traumatic experiences?

## *The Reception of Svinalängorna: a Transnational Work in a Contested Territory*

Literary works do not exist alone but in a number of contexts, which are not always even possible to define. Rita Felski argues that literary works 'are not actors in this rugged, individualist sense, not lonely rebels pitted against the implacable forces of the contextual status quo. If they make a difference, they do so only as co-actors and co-dependents, enmeshed in a motley array of attachments and associations. They gain strength and vitality from their alliances' (2011, 589). Works of art arise from and move back into the social world in different ways and this is the reason why I see the reception as a very important area of study; it reveals something about the institutional expectations, but also about the connections of literature to the social world. A work of art is also always its reception; the reception remoulds the work, directs the ways of reading, it solidifies and underlines certain features while ignoring others. There is also a tendency of repetition in the reviews, which then in turn gradually freezes the work into set frames.

The reception of Alakoski's novel was strikingly different in Sweden and in Finland[9]. Most critics in Sweden saw both the subject of the novel (alcoholism, poverty, working-class identity) and the narration (the child's point of view) as something new in the literary field. In Finland, both (the subject and the narration) were treated as already familiar and existing phenomena in Finnish literature. The Swedish reception situated Alakoski in the long tradition of Swedish working-class literature (the most often mentioned examples were Moa Martinson and Ivar Lo-Johansson), while in Finland, the concept of class was not discussed openly, though poverty and social inferiority were often mentioned.

Kaisa Neimala in *Suomen Kuvalehti*[10] paid attention to the fact that 'on the other side of the gulf', the novel aroused a feeling of a story long awaited, when in Finland variations of the theme in literature already existed

---

9   See also Johansson (2008).
10  'Mutta valitettavasti' ['But Unfortunately']. *Suomen Kuvalehti*, 2007:35, 65.

Susanna Alakoski.
Photo: Elisabeth
Ohlson Wallin /
Bonniers.

from early on. Thus, the novel was more original in Sweden than in the Finnish context. Some of the Finnish reviewers referred in their critique to the sensation Alakoski's novel had had in the Swedish reviews and were astonished. For example, Anneli Kajanto in sivistys.net compared *Sikalat* to Kreetta Onkeli's *Ilonen talo* (1997) and Lassi Sinkkonen's working class classic *Solveigin laulu* (1970, *Solveig's song*), and at the same time wondered how typical a subject alcoholism and poverty is in Finnish literature. 'What kind of eye patches do the Swedish literary circles have if this [*Sikalat*] is something they have never seen or experienced before?' she asked.

The statements of the critics also say something about the cultural differences and expectations in Sweden and Finland. In the Finnish context, the narratives of alcoholism are naturalised and seen as a self-evident part of the story of modernization processes (Koivunen 2012, 10–13). This difference is highlighted in the Swedish film version of *Svinalängorna*, where the analysis of the parents' drinking problems and irresponsibility is even more ruthless than in the novel. In Pernilla August's *Svinalängorna*, alcoholism is no longer understood as the reason and consequence of the modernisation distress[11], but instead a serious social problem traumatising children.

The titles of the Swedish reviews reveal the emphasis of them: 'Hjärtskärande om alkoholistuppväxt' [Heartbreakingly about alcoholist upbringing]; 'Lysande porträtt av barn i alkoholismens skugga' [A brilliant portrait of a child in the shadows of alcoholism]; 'En kraftfull röst i Moa Martinsons anda' [A strong voice in the spirit of Moa Martinson]; 'Arbetarklassverige som det var – och kanske är' [Working class Sweden as it was – and perhaps still is; 'Finska invandrare i det folkhemska'[Finnish

---

11 The Finnish translation of the film – *Sovinto* [Atonement] – can be interpreted as part of this typical Finnish way of quiet approval of alcoholism and diminishing the problematic (Koivunen 2012, 10–13).

immigrants in the People's Home [12]]. In all of these reviews, the concern and anxiety of Leena's story comes up; she is a young girl living in the middle of chaos trying to cope with her uncertain everyday life.

Moreover, in the Swedish reviews, the stereotypes of Finns and Finnishness were strengthened and reproduced (Johansson 2008, 12; see also Gröndahl 2012). The heavy drinking and even the mention of stabbing (which is not mentioned in the novel at all) carry on the characteristics usually connected to Finns in Sweden. Satu Gröndahl (2012) argues that the large publishing houses in Sweden, such as Norstedts and Bonniers, have only published novels – such as *Svinalängorna* (2006) and *Ingenbarnsland* (2012) – in which Finns are described through old stereotypes. She raises the question: Why is poverty, misery and alcoholism a Finnish trademark even in the twenty-first century Swedish book market? The enforcing of such stereotypes is a problem concerning, not only the novels themselves, but the reception of the novels too. The same phenomenon can be seen in the case of Hetekivi Olsson. The media attention, nominations and awards can be seen as a cumulative chain, affecting one another. However, the phenomenon or sensation also implicates how, in the praise and awards of a work of art, the dominant (Swedish) culture in a way participates in awkward subjects (socio-political problems) and by doing so claims a better conscience.

A noteworthy point was that none of the Swedish critics referred to the earlier Sweden-Finnish migrant literature tradition. They saw the novel as either something new in itself, or as part of the Swedish working class literature including new features and subjects such as depiction of alcoholism and the way children manage in these desperate circumstances (see also Johansson 2008, 12–13). Most of the Finnish reviewers immediately placed Alakoski in the previous migrant literature tradition (the most frequently mentioned novel was Antti Jalava's *Asfalttikukka* (1980, *Asfaltblomman*). In the contemporary Swedish literary research, Alakoski's novel is discussed in terms of class and ethnicity (Nilsson 2010), which can also be seen as a signal of approval: migrant literature becomes part of the Swedish tradition. The whole concept of Sweden-Finnishness seemed to be unknown to the Swedish reviewers and if the context of immigration was discussed, the reference was only to Swedish writers such as Majgull Axelsson and Kjell Johansson (Johansson 2007, 11). In that way, the history of Finnish migrants still remained unaddressed.

Satu Gröndahl (2009, 174–175) has paid attention to how the so called multi-cultural Swedish literature is usually homogenized even though the diversity of the novels is numerous, depending on the context and the authors. In her words, migrant or multi-cultural literature should be understood as 'cultural political definitions that mirror different groups' interests in a specific historical and sociological situation, rather than literatures that should consist of a certain, definable bulk of works and authors' (Gröndahl 2009, 187). Gröndahl's concept underlines the idea of context; it makes

---

12 'Folkhemska' in Swedish covers a wordplay where the word 'hem' (home) is transformed into 'hemska' (horrible).

a difference whether you are a political refugee or a descendant of a Finnish migrant from the 1960s and 1970s.

In Swedish literary criticism, the works by authors from immigrant communities are made part of contemporary Swedish literature, but usually by essentializing them. They are integrated into the literary canon, but at the same time, categorised under the same heading – immigrant authors. (Gröndahl 2009, 188; compare Nissilä 2009; Rantonen 2009; Löytty 2013; Huttunen 2013, 246–247.) Alakoski's novel was integrated in the Swedish literary canon by categorising it under working class literature, which the author herself has later rejected in many interviews by claiming that she is only a 'class conscious' writer. The tradition of Sweden-Finnish literature indeed exists in a contested territory – and in between two literary canons. The reception highlights the problematic context and underlines the specificity of this. The novel is read differently within different national frames and the reception directs our ways of reading onwards.

The only reviewer referring to the history of Finnish migrants was Daniel Suhonen in *Tvärdrag*[13]. He wonders why there are so few fictional works about Finnish people who had to move to Sweden; he claims that the reason for this may lie in that the Finnish were not political immigrants but instead migrants. According to Suhonen, they were mostly poor and their literary and writing traditions were deficient, which is mostly true. The other reason, in my opinion, lies in the experience of a social trauma when most of the migrants were – at least in the beginning – without skills in the Swedish language and as such 'outsiders' in the country.

## *The Narrating Child and the Trauma of in-between*

As it is often underlined in trauma studies, a trauma is usually remembered and worked through in later years (Löfström 2012; Leydesdorff et. al. 1999). That is why most traumas are handled in fiction or in history research by the second or even most likely – the third – generation, when (grand) parent's life-stories are witnessed or listened to. One of the reasons for the popularity of these unprocessed traumas, worked through in contemporary fiction and film, is that the authors Alakoski and Hetekivi Olsson are both second generation migrants and Härö represents the second generation as to experiences of war. It is worth noting that traumatic experiences, though subjective, are in such cases as mass migration or war, also highly collective. Trauma can be seen through a socio-political and collective definition underlining shared and generational aspects as it 'may arise not only from an acute event but also from a persisting social condition' (Leydesdorff et. al. 1999, 2.) such as social and political inferiority. Trauma has its social roots in 'structural oppression, persecution, devaluation, and official indifference to the sufferings of socially subordinated and powerless groups' (ibid., 9).

---

[13] Swedish Socialdemocratic Youth Organisation's magazine. 'Arbetarklassverige som det var – och kanske är' (The Working class Sweden as it was – and perhaps is) *Tvärdrag*, 2006:2. 34–35.

The generational aspect of a trauma is underlined in a concept where it is seen as inherited. It is contagious through being transmitted from survivors to their listeners and witnesses, both within families and by means of wider, collective processes to subsequent generations (Leydesdorff et. al. 1999, 17). In the works by Alakoski, Hetekivi Olsson and Härö, although their main protagonists are situated in different contexts, they share the same thematic outline – the issue of in-betweenness in narrations of identity or belonging – and what is even more interesting, the same narrative strategy: the child's point of view. They all use the child as the narrator voice, which can be seen as an efficient way to handle difficult or traumatic subjects, a way that affects people. Leena's, Miira's and Eero's life-stories encompass the years from childhood to early adolescence; as such, they can be described as coming-of-age stories.

All of Härö's films, in the previously mentioned trilogy, concentrate on the history of a somehow marginalised child. In one way or another, all the films also tackle the problematic nature of the so called epistemological violence and trauma history. The violence is connected to the official policy of Swedish state ideology; for example, the film *Elina* is a story of a 'Meänkielian'[14] young girl who is denied the right to speak her mother tongue at school.[15] Härö's films deal with the question of Swedish nationalism and the dubious policies underpinning it.

*Mother of Mine* (2005) is loosely based on the novel *Äideistä parhain* (1992) written by Heikki Hietamies (b. 1933). The script was written by the Sweden-Finnish couple, Jimmy Karlsson and Kirsi Vikman. The Swedish premiere was on the 4th of November 2005 and the film was unusually widely spread in cinemas throughout Sweden. The film was also nominated to represent the Finnish Oscar in the international competition. The mother, the Swedish actress, Maria Lundqvist, won both the esteemed Jussi-prize in Finland 2005 and the Swedish Guldbagge in 2006.[16]

In the reviews, the destiny of the young protagonist, Eero, was at the centre of attention. The history of war children was unknown to many of the critics and now it was told through a child's experiences. One of the Swedish reviews raised the question of a transnational trauma. 'Barn som kom att adopteras i Sverige eller som återvände till Finland och försvann eller aldrig fann ro varken i det ena eller andra landet. Kanske är de finska krigsbarnen också ett svenskt trauma?'[17] [Children that were adopted to Sweden or who went back to Finland and disappeared or never found peace in either country. Perhaps the Finnish war children are also a Swedish trauma?] Härö's film represents this entangled and shared trauma through his protagonist Eero and his two mothers.

---

14 'Meänkieli' = 'Our language', even called Tornedalian Finnish, used in Northern Sweden.
15 The use of the minority language Finnish was stigmatized in Swedish schools in the Tornedalian valley until the 1970s and this was manifested through attitudes or even physical penalties (Gröndahl 2009, 186).
16 Best Actress in a Leading Role; see more http://www.elonet.fi/title/ekqta8/muut
17 Jeanette Gentele: http://www.svd.se/kultur/film/den-basta-av-modrar_23780.svd

## Between Two Mothers/Nations

The protagonist in *Mother of mine*, the 10-year old Eero, is not only situated between two nations and languages, he ends up in an emotionally distressed situation between two mothers. The longing for his biological mother becomes even more intensified through the character of the Swedish mother, Signe, who had openly hoped for a girl.[18] The new mother has severe difficulties in accepting the new child that in her eyes is 'wrong'. In the film, the first dinner at Eero's new home accentuates the feelings of in-betweenness through the unfriendly and rude behaviour of the mother – she treats Eero as if he was a farmhand – and through the cold atmosphere when Eero cannot communicate with his new parents. He keeps repeating the two sentences he has been taught before his journey: 'Jag heter Eero Vilenius. Jag kommer från Finland.' [My name is Eero Vilenius. I come from Finland.]

The story unfolds Eero's gradual but painful identity process in which he finally becomes a Swedish child; he changes his language, he goes native and absorbs new cultural codes. He also fully realizes his new class identity, in one of the ending scenes in the film, when he is given a bicycle as a birthday present in a beautifully filmed outdoor picnic. The differences between his poor past in Finland and his well-off present life in Sweden are underlined. While the mother has been presented as a callous and insensitive person, she gradually gains warm features and her affections towards Eero are strengthened. When they finally seem to have accepted each other and have gained a solid affection, becoming 'mother and son', his biological mother reclaims him back to Finland. Eero has to adjust back to poor Finland and he finds himself again in an in-between situation, when his biological mother has turned into a stranger in his eyes.

The position in-between two mothers can be interpreted as an allegory of being between two nations. The metonymical chain between women, home and the nation represents a strong symbol in nationalism (Yuval-Davies 1998, 29–31; see also Gordon, Komulainen and Lempiäinen 2002); in political rhetoric (Valenius 2004). The image of a woman or mother has formed an embodiment of the nation that emphasizes security, permanence and sense of duty. Being in-between two mothers activates questions of loyalty and identification but also affections. It highlights the difficult position of a person whose identity is uncertain, whose commitments to the nation are unclear and who is thus morally dubious.

The situation of being in-between concerns not only the issue of belonging but also differences in social background. Eero's mothers represent two different class positions as well. Poverty was one of the main reasons for sending children to Sweden and it has been claimed in the latest study of war children that Finnish authorities transferred part of the responsibilities for national child welfare to Sweden through war children (see more

---

18 This detail underlines the fact that most of the Swedish families made choices based on their individual needs and desires and not on the beneficial or social premises that were promoted by the officials in both countries. Siblings were separated and the sick or handicapped children ended up in children's homes. (Kavén 2010.)

Kavén 2010, 196–205). The well-off present and the poor past experienced in the receiving state and in the sending state is also one of the themes in *Svinalängorna*, although in that case, the composition of being positioned between two mothers (nations) becomes even more complicated.

Alakoski's novel tells a story of a young girl, Leena, who moves to Sweden with her family in the 1970s, hoping for a better standard of living and for work in the south of Sweden in Ystad. They move to the new suburb areas built for immigrants. The main theme of the novel is Leena's identity process in a new environment while her parents gradually become addicted to alcohol and are not able to take care of their children properly.[19] The in-betweenness of Leena is constructed through various demarcation lines that intertwine the notions of social class (cf. Kivimäki & Rantonen 2011, 144–145) and nation. Not only is Leena the outsider at her school among wealthy middle class Swedish children – addressed in the novel in a luxurious birthday party at Bo-Peters – but also in her former home land between her two grandmothers from different social backgrounds.

Only once does Leena's family visit Finland in their summer vacation. Leena wakes up in a reality where she grasps the difference between her two grandmothers. Her mother's mother is a poor working class woman from a small town Kokkola on the western coast while her father's mother lives a middle class life in Helsinki. The difference between the grandmothers divides the idea of the united Finnish people and questions the unity of a nation that has been in Leena's mind based on her parents' reminiscences and nostalgia.

> Det var mycket fattigare hos Kokkolanmummi än vad jad trodde. Ingen i hela Fridhem hade det så fattigt. [...] Mummi hade bara ett litet rum och ett pyttelitet kök. Lägenheten låg i ett trähus med två våningar. En smal trappa, som man inte kunde vända sig i, gick upp till henne. Hon delade ett utedass i trä med sina grannar. [...] Mummi hade bara tre tallrikar och några bestick, nästan inga glas och bara två krokiga kastruller. (S 156–157.)

> [It was a lot poorer at Kokkolagrandma's place than what I thought. No one in the whole of Fridhem was so poor. [...] Mummi had only one small room and a very small kitchen. The flat was in a wooden house that had two floors. A few narrow steps, where you couldn't turn, led up to her place. She shared a wooden outdoor toilet with her neighbours. [...] Mummi had only three plates, a few cutlery, almost no glasses and only two crooked pots.]

This short episode in the novel that takes place in Finland makes the poverty that was left behind when migrating concrete and visualises the socio-political reasons for leaving. Leena's other grandmother has been able to climb up the social ladder and has a far better standard of living.

---

19 In the footsteps of Alakoski there have been others with same subjects and themes: for example the Swedish author Åsa Linderborg with her debut in 2007 *Mig äger ingen*, a warm depiction of 1970's working class life and a close relationship between a daughter and her alcoholic father.

> Farmor bodde i en tvårumslägenhet på andra våningen, i ett gammalt stenhus med fyra våningar, mitt i centrala stan. Hon hade det mycket rikare än Kokkolanmummi. Hon hade en kristallampa i taket, bäddsoffa, två fina fåtöljer, riktig bokhylla med fina saker i. [...] Hennes rum var stora, det var högt till tak och hon hade långa vita tunna gardiner med volanger på för fönsterna. (S 159.)

> [Grandma lived in a flat with two rooms in an old four-storey stone house in the centre of town. She was much better off than Kokkolagrandma. She had a crystal chandelier, a bed settee, two fine armchairs, a proper bookshelf with elegant things in it. [...] Her rooms were huge with a high ceiling and she had long white thin curtains in her windows.]

The difference is also about attitudes and ways of living. The drinking, swearing and fighting that seemed 'natural' in Kokkolagrandma's place raise conflicts in Helsinkigrandma's place. The two totally different ways of living reveal the wide gap between the grandmothers; as such, it becomes clear that class is a significant difference that constructs two different worlds or 'nations' in the same way as the Swedish society is based upon distinct class differences. The class frame becomes as important an aspect as the nationalistic frame; they crisscross in *Svinalängorna* in overlapping ways. Nation is an important divider, but the separations and identifications actually always happen through different demarcation lines. Compared to the former tradition of Sweden-Finnish migrant literature where the concept of class was understood as a unified, work-based identity, in the contemporary literature it is intertwined with complex notions of gender and ethnicity (also Gröndahl 2012).

This interrelatedness is most obvious at school. School plays an important role in both Alakoski's and Hetekivi Olsson's novels as well as in Härö's films. It is a place for disciplinary actions, demands of uniformity and national authorial power but also a place for equal education and possibilities in society. School can be a place for conflicts but it also becomes a saviour as Leena puts it, 'Skolan var min oavbrutna räddning. Mina ben hittade den välkända vägen till Maria Munthe dag ut och dag in' (S 184) [School was my constant saviour. My legs could find the well-known way to Maria Munthe [School] day in and day out]. School, and its stability, also helps Eero to settle in little by little and learn the new language. Miira's experiences at school are more complex and critical.

A child's voice can be interpreted as a frame of hope. Both Leena's and Miira's stories end up in a hopeful scene where the future lies ahead unknown but simultaneously full of possibilities that are realizable due to the Swedish welfare state ideology and democratic education system. This interpretation becomes even more accentuated because of the genre of the novels; the coming-of-age stories leave the protagonists in a phase of life of dreaming and anticipation, in an all-powerful state of mind when everything is possible.

## *The Entangled Histories in* No Man's Land

Transnational and entangled history include more than just one specific nation and reject the idea of fixed entities such as the nation-state, 'transcending the boundaries of the entities they analyze by stressing the interactions between them. Their basic assumption is that people have a shared history, though not the same history' (Epple 2010, 156). Actually, as migrants oscillate between two nations, cultures and languages they also de-territorialize the homogenous nature of each nation (Frank 2010, 39–40). In the case of Finland and Sweden, it is fruitful to look at the long history as interwoven and shared. The tradition of Sweden-Finnish literature could be defined as existing in a contested territory – it is given various significations in different contexts. In a way, it exists in no man's land, in between two literary canons, as part of the history of the receiving state and part of the history of the 'sending' state, interweaved intricately.

In *No Man's Land* – in-between – the thematic questions of storytelling also exist. Children are in-between childhood and adolescence, a fruitful position to ponder upon traumatic experiences within a frame of hope and an idea of atonement. The feelings of belonging are manifested through narratives and memory. If trauma arises, not only from an acute event but also from a persisting social condition (Leyerdorff et al. 1999, 2) such as social and political inferiority and it is understood as a collective process, then these stories can be seen as connected to remembrance and memory. With the help of remembrance and narration, it is possible to achieve a feeling of belonging. Storytelling or fictionalizing can be seen as an attempt to come to terms with or even master disturbing experiences (c. Knuuttila 2009, 21–27). Furthermore, the concept of citizenship or identity is usually assimilative, since there has not been much room for the 'old' identities based on collective memories in the new home country. In order to integrate, different groups of people have been forced to look forwards towards the future and not give in to painful memories. Therefore, the memories are usually told by next generations.

The symbolic aspects of no man's land, referring both to the threats of losing one's identity and at the same time to the fruitful possibilities and promises for new openings in art and in constructing identities, resonate with the concept of diaspora by Avtar Brah. Diasporas come to exist through mass emigrations. Though the word 'diaspora' usually evokes stories and pictures of traumatic departures and homelessness, it can also be a place for hope and new beginnings. Diasporas are sites for cultural and political conflicts, where subjective and collective memories collide and change shape into something new (Brah 1996, 196–199). In the tradition of the Sweden-Finnish literature and film, the subjective voices of children are telling the collective stories of a whole generation. Thus, they shape and construct expressions of experiences that used to be unknown.

Diasporic narratives, according to Azade Seyhan, are also an effort to transmit a linguistic and cultural heritage that is articulated through acts of personal and collective memory. She asks, 'What happens to the memory of a nation outside (without) the nation? When origins and heritages become recollections and merge into other histories, who guards and guarantees our national histories and the specificity of our pasts?' (Seyhan 2001, 12). Sweden-Finnish literature is a recollection of different origins and heritages. In the twenty-first century, it has also merged into Swedish history by narrating stories of the different sides of the People's Home: grim suburbs, poverty and inequality but also integration, empowerment and even success.

# Cited Reviews

## Swedish Reviews

Beckström, Liv: Hjärtskärande om alkoholistuppväxt. *Kommunalarbetaren*. 17.5.2006.
Berger, Måna N: Lysande porträtt av barn i alkoholismens skugga. *Nerikes Allehanda*. 14.6.2006.4.
Gentele, Jeanette: http://www.svd.se/kultur/film/den-basta-av-modrar_23780.svd
Johansson, Eva: Lysande debut om den svåra uppväxten. *Västervikstidningen*. 28.3.2006.
Karlsson, Lena S: En kraftfull röst i Moa Martinsons anda. *Dala-Demokraten*. 13.4.2006.
Löfvendahl, Erik: Livet hos de till synes chanslösa. *Svenska Dagbladet*. 24.3.2006.
Nyström, Jan-Olov: Vid sidan av välståndet. *Norrbottens-Kuriren*. 29.3.2006.
Suhonen, Daniel: Arbetarklassverige som det var – och kanske är. *Tvärdrag*. 2006:2. 34–35.

## Finnish Reviews

Hämäläinen, Timo: Ystadin ryysyproletariaatin elämää ja sen kääntöpuolta. *Helsingin Sanomat*. 4.5.2006.
Kajanto, Anneli: Kurjuuskuvaus kaikilla mausteilla. *Sivistys.net*. 12.12.2007.
http://sivistys.net/sivisty_/viikonlopun_kirja/kurjuuskuvaus_kaikilla_mausteilla.html
Lappalainen, Otto: Hakka päälle soumen poika. *Parnasso*. 2007:5. 73.
Neimala, Kaisa: Mutta valitettavasti. *Suomen Kuvalehti*. 2007:35. 65.
Rossi, Oscar: Olen ulkopuolinen. Eija Hetekivi Olssonin romaani kertoo, miksi ruotsinsuomalaiset ajautuivat ja ajettiin syrjään. *Helsingin Sanomat* 12.3.2012.
Rosenqvist, Juha: http://www.film-o-holic.com/arvostelut/aideista-parhain/
Virkkunen, Simopekka: Eija Hetekivi nappaa Ruotsin Finlandian? *Aamulehti* 25.11.2012.
Österberg, Ingalill: Finska invandrare i det folkhemska. *Nordisk alkohol- & narkotikatidskrift*. vol. 24. 2007. 62–63.

# References

Alakoski, Susanna 2006: *Svinalängorna*. Stockholm: Albert Bonniers Förlag.
Brah, Avtar 1996: *Cartographies of Diaspora: Contesting Identities*. London & New York: Routledge.
Epple, Angelika 2012: The Global, the Transnational and the Subaltern: The Limits of History beyond the National Paradigm. *Beyond Methodological Nationalism*.

*Research Methodologies for Cross-Border Studies.* Ed. by Anna Amelina et al. New York: Routledge. 155–175.
Felski, Rita 2008: *Uses of Literature.* New York & London: Blackwell Publishing.
Felski, Rita 2011: Suspicious minds. *Poetics Today* 32 (2). 215–234.
Frank, Søren 2010: Four Theses on Migration and Literature. *Migration and Literature in Contemporary Europe.* Ed. by Mirjam Gebauer and Pia Schwarz Lausten. München: Martin Meidenbauer Verlagsbuchhandlung. 39–57.
Gordon, Tuula, Komulainen, Katri & Lempiäinen, Kirsti 2002: *Suomineitonen hei! Kansallisuuden sukupuoli.* Tampere: Vastapaino.
Gröndahl, Satu 2009: Multicultural or Multilingual Literature. A Swedish Dilemma? *Literature for Europe?* Ed. by Theo D'Haen and Iannis Goerlandt. Amsterdam & New York: Rodopi. 173–195.
Gröndahl, Satu 2012: Sprit och misär som varumärke. *Ny Tid.* http://www.nytid.fi/?s=sprit+och+mis%C3%A4r+som+varum%C3%A4rke
Gröndahl, Satu 2012: Sweden-Finnish Literature: Generational and Cultural Changes. A paper presented in *Ambiguities, Alterations, Alternatives – transforming Nordic literatures.* Uppsala: University of Uppsala 4–5.10.
Hetekivi Olsson, Eija 2012: *Ingenbarnsland.* Stockholm: Norstedts.
Huttunen, Laura 2013: Improvisointi, kitka ja kulttuurin käsitteellistäminen. *Liikkuva maailma. Liike, raja, tieto.* Ed. by Mikko Lehtonen. Tampere: Vastapaino. 245–260.
Johansson, Emil 2008: Ett dubbelt mottagande: Susanna Alakoskis *Svinalängorna* i pressen. Examensarbete för kandidatexamen. Stockholms Universitet, Institutionen för baltiska språk, finska och tyska. Avdelningen för finska. 25 pages.
Kavén, Pertti 2010: *Humanitaarisuuden varjossa: Poliittiset tekijät lastensiirroissa Ruotsiin sotiemme aikana ja niiden jälkeen.* Helsinki: Oy Nord Print Ab.
Kivimäki, Sanna & Rantonen, Eila 2011: Koti ja yhteisöt ruotsinsuomalaisten Susanna Alakosken Sikaloissa ja Arja Uusitalon Meren sylissä. *Vähemmistöt ja monikulttuurisuus kirjallisuudessa.* Ed. by Eila Rantonen. Tampere: Tampere University Press. 132–162.
Knuuttila, Sirkka 2009: *Fictionalising Trauma. The Aesthetics of Marguerite Duras's India Cycle.* Helsinki: Helsinki University Print.
Koivunen, Anu 2012: Sovinnottomuus. *Hiidenkivi* Nr 1:6. 10–13.
Leydesdorff, Selma, Dawson, Graham, Burchardt, Natasha and Ashplant, T.G. 1999: Introduction: Trauma and life stories. *Trauma and life stories. International Perspectives.* Ed. by Kim Lacy Rogers, Selma Leydesdorff & Graham Dawson. London & New York: Routledge. 1–26.
Löfström, Jan (ed.) 2012: *Voiko historiaa hyvittää: historiallisten vääryyksien korjaaminen ja anteeksiantaminen.* Helsinki: Gaudeamus.
Löytty, Olli 2013: Kun rajat eivät pidä, eli mihin maahanmuuttajakirjallisuutta tarvitaan. *Liikkuva maailma. Liike, raja, tieto.* Ed. by Mikko Lehtonen. Tampere: Vastapaino. 261–279.
Nilsson, Magnus 2010: *Den föreställda mångkulturen: klass och etnicitet i svensk samtidsprosa.* Hedemora: Gidlund. 261–279.
Nissilä, Hanna-Leena 2009: Ranya el Ramly ja Auringon aseman vastaanotto. *Kulttuurintutkimus* Nro 26:1. 39–53.
Rantonen, Eila 2009: Muuttavatko maahanmuuttajat suomalaisen kirjallisuuden? *Kiiltomato.* Pääkirjoitus 6.11.
Seyhan, Azade 2001: *Writing Outside the Nation.* Princeton: Princeton University Press.
Valenius, Johanna 2004: *Undressing the Maid. Gender, Sexuality and the Body in the Construction of the Finnish Nation.* Helsinki: Suomalaisen Kirjallisuuden Seura.
Vallenius, Erkki 1998: *Kansankodin kuokkavieraat. II maailmansodan jälkeen Ruotsiin muuttaneet suomalaiset kaunokirjallisuuden kuvaamina.* Helsinki: SKS.
Yuval-Davies, Nira 1997: *Gender and Nation.* London: Sage Publications.

Johanna Domokos
🆔 https://orcid.org/0000-0001-7586-2463

# Multicultural Dynamics and the Finnish Literary Field

*Introduction*

Applying a multicultural analytical perspective to *Suomen kirjallisuus* – the expression most often used for Finnish literature by Finnish authors, readers, and scholars – gives us insights into this literary tradition that would be otherwise difficult to attain. Merely translating the term itself takes us to the heart of the problem, since its most straightforward meaning is 'literature *of* Finland,' but it can be also interpreted as 'literature written *in* Finland.' The rapid growth of ethnic diversity in the Nordic countries, which began at the end of the 20th century, has at long last prompted scholars and readers to question whether the Finnish, Danish, Swedish, or Norwegian literary fields are strongly bound to homogenous national cultures. This development has brought ethnic diversity to the forefront of contemporary Nordic literary studies.

The present article applies a multicultural perspective to the Finnish literary field as well as to general social processes, the configuration individual agents in this literary field, and to the narrative and linguistic structure of multicultural textual worlds. This perspective allows us to examine the role and function of cultural interference, and the value assigned to it, throughout Finnish literary history. Special emphasis will be given to ethnicity, which can be understood as the master code or interpretive key of multiculturality, since it currently poses more serious challenges in Finland than any other source of diversity. The following sections of this paper will argue that one can speak of multicultural writing/*écriture multiculturelle* only to the extent that cultural idiosyncrasy is a relevant issue for the author and/or the reader. This is an intentional and reception-oriented interpretation, and its suggestions can be viewed and valued completely differently by literary and cultural agents. On the other hand, literary scholars are able to apply a multicultural analytical perspective to any work, any literary tradition, and any literary field at any given time.

## From Cultural to Multicultural Studies of Literature

Cultural theorists of recent decades have been attempting to come up with suitable theoretical and terminological differentiations for interference between cultures. To give a few examples, let me recall the theoretical framework of *transculturation* developed by Latin-American scholars (first defined by F. Ortiz 1940 and then rekindled in the 1980s), the spread of a specific usage of the term *multicultural literature* in the United States (growing out of the Civil Rights movement of the 1950s and 1960s), the complex application of *multiculturalism* to the entire literary field in Canada[1], and the theoretical working-out of *intercultural literary studies* by continental scholars.[2] These developments were accompanied and inspired by the outgrowth of *cultural studies*, a discipline created in Britain (e.g. Hoggarts 1957, Hall 1980) and strongly established in the U.S., Australia, and some European states (e.g. Germany and Italy), along with the formation of *post-colonial studies* in the late 1970s in the U.S. and England[3] and the *Kulturwissenschaften* from the early 1990s in Europe (e.g. Bachman-Medick 2006). By the turn of the 21st century, these local schools of theory had achieved a wide reception. This is due not only to the spread of salient theoretical works, but also to radical social changes, of which literature forms a part (e.g. *transculturality* becoming relevant in the Swedish literary discourse, *multiculturality* in the Finnish, and *post-coloniality* in the Sámi literary discourse).

We cannot employ a multicultural analytical perspective without first considering what constitutes the interferencial zone of culture. The interferencial zone of culture underlines the importance of the seminal difference and diversity that are centrally involved in the semiotic processes that bring cultures to life. It also reminds us to be much more aware of ongoing multicultural, intercultural, pluricultural and transcultural discourses. These discourses can be summed up in the following way (for a more detailed description please turn to Domokos 2013b):

> *pluricultural* – when different cultural orders are presented in parallel, e.g. the Sámi and other indigenous voices in Nils-Aslak Valkeapää's multi-modal book *Eanni, eannážan* (2001, [*The Earth, My Mother*]), or the Finnish and Finland Swedish positions in Zinaida Lindén's novels,

> *intercultural* – when cultural interferences are presented between well-delimited agencies in contact, e.g. between 'the Finnish' and 'the Sámi' individuals and communities in the trilogy of Jovnna-Ánde Vest *Árbbolaččat I–III* [The Successors I: 1996, II: 2002, III: 2005], or the 'Finnish' and 'German' perspectives in Roman Schatz's *Der König von Helsinki* (2007, [The King of Helsinki]).

> *transcultural* – when cultural orders overlap in a person or a collective leading to cultural hybridization and ethnic fragmentation in the context of cosmopolitan

---

1   Since the 1970s, e.g. Kamboureli 1996.
2   From the German tradition see the works of Zimmermann 1989, Wierlacher & Bogner 2003.
3   For example, Said 1978, Bhabha 1994, Spivak 1999.

globalization, Rita Magga-Kumpulainen's *Sarvikiela* (2006, [The Antler Language], and Ranya ElRamly's *Auringon asema* (2002, [The Position of the Sun]).

Any literary scholar with an interest in the interferential processes of literary works and fields needs to consider the role literature plays in the processes of covering or uncovering multiculturality. Nordic literary histories mirror both these strategies. The developments of the so-called Finnish, Danish, Norwegian, or Swedish national symbolic orders were, no doubt, a necessity for the modern independent nation-states, and literature has played a crucial role in this process. Since Nordic nation-building processes have always occurred on multicultural grounds, their architects could not ignore multiculturality. Until recently, however, little attention has been paid to their own multiculturality or to that of other nation states.

The establishment of what today we understand as Danish, Swedish, Norwegian, Finnish, and Finland Swedish literary fields goes back to the beginning of the 19$^{th}$ century, to the era of nationalism. At that time literature was understood as the voice of a unified nation, and therefore multiculturality was downplayed. Based on similar, i.e. ethnocentric structures, the field of Sámi and Roma literature appeared in the second half of the 20$^{th}$ century, and e.g. Tornedalian or Kven or local Russian literary fields are acting on the same basis nowadays in order to establish legitimacy. Late 20$^{th}$ century Nordic authors with a background of recent migration have also been fighting for acknowledgement as members of the national literary field, although their emphasis rests on an understanding of literature as the voice of a society conscious of its diversity. This general breakthrough has made multiculturality a common topic in everyday as well as specialized discourses.

The following sections will touch on some Finnish literary examples where cultural diversity has played an important role. When choosing the multicultural analytical perspective from the toolbox of cultural approaches, and applying it to the interferential modalities of the literary field, we must turn our focus to the interferences of diverse symbolic orders manifested in (a) a certain socio-political context, (b) within the literary field and (c) in the text itself. In this sense it means that we pay a great deal of attention to:

a) interrelations within the socio-political context and the resulting structure of the literary field (e.g. what kind of political movements and ethnicities contributed to the establishment of the literary medium; how do national/multicultural political ideologies and marketing strategies affect what is going to be published; what kind of social changes influence the positions and dispositions of majority/minority literary agents; how do certain literary movements contribute to the change of a monocultural social status quo; how are subtle messages about collective identity incorporated into literary work; what kind of multicultural literary work becomes discredited by society, etc.);

b) the cultural and multicultural features of local literatures, also in relation and in comparison to other literary developments (e.g. what has changed in the reception of books with multicultural topics; what causes 'the birth and death' (c.f. Nilsson 2013) of the immigrant/ new Finnish authors; what kind of narrative techniques become dominant through multi/cultural writing; how does the literary horizon get enlarged or reduced; are there local varieties of multicultural literature etc.);

c) the cultural interferences and particularities manifested through various agents of the narrative levels in literary works; it becomes imperative to pay thorough attention to how far fictive multicultural worlds are culturally conditioned and to what degree they act culturally constitutive. As we know, multicultural literary works can also have transformative effects on culture.

The following sections will discuss the multiculturality of the Finnish literary field from the trifold perspective outlined above.

## *The Socio-political Context of Literary Developments*

After being part of Sweden for more than 600 years, the war of 1808–1809 converted the Finnish province into a grand duchy under the rule of the Russian Tsar, and its inhabitants were forced to look for a new political and cultural identity. This is best summarized with the motto (originally in Swedish) ascribed to Adolf Ivar Arwidsson (1791–1858): 'We are no longer Swedes, we do not want to become Russians, let us therefore become Finns!' The establishment of printed media and literature in the Grand Duchy of Finland in the 19$^{th}$ century contributed to the process of Finnish nation-building.

Finnish ethnic nationalism of the 19–20$^{th}$ centuries is a result of a multicultural political movement whose uniqueness has not been considered as much as it should be in the existing scholarship. Finnish nationalism was constructed on German models and spread in its early phase by a mostly Swedish (exolingual) political and cultural elite, whose ancestors had settled down in Finnish provinces when the region was still part of the Swedish kingdom. Most ethnic nationalisms of that time were constructed around a common language and a common ancestry within a defined territory. 'Finnishness' was meant to be a bi-ethnic category based on love and allegiance to the 'patria'. One of the major representatives of the Fennophile movement of the time, Zacharias Topelius (1818–1898) confirms this in his Swedish-language text *Boken om vårt land* (1875/1985, 165 [The book of Our land]) the following:

> Rarely are there families whose ancestors do not have the blood of other ethnicities. But as we used to say, whosoever considers this land a homeland, loves it accordingly, accepts the laws of this country, and works for its good, forms the nation. Their love for the country, respect of the laws, common wealth and common interests unify all them. (my translation)

However, the ethnic diversity so obvious in the birth phase of Finnishness was not extended to ethnicities other than the Swedish-speaking and Finnish-speaking ones. Moreover, after Finland gained independence in

1917, multiculturality was voiced less and less, and Finnishness along with the so-called *Suomen kirjallisuus* (Finnish literature) became more and more monolingual. A high number of Swedish speakers also changed their names and their home language from Swedish to Finnish.

Not only has local multiethnicity and multiculturality become more and more neglected, but also the role of the immigrants – continuously arriving throughout Finland's history – has been completely underestimated. Based on a critical analysis of archival data from the Finnish Immigration Authorities and recent interviews, Antero Leitzinger demonstrates in his 2008 book *Ulkomaalaiset Suomessa 1812–1972* [Foreigners in Finland 1812–1972] that it is a myth that Finland has been a homogenous place for centuries. As Leitzinger shows, the administration just applied different methods to assimilate this stratum of the society, if only in the realm of statistics.

Taking into consideration the points above, the following question arises: how could the image of a monolingual Finnish literature have ever been established? During the early modern period it was natural for up-and-coming intellectuals and writers from Finnish provinces to study at German universities (e.g. Göttingen, Heidelberg) or Sweden ones (e.g. Uppsala or Stockholm). Beginning in the 19th century the Russian sphere also became influential. Finally, in the years since the Second World War, an Anglo-Saxon orientation became more and more dominant, if not the most dominant in the current age of globalization (see Varpio 1999). This has meant a continuous absorption of diverse cultural influences, in order to remain in step with the *Weltgeist* of the time. In spite of the manifold forms of cultural influences, the Finnish literary field created its identity with the help of a widespread framework of the time: homogenization and particularization. Consequently a literary language was created for a nation living within well-defined borders. Until the end of the 20th century the multicultural matrix remained obscured.

Stefan Moster (2006, 411), in an article on the history of Finnish literature, argues that until the 1990s it was very difficult to get publicity for literary works that fell outside the narrow national-cultural framework, or refused to make immediate reference to it. While the multicultural dynamics of the Finnish literary field were dominated by the cultural policy of Finnisation in the 20th century, in recent decades publishers' business interests seem to play the most influential role. Today's large profit-oriented publishing houses, such as Otava or WSOY, usually do not take risks on authors with minoritarian and migrant backgrounds (not to speak of languages), although this barrier has been broken recently by Ranya ElRamly (2002), Roman Schatz (2005), and Sofi Oksanen (2003, 2005, 2008), whose books became bestsellers in a very short time, with tens of thousands of copies sold.

On a more general level, Pasi Saukkonen and Miikka Pyykkönen have reached important conclusions about the role of institutions in sustaining multiculturality by analyzing seven major cultural institutions coordinated through the Helsinki Office of Culture. Keeping in mind that the arts, and therefore also literature, can be used to promote a diverse society, Saukkonen and Pyykkönen conclude their study by asserting that 'there is certainly a need for multi- and intercultural centers that provide facilities for artistic and cultural activities within immigrant groups.' However, they also draw our attention to an even more pressing need, that of setting up of inter- and cross-cultural networking (Saukkonen & Pyykkönen 2008, 8).

## On Field Intern Multiculturality

Starting with Fredrik Polén's *Johdanto Suomen kirjallisuushistoriaan* (1858, [Introduction to the Literary History of Finland]) and V. Tarkiainen's *Suomalaisen kirjallisuuden historia* (1934, [History of Finnish literature]), followed by Rafael Koskimies' *Elävä kansalliskirjallisuus* (1944–1946, [The Living National Literature]) and continuing up to Kai Laitinen's *Suomen kirjallisuus* (1981, [Literature of Finland]) – just to mention the major critical works – literary histories have lent relevance to only those authors whose works contributed directly to the idea of a homogenous national identity. Such pioneering works as Gabriel Lagus' *Den finsk-svenska litteraturens utveckling* [The Development of Finland Swedish Literary history] from 1866, or the Saami literary anthology *Skábmatolak* (1974) have made only a marginal impact. Only in a three-volume work from 1999, edited by Yrjö Varpio, Liisi Huhtala, Pertti Lassila and Lea Rojola (*Suomen kirjallisuuden historia* 1–3 [History of Literature in Finland] is the literature from Finland first presented as trilingual (Finnish, Swedish and Saami), with chapters on Saami and Finland Swedish literature in addition to works in Finnish. At the same time, however, the volume leaves out other minority literary experiments, like those of the Russian, Tatar, Jewish and Roma communities, as well as transit and exile authors. Moreover, any aspect of a multicultural analytical perspective is pushed aside. Such an analytical perspective would seek out hybrid and liminal situations, pluri-, inter- and transcultural issues that are directly and indirectly addressed within a literary text.

In this regard, some new chapters need to be written in order to balance the inequality constantly produced and reproduced by those who participate in the making of the Finnish literary field. Not only are authors with minoritarian and migrant backgrounds in need of greater visibility, but the whole national literary field needs to be reevaluated. This can happen, for example, through critical works on multilingualism, questioning reading and teaching strategies of literary curricula in high schools, and partly de-economizing the book market.[4] It gives us hope that literary critics and scholars can contribute to the change of older literary habits.

*Suomen nykykirjallisuus* (2013, [Contemporary Literature in Finland]) edited by Mika Hallila, Yrjö Hosiaisluoma, Sanna Karkulehto, Leena Kirstinä and Jussi Ojajärvi contains chapters that deal with migrant authors and multiculturality in Finnish literature and society.

---

4 We can also mention pioneering works of literary scholars such as Viola Čapkova-Parente, Heidi Grönstrand, Vuokko Hirvonen, Tintti Klapuri, Olli Löytty, Kai Mikkonen, Hanna-Leena Nissilä and Eila Rantonen. Their articles deal with multiculturality in Finnish literature.

Another internationally exemplary attempt is the *Literary History of Northern Finland* edited by S. Carlsson and co. (*Pohjois-Suomen kirjallisuushistoria*, 2010). This volume brings together the whole region's relevant authors, regardless of their mother tongue. One of the volume's co-authors, Veli Pekka Lehtola, has also published an excellent monograph *Rajamaan identitetti. Lappilaisuuden rakentuminen 1920- ja 1930-luvun kirjallisuudessa* (1997, [*The Identity of Borderland. Building Lapplander Identity in Literature of the 1920s and 30s*]) comparing concepts of alterity used by Finnish (usually of internal migrant backgrounds) and indigenous Saami authors in North Finland. This witty literary analysis shows us how authors with Finnish settler backgrounds described the indigenous Saami, as well as how the Saami authors present themselves and the newcomers in their works.

The ongoing emergence of multicultural narratives in Finland is naturally a direct consequence of recent waves of migration and contemporary political ideology. However in the literary history it has been preceded by several multicultural attempts involved in such movements as the *Tulenkantajat* and the *Dagdrivare* from the 1920s, the modernist poets in the 1960s, and the poets involved with the literary magazine *Nuori Voima* in the 1990s. Their attempts to 'open windows to Europe,' and in turn bring Finland's literary life out of isolation, proved ephemeral. Literary life in Finland has always involved a large number of bilingual authors, or authors with a migrant background, as well as those living abroad. These authors' multicultural experiences were only marginally reflected in literary production and evaluation, since the external and internalized critical social voice did not value most aspects of multiculturality (such as bilingual production, code switching, reflection on cultural diversity etc.). Recent literary life in Finland has gained a great deal of positive momentum. Literary institutions such as FILI (Finnish Literature Exchange) and artistic centers such as Caisa (Multicultural Art Center, Helsinki), have put out several calls for texts reflecting on multiculturality, and readings with migrant authors are held with increasing regularity. Some relevant publications in connection with these institutions are *Hedelmät jotka eivät tuoksu ruudille* (2000, [Fruits that do not smell of gunpowder]), *Mikä ihmeen uussuomalainen?* (2004, [What on earth is a new Finn?]) and *2015: suuret tavoitteet, pieni ihminen* (2005, [2015: big hopes, small people]).

Parallel to local networking, multicultural authors have often profited from international cooperation. Just as the Saami literary movement was supported by the joint work of indigenous people from around the world, global ethnic networking offers much support to a community's mobile members (e.g. the Tatar or Russian networking around the globe). However multicultural networking for multicultural authors brings its own array of difficulties, and such attempts to date have been quite sporadic and ephemeral. Worth noting in this regard are transcultural literary events (e.g. *Supernova* Webstreaming) and a few individual attempts at transcultural, multilingual anthologies (e.g. *Drei Frauen / Kolme naista / Три жени* authored by Inge Kleinert, Orvokki Vironen Vääriskoski and Tzveta Sofronieva).

*Écriture Multiculturelle*

As the two sections above have made obvious, cultural interferences of the literary field play a relevant role on both the macro level (production, distribution, reception) and the micro level (the text itself). On the macro level, we can identify different historical periods and circumstances favoring or disfavoring multiculturality. On the micro level, Nordic literary works of the last three decades have manifested the emergence not only of actual intra- but also inter-systemic challenges. The works of contemporary writers showcase the necessity of new perspectives: re-conceptualizing national/ethnic identities, as in the 2002 novel *Juoksuhaudantie* by Kari Hotakainen, reflecting heterogeneity, as in Ranya El Ramly's *Auringon asema* (2002), and questioning normative homogeneity, as in Roman Schatz's 2005 book *From Finland with love / Suomesta, rakkaudella*, has become more and more obvious.

The three major manifestations of national identity at work in canonical Finnish literature can be described in terms of the narrative perspectives of: *who are 'we'?*, *who am 'I' in the 'we'?*, and *who are 'they'?* While the first question largely dominated the first decades of Finnish literature (e.g. the nation-building literary works of Runeberg and Topelius), and the second one preeminent in the hundred years that followed (starting with Järnefelt's contemplations on the role of the individual in *Isänmaa* (1898, [Fatherland]), the last type of questioning has only popped up in recent decades (a most recent example is Jari Tervo's *Layla*, 2011). However in all of these works multiculturality is addressed from the majoritarian position, and accordingly they bristle with stereotypes. This means that multiculturality is used to support the national position, to give an exotic flavor to the text, but never to question the narrow epistemological field. Therefore the so-called multicultural perspective of these works is in *switched-off* or *switching-off* mode. Of course, there are plenty of other books by now which raise the question *who am I, the other?*, where multiculturality is in constant *switched-on* mode. Let us mention as outstanding examples such works as that of the Russian-born Vepse Raisa Lardot's *Ripaskalinnut* (1978, [Gopak Birds], written in Finnish), the Saami Siiri Magga-Miettunen's *Siirin kirja* (2002, [The book of Siiri]), written in Finnish) or the Finland Swedish and Finland Tatar Sabira Ståhlberg's *Molnvandraren/Pilvivaeltaja* (2006, [Cloud Wanderer]), written in parallel Finnish and Swedish). Additionally, emigré Finnish authors manage more and more to offer feedback on the challenges of migration. Such authors (e.g. Asko Sahlberg or Susanna Alakoski) are more easily welcomed by a broader Finnish readership than writers with no Finnish background.

Inspired by theoretical works on *écriture féminine* (c.f. Jones 1981 or Showalter 1986), I will evaluate multicultural writing as the inscription of cultural interference and cultural difference in language and text. Analytical work on literary multiculturality tends to draw on phenomenology, hermeneutics, semiotics, poststructuralism, gender studies and Derridean deconstruction. Describing the aesthetics of multicultural literature, Szigeti (2002, 23) accordingly notes that works by authentic insiders, who possess multicultural backgrounds and first-hand experience of the psychic and social aspects of multiple identities, reach the readers due to the multiculturalist orientation that both poles share. According to Szigeti, these works make use of multiple choice schemata and salutary role models. Language also contributes to a work's classification as multicultural literature: because such works are created on the bases of several languages and cultures, and they are *received as idiosyncratic* (emphasis mine). Crucial here is the reader's impression that the language or the story or the characters of the book are in some sense 'peculiar' or 'different'.

Looking at the reaction of readers and critics to Ranya ElRamly's novel, *Auringon asema* (2002, [The Position of the Sun]), we can see that the author's name, the topic of the book, and its style were viewed by her critical readers as idiosyncratic, so that the book's 'exoticism' and 'non-Finnishness' came to the fore (Nissilä 2009). Because the author herself voiced very different views on her work, literary scholars could already document the start of a new multicultural period in Finnish literature. Speaking about similar processes and developments that occurred a few decades earlier in Sweden, Magnus Nilsson (2013, 41, italics mine) reports the following:

> The phenomena *immigrant literature* and *immigrant writer* came into existence in the Swedish literary sphere during the second half of the twentieth century, when literature written by authors of non-Nordic origin was more and more often viewed as an expression of ethnic experiences and identities. For a couple of years early in the new millennium, this kind of literature attracted massive attention from both readers and critics. At the same time, an intense critique of the construction of immigrant literature as a literature expressing ethnic otherness was formulated by literary critics and academics, as well as by several leading immigrant writers – a critique foregrounding, above all, the exoticizing, othering, and racializing tendencies of this construction. Thereafter, the literary interest in the literary sphere for immigrant literature seems to have diminished.

Nilsson's description tackles not only the Swedish case, but also the general dynamics of what is labeled as 'multicultural' or 'immigrant' literature, which suggests that Finland will go through the same experiences as the U.S., Canada or Germany. Once critics and readers have ceased to regard multicultural authors and the content of their books as idiosyncratic, and as they become accustomed to authors' names and topics, multicultural literature will be incorporated into the mainstream. After this stage it will also lose its relevance. This kind of literary transformation parallels similar processes in society at large. Consequently we can see that native authors, as well as emigrant Finnish authors (esp. to Sweden) are voicing multicultural topics and employing a multicultural perspective more and more often (e.g. Jari Tervo, Leena Lehtolainen, Anja Snellmann, Eppu Nuotio, Nina Hakalahti or Asko Sahlberg and Susanna Alakoski).

While Finnish canonical literature usually speaks of the identity problems of the individual in an anthropological sense, *écriture multiculturelle* reflects on the individual as a cultural construction. Consequently, in the first case we ask 'how can I be a virtuous human being,' and 'what is my role as a man/woman in this life,' whereas in the second case the question of 'who am

I' is defined in the frame of such cultural categories as ethnicity, religion or gender. One of the best examples of the former is Paavo Haavikko's *Kullervo's story*, while Ranya El Ramly's *Auringon asema* [The Position of the Sun] (2002) is an example of the latter. Haavikko's (1989) lyrical prose reflects on the inner dilemma of its major character in an anthropological (c.f. the nouns *mies* 'man' and *nainen* 'woman' or the verbs 'born', 'killed', 'remember') and mythical sense (since its major intertext is the Finnish national epic, the *Kalevala*).

> I have a good memory. I remember how I was born, not from a woman but from the fire. That was my birth. I wasn't killed. I wasn't given my right, not even the right to die the day I was born. I do remember how the Father woke up, Mother woke up, how they disappeared into the smoke [...] and this master came and took me away. Do I remember this, I don't remember, and I'll never forget. But I don't dwell on it. I don't want it to fade and grow distant in my mind.

While Haavikko's text in translation is still an excellent literary experience, most of the Finnish literary texts with strong connections to nation-building texts fail to become interesting for other literary audiences. The Finnish Swedish author Hagar Olsson commented on this issue in 'Finländsk robinsonad' in 1928 (*Quosego* 1928/3, 130):

> The more nationalistically limited our word is, the less chances does it have to gain a hearing, quite simply because in that case it does not correspond to our true essence, it does not have its source in our actual situation – on the island in the ocean. Only the oceanic winds are able to give our words wings. As nationalists we, citizens of Finland, have little or nothing to win, as internationalist – everything. As such we have a mission to fulfil here up in the North. It might prove that our last winged word was not said with Runeberg or Topelius. A poetic work like that of Edith Södergran is symphomatic. It is international in its essence, born in a process of radical change. (translated by Lars Kleberg see Kleberg 2003.)

Conversely, ElRamly's prose is full of ethnic and geocultural references. Cultural reflection is extremely well expressed in her *Auringon asema* (2002), a book in which the narrator's memories of a multicultural and multilocal childhood are clustered around a reflection on the loss of her mother. Instead of employing ethnic stereotypes, the first-person narrator voices her personal dilemma while often reflecting on different cultural approaches to everyday human tasks.

> When I sat down at the table to peel an orange, I knew that I could make four cuts in the skin so that it would come away easily, that was what my mother did. But I also knew that I could cut the peel away in a long spiral which I could wind around my wrist like a jewel, that was what my father did. And when my mother said that drinking water was fresher if essence pressed from the petals of roses was not added to it, then my father said that drinking water is tastier if essence pressed form the petals of roses is added to it, my father, he would the peel of an orange around my wrist like a jewel. An orange can be peeled in two ways, but

I cannot peel it in both ways, not the same orange in any case, and so I sat at the table for a long time; outsides all sorts of things were happening and I didn't join in, as I did not know how to be in this world with them. Not at all. (El Ramly 2002, translated by Hildi Hawkins.)

No doubt the recent wave of migration to Nordic countries has expanded the cultural horizon of literature. The introduction of new languages and language variations, themes and fields of reference, as well as new aesthetic and formal patterns, has led to the transition of the Nordic national literary field from being tacitly multicultural to being explicitly multicultural and multilingual. As demonstrated by all of the chapters on individual Nordic migrant and minority literatures in *Litteraturens gränsland* (2002, ed. S. Gröndahl), multicultural authors voicing their experience has played the most crucial role in this process.

*Locating Culture Markers of Communicating Agencies, Multicultural Accounts and Culturalia in the Text*

Taking a step away from the hermeneutic analysis of Szigeti, let us consider *écriture multiculturelle* from the point of view of its narrative and linguistic structure. As mentioned above, multicultural writing can be evaluated as the inscription of cultural interference and cultural difference in language and text. Linguistically, it is characterized by the occurrence of a high number of what we might call *culturalia* (verbalized arti-, menti- and sociofacts) of different cultural patterns as well as a high number of multicultural accounts (describing cultural relations). The culturalia and accounts are used in order to pose questions about establishing forms of relationship inside and between cultures, identities and realities. In such writings the interaction of the cultural markers from *all* of the levels of the narrative unit and their communicating agencies (as that of the author/reader, implied author/implied reader, narrator/narratorial addressee, and narrating figure/its addressee) carry semantic relevance, and their horizontal and vertical relationships need to be taken into consideration. However, these categories can be considered in any kind of literary work, not only works of multicultural writing.

According to the cultural sociologist Andreas Reckwitz, the overlapping of diverse cultural orders often obscures personal and collective identity crises (2001, 179). We arrive at the same results when looking to the identity processes of narratives dealing with diverse cultural patterns. In such narratives the interaction of cultural markers (from *all* of the levels) of the communicating agencies carry semantic information relevant to the immediate content of the literary work.

*Example*

The latest multicultural turn in Finnish society and literature was set into motion mostly by agents with migrant backgrounds, rather than deconstructions driven by minoritarian agents. The following text is a first-person narration that includes a great deal of ethnographic observation.

It is good to be a foreigner in Finland. In the land of the blind the one-eyed man is crowned king... Honestly, I'm sure if I were a Finn I would emigrate as quickly as possible. Because I'm a foreigner, I can enjoy Finland; have all the fun without the obligations. I don't have to understand how things work here, nobody expects me to behave like all the others [...]

Last but not least: what's extremely nice in Finland is the fact that the Finns are used to a lot of space around them. That's why they also willingly leave other people a lot of elbow room. They leave you in peace and they let you do your thing without interfering.

I wouldn't go so far as to call Finland a paradise. It's too damned expensive and too damned cold. But to be brutally honest again: As much as I love to complain, I have never really regretted coming here. (Schatz 2005, 119-121.)

In this short prose sample – as so often in multicultural writing – an overt, homodiegetic narrator refers to him/herself in the first person ('I'), and will address his/her narratee directly. Through this technique the reader experiences less psychological distance from the story and more readily develops empathy, effectively slipping into the skin of multicultural characters. Multicultural literature should therefore also be considered initiation literature, especially for readers who are in the dominant/majority position of a society. Besides identifying the cultural markers of communicating agencies and culturalia in our text, I will look also at multicultural accounts. My definition of multicultural accounts goes back to Dausendschön-Gay and Krafft (1998). These two authors define the accounts as textual manifestations of the social order (Dausendschön-Gay and Krafft 1998, 167), and describe four different accounts addressing cultural difference, namely: (1) Cultural difference as difference of background knowledge: anticipation of difficulties in understanding, (2) Setting up and/or deconstructing a hegemonic situation through the representation of incompetence, (3) Perspectivization: using special perspectives in order to address certain thematic aspects and (4) Relationship work: distancing from one's own group. These accounts are not the only ones we can find in multicultural literature and there is a pressing need to map all the cognitive, affective and conative accounts in all of the interferential modalities (cf. Domokos 2013b). Cultural interferences are present not only in intercultural situations, but in all other interferential modalities (c.f. pluri-, inter- and transcultural, Domokos 2013b). At this stage of research I suggest using the umbrella term of multicultural accounts, as well as mapping out all possible variations. The categorization of these accounts will form the next stage of research.

*The cultural level* forming the pillars of the above quoted text reflects an intercultural situation marked by the two major poles of *the foreigners, we, you* as well *the others* and that of *the Finns,* of *the they* of *all the others*. Intercultural dialogue is further particularized with verbs such as: *emigrate, enjoy, understand, expect, behave, use to have, willingly leave*, etc. The text does not feature any accounts that reflect on the power relations between migrants and Finnish society; it is more like a tourist's reflections on his winter holidays. At any rate, the author uses an outsider perspective in order to address certain thematic aspects. His/her positive and humorous attitude definitely opens more hearts in Finland than a critical tone, and indeed the book became a local bestseller.

We are speaking about Roman Schatz's book *From Finland with love/ Suomesta, Rakkaudella* (2005). Though his first language is German, the author chose English and Finnish to be the languages of his debut book. The intercultural relationship work is built up with the help of numerous positive affirmations (e.g. *it is good to be foreigner in Finland; Because I'm a foreigner, I can enjoy Finland; have all the fun without the obligations; nobody expects me to behave like all the others; As much as I love to complain – I have never really regretted coming here* etc.) and several satirical multicultural accounts (e.g. *In the land of the blind the one-eyed man is crowned king; if I were a Finn I would emigrate as quickly as possible; I wouldn't go so far as to call Finland a paradise*). The first person narrator aims to give voice to all migrant agents, though he shares some personal stories in the book. Finnish society is often imagined by migrants as bicultural: with the dominant Finnish, and its dominated but otherwise dominant Finland Swedish poles. Other minorities (the indigenous Saami and the other minorities with hundreds of years of tradition) are seldom mentioned. Rarely do migrants want to see themselves assimilated into those minority groups which occupy a relatively less favorable position.

## Closing Lines

Demographic changes deconstructing the national literary centers can be dated from the 1970s in Sweden, from the mid-1980s in Norway, early 1990s in Denmark and beginning of the 21$^{st}$ century in Finland. Multicultural literature is becoming an import phenomenon in Finland. In local works ranging from little-known to national bestsellers, multicultural literature seeks an ongoing legitimate space in the national context. The explicit presence of multiculturality in Finnish literature makes the literary field appear more updated, and definitely more democratic. How and why the present Finnish situation differs from other contemporary literary multiculturalites will long remain an interesting topic to ponder. Other avenues to explore are the relationship of Finnish literature to other literatures around the globe, as well as comparing the varied multicultural periods of Finnish literature itself.

This article took a heuristic look at multiculturality in Finnish literature on the levels of context, intertext, and text. Such an approach demonstrates why it is important to locate the cultural markers of all communicating agencies and analyze their horizontal and vertical relationships. At the same time we can speak of *écriture multiculturelle* so long as the primary readership experiences a feeling of cultural idiosyncrasy while reading the book, although critics are welcome to apply a multicultural analysis to any work at any time. It is the intention of this author to show how cultural identities are constructed in a literary work, and how diversity affects the power relationships between the characters and their communities, or between communities – questions that should be primary for any literary analysis.

Multiculturality is an increasingly common topic in Finland, both in everyday life and in the world of publishing, where foreign-sounding names are now becoming fashionable. An increasing number of Finnish authors identify with multiple cultural spheres. However, the path to publicity for multicultural works remains narrow. The changes awaiting Finland, Norway and Denmark have already taken place in the literary fields of Sweden and Germany, and they have long been familiar in places like Great Britain, Canada, or the U.S. The task of the Finnish literary field is to contribute to the country's emerging self-image as a multicultural and multilingual society, characterized above all by ethnic diversity. Literature should be experienced as the voice of a society proud of its cultural diversity, just as it was used for voicing national unity long ago. In fact, what multicultural writing does best is to emphasize the organic nature of any literature, since literature is a syncretic and hybridized product of interaction across cultures. Therefore the literary field of *Suomen kirjallisuus* has always been multicultural in its essence, and this fact should be openly and explicitly acknowledged by readers and critics alike.

# References

Amelina, Anna 2010: Searching for an Appropriate Research Strategy on Transnational Migration: The Logic of Multi-Sited Research and the Advantage of the Cultural Interferences Approach. *Qualitative Socail Research/Sozialforschung*. Vol. 11. No 1. http://www.qualitative-research.net/index.php/fqs/article/viewArticle/1279

Bachmann-Medick, Doris 2006: *Cultural Turns. Neuorientierungen in den Kulturwissenschaften*. Reinbek bei Hamburg: Rowohlt.

Bhabha, Homi K. 1994: *The Location of Culture*. London, New York: Routledge.

Bourdieu, Pierre 1992: *Les régles de l'art: Genèse et structure du champ littéraire*. Paris: Éd. du Seuil.

Dausendschön-Gay, Ulrich & Krafft, Ulrich 1998: Kulturelle Differenz als account. *Fremde im Gespräch. Gesprächsanalytische Untersuchungen zu Dolmetsch-Interaktionen, interkultureller Kommunikation und institutionalisierten Interaktionsformen*. Ed. by B. Apfelbaum & H. Müller. Frankfurt a.M.: IKO – Verlag für Interkulturelle Kommunikation. 163–197.

DiMaggio, Paul 1992: Cultural Boundaries and Structural Change: The Extension of the High Culture Model to Theater, Opera, and the Dance, 1900–1940. *Cultivating Differences: Symbolic Boundaries and the Making of Inequality*. Ed. by Lamont, M. & Fournier, M. Chicago. IL: University of Chicago Press. 21–57.

Domokos, Johanna 2011a: *Saami cultural and intercultural conjunctions*. Specimina Fennica 16. Szombathely: Balogh és Társa.

Domokos, Johanna 2011b: Differentiation of cultural interference in the (Uralic) literary fields. *Multilinguality and Multiculturality in Finno-Ugric literatures*. Ed. by J. Laakso & J. Domokos. Wien: LIT Verlag. 12–25.

Domokos, Johanna 2013a: Towards a polycultural narratology. *Kultur-Wissen-Narration. Perspektieven transdisziplinärer Erzählforschung für die Kulturwissenschaften*. Ed. by A. Strohmeier. Bielefeld: Transcript. 122–35.

Domokos, Johanna 2013b: On the ecology of cultural interference. Examples from Nordic and Sami literature. Ritva Hartama-Heinonen & Pirjo Kukkonen (eds.) *Inter Acta Translatologica Helsingiensia* (ATH) Vol 2, 13–24.

ElRamly, Ranya 2002: How to peel an orange. Translated by Hildi Hawkins. http://www.booksfromfinland.fi/2002/12/how-to-peel-an-orange/#more-6737 [17.1.2016]

Gaski, Harald (ed.) 1998: *Sami Culture in a New Era: The Norwegian Sami Experience*. Karasjok: Davvi Girji.

Gaski, Harald 2004: *Den lille forfatterboka: samisk*. Oslo: Biblioteksentralen.

Gröndahl, Satu (ed.) 2002a: Invandrar- och minoritetslitteraturer i Sverige. Från förutsättningar till framtidsutsikter. *Litteraturens gränsland: Invandrar- och minoritetslitteratur i nordiskt perspektiv*. Uppsala Multiethnic Papers 45. Uppsala: Centrum för multietnisk forskning. 35–70.

Gröndahl, Satu (ed.) 2002b: *Litteraturens gränsland: Invandrar- och minoritetslitteratur i nordiskt perspektiv*. Uppsala Multiethnic Papers 45. Uppsala: Centrum för multietnisk forskning.

Gröndahl, Satu 2008: Kön/genus, ras/etnicitet och klass i konstruktion av invandrar- och minoritetslitteratur. – *Gränser i nordisk litteratur – Borders in Nordic literature*. IASS XXVI 2006. Vol 2. Ed. by Clas Zilliacus, Heidi Grönstrand & Ulrika Gustafsson. Åbo: Åbo Akademis förlag. 619–626.

Haavikko, Paavo 1989: *Kullervon tarina/Kullervo's Story*. Translated by A. Hollo. Helsinki: Art House.

Hall, Stuart (ed.) 1980: *Culture, media, language: Working papers in cultural studies, 1972 – 79*. London: Hutchinson.

Hallila, Mika et al. (eds.) 2013: *Suomen nykykirjallisuus 2*. Helsinki: Suomalaisen Kirjallisuuden Seura.

Hirvonen, Vuokko 2008: *Voices from Sápmi. Sámi Women's Path to Authorship*. Translated by K. Anttonen. Guovdageaidnu: DAT.

Hoggart, Richard 1957: *The uses of literacy: Aspects of working-class life with special reference to publications and entertainments*. London: Chatto and Windus.

Jahn, Manfred 2005: *Narratology: A Guide to the Theory of Narrative*. English Department. University of Cologne. http://www.uni-koeln.de/~ame02/pppn.htm.

Jones, Ann Rosalind 1981: Writing the Body: Toward an Understanding of 'L'Ecriture Feminine'. *Feminist Studies*, Vol. 7, No. 2. 247–263. http://www.jstor.org/stable/3177523

Kambourelli, Smaro (ed.) 1991: *Making a Difference: Canadian Multicultural Literature*. Oxford University Press.

Kleberg, Lars 2003: The advantage of the margin. *Swedish–Polish Modernism: Literature – Language – Culture*. Ed. by M. Anna Packalén & S. Gustavsson. Stockholm: Almqvist & Wiksell International. 56–89. http://www.balticsealibrary.de

Koch, Manfred 2005: Goethes 'Weltliteratur' – Ein ambivalenter Erwartungsbegriff. *Weltgesellschaft. Theoretische Zugänge und empirische Problemlagen*. Edited by B. Heintz, R. Münch & H. Tyrell. Stuttgart: Lucius und Lucius. 51–67.

Laakso, Johanna & Domokos, Johanna (ed.) 2011: *Multilinguality and Multiculturality in Finno-Ugric literatures*. Wien: LIT Verlag.

Lehtola, Veli-Pekka 1997: *Rajamaan identiteetti. Lappilaisuuden rakentuminen 1920- ja 1930-luvun kirjallisuudessa*. Pieksämäki: Raamattutalo.

Lehtola, Veli-Pekka 2004: *The Sámi People. Traditions in Transition*. Fairbanks: Alaska University Press.

Leitzinger, Antero 2008: *Ulkomaalaiset Suomessa 1812–1972*. Helsinki: East-West Books.

Mecklenburg, Norbert 2008: *Das Mädchen aus der Fremde. Germanistik als interkulturelle Literaturwissenschaft*. München: Judicium.

Nilsson, Magnus 2013: Literature in Multicultural and Multilingual Sweden: The Birth and Death of the Immigrant writer. *Literature, Language, and Multiculturalism in Scandinavia and the Low Countries*. Ed. by W. Behschnitt and S. De Mul & L. Minnaard. Amsterdam: Rodopi. 41–61.

Nissilä, Hanna-Leena 2009: Ranya ElRamly ja Auringon aseman vastaanotto. *Kulttuurintutkimus* 1. 39–53.
Ortiz, Ferdinand 1940/1991: *Contrapuento cubano del tabaco y el azúcar.* La Habana: Universidad Central de las Villas.
Posner, Roland 2003: Kultursemiotik. *Konzepte der Kulturwissenschaften. Theoretische Grundlagen—Ansätze—Perspektiven.* Ed. by A. Nünning, A. & V. Nünning. Stuttgart, Weimar: J. B. Metzler. 39–72.
Rantonen, Eila 2006: Kirjallisia tuliaisia. Maahanmuuttaja-kirjallisuus kulttuurien välissä. *Fiktiota! Levottomat genret ja kirjaston arki.* Ed. by Kaisa Hypén. Helsinki: BTJ Kirjastopalvelu. 121–135.
Rantonen, Eila 2009a: Pääkirjoitus: Muuttavatko maahanmuuttajakirjailijat suomalaisen kirjallisuuden? *Kiiltomato* 6.11. http://www.kiiltomato.net/?cat=editorial&id=193
Rantonen, Eila 2009b: African Voices in Finland and Sweden. *Transcultural Modernities. Narrating Africa in Europe.* Ed. by Elisabeth Bekers, Sissy Helff and Daniella Merolla. *Matatu. Journal for African Culture and Society.* Amsterdam, New York: Rodopi. 71–83.
Rantonen, Eila (ed.) 2010: *Vähemmistöt ja monikulttuurisuus kirjallisuudessa.* Tampere: Tampere University Press.
Rantonen, Eila & Savolainen, Matti 2002: Postcolonial and Ethnic Studies in the Context of Nordic minority Literatures. *Litteraturens gränsland. Invandrar- och minoritets litteratur i nordiskt perspektiv.* Ed. by Satu Gröndahl. Uppsala: Uppsala Universitet. Institut för Multietnisk forskning. 71–94.
Reckwitz, Andreas 2000: *Die Transformation der Kulturtheorien. Zur Entwicklung eines Theorieprogramms.* Göttingen: Velbrück Wissenschaft.
Reckwitz, Andreas 2001: Multikulturalismustheorien und der Kulturbegriff: Vom Homogenitätsmodell zum Modell kultureller Interferenzen. *Berliner Journal für Soziologie,* 11/2. 179–200.
Said, Edward 1978: *Orientalism.* New York: Pantheon Books.
Saukkonen, Pasi & Pyykkönen, Miikka 2008: *Cultural policy and cultural diversity in Finland.* m.hit.no/nor/content/download/48183/403018/file/SaukkonenPyykkonen.pdf . 24p.
Schatz, Roman 2005: *From Finland With Love. /Suomesta rakkaudella.* Helsinki: Johnny Kniga Kustannus.
Showalter, Elaine (ed.) 1986: *The New Feminist Criticism: essays on women, literature, and theory.* London: Virago.
Sommer, Roy 2000: *Fictions of Migration. Ein Beitrag zur Theorie und Gattungstypologie des zeitgenössischen interkulturellen Romans in Großbritannien.* Studies in English Litearary and Cultural History. Vol.1.Wissenschaftlicher Verlag Trier.
Spivak, Gayatri Chakravorty 1999: *A Critique of Postcolonial Reason: Towards a History of the Vanishing Present.* Boston: Harvard University Press.
Szigeti, László 2002: A multikulturalizmus esztétikája. *Helikon* 2002/4. 395–421.
Topelius, Zacharias 1985: *Maamme-kirja.* Helsinki: Juva.
Zimmermann, Peter (ed.) 1989: *Interkulturelle Germanistik. Dialog der Kulturen auf Deutsch.* Frankfurt am Main.
Varpio, Yrjö 1999: *A sarkcsillag alatt, Európában. Bevezetés a finn kultúrába és irodalomba.* Specimina Fennica VIII.
Wierlacher, Alois & Bogner, Andrea (ed.) 2003: *Handbuch interkulturelle Germanistik.* Stuttgart: Metzler.

Hanna-Leena Nissilä
https://orcid.org/0000-0003-1457-0277

# Women Writers with Im/migrant Backgrounds: Transnationalizing Finnish Literature – Perspectives on the Reception of Debut Novels by Lindén, ElRamly, Abu-Hanna and Salmela

Due to the advancing process of globalization, mass-migration and transportation, the 21$^{st}$ century has witnessed the emergence of transnational and cross-border writers with im/migrant backgrounds in Finland. They have published autobiographical texts, poems in anthologies, short story collections and novels.[1] This diverse group of both professional and amateur transnational and cross-border writers with im/migrant backgrounds has challenged the prevailing concept of national literature in Finland. As a result, the reshaping of Finnish literature and the process of re-evaluating the national literary canon have also begun in Finland. But, as in many other European countries, this literature is still rather peripheral and tends mostly to be confined to small publishing houses or internet sites (Gebauer & Lausten 2010, 2).

In this article, I will analyze the transnationalization of literature in Finland via four women writers, Umayya Abu-Hanna, Ranya ElRamly (now Paasonen), Zinaida Lindén and Alexandra Salmela, and the reception of their debut novels[2]. Although the novels are very different from each other, they deal with common themes, for instance, identity and lives in/between two cultures, which they explore partly through autobiographical elements in the texts. The theme of the struggle for identity has been one of the central themes of women's literature, and highly valued and canonized in western literature, as well. According to Patricia Waugh (1989, 10), '[m]uch [of] women's writing can, in fact, be seen not as an attempt to define an isolated individual ego but to discover a collective concept of subjectivity which foregrounds the construction of identity *in relationship*'. The transnational women writers introduced in this article can be seen as part of the continuum of women's writing. As women have historically been positioned in terms of otherness, also being an im/migrant gives an additional position of otherness and marginality. 'Otherness' is the reason, as Waugh claims, why their desire to become subjects is likely to be strong.

---

1   Even authors belonging to the majority have begun to deal with the themes and problems concerning present migration and multiculturalism in Finland (Rantonen & Nissilä 2013).
2   Before publishing her debut novel *I väntan på en jordbävning* (2004), Lindén had published two short story collections in Swedish.

The studied works span the period from 1996 to 2010. Arguably, it was during this same period, especially during the first decade of the twenty-first century, that the transnationalization of Finnish literary life took place. I understand the conception of Finnish literature as a historical construction, which both reflects and constructs Finnishness and Finnish society. However, literature and literary culture were not born and have never remained within nation-state borders, and, moreover, nation-states also contain cultures other than that which is defined as national (Pollari et. al. 2015; Grönstrand et. al. 2016). There has been, and continues to be, mobility and movement not only between Finland and other countries but within Finland as well.[3] Even in history, there have been multidirectional border-crossing literary activities and movements both in and between Finland and other countries. For instance, literatures of Finland-Swedish, Sámi, Torne Valley Finnish, Yiddish, Finnish Tatar, Finnish Roma, Sweden-Finnish, Kven and Finnish literature published in Carelia are examples of literary cultures, which have historically crossed language and culture borders related to Finland, Finnish language and identity.[4]

These mentioned four women and their books have had a pivotal role in the transnationalization of Finnish literature; they represent the change and problematics connected to the publication, reception and definition of literature by writers with im/migrant backgrounds. They have received a great deal of visibility and media publicity. Critiques, reviews and articles have been written about the works, and the novels have been nominated for various prizes by literary institution and Finnish society.[5] Part of the reason for this publicity has been their relation to Finnish culture, since attention has particularly been paid to the backgrounds of the writers – im/migration – and to their relationships to Finnish literature, the Finnish language and Finnishness. Two central literary debates culminated in discussions of

3   In literary studies, multilingualism, literary minorities and multiculturalism in Finland have been discussed for example in the following works: Savolainen 1995, Hirvonen 1999, Rantonen (ed.) 2011, Grönstrand & Malmio (ed.) 2011.
4   See e.g. Ekman ed. 2014; Gröndahl ed. 2002; 2005; 2011; Gröndahl & Rantonen 2013; Grönstrand & Malmio eds. 2011; Heith 2009; Jama 1995; Kurki 2013; Lehtola 1995; 2013; Maliniemi Lindbach 2002; Parente-Čapková 201; Pelvo 2013; Pynnönen 1991; Rantonen ed. 2010; Tidigs 2014; Viinikka-Kallinen 2010; Wrede ed. 1999; Zilliacus ed. 2000; Hirvonen 1999.
5   These writers have received the following awards and nominations: Abu-Hanna: the Bonnier's Journalist Prize 2002, the Finland Prize 2003, The Finnish Lifelong Learning Foundation Prize 2004, 'the Kristiina of the year' -award 2004 and the Larin Paraske prize 2008; ElRamly: the Kalevi Jäntti Literary Prize 2002, the Runeberg Prize 2003, the Thanks for the Book Award 2003 and nominations for The Helsingin Sanomat Literature Prize 2002 and the Olvi Foundation Literature Award 2002; Lindén: the Prize from the Society of Swedish Literature in Finland 1997 and 2005, the Runeberg Prize 2005, the Finland Prize 2007, awards from the Swedish Cultural Foundation 2006, The Cultural Foundation Längmanska 2010 and the Arts Council of Varsinais-Suomi 2006; Salmela: The Helsingin Sanomat Literature Prize 2010, and nominations for the Finlandia Literary Prize 2010 and the Kalle Kaihari Foundation Cultural Award 2011.

ElRamly and Salmela, even resulting in a change to the rules of the Finlandia Literary Prize[6] so that writers who are not Finnish citizens can also be nominated (Löytty 2013).

Literature and gender have played a significant role in building and defining Finnish national identity since the beginning of the 19th century when Finnish nationalism and Finnish literature were born. I will examine the reception of these debut novels and author interviews in connection to their reception from the viewpoint of challenging the concept and definition of national literature – that is, Finnish literature. Why do these women writers have such an effect on the field of Finnish literature, and why do they have such a central role in transnationalizing Finnish literature? I am interested in the process by which the literary institution receives and canonizes novels, as well as how and on what bases it names, defines and categorizes literature published by authors with im/migrant backgrounds. I am also interested in imagined and real borders framing cultural production, borders that transnational and cross-border women writers cross as im/migrant writers.

In recent years, literary scholars have discussed the usefulness of regarding literature as a national institution, as opposed to a diasporic or transnational institution actualised through language (Huttunen 2013, 247). I will apply an idea of transnational and cross-border literary cultures as imagined (Anderson 1996) and paranational (Seyhan 2010) communities, in which literary culture appears as both local and global. As such, they can be seen as transnational spaces where writers have multiple belongings to linguistically bound, yet transnational and cross-border literary communities. During the last few years, the concept of migrant literature has been widened to encompass literature by non-im/migrants authors. In these cases, migrant literature has not been characterized only by authors' biographies, but also by themes, forms and discursive strategies that have been influenced by im/migrant authors (e.g. Frank 2010). Rather than the concept of 'migrant literature', which emphasizes the background of the author, I prefer the terms 'cross-border literature' and 'transnational literature', which both reach beneath and beyond the level of the nation. The growing discussion on transnational and cross-border studies has challenged concepts and units of analysis that are restricted to the national; it has challenged a way of portraying the world as naturally divided into national societies (Amelina et al. 2012).

The transnational is a starting point for my approach to the reception of novels written by these four women writers with im/migrant backgrounds, who, I argue, are part of the 'transnational turn in literature' in Finland. A transnational or cross-border approach[7] – methodological transnationalism

---

6   The Finlandia Literary prize, presented by the Finnish Book Foundation, is the most prestigious literary award in Finland. The prize was established in 1984, and since then it has been granted annually in recognition of the most deserving Finnish novel.
7   Cross-border studies seems to be more or less synonymous with what is covered by the concept of transnationalism. According to Amelina et. al. (2012), it has 'certainly

– departs from the national research paradigm and pays attention to the relationships between various national and cultural categories (Amelina et al. 2012; Grönstrand et al. 2012). It also critically questions and denaturalizes the concept of nation and the use of an ethnic and national lens to conceptualize migration, and rejects the nation-state as the central relevant context of study (Amelina & Faist 2012; Amelina et al. 2012).

The transnational turn has also resulted, as Paul Jay writes, in remapping the geographical spaces of literary and cultural studies. This has meant, for instance, an interest in tracing complicated histories of displacement, and turning from what used to be a narrow national focus to a global perspective, all of which has helped to recognize that 'we create the spaces we study' (Jay 2010, 8.). Literary spaces include different spatial scales, such as global, transnational, postcolonial, and local dimensions. I understand the literary space and culture also as a meeting point of real and symbolic mobility (Urry 2002) and global flows (Appadurai 1996), and as a landscape where national, cultural, ethnic, linguistic, gender and other categories are constantly transforming. In this landscape, there are no objectively given relations that look the same from every angle. These relations are rather, with regard to Arjun Appadurai (1996, 33), deeply perspectival constructs inflected by different actors, such as nation-states, multinationals, diasporic communities, subnational groupings and movements and face-to-face groups. Transnational or cross-border approaches resonate with intersectionality, and together they offer a fruitful perspective on literary reception and definitions in the context of these four women writers. In combination with the cross-border and transnational approach taken in this article, intersectionality shows how socially and culturally constructed categories, such as nation, gender, race, class, language, and other components of identity, interact on multiple and often simultaneous levels. As Leslie McCall (2005, 1781) writes, 'The intersection of identities takes place through the articulation of a single dimension of each category. That is, the 'multiple' in these intersectional analyses refers not to dimensions within categories but to dimensions across categories.'

Firstly, I concentrate on Zinaida Lindén and bi- or multilingualism as a transnational act operating outside monolingualism, nation and the national canon. What does it mean to be located in/between languages as a bi- or multilingual author choosing to write with her second language? Secondly, I analyze the reception of Ranya ElRamly's novel *Auringon asema* (2002, [The Position of the Sun]) and the first literary discussion about Finnishness and Finnish literature in the context of the so called multicultural literature. Thirdly, I ask why Umayya Abu-Hanna's novel *Nurinkurin* (2003, [Upside down, Inside out]) was interpreted as a memoir and non-fiction, and ended up to be an ethnographical informant from a different culture? Fourthly, I will

> become multidimensional, expanding from an initial focus on international relations and transnational corporations to discussions of global cities, global ethnoscapes and world society. Cross-border studies have subsequently included debates on transnational migration, cosmopolitanism and transnational history writing.'

analyze the second discussion about Finnish literature and its definition, when Alexandra Salmela's novel *27 eli kuolema tekee taiteilijan* (2010, [27 Or The Death Makes An Artist]) ended up changing the rules of the Finlandia Prize. What made the reception different from the earlier reception of and discussion on *Auringon asema*? Finally, I ask if it is somehow significant that it is women who have made such an impact on the transnationalization process of the Finnish literary field.

## Transnational Writers In/Between Languages

The Russian born Zinaida Lindén (b. 1963) published her first collection of short stories, *Överstinnan och syntetisatorn* [The Wife Of a Colonel And a Synthesizer], in 1996, when little if any attention was paid to migrant literature in Finland. She gained prominence in Finland in 2005, after winning the prestigious Runeberg Prize with her novel *Ennen maanjäristystä* ([Waiting For an Earthquake][8], the Swedish edition, *I väntan på en jordbävning*, was published in 2004). The novel depicts a meeting on a train from Moscow to Helsinki between the Russian-born writer Iraida Dahlin, who lives in Finland, and the Russian sumo wrestler Ivan Demidov, who resides in Japan. The train journey is used figuratively to represent how Ivan and Iraida are both constantly on the move and searching for their identity. The international train enables one to momentarily experience a liberating feeling of non-belonging, of being in a 'no man's land' where one does not have to justify one's identity as an immigrant or an emigrant (Klapuri 2012, 402.) *Takakirves-Tokyo* (2007) is an independent continuation of Demidov's story – an epistolary novel in which Iraida, who has now become rooted in the Swedish-speaking literary community in Finland, and Ivan, who still lives in Japan, exchange letters about their experiences of Tokyo and the Takakirves district in the city of Turku. Iraida can be interpreted as Lindén's alter ego: a Russian-born writer settled in Finland, writing in Swedish and pondering the differences between writing in a foreign language as opposed to one's native language, as well as the writing profession in general. In doing so, the novel continues to discuss immigration, especially from the point of view of linguistic and cultural themes related to the preservation and construction of one's identity (ibid.).

Lindén, whose mother tongue was Russian in her childhood, studied Swedish at the University of Leningrad and immigrated to Finland in 1991. Like many other transnational writers, Lindén writes bilingually in/between national paradigms. As a Swedish-speaker in Finland, she has become a part of Finland-Swedish society, and she is regarded as a Finland-Swedish writer, and therefore as part of Finland-Swedish literature. She has written

---

8   In Russian as *V ozhidanii zemletriasenija* (2005), self-translated by Lindén.

*Zinaida Lindén's Takakirves – Tokyo (2007) is about identity, memories and lives in two cultures. Cover: Johan Lindén / Maria Appelberg. Photo: Schildts & Söderströms.*

– self-translated[9] – her novels in both Swedish and Russian;[10] in practice, *Överstinnan och syntetisatorn* was first written in Russian and then self-translated into Swedish (Autio 2001). Tintti Klapuri (2011, 272) posits Lindén as a member of the group of Russian emigrant authors who are familiar with problems related to language and identity, but most of whom write in the language of their new home country. Lindén has also repeatedly been defined as an immigrant author, which is how she perceives herself: 'I'm definitely an immigrant author' (Hämäläinen 2005).

For multilingual authors, languages offer possibilities and alternatives to different identifications, but also the possibility to exist and transnationally belong to different national or linguistic literary cultures and canons.

---

9   Self-translations means an act, when '[T]he author translates his or her own texts and the outcome is two (or more) distinct versions with overlapping content, speaking to two (or more) different audience' (Grönstrand 2014).

10  Lindén has published the following works: *Överstinnan och syntetisatorn* ([The Wife of a colonel and a synthesizer], 1996), *Scheherazades sanna historier* ([Scheherazade's true stories], 2000, in Russian as *Podlinnye istorii Shahrazady* 2003), *I väntan på en josdbävning* ([Waiting for an Earthquake], 2005, in Russian as *V ozhidanii zemletriasenija* 2005), *Takakirves-Tokyo* (2007), *Lindanserskan* ([The Tightrope-walker], 2009, in Russian as *Tantsujusjaja na kanate: Novelly* 2011).

Language belongs to identity and unity, and it offers a framework of reality and identity that speakers can appropriate in their own way (Seyhan 2001, 8). Lindén says that she is often asked how she changed her language. In her experience, one never changes one's language; instead, one's identity fluctuates, because when writing in a different language one is able to play with different roles and identities (Autio 2001; Lehtimäki 2005, 93–94). She describes her relationship with Swedish and Russian as follows: 'I imagine dialogues in Swedish, both in life and in books. […] in Russian, definitely any "jokes, songs and political stories"' (Autio 2001).

Seyhan (2001, 8), addressing the idea of writing between borders and languages, argues that many authors plot complex strategies of translation in an effort to negotiate their loyalties to nation, language, ethnicity, class, and gender. In an interview, Lindén describes her relationship to Swedish, her main working language: 'I write good Swedish, but I have another identity. My struggle is not the same as that of the Swedish-speaking people' (Soto 2005, 24). She also asserts that she has not left the Russian language, and that it is very important for her to write to Russian people also, so that they can read in their own language. The feeling that the text and language are the author's own creations seems to be important, and Lindén describes it in the following way: 'So both versions of my book, Swedish and Russian, are written by my hand'. Self-translation can be seen as a border-activity that operates outside of nation and the national canon. When the author translates his or her own texts and speaks to two (or more) different audiences, with the outcome of two (or more) distinct versions with overlapping content, the act of self-translation challenges the idea of linguistic purity (Grönstrand 2014).

As a Swedish-speaking and a Russian immigrant author Lindén is part of minority and lives between languages and cultures in Finnish society, which has long demanded monolingualism and rendered multilingualism invisible (Grönstrand 2009; Grönstrand & Malmio 2011). The pressures of the monolingual paradigm have obscured multilingualism and multilingual practices, which have also led to processes of monolingualization, which again have produced more monolingual subjects, communities and institutions, despite the continued presence of multilingualism (Yildiz 2012). In Finland, from the majority perspective, national identity and nationalism have been constructed on the idea of monolingualism since the 19th century; since then Finnish literature has been strongly connected to monolingualism and to the idea of a national literature. There have been attempts to include multilingualism, mobility and 'multiculturalism' as part of the national canon or to leave them outside of it (e.g. Grönstrand & Malmio eds. 2011; Grönstrand 2016). For instance, Finland-Swedish literature was left out of national literary histories in Finland until 1960s, Sámi literature until lately (Lehtonen 1999; 2013), and Sweden-Finnish literature was long outside of both the Swedish and Finnish canons. According to Heidi Grönstrand (2016), in the case of bi- or multilingual authors such as Henrik Tikkanen, Elmer Diktonius or Edith Södergran, for instance the movement between languages is disregarded in literature studies and literary histories. Correspondingly, language and nationality are not necessarily linked in Finland any longer, as illustrated by transnational authors and authors who write in minority

Alexandra Salmela's *27* Eli kuolema tekee taiteilijan *(2010) questions the rules of the Finlandia Prize as well as the concept of Finnish literature. Cover: Nina Leino / Teos.*

languages (Grönstrand 2009; Grönstrand & Malmio 2011, 13). Seyhan (2001, 8) asks interestingly that if 'language is the single most important determinant of national identity [...] what happens when the domain of national language is occupied by non-native narratives, writers whose native, mother, home, or community language is not the one they write in?'

In addition to Lindén, Alexandra Salmela and Umayya Abu-Hanna, as multilingual authors who cross linguistic borders, also question the idea of monolingualism and the homogeneous idea of national culture. Alexandra Salmela, who studied Finnish at the University of Prague, wrote her novel *27 eli kuolema tekee taiteilijan* in Finnish in 2010 after having lived in Finland for four years. Salmela (2012, 319, 321) describes herself as a regular 'individual struggling in the maelstrom of multilingualism', who only thought of herself as bilingual after responding to a request to write an essay on bilingualism. She examines the different aspects of becoming bilingual as an adult and emphasizes a person's multiple identities, of which national identity may not be the strongest. Salmela's rapid acquisition of the Finnish language was a cause for much celebration and wonderment: language – both her having learned fluent Finnish as a second language and her creative way of using it – was the central subject of interviews and articles.

The Israel-born Palestinian Umayya Abu-Hanna – a Finnish Palestinian from Israel, as she describes herself (Abu-Hanna 1999) – wrote her first novel *Nurinkurin* in Finnish after having lived in Finland for more than 20 years. Abu-Hanna reflects on her position in relation to a language that can never be her mother tongue:

> I never recognise the person who speaks and appears in public using my name as myself. After all, she is always clumsier both linguistically and in terms of expression [...] That person who focuses all her energy on basic self-expression is worn out and sad over never getting it completely right. It is nice when the community smiles and forgives your comical mistakes. But the real me is neither comical nor clumsy (Abu-Hanna 1999).

In an interview, Lindén also discusses her feelings of helplessness with regard to the Swedish language, stating that even if it is her working language, her profession and her love, she can never learn Swedish like a native speaker. But even if she feels that she is bound by a 'linguistic glass ceiling', when writing her own text she can 'be sly and select strategies' that do not reveal the facts (Lehtimäki 2004, 94–95). Salmela (2012, 323) describes her relationship with her two languages as a balancing act between them. 'Once you enter one language, you exit the other. When absorbing something new you lose something old and constantly balance on the rope of two languages.'

In a sense, balancing between languages illustrates how the authors are trying to work through their situation within a framework of monolingualism and the monolingual paradigm. The acquisition of a language and the choice of im/migrant authors to write in a new language can be seen as cultural improvisation. When improvising, the author navigates in a literary field consisting of various institutionalised, now traditional practices as well as entirely new things, among various actors such as publishers, critics and the reading public. (Huttunen 2013, 253.) Satu Gröndahl (2009) has shown how the language in which literature was written was the most decisive criteria for the inclusion of im/migrant and minority writers in a Swedish canon. For multilingual authors like Abu-Hanna, Lindén and Salmela, languages may offer possibilities and alternatives of identity and existence, as well as belonging transnationally to different literary canons. Through them, literary life therefore appears as a cross-boundary activity, consisting of communities in which authors can reside as members of cross-boundary networks. At the same time, the resilience of monolingualism is strong, and as Yildiz (2012) shows, the mere presence of many languages within one context does not automatically mean that monolingualism has been overcome.

## *Awakening for Multicultural Literature in Finland: An Exotic Author*

Even though Zinaida Lindén's first short story collection, *Överstinnan och syntetisatorn*, was published as early as 1996, the discussion about 'multicultural Finnish' literature only arose after the publication of Ranya

ElRamly's (b. 1974) novel *Auringon asema* in 2002. While in other Nordic countries so-called migrant literature or multicultural literature had long been published, in Sweden since the 1970s and in Norway since the 1980s (e.g. Kongslien 2006), in Finland this literary field only began to emerge in the 2000s. *Auringon asema* is a novel about the daughter of a Finnish mother and Egyptian father reminiscing, in first person, about her parents' bicultural love and her own childhood in Egypt. As in Lindén's novel *I väntan på en jordbävning*, in *Auringon asema* a train is the place where two people from different cultures meet: – Anu and Ismael meet on a train journey from Luxor to Assuan – and fall in love. The novel becomes an identity narrative when the narrator, balancing between Finnish and Egyptian culture, discovers her identity: 'My eyes are green, I'm neither this nor that, yet both. And I no longer want to choose between you' (ElRamly 2002a, 178) (Nissilä 2007).

This thematically and stylistically refreshing work of literature attracted much attention, was the topic of several reviews and articles. It received literature awards and nominations, for instance the prestigious Runeberg Prize – the prize awarded a few years later to Lindén, too, for her novel *I väntan på en jordbävning*. As it also attracted attention in media, it ended up selling very well, even becoming one of the best-selling debut novels in Finland. The relevance of the topic of the novel as a current issue was remarked upon and appreciated in reviews. The novel was seen as creating 'a new kind of Finnish literary tradition', both stylistically and in terms of its subject matter (Paavola 2002, 41). Lindholm (2002, 59), who has analyzed the Runeberg Prize as a literary awarding institution, states that a key factor determining the value of a literary work is related to the ideology of renewal, and even claims that every work that has reformed tradition has received positive feedback from reviewers.[11] The reception of *Auringon asema* reflected the cultural, social and national transformation in Finland that had begun in the 1990s, and ElRamly was inadvertently cast into the midst of an attempt to define both Finnishness and literature. *Auringon asema* was characterized as 'multicultural literature', 'world literature', 'postcolonial literature' and even 'migrant literature', and was said 'to become a symbol of Finnish multicultural literature' (Ratinen 2002, 47).

Nevertheless, most attention was focused on the multicultural background of ElRamly and her relationship to Finland and Finnishness. The child of a Finnish mother and an Egyptian father, the Finnish-speaking ElRamly moved to Finland as a teenager. Before that, she lived in India, Chad, Libya, Saudi Arabia and Egypt. ElRamly was repeatedly asked to describe her 'exotic' childhood, even though she herself wanted to be seen as a Finnish novelist. The novel was made into a kind of a 'cultural ambassador' (Kurkijärvi 2002, 19), meant to function as a reflection of an

---

11 According to Lindholm (2002, 59), the Runeberg Prize citations in the 1990s have featured a demand for freshness, i.e., that a good literary work is defined against contemporary literature as one that reforms tradition. The citations differ from literary reviews in that not one speech compared the award-winning work to the production of canonised authors.

increasingly multicultural Finland (Nissilä 2009). The categorisation of the novel was difficult in terms of both topic and authorship, as reviewers tried to place *Auringon asema* within the field of Finnish literature. In one critique, it was written that 'in a way ElRamly is not an immigrant, because she is also a Finn and she speaks fluent and beautiful Finnish. But yet she is writing as a foreigner, and as a native and a local at the same time' (Hakalahti 2002). According to another reviewer, Finnishness concerns language and the place of publication whereas multiculturality concerns the background of ElRamly and the theme of the novel (Ratinen 2002, 47). Even when ElRamly's 'Finnishness' was also highlighted in the interviews, she was primarily represented as exotic, multicultural and 'ethnic'. The book was seen as containing 'a lot of foreign exotica' (ibid.), and in several interviews ElRamly was described as exotic. According to Satu Gröndahl (2009, 182), many literary reviews of multicultural literature in Sweden have also been characterised by their focus on the 'ethnic' background of the author. Eira Juntti (1998, 69) states that media texts produce 'Finnishness' by delineating borders as to who is accepted as 'Finns' by labelling those who do not meet the criteria of 'Finnishness' as 'different'.

Characteristic of many reviews, critiques and interviews concerning the texts of the other writers too – Abu-Hanna, Lindén and Salmela – is that the media have focused on their ethnic, migrant and linguistic background. In what appears to have been the first paper on migrant literature in Finland, the literary scholar Kai Mikkonen (2001, 553) even then aptly discussed how focusing on the author's background or reading immigrant authors' texts solely from the point of view of cultural identities or windows into Finnishness does not necessarily do justice to literature as literature and language. Satu Gröndahl (2009, 182) has emphasized that expressions like 'second generation immigrant authors' locate certain authors temporally and spatially beyond national culture. It illustrates the essentializing of difference. In other words, an author is represented as 'different' and 'other' because of his/her origin and belonging somewhere else.

ElRamly's voice, emerging from the reception of and the act of speaking against definitions, challenges categorization. The 'talking back' that breaks down the 'us' and 'them' dichotomy portrays a young woman fed up with her role as 'cultural ambassador' and defending her identity, a woman who wishes to be like any other 'Finnish author' – not the 'immigrant author' that the literary institution wants. In interviews and columns, ElRamly comments on the various issues and assumptions linked to her and she is amazed at how foreign and estranged from Finnishness the media has depicted her. She also admits to giving in to her public image, even if she is 'as Finnish as they come' (Sharma 2003, 56–57).

Perhaps ElRamly's Egyptian 'exoticity', her resistance to definitions and the impossibility of fitting her into strict national categories at a time when national and cultural identities were readily perceived as clearly formed is a part of the reason why ElRamly and *Auringon asema* attracted such attention, rather than others. For example, the Iraq-born author Yousif Abu al Fawz, whose short story collection *Taikalintu* ([The Magic Bird], *Ta'ir al Dahsha*) was published two years earlier[12]; or Lindén, whose Swedish-language works failed to attract Finnish-speaking readers before they were translated into Finnish and recognised by Finnish literary institutions. Language is no doubt one notable reason for *Auringon asema*'s success and the attention given to it. Abu al Fawz's book, on the other hand, was published by the then smallish publishing house Like, which did not market the book as a literary event. It was also published in 2000, at which time so-called migrant literature was not discussed in Finland. However, the field was already anticipating the emergence of such literature when *Auringon asema* was published. The literary critic Putte Wilhelmsson (2003, 56) commented almost cynically that the reception of *Auringon asema* constituted infatuation with exoticity and pointed out that the institution had been waiting for new literary voices. 'I correctly assumed that ElRamly would not have what it takes to become Finland's Zadie Smith, even if such a thing seems to be in great demand among Finnish critics and women's magazine editors concerned with their internationality.'

## Literature or Ethnography?

After living in Finland for over twenty years, learning the Finnish language and obtaining Finnish nationality, Umayya Abu-Hanna (b. 1961) published her autobiographical debut novel *Nurinkurin* in Finnish in 2003. The novel describes the history and political position of Palestinians in 1960s and 1970s Israel, where the protagonist, Umayya, grows up as a Palestinian, a Christian and an Arab among political unrest and violence in Haifa. The story is narrated by the first person narrator, Umayya, who is born at the beginning of the novel and has become an adult by the end. She tells the story of her family, of her people, and of Palestinians in general. The endless balancing between peace and war on the part of Jewish people and Arabs leads young Umayya to ponder her identity and sense of belonging to different national, cultural and religious groups[13] (Nissilä 2007; Kervinen 2011; Nissilä & Rantonen 2013).

*Nurinkurin* was published as an autobiography or memoir at a time when different forms of personal texts and auto-fiction had become popular in Finland (Rojola 2002; Koivisto 2011). The back cover characterized the novel as an autobiography of Abu-Hanna by describing it as a story of 'growing

---

12 Yousif Abu al Fawz wrote the short story collection in Arabic while in Finland. The book was published in Cyprus in 1998 and translated into Finnish in 2000 as *Taikalintu* [The Magic Bird]. In critical discussion it was regarded as migrant literature and the first work of Arabic literature written in Finland (Ahtola 2004, 22).

13 The novel *Sinut* (2007, [You]) continues these autobiographical elements, describing the years from the 1990s until the early 21st century, when Umayya settled in Finland. The feeling of otherness and the will to find one's own place are themes in the novel, which describes with self-irony the process of adapting to Finnish society and culture, but also the everyday racism Umayya faces.

up in the North of Israel in the middle of confrontations and conflicts'. In many reviews and critiques, *Nurinkurin* was reviewed as a literary novel that 'resembles a novel more than a typical biography' (Parvikko 2003). Also the literary devices of the novel were highlighted and it was stated that experience is filtered through many different viewpoints. What is more, it was maintained that the narrative voice gushes with 'the buzz of many languages' and that the presence of the narrator is so unconditional that, in its personal nature, the memoir reaches the universal (Riekko 2004, 71). Correspondingly, in the criteria of the Finland Prize,[14] granted by the Ministry of Education and Culture in 2003, the autobiographical character of *Nurinkurin* was understood as 'a very personal way' to consider what it is like when one has to fall silent about one's own identity in a majority culture. The language, which Abu-Hanna had learned so well that she 'had written a linguistically impressive and rich novel' (The Finland Prize citations 2003), was considered to be a literary merit.

It is possible to see *Nurinkurin* as moving across and between two genres; on the one hand, it is an autobiography, on the other, a novel. Despite the fact that critical response highlighted the literary aspects of the novel, *Nurinkurin* never ended up in the fiction section of libraries. It was classified as 'Biographies/memoirs', which is considered 'Non-fiction'. It was not nominated for literary prizes or celebrated as 'a migrant novel' written in Finnish, like *Auringon asema* or the debut novel *27 eli kuolema tekee taiteilijan* of Alexandra Salmela years later.[15] Interestingly, this happened even though Salmela refused to categorize herself as an immigrant and without the novel dealing with common themes in migrant literature, and despite the fact that both novels, Abu-Hanna's *Nurinkurin* and Salmela's *27 eli kuolema tekee taiteilijan*, were written in the Finnish language by persons who had migrated to Finland. After publishing *Nurinkurin*, Abu-Hanna received several non-literary awards, which paid attention to her role as a social actor and as a writer. In the awarding criteria of the Finland Prize, it was stated that 'Abu-Hanna has showed perseverance by migrating to a totally different culture compared to her native one. She has learned the language, which does not resemble any other language in the world, and has done it so well that she has written a very linguistically meritorious novel. Umayya Abu-Hanna has adopted the Finnish language so well that she even dreams in Finnish now'.

Why have the literary merits of *Nurinkurin* been over-shadowed by migration and biography? Why have works such as Pirkko Saisio's novel trilogy, for instance, been received as literary fiction and can be found under

14 The Finland Prize (note the difference to The Finlandia Literary Prize) is 'awarded in recognition of a significant career in the arts, an exceptional artistic achievement, or a promising breakthrough' (http://www.minedu.fi/OPM/Avustukset/palkinnot/?lang=en).
15 *Nurinkurin* was expected to be nominated for the Finlandia Literary Prize for Non-Fiction, which is considered Finland's most significant non-fiction prize, but it never was (Petäjä 2004).

the class 'Fiction' in libraries?[16] A cultural product is said (Lindholm 2002, 53, 56–57) to face two separate 'gatekeeper systems': a first level that accepts a product for the market (publishers and literary marketing), and a second that values and reviews it (the institution of critique and awards). Both of these levels have the power to connect meanings to literary work, which, consequently, affect its value. The criteria of literary value are connected to contexts, in which meanings are connected to works, and in turn, the meanings of texts are also connected to text-external relations. Defining a genre is one of the central functions in literary reviews, because genre frames the reader's interpretation of a text. Genre is not regarded as a fixed form, but rather it is in a constant process of negotiation and change. In different frameworks, the same text can be interpreted and genre can be defined in many ways (Lyytikäinen 2005, 10). In the context of transnational, migrant and diasporic writers, autobiographical texts can be about memories of a subject and a people, about history, about the inconstant line between fiction and non-fiction. Seyhan (2001, 20) remarks that linguistic and cultural transpositions raise new kinds of questions, such as, '[w]hat happens to the memory of a nation outside (without) the nation'.

Migrant authors are often perceived as informants who represent a group of people with an anthropological view, transmitting knowledge from their culture and producing representations of the life of the group. The art produced by migrant authors is often connected to supposed traditions of the author's culture, and, in art projects, im/migrant people are supposed to carry the traditions and views of their groups (Huttunen 2013, 256). Ranya ElRamly (2002b), who was tired of the image of her that was represented in the media, eloquently asks: 'What cultural ambassador am I supposed to be just because my mother happened to fall in love with an Egyptian man?' Similarly, Abu-Hanna has also criticized the assumption that a writer is a representative of a group. She has commented on how ponderous it is to be only a mirror and how it takes one's individuality away. She explains that she has been 'Finland's official foreigner clown', has ended up representing 'refugees, migrants, negroes' (Grundström 2000, 24) and that she has been 'pissed off' when speaking about identities (Vänttinen 2004, 15). Her public role has been strongly societal and political, which was noted by the citation for the Kalevala Women's Association's Larin Paraske Prize: 'Abu-Hanna is known for her versatile way of using words and for an active role as societal conversationalist. […] The experience of an individual, and more generally, themes that concern all people, are compounded in very liberating ways in her texts' (Nuolijärvi 2008, 34). (cf. Nissilä 2007; Nissilä 2009.)

16 Even though the main character was named Pirkko Saisio in the novels *Pienin yhteinen jaettava* ([The Smallest Shared Dividend], 1998), *Vastavalo* ([Against the Light], 2000), and *Punainen erokirja* ([The Red Book of Separation], 2003), and many of the events were from Saisio's real life, the author wanted the trilogy to be read as fiction and a novel, not a memoir (Koivisto 2011, 14).

## Beyond Finnishness

> 'The Finlandia Literary Prize may be granted in recognition of the best novel written by a Finnish citizen by the Finnish Book Foundation.'
> A FINNISH CITIZEN, YOU SAY. FUCK YOU TOO!
> (Schatz 2006.)

This symptomatic text can be read on the back cover of the novel *Rakasta minut* [Love me], written in Finnish by the German citizen Roman Schatz, who has lived in Finland since 1986. At the time, no attention was paid to these sentences; perhaps the deeper meaning of it was not even thought of before November 2010. That is when the Slovakian citizen Alexandra Salmela's (b. 1980) debut novel, *27 eli kuolema tekee taiteilijan*, was nominated for the Finlandia Literary Prize, which according to the rules could only be awarded to a Finnish citizen. In the case of Salmela, the problem was not one of language, but of passport: she was not a Finnish citizen. The nomination created wide debate about the rules of the biggest and most prestigious literary institution in Finland, and therefore about the very conception of Finnish literature. The rules were described as 'embarrassing', and Finnishness was stressed 'as a matter of choice and a relative issue' (Majander 2010). Arts journalists and critics hoped that the Finnish Book Foundation would consider the rules and update them. It was opined that henceforth Finnishness in literature could be related to the fact the writer lives in Finland and writes in Finnish rather than to nationality. Salmela herself was surprised by the importance of nationality, she emphasized 'While living in Finland, I have written a novel for a Finnish publisher' (Mäkinen 2010).

And it happened; the rules were changed so that writers who are not Finnish citizens can also be nominated. The institution showed its flexibility by reacting very quickly, and so the canon reacted reflectively and quickly, as well. Still, the change of rules created confusion in some people's minds, for example on internet sites where some people asked what a Finnish novel really is if nationality or language no longer define Finnish literature (Löytty 2013, 261). Eventually, *27 eli kuolema tekee taiteilijan* ended up challenging and changing the national canon, the process of including literature in the canon and the concept of nationally based literature in two countries. The novel was translated into Slovak (co-translated by Salmela herself), and was a nominee for the biggest Slovakian literary prize, Anasoft Litera, in 2012. Once again, the rules were changed after her nomination; until that moment, only books by Slovakian citizens written in Slovakian could be nominated for the prize. After the change of rules, works by Slovakian citizens that were written in languages other than Slovakian and later translated into Slovakian could also participate in the competition. Like Zinaida Lindén's work, *27 eli kuolema tekee taiteilijan* showed how transnational literature moves across national and linguistic borders and can belong to several literary cultures and national canons at the same time.

*27 eli kuolema tekee taiteilijan* received much positive attention in Finland.[17] The novel was extolled as the 'the long-awaited migrant novel' (Kylänpää 2010, 46). Salmela was celebrated as the 'real' migrant writer, even though she fits no immigrant stereotypes, and even though the themes of the novel did not concern so called 'migrant themes'[18]. An interesting and open question is why it was Salmela who deserved to be the 'real migrant author'. Why were other writers, for example Lindén, Abu-Hanna, the Russian Karelian Arvi Perttu[19] or Yousif Abu al Fawz, not celebrated as such? Is there an idealistic image of an im/migrant author with supposed characteristics of background, as well as those of the theme, style and language of his/her novel? In the case of Salmela and the reception of *27 eli kuolema tekee taiteilijan*, it was rather the background of Salmela and multilingualism that made migrant literature rather than the subject or themes of the novel. The novel is a humorous and satirical story of an artist's development; it has multiple first person narrators, including a pig and a cat, among others. Forced artistic expression and the search for the self are the main themes, and migration from Slovakia to Finland is something that happens only on the level of the plot.

The celebratory reception of the novel was no doubt influenced by the novelty of the structure and the form of the novel. The language was described as 'incredibly skilled' (Moisio 2011, 37) and an 'astonishing performance' (Ropponen 2010, 64). The shine of the language was not dimmed, even though several interviews mentioned how much work the editor did together with Salmela to refine the text. Lindén, Abu-Hanna and Salmela are contemporary examples of, on the one hand, how language, nationality and literature do not self-evidently belong together, and on the other hand, how the romantic assumption of literature written in the 'mother-tongue' does not define literature any longer. Yasemin Yildiz (2012) argues that the modern notion of 'mother-tongue' is a linguistic family romance, constituting a narrative about origin and identity. In this conception, constituted by the mid-nineteenth century, an author might become the origin of creative works only within a native language, and the possibility of writing in non-native languages or in multiple languages at the same time became disallowed.

Like ElRamly and Abu-Hanna, now Salmela also resisted the categorizing reception and partially tendentious definition of her as immigrant. This 'talking back' can be seen as one strategy of resistance. 'Talking back' is subtle negotiation that questions settled categorizations and activates possibilities for alternative identities. Kirsi Juhila (2004, 29) formulates it as 'acts, which oppose or resist and comment upon stigmatized identity, and whose intentions are to represent the difference of this identity in

---

17 *27 eli kuolema tekee taiteilijan* won the Helsingin Sanomat Literature Prize for debut novelists 2010, and was a nominee for the Kaihari Cultural Prize 2010, the Finlandia Literary Prize 2010 and the Anasoft Litera 2012.
18 E.g. the themes of migration and exile, biculturalism and bilingualism, and acculturation and identity formation (ao. Kongslien 2006).
19 In Russia, Perttu had to consider whether to write in Carelian for few people, or in Russian to reach a wider readership. Perttu moved to Finland and chose to write in Finnish.

relation to a prevailing way of categorizing'. On several occasions, Salmela pointed out how questionable it was to gain publicity more because of her immigrant background than her literary merits. The labelling ended up being paradoxical. In the same context, Salmela was known to be opposed to labelling and categorizing, but still she was repeatedly defined as a migrant writer or at least connected to migration. 'Incredibly accomplished playing with the Finnish language, the novel has been extolled as an awaited migrant novel, even though the writer does not identify herself as a migrant, nor do the themes of the novel deal with migration (Moisio 2011, 37)'. Compared to the receptions of ElRamly and Abu-Hanna at the beginning of the decade, it seems like both Abu-Hanna and ElRamly have been given quite narrow and ungraceful public roles, inflected with exoticism, from the perspective of which they were expected to mirror and comment upon Finnishness. Now, in the case of Salmela, she seems to have more space to define herself as neither an immigrant nor immigrant writer, and to be able to concentrate on the matter of writing.

The novel was not published by chance. The impulse to write came when Salmela heard of a literary competition, 'What on earth is a New Finn?' ('Mikä ihmeen uussuomalainen?'), intended for 'New Finns', people with im/migrant backgrounds or who were influenced by or living between different cultures. According to Olli Löytty (2013, 272–275), it was the intention of the organizers to find gifted writers with im/migrant backgrounds. But, contrary to the competition 'New Voices', arranged in Denmark in 2004,[20] they did not want to force texts to have the perspective of an outsider or the other. In all, 108 texts were sent to the competition, from which 13 were selected for the anthology *Mikä ihmeen uussuomalainen?* (What on Earth Is a New Finn?, 2009). Salmela's short story, named 'The real, true migrant blues' ('Se oikea, aito maahanmuuttajablues'), was ranked second in the competition. After this, she proposed to a publisher that she would write a longer text (Pere-Antikainen 2011, 5).

In connection to the writing competition, the concept of the 'New Finn' was now launched for popular use. Before that, the concepts of 'migrant' and 'multicultural' were primarily used in public media to describe literature written by people with im/migrant backgrounds. The 'New Finn' was introduced in several articles and described as a permissive and inclusive term (ao. Ylitalo 2009, 18). Some criticized the concept for its factitiousness and noted that it would end up emphasizing the difference between 'real' or 'old' Finns and 'new' Finns. The literary institution now seems to be conscious about the challenges of defining literature and categorizing writers and their identities with different backgrounds as a single group. Concepts and definitions were in transition at the time when *27 eli kuolema tekee taiteilijan* was received, and there were more alternatives when speaking about writers with im/migrant backgrounds. However, despite the sensitiveness with which the author's own self-definition was listened to (in contrast with

---

20 The literary competition *New Voices* was initiated by the publishing house Gyldendal and the newspaper *Berlingske Tidende* in Denmark in 2006 as an attempt to 'kick-start' a new literature of migration (Schramm 2010, 132, 137).

ElRamly's case), there still was a need and a will to categorize authors and literatures as a single group, such as 'migrant literature' or 'new finn literature' separated from the mainstream of Finnish literature. This all reflects the ongoing change in Finnish society and literary culture – transnationalizing Finnish literature – in which the change in the rules of the Finlandia Literary Prize was just one step (Löytty 2013, 262). During the 14 years, in which the works of Abu-Hanna, ElRamly, Lindén and Salmela have been published, the societal context has changed a great deal in Finland with reference to awareness; each year delivering a growing amount of critical discussion and debates about migration, greater attempts were moreover made to hear the experience and voice of the migrant. When *27 eli kuolema tekee taiteilijan* was published, the literary institution can be seen to be more conscious of the subjects of migration, otherization or exoticization. It received the novel more thoughtfully than at the beginning of decade when *Auringon asema* was published.

## The End: Intertwining Intersectional Dimensions

In the beginning of this article, I asked whether it is somehow significant that women with im/migrant backgrounds have such a central role in the process of transnationalizing Finnish literature. Now at the end, I want to argue that one cannot ignore the fact that it was women who made an impact on the Finnish literary field, even transforming it, during the last decade when speaking of transnationalizing the literary field.

As already mentioned, literature and gender have played a significant role in building and defining Finnish national identity in Finland since the beginning of the 19th century, especially during the late 19th and early 20th century, when Finnishness was under conscious construction and Finnish literature was born (e.g. Valenius 2004, Kivimäki 2012). As feminist scholars have indicated, gender is an important factor when constituting nationality. The borders and boundaries of nations, as well as the ideas of the 'foreign' and the 'familiar' in the past, the present and the future are outlined by gender. Women are said to have an ambivalent position within the collectivity. They are often constructed as the cultural symbols of collectivity, unity and its boundaries, as carriers of honour and the reason for specific national and ethnic projects. But they also have often been excluded from the collective 'we' (Yuval-Davis 1997, 47, 67; Gordon et. al. 2002, 14). A woman's nationality has been more loosely connected to her than a man's nationality to him. In the past, a woman would lose her own nationality and take on the nationality of her husband when marrying a foreign national (Leppänen 2009, 241). The body of a woman is represented and read as a national icon or figure, and different negotiations of the national and nationality have been taking place through women and women's bodies (e.g. Yuval-Davis 1997, Valenius 2004). In light of this, it would be tempting to see these women's texts as metaphors for bodies and as symbolic places, where concepts and definitions of the national and of Finnish literature are negotiated through these four women's different historical, ethnic and cultural relationships to the Finnish nation and nationality.

But these four women and the receptions of their novels end up challenging easy interpretations by adducing complex intertwinings when considering the borderlines of gender, ethnicity, as well as of national and linguistic identity in literary institutions. The national writer has been assumed to be a male writer in Finland, and literature written by women writers has been valuated against literature by male writers; attributes such as inadequate, unfinished or therapeutic have been used to define literature written by women. Men have been actors in relation to literature; they have been 'bringing' or 'giving' something into it (Kivimäki 2012, 57). It would be easy to suppose 'migrant women' to be doubly marginalized as 'ethnic women', neither Finnish nor male. But when observing the reception of their work – the awards, nominations, critiques, sales figures – and comparing them to those of male writers with im/migrant backgrounds, one can see different situations on certain levels.

At the turn of the 20th century, there were many interesting male writers with migrant or transnational backgrounds – such as, for example, Yousif Abu al Fawz[21], Hassam Blasim[22], Alexis Kouros[23], Arvi Perttu[24] and Roman Schatz[25]. They have published novels and short stories, and some of them have even become public personalities, but only Kouros has been recognized by the Finnish literary institution, when the novel *Gondwanan lapset* won the Finlandia Junior Prize, awarded by the Finnish Book Foundation, in 1997. As the example of these women writers shows, on the one hand, the literary institution has made their works more visible with critiques and awards, and on the other, both the works and the authors have gained publicity in media with reviews and interviews. This attention has had a positive impact on the book sales and the visibility of the authors – three of these four debut novels

---

21 Beside the novel *Taikalintu*, while in Finland, Abu al Fawz has also written two novels situated in Helsinki, both of which were published in Iraqi Kurdistan.
22 The Arabic Hassam Blasim lives and writes in Finland and has published his short story collections *The Madman of the Freedom Square* (2009) translated into English in England. It was nominated for The Independent Foreign Fiction Prize 2010 by the British national morning newspaper *Independent*.
23 Finnish-Iranian Alexis Kouros has published the novel *Gondwanan lapset* ([Gondwana's children], 1997), which was the winner of the Finlandia Junior Literary Prize at the same year.
24 Perttu has published the following novels *Skumbria* (Skumbria, 2011), *Kertomuksia Lesosen elämästä ja kuolemasta* ([Stories about the life and the death of Lesonen], 2008), *Papaninin retkikunta* ([The expedition of Papanini], 2006), *Petroskoin symposiumi* ([The symposium of Petroskoi], 2001), and a short story collection *Nuotio hirvenkivellä* ([A campfire on an elk's stone], 1989).
25 Roman Schatz has published novels *Rakasta minut* ([Love me], 2006), *€* ([Euro], 2007), *Telewischn* (2009, novel in German), *Parturi* ([The Barber], 2010) and works like *From Finland With Love / Suomesta, rakkaudella* (2005, satirical texts or causeries), *Osta vokaali. Runoja A:sta Ö:hön* ([Buy a Vowel], 2008, poems) and *Saksalainen rakastaja*, ([A German lover], 2011, collection of newspaper and magazine columns).

have reached the level of 'bestseller', which is considered to be 10 000 copies in Finland (Hypén 2012, 10; Niemi 1997, 13).[26]

Sanna Kivimäki, who has observed connections between nationality and literature in author interviews in magazines[27], has made an interesting note concerning literature, gender, national identity and Finnishness in her study of author interviews. Male authors have discussed Finland, Finnishness, Finnish culture and the future, whereas women have concentrated on 'a women's world' – family, history and the past. Even though magazine journals have highlighted female authorship, nationality and Finnishness have not been subjects. Kivimäki notes that women have not been national actors, and neither have they threatened Finnishness. In contrast to this, in author interviews, Abu-Hanna, ElRamly, Lindén and Salmela have been recurrently invited to discuss and even define national identity, Finnishness, matters of language, cultural differences and cultural identity. Even so, and especially in the case of ElRamly, this role has been limited and confined. An interesting point from the perspective of my article has been made by mentioning traditions of minor literature, for instance Finland-Swedish literature, as examples in which women authors are given some national attachments, and are connected to such cultural contexts as Finland-Swedish (Kivimäki 2012, 72–73; Kivimäki 2002, 15). Even though she does not elaborate on this, it gives support to my observations concerning women with migrant backgrounds and their discussions of nation and nationality in literary contexts, discussions that have even ended up redefining those concepts.

As more critiques have been written and attention paid, it follows that other parts of the literary institution, for instance at the research level, have become interested in these writers and their texts. This is all a part of the process of including the works into the canon, and at the same time, it can also be seen as part of literary publicity and mediatization. In recent years, attention has been paid to the growth of literary publicity and markets (e.g. Lehtonen 2001, Hypén 2002). The mediatization of literature is represented as 'second-level mediatization', which means that the image of the author is not primarily produced through his or her works, but by the media. From this perspective, a literary work is a product, and the writer is a brand. Second level mediatization means that besides literary works and critiques published about them, the writers are also known through columns, interviews, and by being an advertising face or appearing in an entertainment television programme, for instance. Besides literary publicity, all these four women have also taken part in social and cultural conversations by writing columns and essays and giving talks. Having an im/migrant background, being

---

26 Abu-Hanna's *Nurinkurin* has sold 5 000–7 000 copies. ElRamly's *Auringon asema* has sold 33 000 copies in total (hardcover edition 10 000 copies + the paperback edition 21 000 copies + the audiobook 2 000 copies). Lindén's *I väntan på en jordbävning* has sold 11 000 copies and the Finnish edition (*Ennen maanjäristystä*) 2 000 copies. Salmela's *27 eli kuolema tekee taiteilijan* has sold 21 000 copies until the fall 2012. (The sales numbers are delivered by representatives of publishers.)
27 The certain widely circulated magazines published in 1973, 1983 and 1993.

multilingual or in some way 'exotic' and 'different', compared with the majority, catches the attention and is seized upon by the media. It is also possible to see the so-called 'migrant factor' (as one publisher's representative expressed it) as an 'exotic' or 'ethnically characteristic' feature, which may increase the literary publicity and thus media attention paid to the author and the book, and therefore its sales and numbers of published copies. It must also be asked whether women, especially young women, as writers are seen as more interesting by media.

Transnationalism has focused our attention on forms of cultural production that take place in the liminal spaces between real and imagined borders (e.g. Jay 2010). In the context of literary culture and production, borders are not only national, cultural or linguistic, but also religious, class or gender-related, or related to literary production, for instance the genre-defining or culture-based aesthetic values of including works in a literary canon. The complex intersections of various social and cultural categories and different axes of identity interact on many levels also in cultural and literary production. Jay (2010, 19) reminds us of how '[l]iterature, race, gender, and sexuality are defined and regulated by discursive regimes based on difference that operate ideologically and through institutions to both enable and restrict certain forms of agency'. Migrant writers have a more complex relationship to book markets and literary institutions than majority writers have. Rosendahl Thomsen (2010/2008, 62) points out that, taken as a group, there are many distinct differences in their relations with both national and world markets. However, as individuals, they almost always face an awkward relationship with markets, and with national canons and preferences. But even though they have had many borders to cross as non-native, bi-cultural or multilingual women writers, it is possible to say that all these women – Abu-Hanna, ElRamly, Lindén and Salmela – have had a visible, public role with different kinds of agency to act in cultural and social fields.

The role of cross-border and transnational literatures is central in questioning the paradigm of nationalism and monolingualism in the context of literary culture. These four transnational women writers challenge literature committed to the national paradigm, and show how Finnish literature is multilingual, multi-placed and transnational on many levels. Contemporary transnational texts are, as Paul Jay (2010, 8–9; see also Gebauer & Schwarz Lausten 2010) has said, 'transforming the scope of the national literatures to which they belong *and* pushing beyond boundaries to imagine the global character of modern experience, contemporary culture, and the identities they produce.'

# References

Abu-Hanna 1999: Ulkomaalaisena Suomessa. http://www.finnica.fi/seminaari/99/luennot/hanna.htm Quoted in 20.6.2016.
Abu-Hanna, Umayya 2000: Entinen etninen? *Naistutkimus–Kvinnoforskning* 4. 48–50.
Ahtola, Aleksi 2004: Kirjailija Kalevalan ja Gilgamesin välissä. *Hiidenkivi* 4. 22–23.
Amelina & Faist 2012: De-naturalizing the national in research methodologies: Key concepts of transnational studies in migration. *Ethnic and Racial Studies* 35 (10, Special Issue). 1707–1724.
Amelina A, Nergiz DD, Faist T, Glick-Schiller N (eds.) 2012: *Beyond Methodological Nationalism: Research Methodologies for Cross-Border Studies*. London: Routledge.
Anderson, Benedict 1996: *Imagined Communities: Reflections on the Origin and Spread of Nationalism*. London & New York: Verso.
Appadurai, Arjun 1996: *Modernity at Large. Cultural Dimensions of Globalization*. Public Worlds Volume 1. Minneapolis: University of Minnesota Press.
Autio, Milla 2001: Venäläisiä tositarinoita Suomen Turusta. *Helsingin Sanomat* 19.5.2001.
Ekman, Michel (ed.) 2014: *Finlands svenska litteratur 1900–2012*. Svenska litteratursällskapet i Finland, Helsingfors. Stockholm: Atlantis.
ElRamly, Ranya 2002a: *Auringon asema*. Helsinki: Otava.
ElRamly, Ranya 2002b: Egyptiläisen isän tyttärenä. *Helsingin Ylioppilaslehti* 16/2002. The text can be found at http://ylioppilaslehti.fi/2002/11/ranya-elramly-egyptilaisen-isan-tyttarena/ Quoted in 20.6.2016.
Frank, Sören 2010: Four Thesis on Migration and Literature. *Migration and Literature in Contemporary Europe*. Ed. by Mirjam Gebauer & Pia Schwarz Lausten. München: Martin Meidenbauer Verlagsbuchhandlung. 39–57.
Gebauer, Mirjam & Schwarz Lausten, Pia (eds.) 2010: *Migration and Literature in Contemporary Europe*. München: Martin Meidenbauer Verlagsbuchhandlung.
Gordon, Tuula; Komulainen, Katri & Lempiäinen, Kirsti 2002: Kansallisuuden tekeminen ja toisto. *Suomineitonen hei! Kansallisuuden sukupuoli*. Ed. by Tuula Gordon, Katri Komulainen & Kirsti Lempiäinen Tampere: Vastapaino. 10–16.
Grundström, Elina 2000: TV-kiusattu. *Markinointi&Mainonta* 4.
Gröndahl, Satu 2005: Kven, Tornedal and Sweden-Finnish Literature at the Turn of a New Millennium. *Nordic Voices. Literature from the Nordic Countries*. Ed. by Jenny Fossum Grönn. Oslo: Nordbok. 78–91.
Gröndahl, Satu 2009: Multicultural or Multilingual Literature. A Swedish Dilemma? *Literature For Europe*? Ed. by Theo D'haen & Iannis Goerlandt. Amsterdam: Textxet, Studies in Comparative Literature 61. 173–195.
Gröndahl, Satu 2010: Erilaisuuden kokemuksesta moniarvoisuuteen – romanien ja matkaajien kirjallisuus Pohjoismaissa. *Vähemmistöt ja monikulttuurisuus kirjallisuudessa*. Ed. by Eila Rantonen. Tampere: Tampere University Press. 106–131.
Gröndahl, Satu & Rantonen, Eila 2013: Romanikirjallisuus perinteiden ja modernin jatkumolla. *Suomen nykykirjallisuus 2: Kirjallinen elämä ja yhteiskunta*. Ed. by Mika Hallila et al. Helsinki: SKS. 72–75.
Grönstrand, Heidi 2009: Monikielinen kirjailija – harvinainen kirjailija? Tapaus Kersti Bergroth. *Kulttuurintutkimus* 2–3. 19–30.
Grönstrand, Heidi (2014): Self-Translating: linking languages, literary traditions and cultural spheres. Leena Kaunonen (ed.) *Cosmopolitanism and Transnationalism: Visions, Ethics and Practices*. COLLeGIUM. Studies across Disciplines in the Humanities and Social Sciences vol. 15. Helsinki: Helsinki Collegium for Advanced Studies. 116–137.
Grönstrand, Heidi 2016: Kirjallisuushistoria, kansakunta ja kieli: monikielisyys metodologisen nationalismin haasteena. *Kansallisen katveesta – Suomen kirjallisuuden*

*ylirajaisuudesta.* Ed. by Heidi Grönstrand et al. Helsinki: SKS. 38–59.

Grönstrand, Heidi; Kauranen, Ralf; Löytty, Olli; Melkas, Kukku; Nissilä, Hanna-Leena & Pollari, Mikko 2012: Irti kansallisesta kehyksestä. *Kulttuurintutkimus* 3. 64–66.

Grönstrand, Heidi & Malmio, Kristiina (eds.) 2011: *Både och, sekä että. Om flerspråkighet / Monikielisyydestä.* Helsinki: Schildts Kustannus Oy.

Hakalahti, Niina 2002: Kaleidoskooppisilmät. The text can be found at www.kiiltomato.net. Quoted in 9.11.2007.

Heith, Anne 2009: Nils Holgersson Never Saw Us: A Tornedalian Literary History. *Cold Matters Cultural Perceptions of Snow, Ice and Cold.* Ed. by Heidi Hansson & Cathrine Norberg. Northern Studies, Monographs No. 1. Umeå: Umeå University and the Royal Skyttean Society. 209–221.

Hirvonen, Vuokko 1999: *Saamenmaan ääniä. Saamelaisen naisen tie kirjailijaksi.* Helsinki: SKS.

Huttunen, Laura 2013: Improvisointi, kitka ja kulttuurin käsitteellistäminen. *Liikkuva maailma.* Ed. by Mikko Lehtonen. Tampere: Vastapaino. 245–260.

Hypén, Tarja-Liisa 2002: Kirjailija mediatuotteena. *Kurittomat kuvitelmat. Johdatus 1990-luvun kotimaiseen kirjallisuuteen.* Ed. by Markku Soikkeli. Turku: Turun yliopisto, Taiteiden tutkimuksen laitos. 29–45.

Hypén, Tarja-Liisa 2012: Julkkiskirjailijan ja bestselleristin brändi: Jari Tervon tapaus. *Avain*: 2. 5–18.

Hämäläinen, Timo 2005: Zinaida Lindén palkittiin kahdesti Runebergin päivänä. *Helsingin Sanomat.* 6.2.2005.

Jama, Olavi 1995: Haaparannan lukiosta Sipirjaan. Tornionlaakson kirjallisuus kahden kansalliskirjallisuuden marginaalissa. *Marginalia ja kirjallisuus. Ääniä suomalaisen kirjallisuuden reunoilta.* Ed. by Matti Savolainen. Helsinki: SKS. 93–144.

Jay, Paul 2010: *Global Matters: The Transnational Turn in Literary Studies.* New York: Cornell University Press.

Juhila, Kirsi 2004: Leimattu identiteetti ja vastapuhe. *Puhua vastaan ja vaieta. Neuvottelu kulttuurisista marginaaleista.* Ed. by Arja Jokinen, Laura huttunen & Anna Kulmala. Helsinki: Gaudeamus. 20–32.

Juntti, Eira 1998: Pohjolan naisten viemiset Eurooppaan. Suomalaisten naistenlehtien EU-keskustelu. *Kansallisvaltion kielioppi.* Ed. by Marja Keränen. SoPhi 28. Jyväskylä: Jyväskylän yliopisto. 64–89.

Kervinen, Anni 2011: *Sinuiksi itsensä kanssa. Toiseus Umayya Abu-Hannan teoksissa Nurinkurin ja Sinut. A Pro Gradu -study in Finnish Literature.* Tampere: Tampereen yliopisto.

Kivimäki, Sanna 2012: *Kuinka tämän tuntisi omaksi maakseen. Suomalaisuuden kulttuurisia järjestyksiä.* Viestinnän, median ja teatterin yksikkö. Tampere: Tampereen yliopisto.

Kivimäki, Sanna 2002: Kirjoittamisen kokemus. Suomalaisten naiskirjailijoiden haastattelut aikakauslehdissä. *Tiedotustutkimus* 2. 25:2, 4–20.

Klapuri, Tintti 2012: Zinaida Lindén – venäläinen emigranttikirjailija. *Både och, sekä että. Om flerspråkighet / Monikielisyydestä.* Ed. by Heidi Grönstrand & Kristiina Malmio. Helsinki: Schildts Kustannus Oy. 270–291.

Klapuri, Tintti 2011: Matkalla ei-kenenkään-maassa: Zinaida Lindén. *Kenen aika? Esseitä venäläisestä nykykirjallisuudesta.* Ed. by Tomi Huttunen & Tintti Klapuri. Helsinki: Avain. 401–410.

Koivisto, Päivi 2011: *Elämästä autofiktioksi. Lajitradition jäljillä Pirkko Saision romaanisarjassa* Pienin yhteinen jaettava, Vastavalo *ja* Punainen erokirja. Helsinki: Suomen kielen, suomalais-ugrilaisten ja pohjoismaisten kielten ja kirjallisuuksien laitos. Humanistinen tiedekunta.

Kongslien, Ingeborg 2006: Migrant or multicultural literature in the Nordic countries. *Eurozine.* http://www.eurozine.com/articles/2006-08-03-kongslien-en.html Quoted in 20.6.2016.

Kurki, Tuulikki 2013: From Soviet Locality to Multivoiced Borderland: Literature and Identity in the Finnish-Russian National Borderlands. *Region. Regional Studies of Russia, Eastern Europe and Central Asia.* 1. 95–112.
Kurkijärvi, Riitta 2002: Rakkaus loisti kuin majakka ja näytti tien kotiin. *Aamulehti* 1.8.2002.
Kylänpää, Riitta 2010: Vieraassa kielessä. *Suomen kuvalehti* 46. 46–51.
Lehtimäki, Riitta 2004: Kotona kolmella kielellä. *Anna* no 6. 92–95.
Lehtola, Veli-Pekka 1995: Saamelainen kirjallisuus rajoilla. *Marginalia ja kirjallisuus. Ääniä suomalaisen kirjallisuuden reunoilta.* Ed. by Matti Savolainen. Helsinki: SKS. 36–92.
Lehtola, Veli-Pekka 2013: Saamelaiskirjallisuus kriisissä? *Suomen nykykirjallisuus 1: Lajeja, poetiikkaa.* Ed. by Mika Hallila et al. Helsinki: SKS. 220–227.
Lehtonen, Mikko 2001: *Post scriptum. Kirja medioitumisen aikakaudella.* Tampere: Vastapaino.
Lehtonen, Mikko, Löytty, Olli & Ruuska, Petri 2004: *Suomi toisin sanoen.* Tampere: Vastapaino.
Leppänen, Katarina 2009: The Conflicting Interests of Women's Organizations and the League of Nations on the Question of married Women's Nationality in the 1930s. *NORA–Nordic Journal of Feminist and Gender research*, Vol. 17, No. 4. 240–255.
Lindholm, Arto 2002: Katsaus 1990-luvun suomalaisiin kirjallisuuspalkintoihin. Markku Soikkeli (ed.) *Kurittomat kuvitelmat. Johdatus 1990-luvun kotimaiseen kirjallisuuteen.* Taiteiden tutkimuksen laitos, sarja A n:o 50. Turku: Turun yliopisto. 47–68.
Lyytikäinen, Pirjo 2005: Lajit ja kansallinen kirjoittaminen. Ed. by Pirjo Lyytikäinen, Jyrki Nummi & Päivi Koivisto. *Lajit yli rajojen.* Helsinki: SKS. 24–65.
Löytty, Olli 2013: Kun rajat eivät pidä, eli mihin maahanmuuttajakirjallisuutta tarvitaan. *Liikkuva maailma.* Ed. by Mikko Lehtonen. Tampere: Vastapaino. 261–279.
Löytty, Olli 2015: 'Immigrant Literature in Finland. Uses of Literary Category'. *Rethinking National Literatures and the Literary Canon in Scandinavia.* Ed. by Ann-Sofie Lönngren, Heidi Grönstrand, Dag Heedo and Anne Heith. New Castle Upon Tyne: Cambridge Scholars Publishing. 52–77.
Majander, Antti 2010: Nolo sääntö ja nuorennusleikkaus. *Helsingin Sanomat* 12.11.2010.
Maliniemi Lindbach, Kaisa 2002: 'Drømmen om Ruija – havlandet.' Kvenlitteratur i Nord-Norge. Satu Gröndahl (ed.) *Litteraturen i gränsland.* Uppsala: Uppsala Universitet. Institut för Multietnisk forskning. 117–138.
McCall, Leslie 2005: The complexity of intersectionality. *Signs: Journal of Women in Culture and Society.* Vol. 30, no. 3. 1771–1800.
Mikkonen, Kai 2001: Muukalaisten kielellä: Maahanmuuttajien kirjallisuus ja monikulttuurisuuden merkitys. *Kanava* 8/2001. 553–559.
Moisio, Mikki 2011: Sattuma teki kirjailijan. *Anna* 6/2011. 34–37.
Mäkinen, Esa 2010: Kirjasäätiö moittii Teosta. *Helsingin Sanomat* 12.11.2010.
Nissilä, Hanna-Leena & Rantonen, Eila (2013): Kansainvälistyvä kirjailijakunta. *Suomen nykykirjallisuus 2: Kirjallinen elämä ja yhteiskunta.* Ed. by Mika Hallila et al. Helsinki: SKS. 55–71.
Nissilä, Hanna-Leena 2009: Ranya Elramly ja Auringon aseman vastaanotto. *Kulttuurintutkimus* 26: 1. 39–53.
Nissilä, Hanna-Leena 2007: Jälkikoloniaalinen naiskirjoitus – suomalaisen kirjallisuuden uudet tulokkaat. *Kolonialismin jäljet. Keskustat, periferiat ja Suomi.* Ed. by Joel Kuortti, Mikko Lehtonen & Olli Löytty. Helsinki: Gaudeamus. 209–226.
Nuolijärvi, Pirkko 2008: Vuoden 2008 Larin Paraske on Umayya Abu-Hanna. *Pirta* 4.
Paavola, Elisa 2002: Naisena kahden kulttuurin välissä. *Opettaja* 49–50/2002.
Parente-Čapková, Viola 2011: Kotimainen toinen. Romanit suomalaisuuden kirjallisena rakennusaineena. *Kulttuurintutkimus* 28. 3–18.

Parvikko, Tuija 2003: Kielletyn kansan tytär kertoo. Umayya Abu-Hannan lapsuus on erittäin avartavaa ja ajankohtaista luettavaa juuri nyt. *Helsingin Sanomat* 26.10.2003.

Pelvo, Martti 2013: Evakossa. *Suomen nykykirjallisuus 2: Kirjallinen elämä ja yhteiskunta.* Ed. by Mika Hallila et al. Helsinki: SKS. 53–54.

Pere-Antikainen, Gyöngyi 2011: Turvallisesti yli 27. *Kajastus* 1. 4–6.

Petäjä, Jukka 2004: Soi sana kultainen. *Helsingin Sanomat* 9.1.2004.

Pynnönen, Marja-Liisa 1991: *Siirtolaisuuden vanavedessä: tutkimus ruotsinsuomalaisen kirjallisuuden kentästä vuosina 1956–1988.* Helsinki: SKS.

Rantonen, Eila (ed.) 2010: *Vähemmistöt ja monikulttuurisuus kirjallisuudessa.* Tampere: Tampere University Press.

Rantonen, Eila & Nissilä, Hanna-Leena 2013: Pelottavat ja tavallisemmat maahanmuuttajat. *Suomen nykykirjallisuus 2: Kirjallinen elämä ja yhteiskunta.* Ed. by Mika Hallila et al.. Helsinki: SKS. 76–91.

Ratinen, Suvi 2002: Järkevä ja jumalallinen tapa kuoria appelsiini. *Etsijä* 4.

Riekko, Iida 2004: Palestiinalaistytön maailma väärin päin. *Parnasso* 1. 70–71.

Rojola, Lea 2002: Läheisyyden löyhkä käy kaupaksi. *Kurittomat kuvitelmat. Johdatus 1990-luvun kotimaiseen kirjallisuuteen.* Ed. by Markku Soikkeli. Turku: Turun yliopisto. 68–99.

Ropponen, Ville 2003: Kliseissä versoo tuoreus. *Parnasso* 7/2010. The text can be found at http://plaza.fi/lukeminen/parnasso/parnasson-arviot-alexandra-salmela-27-eli-kuolema-tekee-taiteilijan Quoted in 20.6.2016.

Rosendahl Thomsen, Mads 2010/2008: *Mapping World Literature. International Canonization and Transnational Literatures.* London & New York: Continuum International Publishing Group.

Salmela, Alexandra 2012: Mietteitä kielten törmäysvyöhykkeiltä. *Både och, sekä että. Om flerspråkighet / Monikielisyydestä.* Ed. by Heidi Grönstrand & Kristiina Malmio. Helsinki: Schildts Kustannus Oy. 318–336.

Savolainen, Matti 1995: *Marginalia ja kirjallisuus. Ääniä suomalaisen kirjallisuuden reunoilta.* Helsinki: SKS.

Schramm, Moritz 2010: After the 'Cartoons': The Rise of a New Danish Migration Literature? *Migration and Literature in Contemporary Europe.* Ed. by Mirjam Gebauer & Pia Schwarz Lausten. München: Martin Meidenbauer. 131–148.

Seyhan, Azade 2010: Unfinished Modernism: European Destinations of Transnational writing. *Migration and Literature in Contemporary Europe.* Ed. by Mirjam Gebauer & Pia Schwarz Lausten. München: Martin Meidenbauer Verlagsbuchhandlung. 11–22.

Seyhan, Azade 2001: *Writing Outside the Nation.* Princeton, N.J. and Oxford: Princeton University Press.

Sharma, Leena 2003: Suomalainen kirjailija. *Suomen Kuvalehti* 8.

Soto, Adrian 2005: Runeberg-palkinnon voittanut kirjailija Zinaida Lindén: Haluan kertoa tarinoita omalla sielullani. *Monitori* 4. 24–25.

Stenbäck, Irma 2003: Valtio palkitsi taiteilijansa: palkittu palestiinalainen Unayya Abu-Hanna kirjoitti kipunsa kirjaksi – suomeksi. *Helsingin Sanomat.* 10.12.2003.

The Finland Prize citations 2003. http://www.minedu.fi/OPM/Tiedotteet/2003/12/opetusministerio_jakoi_vuoden_2003_suomi-palkinnot Quoted in 20.6.2016.

Tidigs, Julia 2014: *Att skriva sig över språkgränserna. Flerspråkighet i Jac. Ahrenbergs och Elmer Diktonius prosa.* Åbo: Åbo Akademi University Press.

Valenius, Johanna 2004: *Undressing the Maid. Gender, Sexuality and the Body in the Construction of the Finnish Nation.* Helsinki: SKS.

Viinikka-Kallinen, Anitta 2010: While the wings grow – Finnic minorities writing their existence onto the world map. *Planning a new standard language. Finnic minority languages meet the new millennium.* Ed. by Helena Sulkala & Harri Mantila. Helsinki: SKS. 147–177.

Vänttinen, Pekka 2004: Umayya Abu-Hannalla on tehtävä Suomessa. *Anna* 8.
Waugh, Patricia 1989: *Feminine Fictions. Revisiting the Postmodern.* London & New York: Routledge.
Wilhelmson, Putte 2003: Retrospektiivisen hallusinaation eräs lajityyppi. Mantran muminaa Argentiinan pustalla. *Nuori Voima* 2.
Wrede, Johan (ed.) 1999: *Finlands svenska litteraturhistoria. Första delen, Åren 1400–1900.* Helsingfors: Svenska litteratursällkapet i Finland.
Yildiz, Yasemin 2012: *Beyond the Mother Tongue. The Postmonolingual Condition.* New York: Fordham University Press.
Ylitalo, Silja 2009: Kirjailija vai(n) maahanmuuttaja? *Kumppani* 10.
Yuval-Davis, Nira 1997: *Gender & Nation.* London: SAGE Publications.
Zilliacus, Clas (ed.) 2000: *Finlands svenska litteratur 1900–2012.* Svenska litteratursällskapet i Finland. Helsingfors, Stockholm: Atlantis.

# Writing Migrant Identities IV

Anne Heith
https://orcid.org/0000-0002-0682-2668

# The African Diaspora, Migration and Writing: Johannes Anyuru's *En civilisation utan båtar*

As a consequence of migration, national identities have been de-naturalised and boundaries of national belonging are becoming unsettled through representations shaped by multidirectional patterns and cross-appropriation of elements from diverse cultural traditions. New modes of perceiving imagined communities and home are emerging. 'Migration throws objects, identities and ideas into flux' is an observation which provides the vantage point for a collection of articles entitled *Exiles, Diasporas & Strangers*. The explored theme is the critical and creative role of estrangement and displacement of modern art (Mercer 2008, 7). This article will discuss intersections between migration, diaspora and the formation of new kinds of identities, belonging and aesthetics in a Swedish context by means of an analysis of Johannes Anyuru's autobiographical book *En civilisation utan båtar* [A Civilisation Without Ships] published in 2011. The book is about Anyuru's stay in Athens, where he waited with other activists to sail for Gaza as a manifestation of solidarity with the Palestinian people. Anyuru himself is both the narrator and focalizer and to a large extent the book consists of his reflections upon issues of identity and belonging, homelessness, solidarity, migration and writing.

When discussing transformations of present-day Europe related to migration, Gebauer and Schwarz Lausten (2010, 1) suggest that 'the migrant has come to stand as the symbol of all that is disconcerting'. This is likely to be true in contexts where 'the migrant'[1] is viewed from the vantage point of categories such as ethnic majorities, decision makers and xenophobic groups concerned with the erosion of welfare systems and/or transformations of national culture conceived of as threatened by alien influences. However, it is not true when 'the migrant' and migration are viewed from the perspective of migrants themselves or their descendants. Rather, literary writing in which the world is seen with the eyes of 'the migrants' may transform ideas

---

1 The category of 'the migrant' is quite problematic. There has always been a hierarchisation in the Nordic countries (as elsewhere) when it comes to the view on immigrants. People from various parts of the world have been seen as more, or less, different, 'strange' and desirable from the vantage point of the ethnic majority and majority culture.

of the nation and problematize aspects of majority cultures that may be disconcerting for migrants. It may also challenge the status of the ethnic majority as a tacit norm that minorities and migrants are expected to conform to. Ethnicity researchers Fenton and May emphasise that all groups, both minority and majority ones, 'incorporate an ethnic dimension and the failure of the latter to recognise or acknowledge this has more to do with differential power relations between groups than with anything else' (Fenton & May 2002, 10–11). As ethnicity and minority status matter for how the world is perceived and experienced, focalization in literary writing matters. It is of importance whose view of the world that is being represented.

## *Johannes Anyuru: A Successful Afro-Swedish Author*[2]

Already in Afro-Swedish Johannes Anyuru's (b. 1979) first collection of poetry, *Det är bara gudarna som är nya* [Only the Gods are New] from 2003, the practice to mingle influences from diverse literary, geographical and historical traditions prevails. The poems juxtapose elements from Homer, the Swedish poet Göran Sonnevi, rock lyrics and hip hop; the latter by loans and allusions to the Swedish group, the Latin Kings, who received a great deal of media attention a decade ago. The theme of Anyuru's second collection of poems, *Omega* (2005), is the death of a close friend in cancer. The third, *Städerna inuti Hall* (2009, [The Cities Inside Hall]) is more explicitly political than the previous ones.[3] In December 2009, the political drama *Förvaret* [The Deposit] by Anyuru and the philosopher Aleksander Motturi had its premiere at Gothenburg City Theatre. The title refers to Detention Centres where refugees are kept as detainees while waiting to be deported out of the country as a result of the implementation of Swedish Immigration Law. Anyuru has performed live extensively. During 2003, he toured with the

---

2   I choose to use the term 'Afro-Swedish' as it corresponds with the denomination used by Swedes of African descent themselves, for example in the name of the NGO 'Afrosvenskarnas riksförbund', 'The National Association of Afro-Swedes.' I have also had the name of the series of conferences called 'Afroeurope@ns: Black Cultures and Identities in Europe' in mind. The term 'Afro-Swedes' is furthermore used in *Encyclopedia of Afroeuropean Studies* (McEachrane 2012, Heith 2012a). The term is discussed more in detail in the article 'Displacement and Regeneration: Minorities, Migration and Postcolonial Literature' (Heith 2016, 50–52). When writing an entry about Johannes Anyuru for *Encyclopedia of Afroeuropean Studies*, I asked Anyuru if he had any objections to being called an 'Afro-Swedish' author. The answer was negative. The debate in the USA has shown that many Americans prefer the term 'black' rather than 'Afro-American' or 'African-American'. One reason for this is that they do not see any reason for emphasising geographical affiliations to Africa. The backdrop is that the majority of blacks in the USA are descended from slaves (Piety 2013, Santarelli 2012). The situation is different in Sweden where the presence of people of African descent is related to recent migration. This means that there are connections to the African continent through writers, like Sami Said, who was born there, and Anyuru, whose parent was born there (Heith 2016).
3   'Hall' is the name of a well-known Swedish prison.

National Theatre Company with a performance called *Abstrakt rap*. He is a member of the spoken word group *Broken word*, which released the album *Anatomy of a Dying Star* in 2005. In 2010, his first novel, *Skulle jag dö under andra himlar* [If I Were to Die Under Other Skies], was published. His second novel, based on the life of his refugee father, *En storm kom från paradiset* was published in 2012. An English translation, *A Storm Blew in from Paradise*, by Rachel Willson-Broyles was published in 2015.

In 2011, Anyuru went to Athens, Greece, in order to join the 'Freedom Flotilla', also called Ship to Gaza. The plan was that together with other activists he would go to Gaza on a ship carrying supplies that would be distributed to the Palestinian people. The aim of the manifestation was to protest against the Israeli blockade of Gaza and to support the Palestinian people. According to the plan, the ships were to leave Athens where the activists would embark. The participants of the project were counting on the support of international law, which if implemented properly would grant them the legal right to sail on international waters. After preparations and waiting, they finally received the news that the ships were not allowed to leave. The Greek authorities would not grant them the permission to leave for Gaza, and the participants had to leave Athens without having started the planned voyage. Later the same year, a short book by Anyuru, *En civilisation utan båtar* [A Civilisation Without Ships] was published.

*Diaspora, Aesthetics and Identity Formation*

The term 'diaspora aesthetic' is used by Stuart Hall in 'Cultural Identity and Diaspora'; the theme of this article is the emergence of new cultural identities and artistic forms of representation related to 'the diaspora experience'. Hall (1997, 58) connects the formation of a diaspora aesthetic with the postcolonial experience. With an example from the Caribbean, he concludes that it was not until the 1970s that an Afro-Caribbean identity became available as in that historical moment Jamaicans 'discovered themselves to be "black" and to be the "sons and daughters of slavery"' (Hall 1997, 55). Hall makes the point that artistic representations play a vital role for the formation of diasporic, hybrid identities. The theme of identity and difference in the African Diaspora is also elaborated upon by Paul Gilroy; he proposes that the concept of 'diaspora' should be cherished for 'its ability to pose the relationship between ethnic sameness and differentiation: a *changing* same.' (Gilroy 1993, xi).

The presence of people of African descent in Sweden is related to migration. This has consequences for bordering practices on various levels. In our time, migration has become one of the most influential factors shaping the nature and effects of borders: 'Constant border work is being carried out to try to separate the wanted from the unwanted, the imagined barbarians from the civilized, and the global rich from the global poor' (van Houtum 2012, 405). In a discussion of mapping and (b)ordering, van Houtum emphasizes that migration ought not be represented as a unidirectional line in the shape of an arrow indicating the origin and destination of migrants. Instead of uniformity and fixation, he proposes the use of mapping which acknowledges 'the human rhizomatic *becomings*, zig zag connections, traces, tracks and linkages, and the movements and (e)motions that cannot be universally rationalized, yet are felt, sensed and believed' (van Houtum 2012, 413)[4].

The complexity and diversity of present-day migration is an important theme of Anyuru's book. The narrator reflects upon the first African Diaspora related to slave trade, contemporary migration from Africa and migration related to the war in Bosnia. Migrants are depicted as groups whose movements are multidimensional, diverse and at times contingent. For some, as a group of Iranian refugees Anyuru encounters in Athens, migration takes on the shape of waiting for permission to stay. The mobility and migration of today and the emergence of transmobility and transmigrants are trends reflected in the book. Van Houtum describes the implications of this development for conceptualisations of borders and bordering.

> The fact that many mobile people and migrants are crossing borders and have become transmobile and transmigrants – and thus find themselves neither only here nor only there, but mentally, virtually and digitally in several places at the same time – has therefore important consequences for the concepts of borders, nation and identities. It implies that geopolitical borders cannot be understood as discrete, fixed and dichotomous (van Houtum 2012, 406).

One effect of migration, exemplified by the status of some Iranian men Anyuru encounters in Athens, is that of being situated in-between: 'somewhere between two extremes or recognized categories' (*The Oxford Pocket Dictionary of Current English*). The Iranians have left their country of origin, but they are not recognized as legitimate immigrants in Greece.[5] Their situation may be described as that of people being at a halt, not knowing if they will get to the destination they hoped for and not being able to return to where they came from. Another instance of an in-between status is exemplified by the situation of Anyuru's Ugandan father in Sweden, who waits for life to begin while the years pass by and he gets old and ill.

Eventually, he realizes that he will not return to Africa and that he has spent a large part of his life waiting for something that will not happen. These in-between situations experienced by the Iranian migrants and Anyuru's refugee father depict the condition of living neither here nor there, an indeterminate status experienced like a limbo.

---

4   This conception of migration is inspired by Deleuze and Guattari's *A Thousand Plateaus* (Deleuze & Guattari 1987) and *Escape Routes, Control and Subversion in the 21st Century* by Papadopoulos et al. (Papadopoulos et al. 2008) whom van Houtum refers to.

5   This kind of in-between position is of course drastically different from Bhabha's notion of the hybrid positions made available in in-between spaces, which he proposes may contest centres of power (Bhabha 2008, 199–244).

Johannes Anyuru. Photo: Khim Efraimsson / Norstedts.

## *The Story of a Multifaceted Journey*

On the surface level, *En civilisation utan båtar* [A Civilisation Without Ships] is a kind of diary about some days and nights spent in Athens told in the first person by the narrator and focalizer Anyuru. However, it is also a book about writing, as an open-ended process, the direction of which Anyuru is uncertain. Before it was published in book form, the text was available on a blog, which was published on the website of the publisher Glänta. The book contains a poem that consists of texts and fragments that people mailed to Anyuru. Thus, part of the text was co-authored by a number of people.[6] The motif of collective action is varied throughout the text and the theme of writing and producing a new kind of text is interwoven with the

6   This was confirmed by Anyuru himself in an e-mail dated 25 July 2013: 'Ja, det finns en dikt i boken som består av texter och fragment som andra har skickat till mig. Den heter, har jag för mig, Utan namn. I övrigt är det jag som har skrivit. Boken är i stora drag (minus förord) en blogg som jag skrev under resan – den publicerades på Gläntas hemsida. Vet inte om den ligger kvar där.' [Yes, there is a poem in the book that consists of texts and fragments that other people have mailed. Its title is, if I remember correctly, Without name. Apart from that, I have written the book. To a large extent, the book is (minus the preface) a blog I wrote during the journey – it was published at Gläntas website. Don't know if it is still there.]

Johannes Anyuru's autobiographical book En civilisation utan båtar *(2011, 'A Civilisation Without Ships') primarily concerns reflections on identity and belonging.*

narrative of the narrator-focalizer's inner and outer journey. As the story is told in the first person, there is a strong focus upon the inner journey. This is conveyed by means of the narration of the main character's reflections upon events, texts he reads and people he encounters. The concept of focalization is important as it takes into account the cognitive, emotive and ideological orientation, which gives the text specific moods and meanings (cf. Rimmon-Kenan 1999, 71). Anyuru exists in the text not only as a narrating voice, but also as a depiction of an embodied human, who filters subject matter through his mind, senses and psyche. Thus, the text presents a subjective, embodied way of seeing and experiencing the world.

The book opens with a section about Anyuru's hesitation when he gets the request to join the voyage. While still at home in Gothenburg, he initially finds a number of reasons for not joining the activists who are going to Gaza. A number of thoughts run through his mind. He experiences fear at the thought of possible confrontations with Israeli soldiers. The voyage is to take place the year after some members of the first flotilla had been killed when attempting to defy the Israeli blockade. When mentally confronting his fear, Anyuru dwells upon the emotions he experiences vis-a-vis his Afro-Swedish descent, which makes him feel vulnerable, and potentially not being seen as a Swede: 'I believe that my fear, which I had not been aware of, was related to not having an evident feeling of being protected by my Swedishness. Do I look like a Swede in the eyes of a foreigner? In the eyes of a foreign soldier?'

($E$ 9[7]). As this reflection reveals, the narrator confronts the implications of the African Diaspora for his own sense of who he is and for how he is perceived by others. He is aware of the fact that it is visible that he is of African descent and that this might make him more vulnerable than participants whose appearance does not reveal a non-Swedish, non-European, non-White ancestry.[8] By means of the reflection, Anyuru acknowledges that 'Africa speaks' through his skin colour. From a Jamaican context, Hall mentions brown or black skin as a sign of 'Africa of the diaspora' using the metaphor 'Africa speaks' (Hall 1997, 55). A major theme of Anyuru's text is how, or if, the 'old' Africas of the first diaspora and the subsequent waves of migration of black people from Africa may be reconciled with the 'new' Africas emerging in Europe, and specifically in Sweden where he was born and where he has his home (cf. Hall 1997, 55). This implies a new construction of a hybrid form of 'Swedishness', which uses elements from 'old' Africa together with elements from Swedish and other cultural constellations, transforming 'old' Africa to something 'new' in the process (Heith 2012, Heith 2014).

The notion of cross-influences between black intellectuals and artists within a transnational framework is central to Gilroy's idea of the 'Black Atlantic' (Gilroy 1993). In the last chapter of *The Black Atlantic: Modernity and Double Consciousness* Gilroy presents a critical analysis of 'Afrocentrism' and the way it has understood tradition as invariant repetition instead of a stimulus for transformations and innovation (Gilroy op. cit., 187–223). Like Hall, Gilroy highlights 'Africanness' as a category which is invented and changed through cultural production related to African diasporas. Today the term 'Black Atlantic' has 'become a shorthand reference to any and all projects which have a transcultural dimension across one or more sections of the black African *diasporic* cultures of the region' (Ashcroft, Griffiths & Tiffin 2007, 22). One proposal of this article is that the notion of cultural cross-fertilization and interaction within a transnational global framework also provides a framework for conceptualizing the implications of Anyuru's juxtaposition of elements from American popular culture, the Muslim tradition, and traditional African subject matter like the figure of the 'Jali'. Such a framework might be an aid in exploring the coming into being of a new kind of text, which also integrates collective writing and elements

---

7   All the translations of the book are mine.
8   In my reading of Anyuru's literary texts, skin colour is an important theme already in the first collection of poems. So is religion (Heith 2008, Heith 2014). The concept of 'migration literature' is problematic as it tends to essentialise 'the migrant' and reduce differences between various writers. Behschnitt for example describes the early books of Khemiri, Anyuru, Bakhtiari and Wenger as the results of a shared vision of migrants, Sweden and the intended readership in a way that reduces the considerable differences between the respective authors. 'In the unprecedented success of Khemiri's, Anyuru's, Bakhtiari's and Wenger's books, *they* are confirmed in *their* vision of the integrated migrant, *they* see a symbol of success for several decades of integration policy within the Swedish welfare state. From the perspective of the literary texts, the analysis has shown that the authors know exactly what *they* are talking about and whom *they* are talking to. *They* all engage in a play with reader expectations [...]' (Behschnitt 2010, 89, my italics).

from a specific Swedish literary tradition. In a literal sense, this makes the text a flow of sections of words from various stylistic registers and cultural traditions. As such the text exemplifies a form of cross-cultural literary writing (Ashcroft, Griffiths & Tiffin 2009, 214). The term 'cross-cultural writing' has been proposed as being more adequate than the terms 'diasporic literature' or 'post-colonial literature' when it comes to denominating texts that blend elements from various traditions both from within and outside national borders.

*Becoming Black: Exclusion, Racism and Formation of Identity*

When analyzing the formation of black identity and subjectivity in Europe Michelle M. Wright emphasizes the contradictory nature of this process:

> Although there is no biological basis for racial categories (there is no such thing as a 'black', 'white', or 'Asian' gene, the amount of genetic disparity between persons of different races is the same as that between persons in the same racial category), Blacks in the West have nonetheless had their history shaped by the very concrete effects of Western racism (Wright 2004, 2).

The history, and still existing reality, of racism directed against black and brown-skinned people is conjured up by the narrator Anyuru's reflections about how he himself might be seen and treated if he were to join Ship to Gaza. Wright depicts racist discourse as deeply embedded in European culture and modernity, legitimized by the works of philosophers like Hegel who posited that the 'Negro' stands outside the history of intellectual, technological, moral, and cultural progress 'guided by the Absolute of reason' (Wright 2004; 8, Heith 2012b; Hegel 1956). Although this is not always openly acknowledged, racism still exists also in modern 'enlightened' societies. Within the field of ethnic and racial studies, it has been highlighted that the fact that multiculturalism may be a cherished concept in modern liberal democracies does not guarantee that these societies are anti-racist in praxis. Gabrielle Berman and Yin Paradies for example emphasize that: 'It is only through a clear understanding and inclusion of anti-racist praxis that the potential of multiculturalism to address the challenges of racial diversity in modern liberal democracies can be realized' (Berman & Paradies 2010, 214).

Anyuru implicitly hints at the existence of history and philosophical tradition, which have posited blacks as the Others of White Europe. However, he does not engage in a mode of writing, which involves that he actively positions himself as the Other, producing a discourse in a binary, dichotomous relationship to the Hegelian tradition. Rather, Anyuru explores another option discussed by Wright, and Gilroy, namely that of blackness as 'fluidity', which may both harm and heal the black individual (Wright 2004, 2; Gilroy 1993). Wright herself proposes an understanding of black subjectivity, which implies that the category is seen as produced through negotiations between the abstract and the real, or in other terms 'between the ideal and the material' (Wright 2004, 3). Without going in detail into

Wright's analysis, this article will discuss some aspects of how the real and ideal are negotiated in Anyuru's text and how the fluid character of blackness contributes to shaping the narrator's idea of who he is and what role he may shoulder as a writer.

Another theme connected to the African Diaspora, which the narrator-focalizer Anyuru grapples with, is his own feeling of homelessness, which initially gives him some problems in appreciating the Palestinian struggle for a Palestinian state: 'Why did they [the Palestinians] have to live exactly on that piece of land? There wasn't a place on earth which I had that feeling for, and I wondered what it meant' (*E* 11). He also thinks of himself as a member of a transnational, community of homeless people: 'We who are in search of a home' (*E* 12). This feeling makes him sympathize with the Sionist movement too as he sees the affinities between the Sionist and his own quest: 'I myself seeking a home which God shall grant me' (*E* 16). One aspect of Anyuru's identity formation involves a linking to post-Western Europe through religion.[9] In 2007, he converted to Islam and there are frequent references to Islam and religious practices in the book (Heith 2012; Heith 2014).

## *The African Diaspora: Migration, Transnationalism and Hybridity*

During the inner journey of the narrator-focalizer, analogies are created between groups of people in search of a home: Sionists, Palestinians, refugees and Africans scattered in Europe. Emotionally and intellectually, Anyuru establishes links between himself and groups of people that have been violently uprooted.

> You are my cousins and I know like you what history is, that it does not pass without making an impact, that it is stuck in the bodies and the dreams, and that it is a waterfall of chains, and that you inherit something although you don't want to. I have a father, I have my childhood, I have the history books with pictures of people, who look like me in chains (*E* 34).

The section exemplifies how Anyuru creates a transnational imagined community of people who share painful histories and memories that dwell in their bodies and minds. When discussing histories of traumatic ruptures and enforced separations from Africa, Hall (1997, 53) uses the metaphor 'The past continues to speak to us'. While emphasizing the differences between peoples of the African diasporas, Hall also highlights sameness manifested in the construction of an imagined community of Africans of the diaspora. There is a common history of transportation, slavery and colonization shared by a large number of people, but this does not constitute a common origin (Hall 1997, 54).

9   The concept of 'Post-Western Europe' is explored by Delanty and Rumford who discuss various factors which contribute to a shifting understanding of what it means being European. They particularly mention migration, globalisation and an increasing awareness of the existence of different cultural heritages for the emergence of new ways of conceptualising Europe (Delanty & Rumford 2006).

In Anyuru's personal case, the event of the first African Diaspora is evoked by memories of pictures in history books illustrating the slave trade. In the articulation of an identity, which transgresses Swedish national borders, the visual imprints of black people chained aboard slave ships contribute to the shaping of a transnational, global identity shared by people of African descent around the world. Anyuru was born in Sweden. His mother is Swedish and his father is from Uganda. As a result of Idi Amin coming to power, Anyuru's father fled to Sweden in the 1970s. Although Anyuru has never lived in Africa, ideas of Africa and linking to Africa are recurring themes in his writing. The idea of Africa that is explored may be described as a 'home in the heart'.[10] This theme is connected to that of a black, 'racial' identity and the tensions between this form of identification and a Swedish national identity. As Wendy Walters (2005, xvii) points out the issue of 'home' may be quite complex in the writing of black authors who have experienced racial exclusion 'at home'.

Although Anyuru creates links to Africa in his writing, he does not enact any return to Africa, or an African country of origin. The theme of return is touched upon in a section about his father, who Anyuru has left seriously ill in Gothenburg. While in Athens, Anyuru thinks about his father's experience of the African Diaspora:

> My father told me once: 'My biggest mistake in life was that I waited for life to begin. I waited for Idi Amin to be overthrown so I could return home. Amin was overthrown, but another maniac came to power. I waited. Another man came to power, and then another' (*E* 9).

While the father can think of Uganda as a home he wants to return to in a literal sense, Africa is not experienced in the same way by the son who never has lived there. Still Johannes Anyuru connects to Africa, the country of origin of his father and the continent of origin of people who look like himself, who were chained on slave ships (*E* 34). The sense of 'belonging' connoted by the concept of 'Africa' may be related both to ancestral ties and the 'racial' identification of a person of African descent in Europe where whiteness is the norm.

The issue of belonging is complex and it gains a specific character when related to second generation immigrants. Research on participation and belonging in 'diverse' European cities indicate 'high degrees of local involvement in the second generation and the dwindling centrality of single ethnic belongings' which is seen as 'a reflection of the dramatically changing ethnic and (sub)cultural landscapes in cities in Europe' (Crul & Schneider 2010, 1249). One effect of this development is the 'remaking of the mainstream'. In their analysis, Crul and Schenider argue that mobility pathways ought to be in focus in investigations aiming at a better understanding of integration or assimilation as on-going processes (ibid.).

---

10 The expression 'home in the heart' is used in an analysis of the writing of the Black American author Richard Wright. Walters (2005, 5) highlights its shifting character describing it as 'ambivalent, not definitive, shifting rather than fixed'.

In Anyuru's text, 'Africa' functions as an emotional node and imaginary place; in the process of writing, he explores the implications of this for the formation of identity and belonging. This exploration also implies a deconstruction of 'the centrality of single ethnic belonging', which may be conceived of as an exploration of an identity beyond the 'us' and 'them' dichotomy. When analyzing the complexities of the formation of identity, Nira Yuval-Davis (2010, 263) proposes that dichotomous notions of identity and difference are more misleading than explanatory. Identities may connote core aspects of the self, but also 'the development, processual and interactive, of collective self-understanding; or the evanescent products of multiple and competing discourses of self.' (Yuval-Davis 2010, 262). One element of Anyuru's journey is that it stages explorations on various levels and in various contexts. The text is ambivalent. Identities – individual, collective and textual – are evoked as fickle, processual and interactive, evanescent products of multiple and competing discourses, to paraphrase Yuval-Davis.

## *The Jali: The Use of Tradition in Diaspora Aesthetics*

One example of linking to Africa through writing is the exploration of roles and models for the author. This is done in a discussion of the role of the *Jali*, a West-African traditional poet who knows the ancient songs but also sings about contemporary events and matters at hand in the present moment (*E* 91). Anyuru uses the term 'Jali', spelled with a capital 'J', but 'griot' is a term which is more common in English. *The Oxford Dictionary of Literary Terms in Literature* defines 'griot' as: 'A kind of bard or itinerant minstrel found in western African societies, who usually sings of local legends, genealogies, or heroic deeds.' However, there are also connections between the African tradition of griots and contemporary popular culture. In Sage's online encyclopedia on black studies, parallels are drawn between the griot and the contemporary rapper in a characterisation of rap as:

> [...] a continuation of African and Caribbean oral traditions with roots that stretch to West and Central Africa. Like their ancestors, African American male and female rappers – who are essentially contemporary **griots**, praise singers and poets – draw their energy from the combination of personal style, an innovative story, the skillful use of words, and a reading of the nation (Stephens).

This definition fits well with Anyuru's use of the term 'Jali', which is integrated in an exploration of Swedishness, nationality and belonging. The section introducing the figure of the *Jali* is preceded by a section in which the narrator mentions that he started to write in order to remember. As the entire book is a narrative of contemporary events and phenomena that catch Anyuru's attention, interspersed with retrospective elements, a metonymic connection between the *Jali*-figure and Anyuru's own practice as a writer is established. Both the Jali and Anyuru are concerned with memories and the recording of what is going on. The choice of an African term and a traditional African poet, which has influenced today's rap culture in the USA, as a model is one way of establishing connections with various traditions.

The text also mentions and quotes other models, such as the Swedish poet Göran Sonnevi, thus evoking multiple origins, models and directions for the literary text. This is one example of how diaspora aesthetics, combining elements from various cultural traditions may be shaped. In a section which ponders the question of why he started writing, Anyuru suggests that one reason probably was that he wanted oblivion: 'Forget the world, forget my body which always was at the wrong place, which always had the wrong heart, wrong eyes, wrong religion, wrong mouth' (*E* 93). The quote hints to the possibility that literature and imaginative writing may provide a more satisfying reality and 'home' than a reality where feelings of displacement, of being in the wrong place, of having the wrong kind of emotions, the wrong physical appearance, and religion dominate. This kind of view of literary writing, or artistic creation, as the production of alternative realities more satisfactory than the real world is known from Romantic and Modernist aesthetics as an embracement of the notions of the artist as an outsider, as well as from contemporary urban youth cultures (Heith 2004; Heith 2008).

After the introduction of the *Jali*-figure, there is a movement in the text as existential dimensions of writing are evoked. The narrator Anyuru identifies with the figure of the *Jali* by ruminating over his own role as that of a *Jali*. He poses the question of whose *Jali* he is. For whom does he sing? To whom does his voice belong? The answer proposed is that he doesn't know yet, but he knows that his voice as a writer no longer belongs solely to himself: 'I am writing about this journey which is taking a direction that does not yet exist, a direction we will all create together, if our bodies and ships are not broken' (*E* 92). The use of the term 'broken' contributes to the creation of complex (e)motions. The text presents perceptions, sensations and psychic realities in motion and on a metatextual level writing as an ongoing process. Anyuru's oscillation between diverse emotions and contexts is one way of creating movement and moods. The term 'broken', connected to ships and bodies in the quoted passage, exemplifies how complexity is created through a detail which activates motion. It is hardly a coincidence that Anyuru has shown an interest in the theme of 'broken words' as a rapper and writer and that the term is combined here with 'ships' and 'bodies'. Both terms are possible to relate to multiple contexts, for example that of the slave trade of the first African Diaspora and to that of the Ship to Gaza project the previous year when some of the participants were killed.

One theme of Anyuru's narration of a multifaceted journey is the narrator-focalizer's grappling with the role of the writer and of the production of a new kind of text. As mentioned above, an option highlighted by the discussion of the *Jali* is that the role of this traditional West-African figure might be of bearing for Anyuru's own *Bildung* as an author. The narrator mentions that the word 'Jali' comes from the Mandinga word for blood (*E* 93). It is left to the reader to ponder what this means for the interpretation of the text. The text integrates an element linking Anyuru to his ancestral African origin in a vision of the role of the author in a world of flux, migration, diaspora and diversity. One effect of the use of the *Jali* as a model for the contemporary Swedish writer is that an element from the African tradition, dismissed and excluded for being incompatible with progress and modernity by Hegel (Wright 2004, 8), is integrated in present-day Afro-Swedish cultural production. This involves a re-imagination of space 'both in the language of memory and in the politics of the future', characteristic of contemporary 'migrant literatures' (Merolla & Ponzanesi 2005, 15). As Bhabha has suggested, emergent minority communities contribute to symbolic re-mapping, they 'revise our sense of symbolic citizenship, our myths of belonging, by identifying ourselves with the starting-points of other national and international histories and geographies' (Bhabha 2008, xx). This may involve that nation state-centred and Eurocentric cartographies, based on notions of white racial purity, are replaced by migrant cartographies celebrating diversity and hybridity as in Anyuru's text.

## Islam: Deconstructing Orientalism and Constructing New Forms of Community

Another form of linking and hybridization is exemplified by depictions of the narrator Anyuru's spiritual practices as a Muslim. Actively and openly practising Islam in Sweden and other European countries involves a form of self-definition and identification opposed to that of the ideologies of secular and traditionally Christian white Europe (cf. Ballard 1996). When creating the figure of an Afro-Swedish Muslim, content with practicing Islam in Sweden and other parts of Europe, Anyuru performs a hybridization, which undermines prevailing Orientalist constructions of Muslims as alien, threatening and potentially dangerous (Heith 2012; Heith 2014). In Anyuru's text, Islam is presented as a positive element providing opportunities for communion and belonging in the lives of immigrants and converts in Sweden, as well as among Muslims in a transnational global space. For the narrator Anyuru, the reading of the Quran is part of his self-examination and coming into being as a new kind of Swede and European. The narrator's awareness that it involves a risk to confess being a Muslim in contemporary white Europe is revealed in a passage in which Anyuru explicitly disavows the message propagated by *Nation of Islam* which is characterized as a 'racist, distorted version of Islam' (*E* 54).

From the vantage point of Swedish mainstream culture the conversion to Islam represents a move away from what is conceived of as normality (Månsson 2000, 259). According to the dominant media image of Islam and Muslims in Sweden, these are 'strange' and 'different'. It is not unusual that dichotomies are established between Swedish, and Western culture, on the one hand, and Muslim culture on the other.[11] But this is not the 'truth' depicted in the writings of Anyuru where religious rituals and practices provide the basis for a transnational, global community where he belongs and feels at home. This involves the creation of a positive, new, hybrid

---

11 Anna Månsson (2000, 259–288) discusses this theme in an article about women who have converted to Islam in Sweden.

form of Afro-Swedish identity. Evoking the structure of the traditional *Bildungsroman* hybridization is exemplified on the levels of genre and content as the identity formation of a new kind of European, in which 'the Muslim world' and 'Africa 'speaks' is the major theme. When in Athens, Anyuru is invited to dinner in the home of an Egyptian man, who was the cook on the Swedish ship that sailed for Gaza the previous year. While the other guests are talking, he joins the Egyptian in a Muslim evening prayer in the living-room (*E* 123). The episode is described in a way which conjures up a warm and friendly atmosphere. This is one example of a depiction of community and belonging across religious and ethnic borders. While being a recognition of Islam and the Islamic presence in Europe and Sweden, Anyuru's text also provides a response to a historical and still ongoing marginalisation of Muslims. When discussing this theme in an article about politics and Islam in Western Europe, Shadid and van Koningsveld conclude that: 'Europe has had the Islamic world as its neighbour for more than a millenium, but it has never succeeded either to acknowledge it as an equal, or to take its cultural or religious traditions seriously' (Shadid & van Koningsveld 1996, 3).

## *Self-Definition, Self-Knowledge and the Spectacle of Disempowered Africans*

During his stay in Athens, Anyuru encounters Africans living on the margins of society. Shortly after his arrival, he walks to the Syntagma square where he watches the demonstrators and African street vendors (*E* 42). One day he sees a Nigerian man in worn clothes selling old magnifying glasses. The man is standing at a street corner holding the magnifying glasses as if they were a bouquet of flowers (*E* 79). On another occasion, he registers the sight of a large number of African, prostitute women. The narrator makes the remark that these women are found in Athens, everywhere in Europe, even in Gothenburg. They usually stand along the walls outside the hotel and at the traffic lights, as if waiting for nothing (*E* 86). One afternoon, he sees a Greek motor-cycle policeman robbing one of the prostitutes: 'Another of the women is hiding behind a parked car. When I walk by her she looks up at me in horror – her eyes are gleaming in her dark face, in the darkness' (*E* 97). In another section, a square is described as the square of the African pedlars of pirate DVD films (*E* 109).

The Africans are mentioned in a matter of fact way, but there are details revealing feelings of sympathy with the destitute Africans and critique of European politics. It is significant that the Africans are mentioned, and that the presence of the African Diaspora is so conscientiously, even compulsively, registered by the narrator-focalizer. This points to the selection of material. Apparently, the presence of the Africans means something to him. Since they are strangers, it must be their appearance that makes him take notice of them and conclude that they are African. This is another version of the motif 'people who look like me' (cf. *E* 34), of how 'Africa speaks' through skin colour, this time in the form of Africans scattered in present-day Europe. Like Anyuru himself, the Africans he encounters are 'visible minorities' in predominantly white societies.¹² Although the presence of the Africans is registered with few words, there are details revealing a critical view of the Europe of white 'normality'. The depiction of the brutality and inhumanity of the Law, in the person of the robbing policeman, particularly conjures up the image of Athens, and Europe, as a dark place where greedy and morally corrupt representatives of state authorities strike against black migrants with no possibility of raising their voices. The kind of subaltern position held by the prostitute women literally means that they cannot speak, as there is no position from where they can give voice to their stories. There is no position of theirs which will be acknowledged and thus make a dialogue with representatives of white European society possible.¹³

Another aspect of the narrative of the presence of Africans in Athens is that it is a parallel to the story of Anyuru's father, who lived there when he was training to become a fighter pilot in the Ugandan army in the late 1960s. As a result of the political disruption in Uganda, the father's training was interrupted and the planned career came to a halt. This is the theme of Anyuru's second novel, published in 2012. The details about the father are told in the 2011 book accounting for the father's personal reasons for migrating. Although the African Diaspora is a diverse, multifaceted phenomenon, experiences of being scattered, uprooted and homeless are shared by large numbers of people living in the diaspora. Migratory waves are connected with various historical contexts and political, economical and social catalysts, such as the slave trade and contemporary political instability, genocide, poverty and lack of opportunities. The narrator Anyuru specifically draws attention to the slave trade, his father's escape from Uganda, which was the reason why he came to Sweden, and the present-day scattering of Africans struggling as street vendors and prostitutes in European cities.

In an analysis of connections between international migration and the emergence of diasporic communities, Jana Evans Braziel emphasises that migration often is the effect of a crisis, which has a negative impact on the migrants. 'International migrants, uprooted from family, friends and nation-state, dispersed from their homelands, and scattered around the globe in

---

12 The term 'visible minority' is discussed in a Swedish introduction to critical race and whiteness studies. It refers to groups whose physical appearance differs from that of the white majority population. Black people and people who look Asian are mentioned in particular (Hübinette et al. 2012, 67, 69).
13 The idea of the African prostitutes as subalterns who cannot speak is of course inspired by Spivak's analysis of the subaltern and why this category is not listened to and acknowledged as a partner in a dialogue. One form of ultimate disempoverment consists of not being acknowledged and respected as somebody with a voice of ones own. See Morris' introduction to Spivak's *Can the Subaltern Speak: Reflections on the History of an Idea* where she discusses misinterpretations of Spivak's seminal text. Her major point is that Spivak does not write that the subaltern cannot speak, but that she analyses how subaltern women in India have been posited outside discourse and dialogue, thus there have been no position from where they have been able to 'speak'. (Morris 2010.) It seems to me that this idea may be applied to the situation of the African prostitutes in Europe many of whom are illegal immigrants.

one or more countries of adoption, form vibrant diasporic communities' (Braziel 2006, 1). She draws attention to the global refugee crisis of the 1990s, which coincided with increasingly restrictive refugee policies. 'As the number of refugees (blacker, browner, poorer, and Muslim) increased worldwide, so too did the doors to asylum seem to slam shut' (Braziel 2006, 5). Her conclusion is that international migrants and scattered diaspora communities 'remain negatively inflected' and she warns against 'premature celebrations of *poly-scaped* transnational exchanges, the presumed death of nationalism, and hybrid forms of diasporic productions' (Braziel 2006, 6). There are also Swedish studies, which highlight immigration and immigrants as a problem (Rystad & Lundberg 2000). During the last years, the political landscapes of the Nordic countries have shown an increase in open support of xenophobic populist parties. In Sweden, *Sverigedemokraterna*, whose supporters are particularly hostile to Islam and Muslims, have gained seats in the Parliament.[14] This party is mentioned in Anyuru's book, implicitly drawing attention to hostility 'at home' in the social reality experienced by Muslims and black and dark-skinned people.

As a contrast and alternative to racist and excluding discourses, the text also thematises transgressions of binaries, and emancipatory options. The vision of community among migrants and diasporic groups evoked by Anyuru's text has resemblances with the vision of Fanon, who emphasised the need for disempowered groups, who shared similar experiences, to mobilise (Fanon 1968, Fanon 2000). However, there are also examples of present-day diaspora research and fiction, which negate visions of African community and solidarity. The academic, Okpewho, for example, who has migrated to the USA, emphasises problematic aspects of ethnic rivalry and bad leadership in Africa, which cause antagonism between various diasporic groups. When discussing the relationship between the old and the new diaspora, he emphasises that one of the reasons why so many Africans were captured and sold as slaves during the era of slave trade was that they were sold by other Africans: 'Africans in the homeland sold other Africans to white traders' (Okpewho 2009, 11). The backdrop of the present-day diaspora is presented as no less problematic for the formation of a communal African, black identity.

> [T]he resources of Africa continued to be appropriated by the former colonizers working in corrupt collusion with the indigenous political leadership. The

---

14 The collection of articles, *Att möta främlingar* [Encountering Strangers], which is the outcome of a research project with the same name, has the subtitle 'Problem kring flyktingmottagande och kulturkonfrontationer' [Problems related to the Reception of Refugees and Cultural Confrontations]. This focus posing refugees and multiculturalism as problems is opposed to Anyuru's depiction of the same phenomena in the text discussed in this article. The dominant vision, which pervades *En civilisation utan båtar*, is that of a civilisation where people of different origins, ethnic ancestry, nationality and religious convictions can co-exist and work together for a common purpose. This vision is realised in the project of the Freedom Flotilla, Ship to Gaza, which stands as a positive alternative to inertia and division based on ethnicity and religion, as well as misuse of power.

result has been an abysmal lack of commitment to a unified political vision and a perennial crisis of leadership in many African nations, culminating in military coups and, not in a few cases, civil wars and genocidal conflicts. Those who have been lucky enough to escape with their lives, or have simply decided that they needed to carry on their careers in less threatening conditions, have opted to flee the land and live in exile (Okpewho 2009, 7).

Ethnic rivalry, war and oppression are themes that are prominent in literature by black African writers. One Swedish example is Sakina Ntibanyitesha, engaged in writing a trilogy based on her own experiences of abuse, torture, imprisonment and the killing of innocent people in Congo during the war. The first part, *Ormbarn* (2012, [Snake children]) depicts the childhood of the female protagonist, while the second *Farligare än djur* (2012, [More dangerous than animals]) depicts adolescence and the outbreak of the war. The third part will be about her new life as a refugee in Sweden. Another example is the more well-known Ivorian novelist Ahmadou Kourouma (1972–2003), whose *Les soleils des indépendances* (1970) critically depicts post-colonial governments in Africa, and *Allah n'est pas obligé* (2000), about a boy who is forced to become a child soldier. These have both been published in Swedish (*Allah gör som han vill* 2002; *Den siste Doumbouya* 2003). Ntibanyitesha, who lives in the north of Sweden, does not know what year she was born. She grew up with her maternal grandmother who had been a slave and she hardly had the opportunity to go to school as a child and adolescent. Kourouma, on the other hand, was born into a well-established family in Côte d'Ivoire, where he studied before he went to France to study mathematics.

In contrast to narratives of conflicts and disintegration among black Africans, Anyuru's book reflects upon the role of Africa and ancestral ties, tentatively explored by an Afro-Swedish author whose major links to the continent are his own physical appearance, his refugee father and the stories told by the father, which repeatedly are processed in the mind of Anyuru. This also involves confronting emotions conjured up by the vision of diasporic Africans in Athens. One interesting question is what the narrator's comments about the Africans, whose existence he registers while in Athens, mean for the theme of the text. One proposal of this article is that they contribute to the main character, Anyuru's tentative exploration of a black identity across class lines and national borders. As elements of Anyuru's inner journey, they take part in the exploration of group affiliations, which contributes to processes of self-definition and the gaining of self-knowledge. The self-definition and gaining of self-knowledge need not be explicitly formulated. Still the text evokes these themes through the references to 'Africanness' as the element which triggers Anyuru's interest in the vendors and prostitutes as part of the exploration of his ancestral African origin and desire for Africa as a 'home of the heart', as a symbolic imagined community.

There is no way people of the diaspora can go home to Africa literally, but Hall underlines that circular symbolic journeys which bring Africa to the 'New World' are vital: 'These symbolic journeys are necessary for us all – and necessarily circular. This is the Africa we must return to – but 'by another route'. This is what Africa has *become* in the New World, what we have made of 'Africa': 'Africa' – as we re-tell it through politics, memory and desire' (Hall 1997, 56). Anyuru's quest is problematised as the conflict between elements, which construct Africa as a place of desire that is being destabilised and threatened by the un-resolvable problem posed by the existence of destitute, vulnerable people who have escaped from the horrors of their African homelands. Hall makes the point that Africans of the diaspora experience both sameness and difference and that 'boundaries of difference are continually repositioned in relation to different points of reference' (Hall 1997, 55; also see Gilroy 1993, xi). In Anyuru's text, 'Africa' is constructed as a complex site of difference and sameness, as well as a symbolic site for an imagined community (cf. Hall 1997, 56).

## *Migration: Transnationalism, Contingency, Despair*

When depicting the departure for Athens, Anyuru mentions that he is talking to a woman on her way to Sarajevo, while standing in a queue at the airport (*E* 25). Her family was banished from Mostar during the war. Anyuru learns that the inhabitants of the city had fifteen minutes to pack their belongings. Then they were put on buses that drove them to Poland, where they were given the advice that they should continue to Scandinavia. The woman and her husband went aboard the first ferry that departed. That was how they ended up in Sweden. The details mentioned by the narrator concisely summarises the experiences of great numbers of migrants forced to leave their old home-countries due to war. Lack of time for preparations, lack of choice whether to go and where to go when forced to leave, the necessity to rely on unknown advisors, and the randomness of the final destination are experiences reflected in numerous accounts of migration.

The text also describes European asylum politics and the effect it has on desperate people seeking asylum without success. This theme is set in focus in the narration of when Anyuru notices Iranian refugees demonstrating outside a Greek immigration office in Athens (*E* 73–75). The refugees are staying in a tent, which Anyuru walks by every day. One day he notices that the men have blood around their lips. He asks in English if they need help, but they mumble something, not being able to speak. Suddenly he realises that the men have stitched their lips. A man who has fainted is filmed by another man with a mobile phone. A passer-by, a Spanish participant of Ship to Gaza, remarks that the film will probably be published on a website via live-stream. Anyuru is shocked: 'It is crazy, grotesque, like a nightmare' (*E* 74). It is obvious that the men are desperate, but the reader is left just as bewildered as the narrator Anyuru himself of what is going on. The story of the Iranian men remains unknown, untold. They are present in the text as signifiers of despair, contributing to the characterisation of the political and social setting of contemporary Europe. While Anyuru is represented as an individual seeking ways of expressing himself as a writer and as a politically committed person, the Iranians are literally depicted as bodies without voices.

## Words that Matter

For the narrator Johannes Anyuru, Ship to Gaza and the weeks spent in Athens, where popular protest mobilises people to fight for a decent future, function as examples of resistance to political inertia and lack of engagement and solidarity. One of the themes of the story line deals with the coming to insight of the narrator and focalizer about the meaningfulness of trying, at least, to act to change the world, and the role of the written and spoken word for doing this. In this respect, the plot resembles the version of the *Bildungsroman* which thematizes an author-protagonist's inner and outer journey aiming at finding his, or her, role as an author and individual. The motives of 'learning' and 'gaining insight' are mentioned throughout the text. The narrator Anyuru himself points out that the reason for joining Ship to Gaza and going to Athens is that he wants to learn. As Anyuru is the focalizer, the reader gets to know that he learns and experiences a great deal of things. With the theme of the *Bildung* of the author in mind the most important insight is that writing and using words matters: 'I came here to Athens also to see what the words are worth, and this day I learn that the activity of pronouncing them, of writing them down, still is . . . something, in its insufficiency. I will never more be alone' (*E* 122). On the final page of the book, the narrator concludes: 'The person I was when I left will never more return home' (*E* 150).

The inner journey of the narrator is depicted as a deeply transformative process. Yet, the juxtaposition of blocks of words from various stylistic registers and traditions make the text ambivalent. So does the depiction of the focalizer's oscillations between contradictory feelings. The possibilities of collective action, of expressing oneself aesthetically in new, unprecedented ways, and of acting as a social being in political contexts, are presented as positive possibilities, albeit threatened by sensations of despair, chock and lack of belonging and meaning. The narrator-focalizer Anyuru has a body, the colour of which 'speaks' of his African ancestry, and a voice that he ruminates upon how to use. The African prostitutes he registers in Athens are black bodies for sale, without possibilities to voice their experiences. The Iranian men with stitched lips have injured their own bodies in a desperate attempt to draw attention to their lack of voice. The text shows that embodied experiences related to race, ethnicity and outsider-positions in white Europe might constitute some degree of sameness, but also an enormous difference when it comes to the issue of having a voice and being able to express oneself.

## At Home in Diaspora

The concept of *diaspora* has been related to processes of de-territorialization, transnational migration and cultural hybridity. 'These notions, as opposed to more "rooted" forms of identification such as "regions" or "nations", seemed to imply a decline of "locality" as a point of reference for collective identities' (Kokot, Tölöyan & Alfonso 2004, 1). Anyuru and some of the migrants mentioned in the text experience multiple belonging. The negative side of this experience is the feeling of homelessness. However, the migrants of the text are not a homogenous group. There is a huge difference between the situation of the immigrants in Sweden, who can go on holiday to their old home-countries, and the African prostitutes and Iranian men with stitched lips in Athens. The vulnerable situation of migrants not protected by citizenship is part of the social reality that the text depicts. The homelessness of these people, and what it means for their lives, is drastically different from the homelessness experienced by the narrator Anyuru, which has the character of an oscillation between feelings of homelessness and not belonging, on the one hand, and being part of communities and social constellations, on the other. In a literal sense, Anyuru has a home in Gothenburg which he will return to. In the same town, he has a father and friends who he will see again. One of the experiences Anyuru has during his journey is that there actually is a place on earth which he feels is his home.

> I want to get home soon. I want to walk under the trees of Linnégatan [a street in Gothenburg]. No, I never want to come home again. I never want to leave this city [Athens]. But I long for home today. I don't know. I long for the people I know, my father, the trees (*E* 102).

This motif is repeated in a later section in which the narrator continues to enumerate things he misses and things he will do when he comes home. 'I will cycle through the night and sit on the bench opposite to *7Eleven* [a store] with all the brothers ['alla brorsorna'], and we will go to the new mosque, perhaps' (*E* 106). This everyday description of what home connotes is one form of exploration of what belonging means. The theme is varied in the conclusion of the text. The final sentences describe how Anyuru is sitting by the sea in Athens before leaving for Sweden and how he is overwhelmed by the sudden insight that this world is the home he shares with the rest of humanity.

> We share this world with one another – I feel it so strongly, suddenly, and then, unexpectedly, something appears that I had not known that I had been missing: the insight that I belong on this planet, that I am a part of the life of this age, that this is my home (*E* 150).

This rather grandiose account of the outcome of the inner and outer journey of the narrator is accompanied by a final sentence about waves hitting rocks, and drawing back to the open sea in a 'white, foaming roar –' (ibid.). The climax, depicting fulfilment through an epiphanic experience of human community and belonging closes the story-line of the text. At this inconclusive end, a number of significant themes, which previously concerned the traveller Anyuru, have not been resolved. It is significant that the text ends with a dash, and not a full stop, making apparent the inconclusive character of the ending. When the text ends, the outer journey has literally come to a halt in the sense that there will be no voyage to Gaza and the people who have gathered in Athens will return to their homes. As the outer journey is interrupted, the end of the inner journey is synchronized to that.

## Broken Words

The African Diaspora and migration both affect the narrator-focalizer's quest for meaning and belonging; there is an oscillation in the book between diaspora and migration as private experiences on the one hand, and as a transnational global reality experienced by large groups of people, on the other. Through the depiction of the sudden insight and experience of belonging at the end, the text stages a gratifying fulfilment of Anyuru's inner quest. This fulfilment implies feeling at home as a socially engaged writer in the process of exploring his own 'Africanness' in a world of migration and diasporas. The traveller Anyuru experiences both homelessness and multiple belongings. This turns out to be a constructive potential on occasions when he manages to reconcile negative and positive aspects of the reality he encounters with visions of community and belonging.

However, the text is ambivalent, an effect achieved through the depiction of the focalizer's oscillations between feelings of lack of meaning, despair and chock, on the one hand, and hope, contentment and belonging, on the other. While this may be described as an oscillation between emotional extremes, the text is also ambivalent through the 'breaks' in its verbal discourse which juxtaposes elements from various traditions and media. Greek graffiti (*E* 39), the Swedish high culture poetry of Göran Sonnevi (*E* 49), and a multi-authored poem (*E* 132–141) are examples of verbal discourses, which constitute a textual movement of broken words.

The depiction of an epiphany and breaking waves at the end is extremely ambivalent and potentially undermining also when considered from the vantage point of a Swedish literary tradition in which literary presentations and perceptions of the sea became a prominent theme in the reception of a stanza of a poem by Göran Palm frequently called 'Havet' [The Sea]. The stanza which is about the lack of an emotional response from a viewer watching the sea is included in the collection *Världen ser dig* [The world sees you] from 1964. The indifference of the viewer depicted by Palm is in stark contrast to classical and modernist representations of the sea as a mythic, symbolic, overwhelming entity, which profoundly affects the human mind and senses. The final two lines of the poem read: 'The sea. So what./ It is like in the Louvre'. Palm's poem was much discussed and analysed in Sweden; anybody the least familiar with contemporary Swedish poetry is likely to associate to it when encountering lyrical depictions of the sea. Does this make Anyuru's depiction ironical? Or, does Anyuru's grand finale with foaming, roaring waves, which accompany an epiphanic experience, exemplify the deployment of a poetical discourse that has become marginalized in contemporary Swedish literature? Or, is it an example of how a poetics of broken words may be activated?

The outer journey described in the text is circular. Anyuru will return to where he started his journey. But the inner journey and the aesthetic experiment of writing a new kind of text have brought about change: 'The person I was when I left will never return home' (*E* 150). The literary text and the development of the protagonist appear as processes shaped by oscillations between incoherent, sometimes contradictory, material. The cultural identity of the protagonist as well as the generic and stylistic 'identity' of the text are hybrid and fickle. In *The Black Atlantic*, Paul Gilroy (1993) discusses the significance of the travels of African-American writers. He re-interprets their work against the background of a trans-Atlantic context, proposing that there is a double consciousness, which involves that the Black Atlantic strives to be both Black and European. This provides a model for cultural hybridity that refutes ethnic absolutism, essentialism and contemporary forms of cultural nationalism involving exclusion and othering of minorities and racialised others.

Anyuru's book about a journey made in 2011 is a Swedish example of a text extending the waves of the Black Atlantic to the Nordic region. The protagonist recognizes that Africa 'speaks' through him, through his ancestry and skin colour. He has chosen to become a practicing Muslim, and he is at home in various social constellations in Sweden and on a transnational arena. Apart from presenting a text combining elements from various stylistic registers and cultural traditions, the text also describes the becoming of a new kind of hybrid cultural identity, which embraces a symbolic Africa as a 'home of the heart' and locus of desire, as well as being a European and Swede. The performative construction of this new European and Swede in writing involves a deconstruction of absolutist and essentialist notions of cultural identity and the European Enlightenment tradition that posited the 'Negro' as standing outside the history of intellectual, technological, moral, and cultural progress 'guided by the Absolute of reason' (cf. Wright 2004, 8). Anyuru's book about the formation of a hybrid, black, Swedish identity transcends the constraints of ethnicity and national particularity. The text juxtaposes sections of writing that enact how styles and modes for artistic representation travel and interact; it depicts the impact of migration and diaspora for both identity formation and aesthetics. The conclusion of this article is that Anyuru's text is both an exploration of the African disporas *and* a form of cross-cultural literary writing, which blends elements from various Swedish literary repertoires and transnational traditions. In order to highlight the blending of elements from national traditions and traditions originating from locations outside the nation, the term 'entangled literatures' has been proposed (Pollari et al. 2015). This is a perspective which is also relevant for the reading of Anyuru's text if the poetics of hybridisation and the transformation of national narrative modes are themes that are studied. Depending upon what theme is in focus, the text represents an exploration of the African diasporas, transnational literatures and/or entangled literatures.

# References

Anyuru, Johannes 2003: *Det är bara gudarna som är nya*. Stockholm: Wahlström & Widstrand.
Anyuru, Johannes 2005: *Omega*. Stockholm: Wahlström & Widstrand.
Anyuru, Johannes 2009: *Städerna inuti Hall*. Stockholm: Norstedts.
Anyuru, Johannes & Motturi, A. 2009: *Förvaret*. Gothenburg: Glänta produktion.
Anyuru, Johannes. 2010: *Skulle jag dö under andra himlar*. Stockholm: Norstedts.
Anyuru, Johannes 2011: *En civilisation utan båtar*. (*E*) Gothenburg: Glänta produktion.
Anyuru, Johannes 2012: *En storm kom från paradiset*. Stockholm: Norstedts.
Anyuru, Johannes 2015: *A Storm Blew in from Paradise*, translated by Rachel Willson-Broyles. London: World Editions Ltd.
Ashcroft, Bill, Griffiths, Gareth, & Tiffin, Helen 2009: *Post-Colonial Studies: The Key Concepts*. London & New York: Routledge.
Ballard, Roger 1996: Islam and the Construction of Europe. *Muslims in the Margin: Political Responses to the Presence of Islam in Western Europe*. Ed. by W.A.R. Shadid. & P.S. van Koningsveld. Kampen: Kok Pharos Publishing House.
Behschnitt, Wolfgang 2010: The Voice of the 'Real Migrant': Contemporary Migration Literature in Sweden. *Migration and Literature in Contemporary Europe*. Ed. by M. Gebauer, & P. Schwarz Lausten. München: Martin Meidenbauer. 77–92.
Bhabha, Homi K. 2008: *The Location of Culture*. London & New York: Routledge.
Berman, Gabrielle & Paradies, Yin 2010: Racism, Disadvantage and Multiculturalism: Towards Effective Anti-Racist Praxis. *Ethnic and Racial Studies*, 33:2. 214–232.
Braziel, Jana Evans E. 2006: Preface: Between Homelands and Homelessness? New Diasporas, Global Refugees. *Diaspora: An Introduction*. Ed. by Jana Evans Braziel. Malden & Oxford: Blackwell Publishing. 1–10.
Crul, Maurice & Schneider, Jens 2010: Comparative Integration Context Theory: Participation and Belonging in New Diverse European Cities. *Ethnic and Racial Studies*, 33:7. 1249–1268.
Delanty, Gerard & Rumford, Chris 2006: *Rethinking Europe: Social Theory and the Implications of Europeanization*. London: Routledge.
Deleuze, Gilles & Guattari, Felix 1987: *A Thousand Plateaus*. Minneapolis: University of Minnesota Press.
Fanon, Frantz 1968: *The Wretched of the Earth*. New York: Grove Press.
Fanon, Frantz 2000: *Black Skin, White Masks*. New York: Grove Press.
Fenton, Steve & May, Stephen 2002: Ethnicity, Nation and 'Race': Connections and Disjunctures. *Ethnonational Identities*. Ed. by Steve Fenton and Stephen May. Houndmills, Basingstoke, New Hampshire & New York: Palgrave Macmillan. 1–20.
Gebauer, Mirjam & Schwartz Lausten, Pia 2010: Migration Literature: Europe in Transition. *Migration and Literature in Contemporary Europe*. Ed. by Mirjam Gebauer & Pia Schwartz Lausten. München: Martin Meidenbauer. 1–8.
Gilroy, Paul 1993: *The Black Atlantic: Modernity and Double Consciousness*. London & New York: Verso.
Gilroy, Paul 1993: 'Not a Story to Pass On': Living Memory and the Slave Sublime. *The Black Atlantic: Modernity and Double Consciousness*. Ed. by Paul Gilroy. London & New York: Verso. 187–223.
Hall, Stuart 1997: Cultural Identity and Diaspora. *Identity and Difference*. Ed. K. Woodward. London, Thousand Oaks & New Delhi: Sage Publications. 51–59.
Hegel, Georg Wilhelm Friedrich 1956: *The Philosophy of History*. New York: Dover.
Heith, Anne 2004: Postkolonialism och poetic. Alejandro Leiva Wengers Till vår ära. In: *Kulturella perspektiv. Svensk etnologisk tidskrift*, nr 2. 2–11.
Heith, Anne 2008: Invandraren – främlingen – negern. Konstruktioner av utanförskap. *Gränser i nordisk litteratur*. Ed. C. Zillliacus, H. Grönstrand & U. Gustafsson. Turku: Åbo Akademi förlag. 623–631.

Heith, Anne 2012: Beyond Hegel and Normative Whiteness: Minorities, Migration and New Swedish Literatures. *Multiethnica* 34. 18–19.
Heith, Anne 2014. Blackness, Religion, Aesthetics: Johannes Anyuru's Literary Explorations of Migration and Diaspora. *Nordlit* 1 (31). 59–70.
Heith, Anne 2016. Displacement and Regeneration: Minorities, Migration and Postcolonial Literature. *Continental Shifts, Shifts in Perception: Black Cultures and Identities in Europe.* Ed. by Sharmilla Beezmohun. Newcastle upon Tyne: Cambridge Scholars Publishing. 49–71.
Hübinette, Tobias et al. 2012: Om ras och vithet i ett samtida Sverige. *Om ras och vithet i ett samtida Sverige.* Ed. by Tobias Hübinette et al. Botkyrka: Mångkulturellt centrum. 41–75.
Kokot, Waltraud, Tölöyan, Khachig & Alfonso, Carolin 2004: Introduction. *Diaspora, Identity and Religion: New Directions in Theory and Research.* Ed, Waltraud Kokot, Khachig Tölöyan & Carolin Alfonso. London & New York: Routledge.
Kourouma, Ahmadou 2002: *Allah gör som han vill* (Orig. *Allah n'est pas obligé*). Stockholm: Bokförlaget Tranan.
Kourouma, Ahmadou 2003: *Den siste Doumbouya* (Orig. *Les soleils des indépendances*). Göteborg: Papamoscas bokförlag.
Mercer, Kobena 2008: Introduction. *Exiles, Diasporas & Strangers.* Ed. Kobena Mercer. London & Cambridge: MA Iniva & The MIT Press.
Merolla, Daniella & Ponzanesi, Sandra 2005 (ed.): *Migrant Cartographies: New Cultural and Literary Spaces in Post-Colonial Europe.* Lanham, Boulder, New York, Toronto & Oxford: Lexington Books.
Morris, R. C. 2010: Introduction. *Can the Subaltern Speak: Reflections on the History of an Idea.* Ed. by R.C. Morris. New York: Columbia University Press.
Månsson, Anna 2000: Möten mellan 'svenskt' och 'muslimskt'. *Att möta främlingar.* Ed. Göran Rystad and Svante Lundberg. Lund: Arkiv förlag. 259–288.
Ntibanyitesha, Sakina 2012: *Ormbarn.* Stockholm: Blue Publishing.
Ntibanyitesha, Sakina 2012: *Farligare än djur.* Stockholm: Blue Publishing.
Okpewho, Isidore 2009: Introduction: Can We 'Go Home Again'? *The New African Diaspora.* Ed. Isidore Okpewho & Nkiru Nzegwu. Bloomington & Indianapolis: Indiana University Press. 3–30.
Papadopoulus, Dimitris, Stephenson, Niamh & Tsianos, Vassilis 2008: *Escape Routes, Control and Subversion in the 21$^{st}$ Century.* London: Pluto Press.
Palm, Göran 1964: *Världen ser dig.* Stockholm: Norstedts.
Pollari, Mikko et al. 2015: National, Transnational and Entangled Literatures: Methodological Considerations Focusing on the Case of Finland. *Rethinking National Literatures and the Literary Canon in Scandinavia.* Ed. by Ann-Sofie Lönngren, Heidi Grönstrand, Dag Heede & Anne Heith. Newcastle upon Tyne: Cambridge Scholars Publishing. 2–29.
Rimmon-Kenan, Shlomith 1999: *Narrative Fiction: Contemporary Poetics.* London & New York: Routledge.
Rystad, Göran & Lundberg, Svante 2000: Förord. *Att möta främlingar.* Ed. by Göran Rystad and Svante Lundberg. Lund: Arkiv förlag. 7–10.
Shadid W.A.R. & van Koningsveld, P.S. 1996: Politics and Islam in Western Europe: An Introduction. *Muslims in the Margin: Political Responses to the Presence of Islam in Western Europe.* Ed. by W.A.R. Shadid. & P.S. van Koningsveld. Kampen: Kok Pharos Publishing House. 1–14.
Spivak, Gayatri Chakravorty 2010: *Can the Subaltern Speak: Reflections on the History of an Idea.* New York: Columbia University Press.
van Houtum, Henk 2012: Remapping Borders. *A Companion to Border Studies.* Ed. by Thomas Wilson & Hastings Donnan. London et al.: Blackwell Publishin Ltd. 405–418.

Walters, Wendy W. 2005: *At Home in Diaspora: Black International Writing.* Minneapolis, MN: University of Minnesota Press

Wright, Michelle M. 2004: *Becoming Black: Creating Identity in the African Diaspora.* Durham & London: Duke University Press.

Yuval-Davis, Nira 2010: Theorizing Identity: Beyond the 'Us' and 'Them' Dichotomy. *Patterns of Prejudice*, 44:3. 261–280.

## Other Sources

'griot.' *The Oxford Dictionary of Literary Terms in Literature*, 'griot', Oxford Reference Online.: http://www.oxfordreference.com/views/SEARCH_RESULTS.html?y=3&q=griot&x=..., 23 Sep. 2012.

Heith, Anne 2012a: Johannes Anyuru: Literary Explorations of Afro-Swedishness. *Encyclopedia of Afro-European Studies.* http://www.encyclopediaofafroeuropeanstudies.eu/encyclopedia/johannes-anyuru/.

in-between. *The Oxford Pocket Dictionary of Current English*, 2009. *Encyclopedia.com*.: http://www.encyclopedia.com, 28 Sep. 2012.

McEachrane, Michael, 2012: Afro-Swedes. *Encyclopedia of Afro-European Studies*,: http://www.encyclopediaofafroeuropeanstudies.eu/encyclopedia/afro-swedes/.

Piety, M. G. 2013: Why 'African-American' is a Patronizing, Even Racist Term. *Counterpunch*, May 2013, http://www.counterpunch.org/2013/05/20/why-african-american-is-a-patronizing-eve... 26 Aug. 2013.

Santarelli, Christopher 2012: Is the Term 'African-American' Accurate in 2012? In: http://www.theblaze.com/stories/2012/02/04/is-the-term-african-american-accurate-in..., 26 Aug. 2012.

Stephens, Ronald J.: Hip-Hop. *Sage Knowledge*, online encyclopedia on black studies: http://knowledge.sagepub.com/view/blackstudies/n137.xml?rskey=FVGNWg&row=1, 23 Sep. 2012.

Pirjo Ahokas
https://orcid.org/0000-0001-6638-4754

# Is Love Thicker Than Blood? A Bi-cultural Identity Process in Astrid Trotzig's *Blod är tjockare än vatten*

*Introduction*

Sweden has not only received a large amount of immigrants and refugees after World War II, but it also has historical and national minorities such as the Sami, the Roma, the Jews, the Tornedalians and the Finnish Swedes. All these groups have contributed to Swedish literature. A significant and far-ranging decision about its immigration was made by Sweden in 1975 in emulation of a new American model of integration. This model was proposed by the Civil Rights Movement and a number of the other American social movements of the 1960s and early 1970s in order to contest the earlier, normative 'melting-pot' assimilationism. In contrast to the previous emphasis on assimilation, the government of Sweden began to promote equality, freedom of choice and co-operation as goals of its immigrant and minority policy (Gröndahl 2007, 23). Subsequently, the official discourse in Sweden has not only supported cultural diversity, but also propagated an emerging image of Sweden as a colour-blind multicultural society. In the meantime, changes have taken place in the composition of the immigrant population in Sweden and therefore also in literature produced by authors of foreign descent. In the 1990s and after the turn of the millennium, new authors whose backgrounds speak of globalization and contemporary migration have come into the limelight. For instance, authors of Kurdish, Iranian and Somali descent have emerged as representatives of diasporic Swedish literatures (Gröndahl 2007, 22). Moreover, it has been argued that a new kind of ethnic minority identity has developed in Sweden in the mid-1990s.

In her analysis of Dogge Doggelito's rapping, The Latin Kings' rap poetry, Jonas Hassen Khemiri's novels, and Josef Fares's films, Corina Lacatus claims that, alongside other artists and writers, they have given artistic form to this new diasporic Swedish identity that is grounded in hybridity.[1]

---

1  As Jonas Hassen Khemiri's open letter to Beatrice Ask, the minister of justice in Sweden, shows, constructions of hybridized identities do not mean that racial discrimination has ended in Sweden. On the contrary, Kherimi suggests that they change bodies for 24 hours, which would help her to understand what it is like to be racially discriminated on the base of one's skin colour. Kauhanen 2013, C 1.

Astrid Trotzig. Photo: Cato Lein. Private collection, Astrid Trotzig.

Thus, the prominent figures she mentions resist the earlier notions of the national identity of Sweden as fixed and homogeneous (Lacatus 2008, 122). Hybridization of identities involves cultural and social negotiations, which undermine whiteness as a sign of privilege by affirming difference in white-dominated societies. A sense of diaspora and displacement also pervades some of the writings representing the tiny but highly intriguing body of literature produced by Korean-born adoptees in Sweden. However, their identity processes are markedly different due to their early separation from their birth mothers and birth nations as well as their subsequent integration into white adoptive families and a white-dominated nation. Furthermore, while the works by the definers of hybridized Swedishness are seen against the backdrop of segregated high-rise immigrant suburbs, David L. Eng contends that transnational adoption from Asia fits within a 'postwar pattern of privileged immigration' (Eng 2003, 10).[2] Nevertheless, as he also points out, simultaneously transnational adoptees suffer from psychic displacement in their new home countries (Eng 2003, 1, 22).

International adoption from Korea to about twenty Western countries started as a rescue operation of orphaned or abandoned children after the end of the Korean War in 1953, and the first adoptees were sent to Sweden in 1957. Since the end of the 1960s, due to a shortage of adoptable white

2   Eng's other examples from the United States are war brides and mail-order brides. Eng 2003, 10–11.

children, worldwide interest in international adoptions grew among both white heterosexual upper- and middle-class couples and single people in the Western countries like Sweden.³ Consequently there are approximately 9000 Korean-born adoptees in Sweden. Proportionally, Sweden is regarded as 'the leading adopting country in the world, and, in absolute numbers, the second only after the United States' (Hübinette 2005a, 77–78).⁴ The first anthology written by Korean-born adoptees is entitled *Seeds from a Silent Tree: An Anthology of Korean American Adoptees* (1997). Its Swedish counterpart, entitled *Hitta hem. Vuxna adopterade från Korea berättar* (2003) was edited by Astrid Trotzig and Sofia Lindström. Both anthologies indicate that Korean adoptees are socialized to identify with their white adoptive parents' whiteness and a dominant white mainstream.

Unlike the artists and authors who are said to construct hybridized Swedish identities in their works, many of the Korean adoptees disidentify with their Koreanness and desire an idealized whiteness. Nevertheless, even if Sweden's self-image is that of the most progressesive, tolerant, antiracist and liberal of all countries (Hübinette 2005b, n. pag.; Hübinette and Lundström 2011, 45), experiences of racialization inescapably draw their attention to their Asian appearance in a white-dominated society. This is why processes of identification with Swedishness can become conflicted and suspended even for Korean adoptees, who might not accept themselves as a minority but who, in spite of it, are seen as a visibly different group in Sweden. The difference in appearance installs traumatic effects and not only can this lead to an emotional cleaving in the adoptive family, but can also exacerbate the psychic dilemmas related to transnational/transracial adoption.⁵ Significantly, racism and racialization undermine the image of contemporary Sweden as a country that supports colour-blind multiculturalism as the official discourse bolstering ethnic diversity.

In this essay, I examine the ambivalent and vexed identity process in Astrid Trotzig's autobiographical work called *Blod är tjockare än vatten* (1996).⁶ Trotzig is a Swedish author and a Korean adoptee. According to her, 'writing is a process of discovering one's history, and a way to heal an identity crisis' (Kim 2002, non pag.).⁷ Although a reading of Trotzig's debut book

---

3 Hübinette2003, 124; cf. Sweden Statistics 2015.
4 For a concise history of adoption in South Korea, see Hübinette 2003, 117–125; see also Hübinette 2005a, 52–80.
5 The terms 'transnational' and 'transracial' are often used interchangeably, but Callahan points out that 'transracial generally connotes the adoption of African American or biracial children by white parents, unless otherwise indicated.' Callahan 2011, 6. Jerng emphasizes that he employs 'these terms as shorthand and sometimes interchangeably for a broader conception that attends to the mutually imbricated relationships among kinship, national belonging, citizenship, race, and religion and not just to questions of race and nationality, respectively.' Jerng 2010, xii.
6 The book has been classified as a biography, but also as fact in 'faktaklassen,' while the author herself has also referred to it as 'my debut novel.' See Duric 2003, 5.
7 Trotzig attributes the success of *Blod är tjockare än vatten* to the fact that the question of identity is something the large population of foreign adoptees in Sweden, as well as by others, can relate to. Kim 2002, non pag.

shows that the title's reference to the importance of blood relations is ironic, the work addresses the psychic and social problems involved in the identity construction of transnational adoptees in contemporary multicultural Sweden. Trotzig's style has been called 'Spartan' (Waern 1996, B 2), and the fragmented narrative of *Blod är tjockare än vatten* consists of short chapters and paragraphs that move between different time levels and are interspersed with official documents and dream sequences. When discussing the medium of written autobiographical testimony and traumatic experience, Suzette Henke points out that 'prevalent notions about literature and psychoanalysis began to change radically in the early 1990s' (xiii). Trotzig's book from the mid-1990s is not only suggestive of postmodern and postcolonial writing, but also of trauma narratives and trauma fiction, which flourished in the 1980s and 1990s and are also characterized by the fragmentation of narrative and identity (Vickroy 2002, 2, xi). Moreover, *Blod är tjockare än vatten* can be regarded as representing the genre of women's life writing,[8] because it reassesses the past when attempting to fashion an enabling discourse from a traumatic experience that generates psychic fragmentation, which is mirrored in the fragmented form of the book.[9] When taking the readers through a process of working through trauma, Trotzig's book not only implies a personal and communal healing process, but it also serves an important function of revealing repressive socio-political ideologies.

In spite of their significance, *Blod är tjockare än vatten* and other writings by Korean adoptees in Sweden have not received much critical attention to date, and therefore I find it useful to turn to Asian American literary studies for a theoretical framework of my study. This academic field grew out of the social and political movements of the 1960s and the 1970s, and it is still a rapidly developing area of scholarly inquiry. Importantly, it also offers new critical tools for the study of representations of Korean adoptees and their identity formation. At the turn of the 21$^{st}$ century, there was a discernible shift in Asian American studies from nationalism to transnationalism and diasporic identity constructions as well as psychonanalytic criticism (Li 2003, 613). In her pioneering book entitled *The Melancholy of Race*, Anne Anlin Cheng used psychoanalytic tools to scrutinize a melancholic construction she calls 'racial melancholia' in the American context. She characterizes racial melancholia in the following way: 'it has always existed for raced subjects as a *sign* of rejection and as a psychic *strategy* in response to that rejection' (Cheng 2001, 20). Subsequently, literature scholar David L. Eng and Shinhee Han, a New York based psychotherapist, have elaborated

---

8  The term life-writing has been attributed to feminist critics such as Shari Benstock. It has been proposed in order to challenge the traditional limits of autobiography. Suzette A. Henke has defined the genre life-writing 'broadly, and sometimes metaphorically, to include confessional forms, autofictions, diaries, journals, and the bildungsroman, as well as autobiography and biomythography.' Henke 2000, xii, xvi.

9  At the Symposium on Literature and Translation organized by the Korea Literature Translation Institute in Seoul in 2002, Trotzig stated: 'I do not believe that my authorship started with the trauma of being adopted, although my first book dealt with this subject.' Kim 2002, non pag.

the concepts of 'racial melancholia' and 'racial reparation' in the context of transnational adoption.

In contrast to Freud's initial formulation of melancholia as a pathological psychic condition, Eng describes a largely unconscious and intrasubjective racial melancholia as 'a psychic process by which vexed identification and affiliations with lost objects, places, and ideals of both Asianness *and* whiteness remain estranged and unresolved' (Eng 2003, 17; emphasis in the original). In Eng and Han's estimation, racial melancholia also differs from Freud's separation between 'mourning *or* melancholia,' because it involves 'negotiations between mourning *and* melancholia' (Eng and Han 2006, 154). Their theoretical framework is also informed by Melanie Klein's psychoanalytic thinking about the earliest infantile development, which they modify for their studies of the affective problems of transnational adoptees. In addition to Eng and Han's two co-authored articles, one of which is on the case history of a Korean transnational adoptee, a ballet dancer called Mina, Eng has applied their notion of racial melancholia in his analysis of Deann Borshay Liem's documentary film entitled *First Person Plural* (2000). It recounts the American filmmaker's own story as an adoptee from South Korea. I will employ Eng and Han's theoretical insights into Korean adoptees' psychic predicaments in their new home countries, but apply them on a literary text, Trotzig's *Blod är tjockare än vatten*. I will also draw briefly on Cheng's work on the psychic implications of discrimination on the identity formation of racialized others.

According to Mark C. Jergn, adoption stories began to emerge as a recognizable genre in the 1970s, but stories that centre on transracial adoptees are more recent (Jergn 2010, 170). In his book, Jerng explores the subject of transnational/transracial adoption and its centrality to issues of race and nationality. Like Eng and Han, he pays attention to the collective and communal nature of individual identity formation in transnational/transracial adoption stories. In addition to Eng and Han's work, I find studies of trauma fiction, as well as Jergn's work on the different models of narrating transnational/transracial adoption, helpful when examining Trotzig's representation of the processes of identification and identity formation in *Blod är tjockare än vatten*.

## *From South Korea to the Kingdom of Sweden*

Adoption narratives have been linked to trauma by adoption scholars, who point out that infant abandonment 'is not only like trauma (an unremembered yet life-altering event): it has itself been called a form of trauma' (Homans 2006, 4). As Jergn points out, birth and lineage often play an implicit role in the way in which important social categories such as nation, family and race are constituted (Jergn 2010, x). In the introductory chapter, Trotzig's narrator emphasizes that even if a sense of being an outsider and a search for identity are universal ('allmänmänskligt') experiences, she has no answers to questions such as: 'Vem är jag' [Who am I?] (Trotzig 1996, 7–8). The reason is a lack of any information about her biological parents in South Korea.

This is why other painful questions pertaining to the complexities of identity formation also remain unanswered. Similar to many other transnational adoptees, a sense of being an outsider haunts Trotzig into adulthood.

Some of the problems connected with post-war adoption from South Korea derive from ancient Korean history and the tradition of agnatic adoption. This meant that legislation only allowed patrilineal male relatives of a younger generation to be adopted (Kim 2010, 33). Thus the purpose of adoption used to secure a male heir in ancient Korea (Hübinette 2005a, 44). According to Eleana J. Kim, due to this practice, women's value became totally dependent upon their ability to bear sons for their husband's lineage (Kim 2010, 38). Moreover, this tradition explains even the currently common belief that the traditional Korean family is based on blood ties, even though recent social changes have lessened the social stigma of adoption (Kim 2010, 30. 31). Initially, post-war adoptions from Korea were motivated by an urge to rescue homeless mixed-race children, the offspring of UN soldiers and Korean women, who were stigmatized by the patriarchal Korean society. In the 1960s, the mixed-race children were replaced by full Korean children, mostly girls due to the local preference for boys. These children were often born to young female factory workers and abandoned during the brutal transformation of South Korea into an industrial country (Hübinette 2003, 119, 120). However, since the end of the 1960s, increasing numbers of babies born to young unmarried mothers of middle-class backgrounds were also given up for adoption in order avoid social stigmatization. South Korea's practice of overseas adoption has been criticized throughout its history, and a special agency for domestic adoption was created as early as 1962.[10] Nevertheless, overseas adoptions to countries like Sweden still continue.

In the meantime, as Eng propounds, the position of a parent has become 'the primary contemporary measure of social respectability and value' in the Western world (Eng 2003, 7–8). This is why he claims that childless couples are willing to adopt in order to form the biologized ideal of the nuclear family.[11] To return to *Blod är tjockare än vatten*, the Trotzigs already had two Korean-born adoptees, when they applied for a third child from South Korea in 1969. It appears from the beginning of Astrid Trotzig's book that, in retrospect, the narrator experiences her identification with the new adoptive family as problematic even when she remembers her earliest childhood. Subsequently, she is disturbed to find out that she did not correspond to the ideal Korean child the adopting family had in mind, when they filed their third adoption application. The parents had asked for a boy between the ages

---

10  Instead of helping single mothers outside of marriage to keep their babies, adoption rights in South Korean internal adoptions have been extended to 'never-married, divorced, or widowed individuals.' Kim calls the privileged single women for whom unwed motherhood has become a choice through adoption 'the neoliberal doublegangers' of the single birth mothers, who are not able to raise their own children in the face of social stigma and inadequate financial support. Kim 2010, 34, 37, 38.

11  Transnational adoption was the main response to involuntary childlessness in Sweden until the coming of assisted reproductive technologies as a new mode of family formation. Gondouin 2012, 2.

of three and five, but they were offered a baby girl for acceptance. Moreover, the family was contacted by the South Korean adoption agency called Child Placement Service prior to receiving a letter with her social study. The agency inquired, whether the family would be willing to adopt immediately a boy whose prospective Swedish adoptive parents had not wanted him. The narrator also hears about a family friend who turns down an adoptive baby whose hearing is not perfect. This and the fact that the comments on an adoptable baby in her Swedish siblings' social studies resemble those in hers make Trotzig wonder about the arbitrariness of the entire adoption process. This reinforces her sense of abandonment and alienation.

In the 1980s, critical voices were raised against the adoption programme, and South Korea was accused of selling its own children (Hübinette 2005a, 85, 86). In his article on Liem's *First Person Plural,* Eng underlines the commodification of helpless transnational adoptees (Eng 2003, 8–9). When looking at the letter from the South Korean adoption agency, Trotzig appears to be annoyed to see that the agency promises to speed up her delivery on the condition that the family pays the adoption processing cost at their earliest convenience. In retrospect, she also compares the price of her adoption with the corresponding price in the mid-1990s, stressing the vast discrepancy by placing the sums on opposite pages of her book. Moreover, the narrator regrets that, in addition to a couple of photos, the only objects she has from South Korea are the playsuit that she was wearing as a baby on the flight to Stockholm and a silk bag all adoptive children were given before their departure from South Korea. Self-evidently Trotzig has no conscious memories from South Korea. Korean history and culture are mentioned only in connection with her attempt to write an essay about them in middle school. Looking into the historical contexts of transnational adoptions, Eng claims that generalized narratives attached to transnational adoption often displace and erase global and local histories by contracting them into the privatized space of the reconstituted adoptive family. Thus, the particular histories of the adoptees' past 'are denied, repressed, and effaced' (Eng 2003, 9, 14). This is also the case in the Swedish adoptive family in the privatized space in which Trotzig's identity is initially constructed.

Like other trauma narratives, *Blod är tjockare än vatten* begins by resisting normal chronological narration by harking back from adulthood to Trotzig's life as an infant and a child. She was brought from Seoul to Sweden as a five-month old baby in June 1970, which makes her into one of the 3 400 Korean-born adoptees who arrived in Sweden in the years 1967–1974.[12] Indeed, the 1970s was a decade when adoption flourished in Sweden and when it was also considered as an act of solidarity with the so-called third world (Gondouin 2012, 9). As Jerng points out, in a sense, adoption assumes that the adopted person changes identity: 'they will take on a new name, become part of a new family and sometimes a new country' (Jergn 2010, vii-viii). A good example of the fragmentary nature of Trotzig's writing is that she has placed a transcript of her social study from South Korea by itself right after her short introduction to the book: she was born as Suh-Yeo

---

12  Quoted in Hübinette 2005a, 69.

Park in an unknown place in January 1970 and was found abandoned in the city of Pusan (Busan) in South Korea.[13] As Trotzig indicates in a subsequent fragment, even the date of her birth is shrouded in obscurity, because the permission to travel to 'The Kingdom of Sweden,' signed by the South Korean minister of foreign affairs, has a different date from the other official documents. Indeed, as the narrator-protagonist underscores, the baby Suh-Yeo not only travels to 'en annan värld' [a different world] (Trotzig 1996, 29), but, like her Korean-born Swedish siblings, she is also given a new name. Significantly, Astrid, a popular name in Scandinavia, is of Old Norse origin and means 'fair, beautiful goddess.' This first name marks Suh-Yeo's new Swedish identity. Names can be powerful sites of identification, but for the narrator as a child, her Korean and Swedish names signify the problem of her divided cultural identity. She reads the Korean name as a painful reminder of her biological origin and regards it as ugly. Yet, she would like to erase her other names, too. For her, her then old-fashioned Swedish first name does not connote a shared Scandinavian historical heritage, but, is the name of somebody else's grandmother.

Referring to Asian American immigrant parents and their children, Eng and Han argue that they 'negotiate problems of immigration, assimilation, and racialization as *intergenerational* and *intersubjective* conflicts' (Eng and Han 2006, 142: emphasis in the original). In contrast, the transnational adoptee has to struggle with similar issues in social and psychic isolation.[14] According to Melanie Klein, the process of an infant's loss of, and separation from, the mother begins around the age of four to five months (Eng 2010, 152), exactly at the age when Trotzig leaves Korea as a baby. Like the Korean-born ballet dancer, Mina, in Eng and Han's case study, Trotzig mourns the loss of her birth mother and motherland, even if the past prior to her arrival in Sweden becomes repressed after her childhood.[15] While Mina and Liem try to create psychic space for two mothers, Trotzig originally struggles with three mothers: her unknown birth mother, her Korean foster mother with whom she lived during her first five months, and the Swedish mother. Even if the processes of splitting, projection and introjection around the maternal figure cannot be characterized as extreme in *Blod är tjockare än vatten* as in Mina's case study,[16] little Astrid misses the birth mother. However, like the two American adoptees, she finds it very difficult to accept that she has been abandoned by her birth mother. Indeed, in her childhood fantasies Trotzig's narrator sometimes wishes that her birth mother had died when giving birth to her. Even this thought is so painful that she revises it into a paradoxical wish-fulfillment: 'Jag vill inte att hon ska vara död, men inte heller att hon skall leva' [I neither want her to be dead, nor to be alive] (Trotzig 1996, 41). Like in the case of the two other melancholic adoptees, Trotzig's refusal to relinquish the lost birth mother indicates that she continues to live on unconsciously in the psychic realm.

---

13 See Trotzig 1996, 9–11.
14 Cf. Eng and Han 2006, 142.
15 Cf. Eng and Han 2006, 142–43.
16 Cf. Eng and Han 2006, 160.

Trotzig's narrative is not only punctuated by the adult narrator's comments on her present life, but also by her reminiscences of her early attempts to solve the conflicted situation with the help of imagination. Even if the word 'invandrare' [immigrant] has negative connotations in Swedish, Trotzig's memories are consonant with Eng and Han's observation about first generation immigrant Asian parents and their children, when she remembers how she wished that she was 'en "riktig" invandrare' [a 'real' immigrant], a Korean child who shares a new country with her Korean family (Trotzig 1996, 49).[17] Another wish is that she had been adopted by an Asian family and had grown up believing that she was the family's biological child. Like many other adoptive parents of Korean-born children, the Trotzigs do not appear to have any contact with South Korea other than their children, who were brought to them at the airport in Stockholm by their Korean escort women. Subsequently, the Trotzigs were particular about persuading their children to be proud of their having been adopted and convincing them that they should not feel different in Sweden.

Eng and Han point out that white adoptive parents do not necessarily identify with their Asian adoptees' Asianness but are devoted to denying their racialized difference (Eng and Han 2006, 156; Homans 2011, 187). In their case study, the adult Mina's de-idealizing her adoptive mother appears to stem from the fact that she has not exposed her to anything Korean (Eng and Han 2006, 150). This is connected with the adoptive parents' failure to recognize their Asian-born adoptees or themselves as racialized subjects. This failure is also the reason why adoptive parents do not easily understand that transnational/transracial adoption involves loss, and that they also fail to understand the symptoms of racial melancholia.[18] Their behavior is in agreement with the so called 'clean break' principles, which prevailed in the adoption discourse of the 1960s, 1970s and 1980s. According to this line of thinking successful adoption requires forgetting the child's past and aiding her full assimilation into the new country (Homans 2011, 186).

In general, the Trotzigs seem to keep their adoptees away from everything related to their Korean background. The only exception is the Korean flag, which the parents give their youngest child, Astrid, when the older siblings move out. The parents have received the flag, an obvious symbol of their adoptees' country of birth, at a meeting for adoptive parents. Although they remain curiously silent about the purpose of their present, the child-narrator surmises that they may have meant her to take pride in it. Not surprisingly, she resents the present and throws it away claiming that without her knowing the language and the national codes of Korea the flag has no meaning to her. The other rationalization for rejecting the flag is that she does not want to be reminded of the strange country on the other side of the globe. In her early teens, Trotzig represses her adoption history and decides to keep identifying with her white Swedish parents and Sweden as her home country: 'Jag var

17 In an article published in 2005, Trotzig opposes to being regarded as an 'invandrare,' and also claims that she has nothing to do with the so-called 'invandrarlitterature' [immigrant literature]. Trotzig 2005, 106.
18 Cf. Eng 2010, 122.

svensk. Punkt.' [I was Swedish and that's it.] (Trotzig 1996, 54). Indeed, Western colour-blind multiculturalism supports the idea that one is free to choose one's ethnic identity. However, as Lacatus notes, migratory identity formation processes require constant negotiations, and once people are subsumed under certain ethnic categories in a dominant society, there is little room left for the exercising of free will (Lacatus 2008, 2, 3). Not even the protagonist of *Blod är tjockare än vatten* is saved from this fate.

Historically race has been used as a means of ranking a range of people labelled as others, 'naturally' inferior in contexts, in which normative whiteness has been associated with superiority and racial dominance. For obvious reasons the term has been shunned in the West since World War II. This is also true about Sweden, the world's first country to establish a government-sponsored institute for racial research, focused on racial hygiene. The currently notorious State Institute for Racial Biology was founded in 1922 and operated until the 1950s, when it was integrated into Uppsala University.[19] Even if 'race' has been understood as a social construction in cultural and literary studies since the late 1980s,[20] it does not mean that racism and racialization have vanished from Western multicultural countries. People from East Asia are rarely objects of discrimination in contemporary Sweden,[21] yet Trotzig's narrative offers ample evidence of the fact that the physical appearance plays a crucial role in defining the other and in orientalizing Asians even there. In the past decades, social constructionist analyses of race and whiteness have been undertaken in order to interrogate whiteness as a site of racializing and racialized privilege. Such an analysis also regards other relations such as gender, sexuality, class and nation which intersect with constructions and representations of race. In my reading of *Blod är tjockare än vatten*, I perceive these other categories as inextricably tied to the constructedness of race.

## *The White Ideal and Racist Stereotyping*

Ethnic and racial stereotyping is part of the maintenance of the social and symbolic order, as it sets up a symbolic frontier 'between "insiders" and "outsiders", Us and Them' (Hall 1997, 258). Even if fighting against different forms of discrimination can be seen as a one of the foremost challenges of a multicultural society (Roth 2008, 22), there exists a hierarchical difference between ethnic Swedes and non-ethnic Swedes or immigrants even in

---

19 The institute served as a model for the corresponding Kaiser Wilhelm Institute founded in Germany in 1927. For the activities of the institute, see Björkman and Widmalm 2010, passim.
20 Samina Najmi and Rajini Srikanth name two books in which a social constructionist approach to race gained ground in 1986. They are Michael Omi and Howard Winant's *Racial Formation in the United States* and *"Race," Writing and Difference*, edited by Henry Louis Gates. Najmi and Srikanth 2002, 7.
21 In addition to East Asians, Lacatus includes people moving to Sweden from the other Scandinavian and West European countries and North America in this group. Lacatus 2008, 13.

contemporary multicultural Sweden.[22] Trotzig's memoir keeps returning to the loss of the birth mother and the crucial moments of her racialization in Sweden. In Klein's theory, the early stage of infantile psychic development involves the creation of two internalized images: good (gratifying) and bad (frustrating) objects, or the 'good mother' and the threatening 'bad mother' (Eng and Han 2006, 158; Klein 1986, 116, 176–178). As in Eng and Han's case study of the South Korean adoptee Mina, the two mother figures are racialized in Trotzig's narrative and subsequently, 'good and bad objects become racially segregated into "white" and "Korean" ' (Eng and Han 2006, 160).

Perceptively, Trotzig alerts the reader to visible differences as early as in her depiction of her arrival as a baby in Sweden: 'Plötsligt är jag här. I Sverige. I detta land bland långa blonda.' [Suddenly I am here. In Sweden. In this country among the tall blond people.] (Trotzig 1996, 30). Associating differences in appearance within primal fantasies of infantile development, this quotation underlines whiteness as the unchallenged national norm: Swedishness denotes whiteness. Time and again, the grown narrator hears flattering comments on her exotic looks, but she reminds herself of the fact that the white ideal also equals the Western standards of beauty: 'Men det västerländska skönhetsidealet är en vit kvinna.' [The Western ideal of beauty is a white woman.] (Trotzig 1996, 91). Mina's problems with interpersonal relationships and her adoption issues make her seek Han's psychotherapy. From the very beginning of their work together Mina argues: 'I'm American! I have an Asian face but I'm white! My parents are white, and I grew up in a white suburb, and I feel most comfortable around white people' (Eng and Han 2006, 149). In a similar fashion, Trotzig's protagonist represses the lost birth mother and motherland. Just like Mina, she wants to emulate the white ideal: 'Jag ville vara som alla andra. Blond och svensk.' [I wanted to be like everybody else. Blond and Swedish.] (Trotzig 1996, 75). Simultaneously, however, her physical appearance continues to be a significant marker of racial difference in Sweden.

One of the terms used in Sweden to differentiate between 'us and them' is the previously mentioned word 'invandrare' [immigrant], which has been manipulated for diverse discriminating purposes to indicate that some of the immigrant groups are foreigners to a higher degree than some others (Roth 2008, 29). In her depiction of a school scene, Trotzig observes how her classmates use derogatory words such as 'blattar' and 'svartskallar' [black heads] about immigrants to Sweden. In her study, Lacatus points out that the Swedish word 'blatte' is a concept that is used interchangeably with 'black head' and 'immigrant' (Lacatus 2008, 11). While black head initially referred to South European immigrant labourers to Sweden, 'blatte' is employed as a similar marker of social and cultural otherness (Lacatus 2008, 10–11). According to Lacatus, the currently more popular term blatte refers to immigrants from 'the Middle East, Eastern Europe and Eurasia, Africa, and South America,' whose 'skin or/and hair color' sets them apart from the white majority or what Lacatus calls 'heritage Swedes' (Lacatus 2008, 13, 14). Even if the self-

---

22  Cf. Lacatus 2008, 1, 9.

referential use of both black head and blatte has been employed in the sense of 'the affirmation of immigrant identity grounded in ethnic pride' since the mid-1990s, the words are not only linked to the discourses of ethnicity and race, but also to a working class background (Lacatus 2008, 11, 19). In contrast to fairly recent immigrants, the Trotzigs are an old Swedish family of German ancestry, and thus the adoptive family's class status separates Trotzig from non-heritage Swedes.[23] In school, too, the narrator is told by her class mates that she is not an immigrant but an adopted child, and that is why she is saved from the worst forms of school bullying. However, when she is alone, she also becomes a target of racist remarks and is always afraid because of her different looks.

As a child other children call Trotzig 'tjing tjong eller något liknande' [tjing tjong or something like it] (Trotzig 1996, 59). Later on both children and adults look at her condescendingly and, according to her, they cannot help saying or even screaming that she should go back to China. Each racist encounter with 'ordinary Swedes' that links the narrator with Asia shocks and depresses her. These incidents exasperate her racial melancholia and lead to attempts at effacing her Koreanness. When she is a young adult the racist remarks become gender-specific and rudely sexist. Skin colour is mentioned as one of the differences between Korean adoptees and heritage Swedes, yet, the few episodes in which Trotzig's narrative touches upon the fate of black people in Sweden ruthlessly reveal their place on the lowest rung of the racial hierarchy.

Linear time is constantly broken as Trotzig's narration intersperses childhood memories with episodes from the narrative present. If anxieties of persecution increase her doubts of ever fully belonging in Sweden, a shocking instance of being subjected to a racist gaze occurs in an episode that describes the adult narrator on a ferry trip in Greece. It is evocative of the opening lines of Frantz Fanon's famous essay 'The fact of blackness,' because the perpetuator of virulent racism is a child in each text. While the traumatizing opening words 'Dirty nigger!' or 'Look, a Negro' are attributed to a young French boy in Fanon's essay (Fanon 1986, 109), Trotzig's narrator encounters a little Greek girl. She keeps pulling the corners of her eyes in order to imitate the narrator's eyes with an epicanthic fold. While the racist words keep ringing in Fanon's ears throughout the essay, the little girl follows the narrator and her female friend to the different parts of the ferry always stopping by the narrator's side talking, smiling and giggling at her. As the Greek friend leads Trotzig away from the girl, she in tacit consent does not want her to translate the girl's words.

Another key episode in Trotzig's fragmented narrative points to the intra-ethnic dimensions of internalized racism. It takes place in a kindergarten

---

23 Astrid Trotzig explains that the family history of the Trotzigs can be traced to the 16th century. The family ancestor moved from Germany to Sweden; his picture is at the top of the family tree in the possession of her paternal grandmother. A narrow street in the Old Town of Stockholm has been named after Mårten Trotzig, the ancestor. Every time the author passes by the street she thinks: 'Detta är mina svenska rötter' [These are my Swedish roots]. See Trotzig 1998, 85–86.

between the child-narrator and another adopted girl called Mi. This cruel scene is reminiscent of a traumatic encounter between two Chinese American girls in the school lavatory in Maxine Hong Kingston's famous autobiographical work *The Woman Warrior* (1976). This episode has attracted critical attention in terms of Asian American ego formation. In Kingston's book the Chinese American protagonist attacks and torments a quiet classmate, whereas the roles are reversed in *Blod är tjockare än vatten*. Mi is often mean to the narrator and even goes as far as to scratch her face. According to Cheng, the episode in Kingston's book 'signals a moment of disidentification predicated on identification' (Cheng 2001, 75). She suggests that, in this scene, Kingston attempts to theorize 'the constitutive racial element *at work* in the interplay of projection and introjection' (Cheng 2001, 76: emphasis in the original). To begin with Trotzig's narrator claims that she does not know why Mi's aggression is directed towards her, thinking that there should be a bond of solidarity between them. However, her insight into their similarity is consonant with Cheng's reading of the school lavatory scene. Indeed, the narrator surmises that Mi dislikes her, because she reminds her of the fact that they are both adopted. While this may imply that Mi is also an Asian adoptee, the narrator's insight is in agreement with Cheng's assessment of the incident in Kingston's book. Cheng points out that 'the aggression is being performed by someone repeating her own trauma in the form of persecution' (Cheng 2001, 75). Mi's abusing of the narrator allows her to identify with whiteness, but at the same time as she is also reproducing her own traumatic experiences.

Eng and Han observe in their case study of Mina that her psychological difficulties, diagnosed as symptoms of unconscious racial melancholia, are connected with her negative feelings toward Korea, Koreans and Korean adoptees, in particular (Eng and Han 2006, 144, 148, 149, 163, 169). Mina has a younger brother, also adopted from Korea, whom she describes as an 'easy going kid': according to her, he is troubled by neither his adoption nor his Koreanness (Eng and Han 2006, 145). The older brother of the protagonist of *Blod är tjockare än vatten* has been one of the first adoptees from Korea to Sweden. Even if she is jealous of his memories from his birth family and South Korea, she empathizes with his numerous difficulties on his arrival in Sweden as a little boy at the age of three and a half. Surrounded solely by Swedish-speaking white Swedes, he is said to have not allowed his new parents to remove a name tag hung around his neck and he also held tight a bunch of papers. Moreover, unlike Mina, who devalues her Korean class mates at the dance school and also looks down on other Korean adoptees, the protagonist of Trotzig's book maintains a degree of sympathetic identification with other Asians. For instance, she misses a 'real' Korean sister, and in the subway she identifies with a little Asian-looking girl, a look-alike of her younger self, since the appearance of her parents makes it clear that the girl is adopted. She goes on to imagine that they are biological sisters who must belong to the same family 'någonstans' [somewhere]. Unlike Mina, the adult protagonist also reports pleasurable experiences not only with other Asian-looking people, but also with other immigrants to Sweden.

Eng and Han link Mina's psychic strategies of splitting and idealization to her effort to unconsciously preserve a space of goodness for the Korean mother and link this to her gradual move toward a reparative position for race (Eng and Han 2006, 161). In Trotzig's book, Astrid's healing process also involves the desegregation of the racialized mothers. Furthermore, an important sign of the protagonist's beginning to come to terms with the difference is her relationship to her older adoptive sister. They share a similar past, but Astrid calls her 'tuffa syster' [cool sister], who does not want to discuss adoption issues with her (Trotzig 1996, 101). However, as an episode from the summer of 1993 proves, the adult narrator is empowered by her cool Swedish sister, because she helps her to understand that they can resist racism. When the family by accident finds itself in the middle of an outdoor meeting of the Sweden Democrats, a populist anti-immigrant party, the mother is frightened and wishes them to leave, but the adoptive daughters insist that they do not want to hide. 'Tillsammans med tuffa syster blir jag stark, men inom mig är jag lika rädd som mamma.' [Together with my cool sister I become strong, but inside I am as frightened as mother.] (70), concludes the protagonist about her divided feelings.

Undoubtedly, the existence of a party like the Sweden Democrats contradicts the ideology of colour-blindness. It is also contradicted on the other side of the national borders of Sweden. The adult narrator's story about her trip to Denmark together with her beloved ['min älskade'] once again confirms her doubts about the self-evidence of her national belonging. Nordic citizens are allowed to cross the borders of the Nordic countries without a passport, but as soon as the ferry from Sweden arrives in Copenhagen passengers who do not look Nordic, i.e. are not white, are asked to come to the passport control. The narrator's claim to her Swedish citizenship does not mean anything until the Nordic-looking beloved explains that they travel together. On the way back she is the only passenger in their train compartment who looks different from the rest. Consequently, she is the only one who is asked to explain what she has been doing in Copenhagen for three days.

The encounters with white people who take recourse to racist stereotypes in order to maintain their white privilege, both in Sweden and abroad, urge the narrator to flee into huge crowds of people where she can hide from the gaze of the dominant culture. However, narratives of transnational adoption also involve intersubjective processes such as identification. A visit to the Asian quarter of London provides signs of the adult narrator's gradual move toward a reparative position for Asianness. She has previously admitted to herself that it is as impossible to wash away the colour of one's skin as it is to remove the stripes from a zebra. A bond of identification arises between her and a Japanese green grocer when the man addresses her in Japanese. Suddenly the protagonist, not only wishes that she could answer in Japanese, but also that she could speak the language of her birth country. This productive train of thought leads her to think how much more she should actually know about Korea.

According to Freud, ambivalence is the psychic mark of melancholia (Freud 1957, 258). The narrator calls Sweden her 'hem-land' [home-country]

(70). However, in spite of her disidentification with South Korea, she admits that there is another country inside her and that she misses it. Jergn argues that the desire for returning to one's roots has become a narrative 'through which transracial and transnational adoptees have gained legibility and articulated their claims' (Jergn 2010, 129). The episode in London appears to be the turning point in Trotzig's relationship to her birth country. It is there that she concludes: 'Borde resa dit. Till Sydkorea.' [Should travel there. To South Korea.] (Trotzig 1996, 120). Historically, the signing of the Hague Convention[24] in 1993 was a milestone in the discourse of contemporary transnational adoption. The convention insisted on a transnational adoptee's full membership in the adoptive family, but it also stressed the transplanted children's right to support in the formation of a culturally rooted identity (Homans 2011, 186). Although Trotzig's adoptive siblings do not have a similar need to explore their erased Koreanness, she becomes one of the thousands of young-adult Korean adoptees who grapple with their divided identity in their birth country, when her plane descends in Seoul on June 22nd, 1995.

## A Foreigner in the Birth Country

The birth mother and motherland are not only linked to the search and reunion narratives, which Jergn regards as the dominant form of adoption narratives, but also to roots trips and return narratives. The first generation of adult Korean adoptees began to visit their birth country as early as the mid-1970s. They travelled there as individuals or took part in tours organized by friendship associations and adoption agencies (Hübinette 2005a, 89). One of the adoption agencies arranging these visits is the Adoption Center of Sweden, a voluntary non-profit adoption organization authorized by the state of Sweden. Founded in 1969, it launched its first 'Motherland Tour' in 1983. The so called roots trips are organized for adoptive parents and their adopted children, who return to the site of adoption in order to construct 'a narrative of origin and beginnings' (Jerng 2010, 171). Some of these trips are generated as part of the adoption rights movement with the intention of looking for the adoptees' biological parents. Subsequently, several native Korean organizations have been involved in setting up visiting programmes. All the visiting programmes include field trips to important national sites, a Korean language course, the tea ceremony, and other practices deemed to be genuine Korean traditions (Hübinette 2005a, 91). While the purpose of the visiting programmes 'with the best of intentions is to produce domestic Koreans out of Westernised adoptees' (Hübinette 2005a, 91, 92–93), the Korean media attention has focused almost exclusively on successful adoptees as 'model citizens' since the mid-1990s (Hübinette 2005a, 91, 92–93). The adopted Koreans were also presented as a unique bond between Korea and the West in the apology president Kim Dae Jung delivered in the

---

24 The full term is the Hague Convention on Protection of Children and Co-operation in Respect of Intercountry Adoption.

presence of officially invited adopted Koreans in Seoul on October 23, 1998 (Hübinette 2005a, 97–99).

The previously mentioned anthology entitled *Hitta hem* includes writings by members of the first generation of Korean adoptees in Sweden. The explicit aim of the anthology is to offer inspiration and support to a younger generation of transnational adoptees and other young people with a foreign background (Lindström and Trotzig 2003, 8). While Jergn criticizes the American anthology *Seeds from a Silent Tree* for its tendency to rely 'on imagining one's birthplace as a kind of originary relation that needs to be negotiated at some level' (Jergn 2010, 189), the editors of *Hitta hem* stress that their ambition is not to put forward any kind of absolute truth about how to be a transnational adoptee (Lindström and Trotzig 2003, 8). Consequently, some of the contributors to the Swedish anthology show no signs of an urgent need to visit Korea, whereas others join the so-called motherland tours, decide to study in Korea or visit the country on their own. Trotzig is the first member of her Swedish family to travel to South Korea: she flies there at the age of twenty-five. Unlike Borshay Liem, who attempted to solve her emotional cleaving through a long-anticipated 'reunion' with her two mothers (Eng 2003, 26), Trotzig, in spite of her contacting NIA (Myndigheten för internationalla adoptionsfrågor) and the Adoption Center as part of her preparations for the trip, eventually turns down even the Center's suggestion to have a contact person in Seoul. The only other person with the baby Suh-Yeo, in a picture taken in Korea, is the foster mother. The Adoption Center had previously told Trotzig that she is unlikely to find any more information about her birth parents even if she were to contact the police station in Pusan, because the local authorities destroy the police reports every few years. The purpose of the trip, which the narrator hesitates to call a return trip, is to see the strange country where she was born and to visit the city of her birth in particular.

Throughout *Blod är tjockare än vatten,* it is clear that the Trotzigs are caring and supportive parents. The mother is obviously aware of her youngest daughter's inner suffering, because she remarks upon hearing about her planning a trip to South Korea: 'Du är på väg att hitta nyckeln' [You are on your way to find the key] (Trotzig 1996, 144). The narrator's irritated reaction reveals that even if she also anticipates that the trip is likely to bring her closer to 'ett jag, en identitet' [an I, an identity] (Trotzig 1996, 144), she is not expecting an immediate transformation. It is also important to notice that the trajectory of her narrative about the trip deviates somewhat from the teleological narratives Jergn outlines as the dominant form of narrating adoption. Significantly, repetitive reappearances of traumatic experiences not only mark the inner lives of traumatized individuals, but repetition also marks trauma narratives as a stylistic device. As Trotzig's book progresses to the trip to Korea, the flashbacks to her past almost disappear and the temporal succession assumes linear chronology, which is punctuated by the narrator's dream sequences in South Korea. The protagonist and the man she calls my beloved have signed a contract on a new apartment before she leaves Stockholm, and the new home figures in several of her dreams during the trip. The dreams seem to be related to the narrator's search for identity:

in the first dream, the new house lies in the middle of Seoul, whereas it has moved to the suburb where she used to live as a child in the next one. The last dream occurs towards the end of the trip to Pusan and close in time to the journey back home. It is a nightmare in which the apartment is in a different house, and it appears to foreshadow the narrator's anxieties about returning to Sweden.

Like many other Korean adoptees visiting South Korea, the narrator realizes that her difference in physical appearance disappears there and she blends into the majority.[25] Similarly, in contrast to Sweden, she reveals her foreignness when people address her in the Korean language, which she does not know. However, during her visit to Pusan, which is the second largest city in South Korea located at the southeast tip of the Korean peninsula, she observes that, just like in Sweden, people ask her, where she is from even before she opens her mouth.[26] From the very beginning, Trotzig is aware of how differently her femininity is constructed from that of the South Korean women she meets. At first glance, they are heavily made-up and look tall and slender in their very high heels. Moreover, when the narrator sees two bridal couples in the palace area in Seoul, she pays attention to the fact that both the bride and the groom wear make-up. On the other hand, there are also instances in which South Korean men treat her in a patronizing manner. During the trip, Trotzig challenges the prevailing Korean gender roles. For instance, even if her guide book says that women should not smoke in South Korea, she transgresses the prohibition by going to smoke in a smoking square which is reserved for men and forbidden to women at the central station in Seoul.

In the course of the trip, Trotzig admits that she does not feel at home in South Korea and mainly assumes the role of a Western tourist, although it does not always feel comfortable. She visits many of the same sites such as famous parks, museums, palaces and temples, which are included in the motherland tours, and which Jane Jeong Trenka 2003, for instance, depicts as part of her first trip to South Korea.[27] Trotzig's impressions about the country are divided. There are moments when she thinks that she can imagine what Seoul looked like 20–30 years ago without the skyscrapers. On the other hand, in certain parts of the city, in spite of the saying that seven years in South Korea correspond to seventy years in Europe, she observes no signs of the rapid development. As Trenka's narrative shows, motherland tours often bring adoptees to South Korean orphanages and homes for unwed mothers (Trenka 2003,100; Kim 2010, 254). Sometimes adult adoptees are even permitted to volunteer in orphanages or baby reception centers (Kim 2010, 183–184), as the narrator in Sofia French's (née Lindström) *På jakt efter Mr Kim in Seoul* does on her second trip to South Korea. According

---

25 Cf., for instance, Persman 2003, 87.
26 In her contribution to *Hitta hem*, Ahn-Za Hagström points out that before she opened her mouth in South Korea local people had concluded on the basis of her body language and her manner that she was not South Korean. Hagström 2003, 213.
27 Cf. Trenka 2003, 100.

to Anne Whitehead, a traumatic memory is evoked only under particular conditions, which are reminiscent of the original event (Whitehead 2004, 141). Trotzig does not visit any orphanages but, in her case, the memory of her adoption is triggered as soon as she arrives at the airport in Seoul, where she sees a group of Western women carrying their Korean babies and notices a little baby girl looking at her.

When Trotzig meets Koreans who are curious about her background, she tries to explain that she was adopted from there to Sweden, but they fail to comprehend what she means. Pusan, the city where she was found, is evocative of melancholic feelings of loss and sadness connected with her adoption. War monuments and the frequent military presence remind her of the Korean War. The closest Trotzig comes to imagining Pusan 'as a kind of originary relation that needs to be negotiated on some level' (Jerng 2010, 189), is when she surmises that her love for the sea and harbours may derive from that fact that she was born in the harbour area of the city. Although Trotzig is not looking for her biological roots, like many other Korean adoptees, she cannot help fantasizing about what her life would have been like if she had grown up in her birth country. After having visited the drab and stuffy café of the Pusan Tower she toys with the idea that if she had stayed in the city, perhaps she would have worked there.

Trotzig's displacement in South Korea is symbolized by the fact that she cannot always trust her maps and that she often finds herself in places where the public is not supposed to enter. Yet, there are also instances when she admires the mountain and sea landscapes and even attempts to speak Korean on the basis of what she hears the local people saying. All in all, Trotzig wants to explore and absorb as many facets of South Korea as possible during her short trip. Ultimately, she experiences the trip and the memories she will have from it as meaningful, because they make her recognize her ties to her birth country and help her to move forward psychically. Indeed, one can argue that the trip transforms her racial melancholia into mourning and provides a transition into a reparative position for race, to use Eng and Han's term based on one of Klein's developmental positions (Eng and Han 2006, 143). The reparation of racial melancholia involves Trotzig's identification with the previously disparaged and repressed Koreanness. When she looks at thousands of young Korean people milling about the shopping streets of Seoul soon before her departure, she ponders: 'På sätt och vis är jag en av dem.' [In a way, I am one of them.] (Trotzig 1996, 259). The Korean flag is based on the Yin and Yang symbol of complementary opposites which expresses the perfect balance of the universe. Whilst the Korean flag Trotzig received from her parents as a child came to signify her vulnerability and her conflicting relationship to her bi-cultural identity, the flag she buys before her departure is a token of her reconciliation with her 'original' Korean identity.

The third and last part of the book records Trotzig's life back in Sweden and signals that even if she has come to terms with the Korean component of her identity, her Swedish and Korean identities do not harmonise with each other: 'Jag kan aldrig känna mig som enbart svensk i Sverige. Jag kunde aldrig känna mig som enbart korean i Sydkorea.' [I can never feel as only Swedish in Sweden. I could never feel as only Korean in South Korea.]

(Trotzig 1996, 278). Trotzig is not able to use the two cultures as a means of empowerment, since they fail to merge and fuse into enabling cultural hybridity. Instead, she still suffers from a cleaving of the psyche by holding on to her painful identity as an adoptee in spite of the fact that towards the end of the book there is an occasional and apparently hopeful reference to the possibility of the discontinuation of adoptions from South Korea. Ultimately, the significance of the bonds of the adoptive family in Sweden is highlighted, when she plans her future trips to South Korea in the company of the various present and future family members. Even the adoptive mother's positive role in constructing her adoptees' Koreanness is highlighted, when she, the mother of three Korean-born children, begins to pose questions about South Korea and thereby recognizes their racialized difference. Klein claims that the integration of split-off and despised parts of the self into the psyche increases the capacity of love (Klein 1986, 227).[28] Finally, Trotzig also stresses the meaning of love. Stating that she has always loathed the saying 'blod är tjockare än vatten' [blood is thicker than water] (Trotzig 1996, 287), she places love above biological family ties. 'Men kärlek är tjockare än blod.' [But love is thicker than blood.] (Trotzig 1996, 287) is the last sentence of her book, which can be interpreted to echo not only the discourse of 'the happy adoption story,'[29] but also the rhetoric of multicultural harmony in relation to the narrator's privatized, extended family in Sweden.

## Conclusion

Trotzig's *Blod är tjockare än vatten* addresses crucial issues connected with transnational adoption and Korean-born adoptees' identity formation in a white-dominated Western society. It reveals that in spite of the rhetoric of officially supporting ethnic diversity and neoliberal colour-blind thinking, contemporary multicultural Sweden, which Allan Pred calls 'the world's capital of good intentions and civilized behavior toward others' in his fittingly titled, antiracist work *Even in Sweden* (Pred 2000, 6), is by no means free from racialization and various forms of racisms. This obliges the readers of Trotzig's book to rethink the idea of nation and national belonging. In my reading of the bi-cultural identity process at the centre of *Blod är tjockare än vatten*, I examine how the protagonist learns to repress her Koreanness and to identify with the idealized white mainstream. However, by utilizing the conventions of trauma narrative, the book throws light on the persistence of racial melancholia. A significant psychic shift can be discerned to occur when the narrator travels to South Korea and gradually begins to repair the lost ideal of Koreanness. Although the protagonist ultimately has psychic room for both the previously segregated white and Korean components of her identity, they remain apart. However, the ending hints at the healing

---

28 Cf. Eng and Han 2002, 364–365.
29 According to Monika Zagar (2008, 495), 'the memory of the genetic parents does not intervene in the daily life of the reconstructed family' in the happy adoption story.

power of love. With its orientation to the future, the book can be claimed to suggest a nascent possibility of creating what Eng calls 'new global families.' While *Blod är tjockare än vatten* neither addresses the causes of European racisms nor the power and gender imbalances involved in transnational adoption, it opens a prospect of an urgent need to negotiate more effective and socially responsible forms of multiculturalism on the local and global level.

# References

Björkman, Maria and Sven Widmalm 2010: Selling Eugenics: the Case of Sweden. *Notes and Records of the Royal Society* 64 (4). 379–400.

Callahan, Cynthia 2011: *Kin of Another Kind: Transnational Adoption in American Literature*. Ann Arbor: University of Michigan Press.

Cheng, Anne Anlin 2001: *The Melancholy of Race: Psychoanalytic Assimilation and Hidden Grief*. Oxford: Oxford University Press.

Duric, Dubranko 2012: *Astrid Trotzigs författarskap*. C-uppsats i kulturvetenskap. Malmo: Malmö högskola. Web. 30 July.

Eng, David L. 2003: Transnational Adoptions and Queer Diasporas. *Social Text* 21 (3). 1–37.

Eng, David L. and Shinhee Han 2002: A Dialogue on Racial Melancholia. *Loss: The Politics of Mourning*. Ed. by David L. Eng. Ewing: University of California Press. N.J. 343–371.

Eng, David and Shinhee Han 2006: Desegregating Love: Transnational Adoption, Racial Reparation, and Racial Transitional Objects. *Studies in Gender and Sexuality* 7 (2). 141–172.

Eng, David L. 2010: *The Feeling of Kinship: Queer Liberalism and the Racialization of Intimacy*. Durham: Duke University Press.

Fanon, Frantz 1986: *Black Skin, White Masks*. Trans. Charles Lam Markmann, with a foreword by Homi Bhabha. London: Pluto Press Limited.

Freud, Sigmund 1957: Mourning and Melancholia (1917). *The Standard Edition of the Complete Psychological Works of Sigmund Freud, Volume XIV (1914–1916)*. Trans. and ed. by James Strachey et al. London: Hogarth.

Gondouin, Johanna 2012: Adoption, Surrogacy and Swedish Exceptionalism. *Critical Race and Whiteness Studies* 8 (2). 1–20. [Web. 8 Feb.]

Gröndahl, Satu 2007: Identity Politics and Construction of 'Minor' Literatures: Multicultural Swedish Literature at the Turn of the Millennium. *Multiethnica* 30. 21–29.

Hall, Stuart 2007: The Spectacle of the Other. *Representation: Cultural Representations and Signifying Practices*. Ed. by Stuart Hall. London: Sage Publications. 225–279.

Hagström, Ahn-Za 2003: Adopterad är bara ett ord. *Hitta hem. Vuxna adopterade från Korea berättar*. Ed. by Sofia Lindström and Astrid Trotzig. Stockholm: Ordfront. 206–215.

Henke, Suzette A. 2000: *Shattered Subjects: Trauma and Testimony in Women's Life Writing*. New York: St. Martin's Press.

Homans, Margaret 2006: Adoption Narratives, Trauma and Origins. *Narrative* 14 (2). 4–26.

Homans, Margaret 2011: Adoption and Return: Transnational Genealogies, Maternal Legacies. *Rites of Return: Diaspora Poetics and the Politics of Memory*. Ed. Marianne Hirsch and Nancy K. Miller. New York: Columbia University Press. 185–199.

Hübinette, Tobias 2003: En blick på historien. *Hitta hem. Vuxna adopterade från Korea berättar.* Ed. Sofia Lindström and Astrid Trotzig. Stockholm: Ordfront. 116–125.
Hübinette, Tobias 2005a. *Comforting an Orphaned Nation. Representations of International Adoption and Adopted Koreans in Korean Popular Culture.* Department of Oriental Languages. Stockholm: Stockholm University.
Hübinette, Tobias 2005b: En plädering för utländska adoptivbarns rätt att få behålla sin ursprungsidentitet. *Aktuellt om migration.* 2. n. pag. PDF file.
Hübinette, Tobias and Catrin Lundström 2011: Sweden after the Recent Election: The Double-Binding Power of Swedish Whiteness through the Mourning of the Loss of 'Old Sweden' and Passing of 'Good Sweden'. *NORA: Nordic Journal of Feminist and Gender Research* 19 (1). 42–52. [Web 31 July, 2013.]
Jerng, Mark C. 2010: *Claiming Others: Transracial Adoption and National Belonging.* Minneapolis: University of Minnesota Press.
Kauhanen, Anna-Liisa 2013: Avoin kirje arjen rasismista. *Helsingin Sanomat* 15.3.2013.
Kim, Eleana J. 2010: *Adopted Territory: Transnational Korean Adoptees and the Politics of Belonging.* Duke University Press, Durham.
Kim, Hoo-ran 2016: A sense of who you are. *Korea Joongang Daily.* Dec. 19, 2002. [Web. 14 February 2016.]
Klein, Melanie 1986: *The Selected Melanie Klein.* Ed. Juliet Mitchell. Harmondsworth: Penguin Books.
Lacatus, Corina 2008: *The (In)visibility Complex: Negotiating Otherness in Contemporary Sweden.* Stockholm: The Centre for Research in International Migration and Ethnic Relations.
Li, David Leiwei 2003: The State and Subject of Asian American Criticism: Psychoanalysis, Transnational Discourse, and Democratic Ideals. *American Literary History* 15 (3). 603–624.
Lindström, Sofia and Astrid Trotzig (eds.) 2003: *Hitta hem. Vuxna adopterade från Korea berättar.* Stockholm: Ordfront.
Najmi, Samina and Rajini Srikanth 2002: Introduction. *White Women in Racialized Spaces: Imaginative Transformation and Ethical Action in Literature.* Ed.by Samina Najmi and Rajini Srikanth. Albany: State University of New York Press. 1–26.
Persman, Peter 2003: Resan till helheten. *Hitta hem. Vuxna adopterade från Korea berättar.* Stockholm: Ordfront. 82–91.
Pred, Allan 2000: *Even in Sweden: Racisms, Racialized Spaces and the Popular Geographical Imagination.* Berkeley: University of California Press.
Roth, Hans Ingvar 2008: *Diskriminering.* Stockholm: SNS förlag.
Trenka, Jane Jeong 2003: *The Language of Blood: a Memoir.* St.Paul. MN: Borealis Books.
Trotzig, Astrid 1996: *Blod är tjockare än vatten.* Stockholm: Albert Bonniers förlag.
Trotzig, Astrid 1998: Rotfrukt. *Att Odla papaya på Österlen. Nitton författare om dubbel kulturell identitet.* Ed. Annette Masui. Stockholm: Rabén Prisma. 81–88.
Trotzig, Astrid 2005: Makten över prefixen. *Orientalism på svenska.* Ed. Moa Matthis. Stockholm: Ordfront.
Vickroy, Laurie 2002: *Trauma and Survival in Contemporary Literature.* Charlottesville, V.A.: University of Virginia Press, Charlottesville.
Waern, Carina 1996: Blod är tjockaren än vatten. Bokrecension. *Dagens Nyheter* 23.8.1996.
Whitehead, Anne 2004: *Trauma Fiction.* Edinburgh: Edinburgh University Press.
Zagar, Monika 2008: Crossing Borders and Redefining Family and Kinship through Adoption: Representation in Recent Literature. *Gränser I nordisk litteratur. Borders in Nordic Literature.* Vol. II. Ed. by Clas Zilliacus, Heidi Grönstrand and Ulrika Gustafsson. Åbo: Åbo Akademi Förlag. 493–499.

Marta Ronne
https://orcid.org/0000-0002-2587-0913

# Narratives of Exile, Gender and Disability in Latvian Zenta Mauriņa's Autobiographical Writings

The aim of the article is to study the themes of disability, gender and exclusion in the works of the Latvian writer Zenta Mauriņa (1897–1978), whose work as a writer, editor and literary critic was conducted in Swedish exile since 1946. In her literary oeuvre, various themes can be found: war and exile, the role of the humanities in building a peaceful world, language and identity, mobility and homelessness, and, last but not least, thoughts on European literature of the late 19th and early 20th century. In my essay, she is primarily of interest as an exile writer, making various interpretations of exile, of homelessness and of split cultural identities, the major themes of her writings. Her life and work, in a way, also bridge the gap between the late 19th century and our own time. She was born and educated in a time when women with academic diplomas were still more or less an exception in public debate. Between the lines in her diaries and autobiographies, Mauriņa depicted her life-long efforts to achieve a position as a writer and an intellectual. First, the setting is early 20th century Latvia, where Mauriņa was the very first woman to take a PhD degree, and then Sweden in the late 1940s, where she was trying to become established anew, this time as an exile writer and critic.[1]

In her works, she also depicted her own disability, a theme connected to the question of the body on the one hand, and to exile and exclusion on the other (after a polio infection in her early childhood, Mauriņa was in need of a wheelchair for the rest of her life). My aim is thus to cross-read these themes in order to study how Mauriņa on the one hand created the literary image of a female intellectual in exile and on the other how lack of independence (intellectual as well as physical) was depicted in her works. Here I restrict myself to studying Mauriņa as a German-speaking exile writer in Sweden, and not as a Latvian writer of consequence to Latvian literature. Of interest to my essay are part two and three of the three-volume autobiography, *Denn das Wagnis ist schön: Geschichte eines Lebens* from 1952 and *Die eisernen Riegel zerbrechen* from 1957, and Mauriņa's diaries from

---

1  On Mauriņa as the first Latvian female PhD see Orehovs 1999, 230.

*Zenta Mauriņa (1897–1978). Photo: Gunnar Sundgren / Uppsala University Library.*

exile: *Exilens tragik. Svenska dagböcker* from 1966 and *Befrielsens år. Svenska dagböcker 1951–1958* from 1968.[2]

As the case has been with many women writers in literary history, Mauriņa is both a remembered author and, in a way, a forgotten one. However, her gender may not be the whole explanation to why she seldom is referred to today in literary critique and literary handbooks outside Latvia. Her literary oeuvre consists mainly of essays and books about Latvian, Russian and German authors in the late 19th and early 20th century, as well as of works addressing ethics, human faith and the impact of the two world wars on the condition of Western culture.[3] In this essay, I will also point to some inconsequences in her efforts to write from a position of an objective and idealistic humanist observer. Today, this may make the reading of her autobiographical oeuvre less convincing.

2  The reason why I am reading the diaries in Swedish translation is that the German original is no longer available. *Exilens tragik* was first published in German in 1962 as *Nord- und südliches Gelände: Schwedische Tagebücher 1946–1951* and *Befrielsens år* as *Jahre der Befreiung: Schwedische Tagebücher 1951–1958* in 1965.

3  Her education was based on the late 19th century canon of Western philosophy and literature, and her research interests were restricted to Russian and German 19th century authors and to Nietzsche; Mauriņa's view of what she meant by world culture and literature remained typical of the late 19th century. In her diaries from her Swedish exile, and especially in *Befrielsens år*, she nevertheless commented on contemporary writers she was reading: among others Romain Rolland, Romain Garry, André Gide, Julien Green, C.G. Jung and R. Musil.

Born in Lejasciems in 1897 as a daughter to Robert Mauriņs, a Latvian physician and Melanie Knappe, a pianist of German origins, Zenta Mauriņa was bilingual by birth. Thanks to her education at a Russian secondary school, she also spoke fluent Russian. In 1918, the same year that Latvia gained political sovereignty from Russia, Mauriņa founded a high school in her hometown Grobina, where she also was the head teacher. In 1927, she obtained her degree from the faculty of philology and philosophy at Riga University and was employed as a lecturer at Riga's High School for Pedagogy. She published extensively in Latvian newspapers and periodicals, and in 1929 she founded her own 'Literary Academy' in Riga (which existed until 1940). During the years 1929–1938, she conducted literary research in Heidelberg, Vienna, Firenze and Paris; in 1938, she passed her PhD at Riga University. After that, she devoted herself to lectures and teaching outside the Academy. During the Soviet and then the Nazi occupation of Latvia 1940–1941, she conducted her work in Riga as an editor of collected literary editions and as a critic. However, when Soviet troops marched in again in 1944, Mauriņa and her partner Konstantin Raudive, whom she married a year later, decided to flee Latvia.

In 1945, the couple arrived in Detmold in Germany, where Mauriņa despite her health problems took up her work as a public lecturer. In 1946, the couple came as refugees to Sweden and settled down in Uppsala, where Mauriņa, according to her own account, initially had enormous difficulties. Without any knowledge of Swedish, she tried to make her living as a lecturer at Uppsala University, as an essayist and a writer (Ronne 2011).[4] In 1953, the couple were granted Swedish citizenship and Mauriņa started travelling extensively in Italy, Switzerland and Germany for her lectures. As she insisted on publishing in German, she finally found her editors and audience in West Germany; the couple finally settled down in May 1965, in the German town of Bad Krozingen. From there, Mauriņa could continue her lecturing tours in Italy and her writing. She died in 1978 in Switzerland.

Most of what is known to Mauriņa's readers outside Latvia about her youth, her career and her life before she left her home country in 1944 is based on her own autobiography, her diaries in exile and some of her essays.[5] Through the years, she has been distinguished through several commemorative and biographical publications, most of them in German.[6]

---

4   I have previously analysed Mauriņa's own critical narrative of her first years in Swedish exile.
5   In her home country Latvia, Mauriņa's life and oeuvre has been noticed quite a lot, but the only information I have found about current research on her as well as on her archives is solely accessible in Latvian. See the documentary at http://www.youtube.com/watch?feature=endscreen&NR=1&v=HSSiQSazrpQ and http://www.youtube.com/watch?v=NKTst-pnViM&feature=related (both accessed 2012-08-15, 11:50).
6   It should be observed that almost all German publications by and about Mauriņa were edited by Maximilian Dietrich Verlag in Memmingen who still sells some of her books. See *Buch der Freundschaft für Zenta Mauriņa zum 70. Geburtstag*, Memmingen 1967, *Zenta Mauriņa zu Ehren. Texte zu Ihrem 80. Geburtstag am 15. Dezember 1977*. Ed. by Isa Sigg. Memmingen 1978 and *Zenta Mauriņa: Bilder*

In Sweden, she has been briefly studied previously by Aronson 1969, Tamm 1986, Orehovs 1999 and myself.

## Disability and Exile as Different Metaphors of Exclusion

In my readings, I use several theoretical approaches to exile literature, as well as to disability studies. I also refer to gender research in women's history of education and to the philosophical approach to mind and body presented by Elisabeth Grosz in her writings on 'corporeal feminism'. My aim is to combine theoretical approaches to exile with those to disability, since both can be metaphorically understood as various kinds of exclusion.

The definition of exile that I adopt in this essay is the one by Tabori: 'a flight from a political system rather than from a natural disaster or a general, impersonal threat such as war or famine' (Tabori 1972, 23). According to his definition, persons in exile have been forced to leave their home country, and to remain refugees against their own will, due to their ethnic background, religion, nationality or political views (Tabori 1972, 23). The term exile has also been subject to both semantic and historical discussions in relation to studies of exile literature (Gurr 1981; Strelka 1983 & 2003; Ouditt 2002). Strelka has argued that the definition of exile literature is problematic in regard to defining both the term 'exile' and 'literature' (Strelka 1983, 13-34).[7] Although the notion of exile in the age of globalisation is questioned nowadays by some scholars, the term cannot be fully replaced by mobility.

Even if Tabori's definition of exile is the starting point for my analysis of Mauriņa as a refugee from a political system, I aim to show that her works proposed a broader view of exile than the one rendered by Tabori. That is why I apply a radically different idea of exile on different parts of her works, an idea that has been expressed in Edward W. Said's concept of exile as a metaphor. Drawing on Said, Sharon Ouditt points out that exile may or may not have to do with physical relocation; it can also be 'metaphorical' (Ouditt 2002, xiii, drawing on Said 1993, 177).

> *aus Ihrem Leben*, Memmingen 1983. Für biographical studies see Otto Schepp's biography *Das Herz hat Flugel* from 1953 and Margot Fethke's *Eine Stimme in der Brandung der Zeit* from 1969. In recent years, on February 29, 2012, in the German town of Bad Krozingen, where Mauriņa settled in 1965, she was commemorated by a public lecture, conducted by Dr. Günter Höffker. See http://www.youtube.com/watch?v=_fGdgrkqGng (accessed 2012-08-15, 12:02).
> 
> 7   With a basis in earlier studies on exile and modernism, Anders Olsson has broadened the discussion of exile as well as of nomadism in world literature (Olsson 2011). Olsson points out the relationship between exile literature and the term of 'world literature' in contemporary research: 'It is clear that several basic traits of exile literature are also to be found in what many scholars of comparative literature deal with today under the term of *world literature*. This includes literature transmission, translation, migration and a new cosmopolitan consciousness' (Olsson 2011, 195). 'Det är helt klart att ett antal grunddrag i exillitteraturen också återfinns i det som många litteraturvetare idag sysslar med under beteckningen »världslitteratur«, allt från litterär förmedling, översättning, migration till ett nytt kosmopolitiskt medvetande' (My own translation).

In addition, a gender perspective is of use to my analysis of Mauriņa's narrative of herself as a disabled female writer in exile. Besides Elisabeth Grosz' analysis of Merleau-Ponty's concept of the interrelatedness of mind and body in *Volatile Bodies. Toward a Corporeal Feminism* (1994), I will refer to Susan Wendell's critical thoughts on the dualist view of body and mind. I also use references to disability studies by Lennard J. Davis and G. Thomas Couser in *The Disability Studies Reader* 2006 in my analysis of Mauriņa's particular way to cope with the issue in her narrative.

*Disability and Exclusion*

The theme of disability as both physical and social exclusion can be found already in a recount of Mauriņa's student years in Riga. The dominating theme in 'Glühende Stäbe' ('Red-hot iron'), part one of *Denn das Wagnis ist schön*, is the protagonist being torn between her physical suffering and her intellectual ambitions. It is in this fragment that the way of writing about her disabled self is set; neither sleeplessness nor pain can beat her as an intellectual. Her approach to disability as a lived experience is, as far as I can see, quite a rare European example within the genre of autobiography.[8]

However, as Lennard J. Davis claims in the same volume, disability is rarely a central issue in novels (Davis 2006, 11). Furthermore, as Davies implicates, the narrative tradition of the Western novel has been to connect questions of disability to abnormity, which only tended to strengthen the hegemony of normality. 'I am not saying simply that novels embody the prejudices of society toward people with disabilities. That is clearly a truism. Rather, I am asserting that the very structures on which the novel rests tend to be normative, ideologically emphasizing the universal quality of the central character whose normativity encourages us to identify with him or her', Davis (2006, 11) states. Mauriņa herself tells a critical story of the society's poor understanding of her protagonist's condition. It is, of course, of importance that her approach is autobiographical. In Mauriņa's case, disability is on the one hand depicted both as a burden and as an evil, and on the other, as a resource in her striving after self-discipline. In the beginning of her narration, Mauriņa actually departs from the mind-and-body dualism as described by Wendell and Hall; her ever-aching body might be a possible hindrance to her if it were not for her disciplined mind. This is an interesting aspect, since according to Susan Wendell in her *The Rejected Body. Feminist Philosophical Reflections on Disability* (1996), the Western view of a disabled body – as well as of an ideal body – is very much about the idea of control. Wendell analyses what she calls 'the Myth of Control', an idea

---

8   It can be compared to Couser's observation about North American literature, where practically no accounts on disability from before 1970s are to be found in life writing. As Couser states, disability has been 'hyper-represented' in mainstream human culture and an 'extremely valuable cultural commodity for thousands of years' (spontaneously, I could hardly agree with this), but disabled people were 'subjected to objectifying notice in the form of mediated starring', which means that they could hardly control their own images (Couser 2006, 399). But both first- and third-person narratives on disability have only proliferated for the last three decades (Couser 2006, 399).

she summarises as '[t]he myth that the body can be controlled is part of the general assumption of the modern Western scientific project that nature can be controlled' (Wendell 1996, 94). Here I will only address her reflections on the idea of the mind being able to control a disabled body.

Drawing on feminist analyses of how female bodies have been controlled and disciplined by society over the time, Wendell finds a parallel to disabled bodies. With a point of departure in Michel Foucault's description of the 'disciplinary practices that produce "docile bodies"', Wendell talks of 'disciplinary practices of physical normality that are in many ways analogous to the disciplinary practices of femininity' (Wendell 1996, 87, 88). Disability may be perceived as 'Otherness', which leads to stigmatization, or more generally as a difference, which also includes a view of disability as 'exotic' or 'interesting', or more seldom as valuable. The disabled themselves will not perceive that difference as exotic, Wendell points out, although they may value it as an experience (Wendell 1996, 66). Still, they have to learn 'that most people do not want to know about the suffering they experience because of their bodies', as the Western culture disciplines most people to 'deny bodily weaknesses' and 'to feel ashamed of and responsible for their distance from the ideals' (Wendell 1996, 91). That is why disabled people, among other standpoints, 'may wish for bodies they cannot have, with frustration, shame and sometimes self-hatred' (Wendell 1996, 91). The idea that mind to some extent can control the body and its state of 'normality', as Mauriņa expressed it in her writings, is an old one, although as Wendell points out, since the 1970s it has been fuelled by the development of psychosomatic diagnoses (Wendell 1996, 93–103).[9] Or as Hall summarises Wendell, 'The prevailing Western view, as Wendell explains, associates normalcy with the exercise of proper discipline and control over the body' (Hall 2011, 5). The view of the mind controlling the body becomes an individual's moral duty. Davis observes in a similar manner that although terms describing the spectrum of normality ('normalcy', 'normality', 'average' and 'abnormal') did not appear in the European languages until around 1850, they soon also became connected to the notion of healthy nations and societies, and to moral values (Davis 2006, 3–15). Back to Hall's study, it is of importance to remember that 'disciplined bodies are also properly gendered bodies' (Hall 2011, 5).[10]

*Living One's Body*

However, in Mauriņa's narrative the dualist concept of body and mind will soon be put aside. Not only is the disease haunting her; in a sense, the environment, as well as her material conditions, makes her 'disabled' too. It is clear that Mauriņa constructs her protagonist as an intellectual in opposition to the world she lives in and that the account of her suffering also becomes her credo:

9  However, Wendell does not argue for disability being wholly socially constructed, as some other theoreticians do. See Thomas 1999, 33–45 on the 'definitional riddle' in disability studies.
10 Here Hall draws loosely on Sandra Bartky's *Femininity and Domination. Studies in the Phenomenology of Oppression* (1990).

> Since childhood, I had seen my physical disability as a giant who rolled a heavy stone over me, and against whom not only I, but also Father and all good people were powerless. The suffering put on me by God or by faith was unavoidable. This block of stone, which constantly burdened me, I wished to hammer at and chisel out to a work of art, so that it would make me inviolable. However, even during my first term at the university I had to learn that if you have one enemy, sooner or later you will be attacked by a whole horde. All dark creatures are allied with each other. One dark hour would conjure up another. I believed I had free admission to the spiritual world. [...] But now, I experienced that evil monsters and dragons ambush the wanderer at the gate to the spiritual world; [...] The disease was my enemy number one; [...] people [...] who found satisfaction in persecution were my enemy number two. [...] Poverty making me so tired and limp, was my enemy number three.[11]

The quotation, also giving a taste of Mauriņa's bombastic style of narration, is typical of her narratives of her own life-long and constant physical suffering. One might say, that she represents the traditional view of the body as 'separate from and a hindrance to the mind', as Hall puts it, but I would rather claim that the narrative demonstrates how, speaking in Merleau-Ponty's terms, Mauriņa's protagonist 'lives her body'.

In her *Volatile Bodies. Toward a Corporeal Feminism* (1994), Elisabeth Grosz has analysed Merleau-Ponty's concept of the interrelatedness of mind and body. Some elements of his corporeal phenomenology I find useful for my analysis. In his concept of mind as 'always embodied, always based on corporeal and sensory relations' (Grosz), Merleau-Ponty sees body and mind as necessarily interrelated. He 'begins with the negative claim that the body is not an object'. Grosz states, 'it is the condition and context through which I am able to have a relation to objects. It is both immanent and transcendent. Insofar as I live the body, it is a phenomenon experienced by me and thus provides the very horizon and perspectival point which places me in the world and makes relations between me, other objects, and other subjects possible' (Grosz 1994, 86). According to Grosz, Merleau-Ponty has introduced a new concept of the body being a channel for our communication with the world. As he himself has put it in *The Primacy of Perception*, 'The perceiving mind is an incarnated mind' (Merleau-Ponty 1964, 3). Grosz summarizes it as

---

11 My translation. In original: 'Mein körperliches Behindertsein empfand ich seit meiner Kindheit als einen Riesen, der einen schweren Stein auf mich wältzte und demgegenüber nicht nur ich, sondern auch Vater und alle guten Menschen machtlos waren. Das von Gott oder dem Schicksal mir auferlegte körperliche Leiden war unabwendbar. Diesen Block, der ständig auf mir lastete, wollte ich zu einem Kunstwerk hämmern und meißeln, damit er mich unversehrbar mache. Aber schon im ersten Semester meines Studiums musste ich erfahren, dass, wer einen Feind hat, über kurz oder lang von einer ganzen Schar angegriffen wird. Alle Dunkelwesen sind untereinander verbündet. Eine Schwarze Stunde beschwört die andere herauf. Ich hatte geglaubt, im Reich des Geistes freien Einlass zu erhalten. [...] Und nun erlebte ich, daß am Tor, das in das Reich des Geistes führt, dem Wanderer böse Ungetüme und Drachen auflauern. [...] Die Krankheit, das war der Feind Nummer eins, Menschen [...] dem Verfolgungen Genugtuung bereiteten, das war der Feind Nummer Zwei. [...] Die Armut, die einen so müde und mürbe machte, das war der Feind Nummer drei'. (Mauriņa 1953, 31–32.)

follows, 'the body is my being-to-the-world and as such is the instrument by which all information and knowledge is received and meaning is generated. It is through the body that the world of objects appears to me; it is in virtue of having/being a body that there are objects for me' (Grosz 1994, 87). This can be cross-read with Susan Wendell who, according to Kim Q. Hall, 'examines how Western philosophical conceptions of the body as separate from and a hindrance to the mind form contemporary anxieties about bodies "out of control" in general and disabled bodies in particular' (Hall 2011, 5).

As Grosz has put it, 'For Merleau-Ponty, although the body is both object (for others) and a lived reality (for the subject), it is never simply object nor simply subject. It is defined by its relations with others and in turn defines these objects as such – it is "sense-bestowing" and "form-giving", providing a structure, organization and ground within which objects are to be situated and against which the body-subject is positioned. The body is my being-to-the-world and as such is the instrument by which all information and knowledge is received and meaning is generated' (Grosz 1994, 87).

In Mauriņa's account of her 'double life' as a disabled intellectual, the concept of the body as 'sense-bestowing' and 'form-giving', becomes very clear. The body and its disability becomes one and both become a context through which she both upholds a relation to the world and defines herself as an intellectual. She often concludes that it is the environment that is disabled. This makes her narration a very early contribution to the constructionist view of disability represented by many contemporary scholars (Thomas 1999, 11–32). It may be the people who do not understand that her needs are like everybody else's, or maybe material things hinder her to move in her wheelchair: the stairs or the wagons. The protagonist's choice to make Nietzsche her prophet is not only meant as an intellectual manifesto but also as a manifesto of both exclusiveness and independence.

> 'Fate had marked me as an extraordinary being and an extraordinary existence had been forced upon me. I did not know anybody to whom I could turn with my sorrows and worries. [...] The broken wings dimmed my days. I held on to Nietzsche's wisdom and I turned away from the pitying ones, the small, kind, ordinary people'[12] (Mauriņa 1953, 42).

The protagonist's view of the world is often narrowed to her own room, as she cannot move around freely on her own. Still, on the other hand, the experience of constantly living in the shadow of death had furnished her with two skills: her knowledge of literature and philosophy and her ability to endure her physical suffering (Mauriņa 1953, 132). Sleeplessness can be fought by reading poems, she states (Mauriņa 1953, 133). She has also learned to oscillate between those among her acquaintance who, in her own

12 My translation. In original: 'Das Schicksal hatte mich zu einem Sonderwesen gestempelt und mir ein Sonderdasein Aufgezwungen. Ich kannte niemand, zu dem ich meinen Kummer und meine Sorgen tragen konnte. [...] Und die gebrochenen Schwingen verdunkelten den Tag. Ich hielt mich an Nietzsches Weisheit und wandte mich von den Mitleidigen ab, von den kleinen, wohlwollenden, grauen Leuten' (Mauriņa 1953, 42).

eyes, humiliate her by pity, and those who lack the understanding of her situation, something that brings up the view of disability as either a stigma, or as 'exotic' or 'interesting':

> To live a double life became my lifestyle. In order not to frighten these people away, whom I must or wanted to be together with, and so as not to be misunderstood by them, I had learned never to talk about myself. [...]
>
> With my fellow-students, I talked about the exams or about the latest literary events. I could divide my guests into two groups. The simple souls were those who treated me as ill, that is as a creature who is capable of nothing, fit for nothing and thus forced to be grateful for people having patience with her. If these people helped me with some of the small everyday problems, their helpfulness was either condescending or theatrical. [...]
>
> The other kind, the intellectuals, worshiped and admired me, but their admiration was of the kind that deprived me of the possibility of being an ordinary and outspoken person.[13]

The 'double lifestyle' Mauriņa talks about, as well as her ever-lasting sense of alienation, leads me back to Ouditt's thoughts on different kinds of exile. 'The condition of exile may not be consequent on the literal event of relocation: it may also, as Said makes clear, be metaphorical. In other words, any intellectual community may be made up of insiders and outsiders: those who feel at ease with the structures they inhabit, and those who are driven by the sense of dislocation, of dissonance' (Ouditt 2002, xiii). Mauriņa's narration, constantly playing on the concept of being an outsider, is an illustrative example of both kinds of exile. One is the metaphorical exile she is said to experience in Latvia, where she is seen as a pitiful cripple and her language and other skills are misjudged, and the other is the physical political exile in Germany and Sweden, where she is an anonymous (disabled) female intellectual. Thus, her way of depicting exile cannot be captured solely by using Tabori's strict definition of the term.

*Boundaries of Gender versus Boundaries of Disability*

The story of both Mauriņa's disability and of all her diseases that make a part of her existence is throughout the first volume interwoven with the narrative

---

13 My translation. In original: 'Ein Doppelleben zu führen ward zu meinem lebensstil. Um die Menschen, mit denen ich zusammensein mußte oder zusammensein wollte, nicht abzuschrecken und von ihnen nicht mißverstanden zu werden, hatte ich gelernt, nie über mich zu sprechen. [...] Mit meinen Kommilitoninnen erörterte ich gern Examensfragen oder die letzten Ereignisse der Literatur. Meine Besucher konnte ich in zwei gruppen einteilen: die Primitiven behandelten mich als krank, das heißt als ein Wesen, das nichts kann, zu nichts Rechtem taugt und mit einem Geduldetwerden sich zufrieden geben muß. Halfen mir die Menschen dieser gruppe eine der kleinen Alltagsfragen regeln, lag in ihrer Hilfsbereitschaft etwas Erniedrigendes oder auch etwas theatralisch Komisches. [...] Die anderer Typ meiner Gäste, die geistigen, verehrten und bewunderten mich, aber diese Bewunderung war so geartet, daß sie mir die Möglichkeit zu einem einfachen, schlichten Menschen nahm' (Mauriņa 1953, 101–102).

of several different subjects. These include her intellectual ambitions and her encounters with literature and music, as well as her hard-earned economic independence, her journeys in Europe and her achievements as literary historian, essayist and editor. It is through her aching body that she perceives infatuation (the story of her meeting the poet Janis Akuraters), friendship (the story of Anna-Antigone), deep sympathy or deep antipathy, and also empathy with those whose own physical sufferings remind her of living in the shadow of death.

Already in the first autobiographical volume, it is clear that the protagonist does not wish to talk of her situation as a disabled *female* intellectual. In *Denn das Wagnis ist schön* she only seldom alludes to her situation as a disabled woman, as in the passage about those who worship her. 'They admitted my achievements but regarded it as natural that I could manage without fresh air and with only a few hours sleep, not to mention other purely female wishes [sic!] and human needs'.[14] Despite being the first Latvian woman to obtain a PhD, Mauriņa did not occupy herself with women rights or the question of gender whatsoever. In one of the very few exceptions, in a short passage in *Denn das Wagnis ist schön*, we find the protagonist reasoning with her friend Anna on biological differences between men and women and on women's ever-lasting desire to be confirmed by the male gaze.

> "Men are so terribly stupid." Anna lightened her cigarette and answered thoughtfully: "Yes, that's what one usually says. One also says, for me men are air, and still air is something one cannot live without. Somehow or other you need a man, you need him as a confirmation of yourself."
> "But a woman could do that too."
> "Not to the same extent as a man. It seems to be a law of Nature."
> "I do not agree to such laws of Nature."
> "Do not say that. Laws of Nature are omnipotent, and we must try to comprehend and cultivate them and to fit into them."
> "I only admit the laws of the spirit."
> "Yes, you are fighting against Nature."
> […]"It is a cruel and hopeless fight."[15]

---

14 My translation. In original: 'Sie erkannten meine Leistungen an und nahmen es als selbstverständlich hin, dass ich ohne frische Luft mit wenigen Stunden Schlaf auskam, von anderen, rein weiblichen Wünschen und menschlichen Bedürfnissen gar nicht zu reden.' (Mauriņa 1953, 102.)

15 My translation. In original: '»Die Männer sind eben schrecklich dumm.» Anna zündete sich eine Papyros an und erwiderte nachdenklich: »Ja, das sagt man so. Man sagt auch, die Männer sind für mich Luft, und doch kann man ohne Luft nicht leben. Irgendwie braucht man den Mann, man braucht ihn zur Bestätigung des eigenen Ich.» »Aber das kann doch auch eine Frau. » »Nie in dem Maße wie ein Mann. Dies ist wohl ein Naturgesetz.»»Ich erkenne solche Naturgesetze nicht an. »» Das müssen Sie nicht sagen. Die Naturgesetze sind allmächtig und wir müssen versuchen, sie zu ergründen, ze veredeln und uns in sie einzufügen. » »Ich erkenne nur die Gesetze des Geistes an. »Ja, Sie kämpfen gegen die Natur.[…] »Das ist ein grausamer und hoffnungsloser Kampf.'(Mauriņa 1953, 95–96.)

The quotation is a very good example of how the protagonist refuses to admit the traditional boundaries of heteronormativity and rather talks of herself as a spiritual and intellectual being. In Mauriņa's autobiographical writings, this seems to be a rule. On this point Anna is her antagonist, in her lines one perceives echoes from both Otto Weininger's popular misogynous opus *Geschlecht und Character* from 1903 and the debate on femininity and masculinity that was typical of radical early 20th century female intellectuals.[16] The subject is never discussed by Mauriņa again, which makes her narration as a female academic differ from many of her contemporary female authors with academic backgrounds. Instead, her rhetoric seems strongly influenced by Christian humanist thought and her divagations about freedom and justice are all about general human rights and responsibilities in the world. Her story of a (disabled) female intellectual in early 20th century Riga has to be read between the lines. Here, we read about her small chances as a female student to earn her living by giving private lessons, the confusion the male admirers of her intellect show when it comes to a more practical manner of help, or the way her language skills at first were underestimated at the university.[17] The following parts of *Denn das Wagnis ist schön* instead depict the protagonist's life as a European intellectual who despite both her disability and gender is free to study in Florence, Rome, Venice and Paris.

*Becoming a Political Refugee pitkä väliviiva 'Exile as Relocation*

In the second volume of Mauriņa's autobiography, *Die eisernen Riegel zerbrechen*, the theme of disability and of the body is integrated in her narration about the war years in Latvia and in the story of her and Konstantin Raudive's flight to Germany through the occupied parts of Poland. Being both a member of the German minority and a Latvian patriot, during the Nazi occupation of Latvia, she felt 'squeezed between two rocks, of which the one was called despair and the other one powerlessness', when a German officer talked of Latvia as a future federal country of Germany.[18] Still, she managed to continue working as a lecturer and a writer, while Raudive was editing J.W. Goethe's collected works. It was not until the recapturing of Latvia by the Soviet army in the summer of 1944 that Mauriņa and Raudive decided to flee the country. Here the narrative of their escape and political exile begins. Her message is that no real peace is obtained even though Nazi Germany has been defeated. As she puts it: 'the devil they had fought was dead, but many of the survivors were left to the power of the arch-devil' (i.e. into the new

---

16 This can be compared to the debate of Swedish female authors on women's ambivalent image of themselves. Weininger's view of the sexes was both influential and hardly criticised. See Ronne 2000, 222–229; Markusson Winkvist 2003, 195–196. On the polemic against Weininger's bestselling *Geschlecht und Charakter* in Austria and Germany in the early 20th century see Melander 1990, 49–56.
17 See for example the chapters 'Beelzebub' and 'Der Kampf um das tägliche Brot' In Mauriņa 1953, 50–60 and 77–87.
18 My translation. In original: '[…] jetzt war ich zwischen zwei Felsen eingeklemmt, der eine hieß Verzweiflung, der andere Ohnmacht.' (Mauriņa 1957, 288.)

geopolitical order dictated by the Soviet Union).[19] The protagonist's physical suffering and her nomadic life can be read as a symbol of the destroyed and bleeding central Europe she is travelling through. Her and Raudive's journey is interrupted, not only by the war going on and other outer circumstances, but also by her many stays in hospital and her poor health.

It has nevertheless to be observed that Mauriņa's narrative of her flight through the occupied Silesia and of her stay in Germany in 1945 seems ambiguous; it indicates her unequivocal condemnation of the war on the one hand, and on the other, her slight interest in the sufferings of other peoples than Latvians and German civilians. In *Befrielsens år* (*Die Jahre der Befreiung*), the protagonist declares that she has always been against 'all kinds of violence. As in my childhood, I am followed by the old Latvian Daina, who considers that the biggest sin is to trample somebody who is defenceless' (*Befrielsens år*, 11).[20] Nevertheless, in her diaries from her Swedish exile, the issue of the Holocaust is practically missing, although the problems of war and suffering (German and Latvian) civilians occupy her a lot, as well as the sufferings of German soldiers (Ronne 2011).[21] In a short passage of five lines in *Die eisernen Riegel zerbrechen*, Mauriņa mentions the Riga ghetto. In the same volume, the protagonist conducts three conversations about the fate of the Latvian Jews, where she is the one to defend them and to condemn Nazi persecutions of the Jewish people. Still, the discussions are rather philosophical. She also tells the story of a single Jewish refugee who steps into her home, and whom she supplies with food. Her narration of both the Jewish people and the Polish slave workers whom she meets while staying in a German land-owner's house in Silesia is full of empathy, but it also puts them in the position of pitied 'Others'.[22]

19 My translation. In original: 'Der Teufel, gegen den man gekämpft hatte, war tot, aber ein großer teil der Überlebenden war der Macht des Erzsatans ausgeliefert.'(Mauriņa 1957, 502.)

20 My translation. In original: '[...] mot varje slags våld. Som i min barndom följer mig den gammallettiska Daina, som anser det för den största förseelsen att trampa ner en värnlös.' (Mauriņa 1968, 11.)

21 In *Die eisernen Riegel zerbrechen* Mauriņa makes an effort to picture a German soldier's ambivalent view of his own army. She also addresses the controversial subject of Latvian women's relationships with Nazi soldiers; her character, the German Heinz Riedel, takes them into defence (Mauriņa 1957, 293–294). It is in some parts difficult to define Mauriņa's position as a humanist, and thus there is a risk of trivialising her narrative project. A much deeper analysis is needed than what is possible here.

22 Gertrude Schneider has in her *Journey into Terror: Story of the Riga Ghetto* (2001) commented on Mauriņa's seemingly ambivalent attitude towards the Nazi occupation; Schneider points to this in *Die Eizernen Riegel Zerbrechen*. 'Mauriņa, a loyal Latvian, presents an exact description of how pleased even well-educated Latvians were about the terrible fate of the Jews. She tried to be even-handed in her anecdotes about Jews, although some anti-Jewish bias is discernible. While her report is very detailed on horrors allegedly perpetrated by the Russians, whom she hates, she manages to say little about the fate of the Jews in Riga and environs, although she was there throughout the time of their destruction. She left her country in the summer of 1944, so as to avoid falling into the hands of the Soviet

*'Rancour and Regret'*

In *Exilens tragik* (*Nord- und südliches Gelände*), volume one of her Swedish diaries, her tone is critical and harsh when she narrates the stories of other (that is non-Latvian) refugees. According to the protagonist, her room-mate in the refugee camp in Landskrona, a female Dutch refugee from the Soviet occupation zone, tells her 'not without voluptuousness, how she during one and the same night was raped twenty times by Bolshevik soldiers'.[23] The only thing the protagonist remembers about an Italian-Polish couple who had come to Sweden after surviving forced labour in Germany is that they talk a German that only they understand and a 'gibberish that gives her nausea'.[24] As Said (2003, xxxv) puts it, 'exile can produce rancor and regret, as well as a sharpened vision'. In Mauriņa's way of portraying many of those whom she met in exile, there was sometimes much more rancour and regret than sharp observations. On the other hand, what we see in both the passages mentioned above and other parts of her narratives may be precisely what Said talks about when he calls exile 'a jealous state'. He observes the following in his *Reflections on Exile*:

> 'What you achieve is precisely what you have no wish to share, and it is in drawing of lines around you and your compatriots that the least attractive aspects of being in exile emerge: an exaggerated sense of group solidarity, and a passionate hostility to outsiders, even those who may be in fact in the same predicament as you' (Said 2003, 178).

However, the narrator's cold eye may also indicate the author's wish to write from a position of a distant and 'objective' observer; on the other hand, unfortunately, this does not fit into the dramatic account she gives of her own life. One might of course argue that *Die eisernen Riegel zerbrechen* should be read as a metaphor of the ever-lasting conflict between good and evil, rather than as an autobiographical narrative on Mauriņa's own life in exile. It is not without a reason that *Die eisernen Riegel zerbrechen* as a whole alludes to Dante's *Inferno*.[25] The whole story of her life as a refugee is also – in some way – a novel of ideas, where the protagonist's thoughts on literature and philosophy, often pictured as dialogues with people she meets during her flight, are a part of her divagations on how a better and more human world could be built. In the prologue, the author declares: 'The most important for me is not a pedantic account of facts, but what the soul experiences as truth'.[26] The autobiographical element is nevertheless still the main one. As

forces, who would not have looked kindly upon her literary output during the German occupation' (Schneider 2001, 163).
23 My translation. In original: '[Sävligt brett berättar hon] inte utan vällust om hur hon på en enda natt blev våldtagen tjugo gånger av bolsjeviksoldater.' (Mauriņa 1966, 21–22).
24 My translation. In original: 'en rotvälska som framkallar sjösjuka'(Mauriņa 1966, 22).
25 See the explicit evocation of Dante in Mauriņa 1957, 485.
26 My translation. In original: 'Nicht die pedantisch genau aufgezeichneten Tatsachen sind mir das Wichtigste, sondern die seelische Wahrheit.' (Mauriņa 1957, 12.)

the author puts it in *Die eisernen Riegel zerbrechen*, the book 'narrates the story of a life in which living against all odds is the core'[27]; so do her exile diaries from the years 1946–1948 and 1951–1958, published 1962 and 1965 respectively (to Swedish in 1966 and 1968). The main interest here is the intersection between the notion of exile and physical disability, an ever-present motive in the story.

In the first chapters of *Exilens tragik* (*Nord- und südliches Gelände*), Mauriņa uses the picture of her aching body in order to emphasise the fragility of a refugee, as if making herself an object of study. This is the case, whether she writes about the brutal treatment of her in the Swedish refugee camp in Landskrona, the indifference she meets among Swedish middle class and writers who mostly see her as a worthless cripple, or all physical obstacles that reduce her freedom. 'It is difficult to be ill, even more difficult to be ill and poor, but when you are both ill and poor and in a foreign country, you better search for a rope', she states.[28] In another fragment referring to a visit to a well-off Swedish home, where she found her way to the kitchen and there found a gas tap, she alludes to the possibility of taking her own life by using a gas oven. 'The gas tap! If only I knew how to use such a thing. In Riga, we had an electric oven. I have often read that the gas tap can be a relief from the unbearable. Open the gas tap, take a pill, lie down on a kitchen sofa and fall asleep forever.'[29]

As read between the lines, the motive of disability in both *Exilens tragik* and *Befrielsens år* also introduces the theme of reversed gender roles. The protagonist feels useless, lonely and chained to her room during her and Raudive's first months in Uppsala. She takes upon herself the traditionally male role of a lonely genius, whose primary goal is to create against all odds. In the mean time, Raudive who also is a writer, a translator and a scholar in psychology, becomes partly Mauriņa's muse and partly a maid-of-all-work, since he literally has to solve the most trivial everyday problems, as well as being both her literary impresario and a link between her and their acquaintances (Ronne 2011; Mauriņa 1966, passim). 'The first six years in Sweden were a drowning person's struggle. I would never have reached land if Albatross had not been here', she notes in *Exilens tragik*, in her usual way referring to Raudive as 'Albatross' (Mauriņa 1966, 12). Mauriņa, for her part, translated a number of his literary works from Latvian into German.[30]

'My life is not an organised ascent à la Dante, it is a raft steered by gusts

---

27 My translation. In original: 'Es erzählt die Geschiche eines Lebens, deren Kern ein Trotzdem ist.' (Mauriņa 1957, 11.)
28 'Det är svårt att vara sjuk, ännu svårare att vara sjuk och fattig, men den som sjuk och fattig hamnat i främmande land, den ser sig om efter ett rep.' (Mauriņa 1966, 24–25.)
29 'Gaskranen! Om jag bara visste hur man hanterade en sådan tingest. I Riga hade vi elektrisk spis. Jag har ofta läst att gaskranen befriar från det outhärdliga. Öppna gaskranen, ta en tablett, lägga sig på kökssoffan och somna för att aldrig mer vakna.' (Mauriņa 1966, 24.)
30 See the list of Mauriņa's translations from Latvian to German in *Zenta Mauriņa. Bilder aus ihrem Leben* 1983, 153.

of wind – coincidence, faith or providence, who can tell' she concludes.[31] In her own picture of her life in exile she repeatedly stresses the power of coincidence and chance, which, of course, can as much be read as a narrative on melancholy and depression as on conditions of political exile ('the unforeseen rules my life; a number of seemingly meaningless coincidences keep on placing new obstacles in my way').[32] Maybe she tries to express something similar to Said's later concept. 'The sense of dissonance, engendered by estrangement, distance, dispersion, years of lostness and disorientation – and, just as important, the precarious sense of expression by which what "normal" residents find easy and natural to do requires in exile an almost excessive deliberation, effort, expenditure of intellectual energy at restoration, reiteration and affirmation that are undercut by doubt and irony' (Said 2003, xxxiii). As I have pointed elsewhere, in her narratives she was very much occupied by dispersion, lostness and disorientation, precisely in the sense Said writes about it (Ronne 2011, 200; 202–211). In a passage in *Exilens tragik*, notes on small slips of papers are used brilliantly as a symbol of dispersion, physical as well as linguistic and intellectual.

> In Riga, I had a row of very small compartments in my desk; my thoughts, noted on small slips of paper, were sorted in these drawers. […] People are my passion, my landscape. In my isolation, these diaries and noctuaries [*sic!*] are a surrogate for the dialogue that includes me, my isolated self, among my friends. […] These notes are my only living contact with the spiritual world, an alliance with the beloved language. In a foreign language and especially one you learn late in life, both undertones and overtones are lost.[33]

Still, in *Befrielsens år*, the main tone in her narrative of the conditions of her exile shifts slightly from dark to light. Liberation can be obtained if one's inner possibilities are carried out, she says in her foreword, alluding to the title (German 'Befreiung' and Swedish 'befrielse' meaning 'liberation') (Mauriņa 1968, 7). In her own case, her life in Sweden after 1950 meant that many of her dreams as a writer gradually came true.[34] The volume is

---

31 My translation. In original: 'Mitt liv är ingen ordnad dantesk uppstigning, det är en flotte, driven av vindstötar – slumpens, ödets eller försynens, vem förmår avgöra det?' (Mauriņa 1968, 7.)

32 My translation. In original: 'det oförutsedda behärskar mitt liv; en rad skenbart meningslösa tilldragelser lägger nya hinder i vägen' (Mauriņa 1968, 8).

33 My translation. In original: 'I Riga hade jag en rad mycket små fack i mitt skrivbord; mina på papperslappar antecknade tankar ordnades i dessa lådor. […] Människor är min passion, mitt landskap. I min avspärrning är dessa dag- och nattböcker ett surrogat för dialogen som innesluter mig, den isolerade, i vännernas skara. […] Dessa anteckningar är min enda levande relation till andens värld, en förbundenhet med det älskade språket. I ett inlärt språk och i synnerhet i ett som man lär sig under senare hälften av sitt liv går under- och övertoner förlorade.' (Mauriņa 1968, 82). Also quoted by myself in Ronne 2011, 200.

34 As Orehovs observes, regardless the initial problems Mauriņa experienced as an anonymous Latvian intellectual in Sweden lacking books, connections and economical means, the Swedish exile allowed her to get the 'view over the world' she claimed was essential to her (see Mauriņa 1968, 7). It also provided her with two

thus mostly devoted to her work as a public lecturer in Sweden, Germany, Italy and Switzerland and to her life as an acclaimed German-speaking Latvian intellectual in exile. 'It is a hard and irrevocable fact in my life that my body is irreplaceably connected with myself, and that my never-ending task is to subordinate my physical I under my inner self, and to integrate the world into that', she concludes (Mauriņa 1968, 7).[35] In the narration of her many journeys, her disability and her poor health nevertheless becomes an immanent element of her everyday life, an everyday suffering to deal with, and an obstacle possible to overcome. *Befrielsens år* is no longer a story of loneliness, passivity and hopelessness but one of growing hope, mobility and spiritual freedom. A visit to Germany is said to have awakened 'new energy' in the protagonist and 'a spiritual freedom I did not believe I had any more' (Mauriņa 1968, 28). She feels at home in Germany in the fifties, as in all places where growing 'critical tolerance' has replaced 'aggressive nationalism' and where there is a hope for 'a religious-social humanism' (her Christian background is not to be forgotten here) (Mauriņa 1968, 29).[36]

# References

Aronsson, Asta 1969: Zenta Mauriņa und Schweden. An unpublished student essay from the Department of German Language. Stockholm: Stockholm University.

Bartky, Sandra 1999: *Femininity and Domination. Studies in the Phenomenology of Oppression*. New York: Routledge.

Couser, Thomas G. 2006: Disability, Life Narrative, and Representation. *The Disability Studies Reader*. Ed. by Lennard J. Davis. New York & London: Routledge. 399–401.

Davis, Lennard J. (ed.) 2006: *The Disability Studies Reader*. New York & London: Routledge.

Grosz, Elisabeth 1994: *Volatile Bodies. Toward a Corporeal Feminism*. Bloomington and Indianapolis: Indiana University Press.

Gurr, Andrew 1981: *Writers in Exile. The Identity of Home in Modern Literature*. Sussex & New Jersey: The Harvester Press.

Hall, Kim Q. 2011: Imagining Disability and Gender Through Feminist Studies. An Introduction. *Feminist Disability Studies*. Ed. by Kim Q Hall. Bloomington. 1–10.

Melander, Elinor 1990: *Den sexuella krisen och den nya moralen. Förhållandet mellan könen i Grete Meisel-Hess' författarskap*. [diss]. [Acta Universitatis Stockholmiensis. Stockholm Studies in the History of Ideas, 1]. Stockholm: Stockholms universitet.

Markusson Winkvist, Hanna 2003: *Som isolerade öar. De lagerkransade kvinnorna och akademin under 1900-talets första hälft*. Symposion. Stockholm: Stehag.

Mauriņa, Zenta 1953: *Denn das Wagnis ist schön. Geschichte eines Lebens*. Memmingen/Allgäu: Maximilian Dietrich Verlag.

parallel identities, an 'ethnic' one, as Orehovs calls it, and a European one (Orehovs 1999, 231 and 233).

35 My own translation. In original: 'Att min kropp outbytbart är förbunden med mig hör till mitt livs svåraste, oåterkalleliga fakta, den aldrig slutande uppgiften att underordna det kroppsliga jaget mitt andliga väsen och att integrera världen i detta.' (Mauriņa 1968, 7.)

36 She also followed the political situation in Eastern Europe, for example the Soviet invasion of Hungary in 1956 (189–193).

Mauriņa, Zenta 1957: *Die eisernen Riegel zerbrechen. Geschichte eines Lebens.* Memmingen/Allgäu: Maximilian Dietrich Verlag.

Mauriņa, Zenta 1966: *Exilens tragik.* Svenska dagböcker. [1962: *Nord- und südliches Gelände: Schwedische Tagebücher 1946–1951.* Maximilian Dietrich Verlag, Memmingen/Allgäu]. Stockholm: Norstedt.

Mauriņa, Zenta 1968: *Befrielsens år.* Svenska dagböcker 1951–1958. [1966: *Jahre der Befreiung: Schwedische Tagebücher 1951–1958. Memmingen/Allgäu]*Maximilian Dietrich Verlag]. Stockholm: Norstedt.

Merleau-Ponty, Maurice & Edie, James M. 1964: *The Primacy of Perception and Other Essays on Phenomenological Psychology, the Philosophy of Art, History and Politics.* Evanston: Northwestern University Press.

Olsson, Anders 2011: *Ordens asyl: en inledning till den moderna exillitteraturen.* Stockholm: Albert Bonniers förlag.

Orehovs, Ivars 1999: Erfarenhet av verkligheten i Zenta Mauriņas svenska dagböcker. *Litteratur och verklighetsförståelse. Idémässiga aspekter av 1900-talets litteratur.* Ed. by Anders Pettersson & Torsten Pettersson & Anders Tyrberg. Umeå: Umeå universitet. 230–233.

Ouditt, Sharon (ed.) 2002: *Displaced Persons: Conditions of Exile in European Culture.* [Studies in European Cultural Transition 14]. Burlington: Ashgate.

Ronne, Marta 2000: *Två världar – ett universitet: Svenska skönlitterära universitetsskildringar 1904–1943. En genusstudie.* [Skrifter utgivna av Avdelningen för litteratursociologi vid Litteraturvetenskapliga institutionen i Uppsala, 44]. Uppsala: Uppsala universitet.

Ronne, Marta 2011: A Foreigner to Her Mother Tongue. Zenta Mauriņa (1897–1978) and Konstantin Raudive (1909–1974) as German-speaking Latvian Writers in Swedish Exile. *The Invasion of Books in Peripheral Literary Fields. Transmitting Preferences and Images in Media, Networks and Translation.* Ed. by Petra Broomans & Ester Jiresch. [Studies on Cultural Transfer and Transmission, 3]. Groningen: Barkhuis.181–211.

Said, Edward 1993: Intellectual Exile: Expatriates and Marginals. *Grand Street* 12/3.

Said, Edward 2000: *Reflections on Exile and other Essays.* Cambridge Massachusetts: Harvard University Press.

Schneider, Gertrude 2001: *Journey into Terror: The Story of the Riga Ghetto.* Westport: Praeger Publishers.

Strelka, Joseph P. 1983: *Exilliteratur. Grundprobleme der Theorie, Aspekte der Geschichte und Kritik.* Frankfurt am Main & New York: Peter Lang.

Strelka, Joseph 2003: *Exil, Gegenexil und Pseudoexil in der Literatur.* Tübingen: Francke Verlag.

Tabori, Paul 1972: *The anatomy of exile: a semantic and historical study.* London: Harrap.

Tamm, Maare 1986: En kvinna förtrogen med lidandet. *Svenska kyrkans tidning* nr 48.

Thomas, Carol 1999: *Female Forms. Experiencing and Understanding Disability.* Buckingham & Philadelphia: Open University Press,

Wendell, Susan 1996: *The Rejected Body. Feminist Philosophical Reflections on Disability.* New York & London: Routledge.

http://www.youtube.com/watch?feature=endscreen&NR=1&v=HSSiQSazrpQ (accessed 2012-08-15, 11:50)

http://www.youtube.com/watch?v=NKTst-pnViM&feature=related accessed 2012-08-15, 11:50).

http://www.youtube.com/watch?v=_fGdgrkqGng (accessed 2013-02-26, 23:01)

*Zenta Mauriņa. Bilder aus Ihrem Leben.* 1983. Memmingen: Maximilian Dietrich Verlag.

http://www.youtube.com/watch?feature=endscreen&NR=1&v=HSSiQSazrpQ (accessed 2012-08-15, 11:50)

http://www.youtube.com/watch?v=NKTst-pnViM&feature=related accessed 2012-08-15, 11:50).

http://www.youtube.com/watch?v=_fGdgrkqGng (accessed 2013-02-26, 23:01)

Eila Rantonen
https://orcid.org/0000-0002-1807-4361

# Writing Biography by E-Mail – Postcolonial and Postmodern Rewriting of Biographical and Epistolary Modes in Jonas Hassen Khemiri's *Montecore*

Jonas Hassen Khemiri's second novel *Montecore. En unik tiger* (2006, *Montecore. The Silence of the Tiger*, 2011) emblematizes postcolonial and migration writing, where different culturally marginalised identities are explored. In his highly acclaimed novel, Khemiri uses in an intriguing and subversive way such literary genres as the *novel of letters* (or *epistolary novel*) and *biography* in his portrayal of migrant identities and histories. Moreover, Khemiri's inventive use of genres is linked with the postmodern literary devices employed in *Montecore*. The text plays with genres, metafictional elements, truth claims, narrative modes and linguistic forms as in postmodern novels. Thus in *Montecore* many kinds of narrative devices are employed, by which the author moulds and mocks the generic conventions and expectations of the reader. Metafictional play between the fictional protagonist Jonas Khemiri and the real author Jonas Khemiri, for example, represents the postmodern lucid irony in the novel.

Apart from its postmodern veins, *Montecore* can also be conceived as postcolonial rewriting of epistolary, biographic and autobiographic modes. The multiple voicing of characters in the novel especially illuminates the innovative ways in the presentation of Tunisian migrants' lives in Sweden. In this article, I will explore how the dialogic and perspectival technique employed in the epistolary and biographic form is intertwined with the themes of migration and voicing of migrant identity.

Before exploring more closely the generic innovations, I will shortly outline the main events of *Montecore*. The novel unfolds the story of Tunisian Abbas Khemiri, who has migrated to Sweden and finally disappeared. Other main characters are his Swedish-born son Jonas and his old friend Kadir, who lives in Tunis. The novel starts with Kadir's correspondence with Jonas, who has made his début as a novelist in Sweden. In his email-letter, Kadir suggests that they should write a biography of Abbas together, which would be based on their memories of him: 'Let us collide our clever heads in the ambition of creating a biography worthy of your prominent father!' (*M* 2011, 4).[1]

---

1 'Låt oss kollidera våra kloka huvuden i ambitionen att kreera en biografi värdig din prominente far!' (*M* 2006, 14.)

In his letters, Kadir describes his memories of Abbas in Tunisia in 1958, which was bombed by the French troops in the Algerian war. Originally the friends had met in the orphanage, where Abbas had ended up after his parents had died in a bomb attack. In the first part of the novel, is outlined briefly the political conflicts and history of Tunisia and Algeria in the 1950s, 1960s and early 1970s are briefly outlined. Abbas meets his wife Pernilla in Tunisia, in a tourist-resort Tabarka in the 1970s, with the result that he moves to Sweden and has three sons with Pernilla. In fact, large parts of the novel concentrate on depicting how Abbas tries to find his place in the Swedish society and how the cultural differences affect a bicultural family. While *Montecore* is a moving depiction of the relationship between son and father, it is also an incisive study of Swedish society with its increasing number of immigrants and hostility towards them in the 1980s and 1990s. It also reflects the growth of neo-Nazi movements in the 1990s in Sweden.

The last part of the novel concentrates on Abbas's downfall in Swedish society, where hostility to foreigners is on the increase. In his letter to Kadir, Abbas is worried that his children will be outsiders in Sweden with their black hair and brown skins in a country where neo-Nazis demonstrate openly in the streets and attack with fire bombs (*M* 2011, 135–136; *M* 2006, 164). Abbas does not want a situation in which migrants become segregated or secluded groups in Swedish society. Instead, he wants to promote integration and even ends up forbidding his sons to play with other children of immigrant descent (*M* 2011, 242; *M* 2006, 284). Furthermore, Kadir humorously describes that Abbas starts to emblematise a hybrid European and North-African identity in Sweden, symbolising 'the globally modern meeting place where East crosses West, where Jesus crosses Muhammad' (*M* 2011, 49; *M* 2006, 64).

The second-generation perspective is presented in Jonas's characterization. Similarly, Khemiri has also dealt with the second-generation identity in his first novel *Ett öga rött* (2003, [One Eye Red]). Thus, the children of migrants portrayed in both of Khemiri's novels skilfully represent the dual or hybrid perspective on Arab and Swedish cultures. This kind of dual cultural positioning of children renders them useful literary devices for depicting various aspects of multicultural societies such as Sweden.

Abbas's son Jonas demonstrates how migrant children represent the voice of conflict between cultures, which arise between and among native and immigrant groups. Khemiri seems to employ the child protagonist to introduce and negotiate the tensions arising between the host and original cultures, which often culminates as generational conflict. Children thus become literary devices that allow insights into disparate cultural issues. (Campbell-Hall 2009, 292–293.) In *Montecore*, Abbas's attempts to 'Swedify' himself and his sons are strongly opposed by Jonas who even deliberately begins to speak Swedish with an Arabic accent. Together with his friends Nigerian-descendent Melinda, Balochian Imran and Chilean Patrick, he starts a political movement, an antiracist organisation *BFL* (Blatte for Life), promoting the rights of migrants. Jonas calls his revolutionary group 'the unidentifiable creoles, the blend of everything, all the pigeonhole-free border people' (*M* 2011, 274)² who cannot be categorised. In their correspondence, both Abbas and Kadir criticise the children, who want to give a decisive weight to the valour of ethnicity: 'And who becomes a better pet of racists than people that accept the existence of an us and a them?' (*M* 2011, 275)³

## Three Informants and Writers Composing the Story of Abbas. The Relational Identity and Family Histories

*Montecore* recounts Jonas's and Kadir's attempt to reconstruct the life story of Abbas. In a postmodern vein, the novel conveys a constant play with truth-claims. In many passages, Kadir makes a direct claim to the 'real,' and the truth of lived experience in the shaping of Abbas's biography, 'THE TRUTH and nothing but THE TRUTH must be our lighthouse in the shaping of a literary master opus' (*M* 2011, 15–16).⁴ Moreover, in his letter to Jonas, Kadir recommends that they should use a pseudonym in their biography of Jonas's father in order to protect Abbas's anonymity. 'I also agree that certain people's need for anonymity could be damaged if we employ real names. So let us call the book "fiction" and modify certain names. What shall we name your father?' (*M* 2011, 18)⁵ Therefore, Kadir invents the pseudonym 'Abbas' for Jonas's father in order to illustrate his relocation in Sweden. This name combines the Swedish pop-group Abba with a typical Arabic name, Abbas. In fact, playing with proper names is paradigmatic of toying with identity markers in bilingual literature, where names are part of the game of border crossing (Cortés-Conde & Boxer 1992, 143). Moreover, the anonymity of Abbas, is motivated by political reasons, too. In a footnote, Kadir warns Jonas that all information about the contemporary political situation of Tunisia must be excluded from the biography of Abbas since it may cause problems with his Tunisian passport (*M* 2011, 76; *M* 2006, 94).

Although *Montecore* cannot be conceived as a biography or memoir, it uses the literary devices of these genres. The researchers of autobiographical and biographical mode have pointed out the extent to which the self is defined by its relation with others. For instance, Paul Eakin appropriates the term *the relational life*⁶ to describe the story of a relational model of

2   '[...] vi dom oidentifierbara kreolerna allas blandningar alla fackfria gränsfolk.' (*M* 2006, 322.)
3   'Och vem blir en bättre kelgris till rasister än personer som accepterar existensen av ett vi och ett dom? Vem blir mer tandlöst ofarlig än "blatten" som accepterar sin existens som "blatten"?' (*M* 2006, 322.)
4   'SANNINGEN och inget utom SANNINGEN måste bli vårt fyrtorn i skapandet av ett litterärt mästeropus' (*M* 2006, 27.)
5   'Jag håller också med om att vissa personers behov av anonymitet kan skadas om vi brukar deras riktiga namn. Låt oss således kalla boken "fiktion" och modifiera vissa namn. Hur ska vi namnge din far?' (*M* 2006, 30.)
6   Eakin is inspired in his discussion of 'relational life' by feminist theories of relational selves and autobiographical writing. (Cf. Bella Brodski's and Celeste Schenk's essay 'Other Voice' in *Life/Lines: Theorising Women's Autobiography* (Ithaca: Cornell University Press, 1988) or Domna Stanton's introduction 'Autogynography: Is the

identity, developed collaboratively with others, often family members.[7] He mentions both autobiographic and fictional family memoirs, in which the lives of other family members are rendered as either equal in importance to or more important than the life of the reporting self. Thus the self's story is viewed through the lens of its relation with some other key person, most often a parent. Eakin (1999, 85–86) calls such an individual 'the proximate other' to signify the intimate tie to the relational autobiographer.

Among others, Eakin's examples consist of ethnic minority writers, whose writing strategies can be compared with Khemiri's *Montecore*. For example, Eakin (1999, 58–59) mentions Jewish-American Art Spiegelman's *Maus: A Survivor's Tale* (1986, 1991), where the cartoonist Spiegelman records and translates into comic strip form his father's tale of his survival at Auschwitz. Eakin claims that in this text the autobiographical act is doubled, since the story of the other, of the informant (Art Spiegelman's father, Vladek), is accompanied by the story of the individual gathering this oral history (Art Spiegelman himself). This second narrative, Eakin (1999, 59) terms 'the story of the story' that structures the text. The stress is on the performance of the collaboration and therefore on the relation between the two individuals involved. However, in *Montecore,* we can note that the narrative position is tripled. Apart from Abbas, whose voice is presented in his letters to Kadir, both Jonas and Kadir collaborate as informants and witnesses in the telling of the life history of Abbas. Notably, we can claim that mediated by Jonas's and Kadir's memories, Abbas's story is also partly both Jonas's and Kadir's life story.

Gayatri Spivak's famous question of whether marginalised people can have a voice of their own and speak for themselves, which Spivak handles in her book *In Other Worlds* (1986), is also dealt with in *Montecore*. In fact, it is suggested in the text that Abbas is not able to write his own autobiography although he would like to do it. He even confides in his letter to Kadir that it is very difficult to bring order to his life since all of his memories are mixed and he cannot even know how he should begin his history (*M* 2011, 298; *M* 2006, 347). When sketching Abbas's biography in his letter, Kadir suggests that they should start the writing process of the book by recalling their memories of Abbas.

> Recall you father citing the Baudelaire photographer Félix Nadar: "The best portrait is made by the person one knows best." This rule also applies to authors. How can you (and the reader) know you father's contours and understand his later actions without the forming of his historical history? (*M* 2011, 40.)[8]

Subject Different' in *The Female Autobiograph: Theory and Practice of Autobiography from the Tenth to the Twentieth Century* (Chicago: Chicago University Press, 1987). However, Eakin wants to extend its use as a cross-gender phenomenon especially in autobiographical writing.

7   Here Eakin (1999, 85–86) mentions, among others, Maxine Hong Kingston's *The Woman Warrior* (1976) and Michael Ondaatje's *Running in the Family* (1982).

8   'Erinra din far citerande Baudelairefotografen Félix Nadar: "Bästa porträttet görs av den person som man känner bäst." Denna regel gäller också författare. Hur ska du (och läsaren) känna din fars konturer och förstå hans senare aktioner utan gestaltandet av hans historiska historia?' (*M* 2006, 53.)

As it follows, Jonas's childhood memories in Tunisia are inserted in the text:

> Here I propose that you inject some of your own memories from your yearly vacations in Tunisia. If you fear needing to compete with my metaphoric magnificence you can vary your font. Do you memorize anything from Jendouba. **Sure you remember Jendouba...**
> The city in western Tunisia where Dads grew up. The city where wrinkly, straw-hatted farmers sit crookedly on horseback and red trailers rattle iron bars. (*M* 2011, 10.)[9]

In this passage the shift from Kadir's letter to Jonas's memories is textually marked in bold letters. Noticeably, Jonas's memories, presented in the present tense, are conveyed in the unconventional second-person mode, 'You remember the pounding at the hamam, the eternal rubbing out of sweat dirt, Dads's hairy bodies, and then go home on the truck bed with cactuses whizzing by and stacked mountains of garlic' (*M* 2011, 10)[10]. This distancing device in *Montecore* may promote the idea of studying Jonas from a distance, as if the adult Jonas were discussing with his younger version.

How are then the disparate bits and pieces of Abbas's life story assembled and put together in the text from a variety of sources? Indeed, in *Montecore*, the opacity of creating a life story of a real person is illustrated to the reader. The result is that it is left for the reader to make a connected and coherent story of Abbas's life. Thus the reader has to compose the biography of Abbas from the different kinds of representative modes and sources, such as letters between Jonas and Kadir, reminiscences of Jonas presented in the second person, and Abbas's own letters. With these kinds of fragmentary narrative forms, the text illustrates how the biography of Abbas is a hypothetical and relative construction, composed of many different fragmentary sources and written from different angles.

In fact, Abbas's life story can be viewed in the context of *witness biography*, which Cohn (1999, 43, 87) distinguishes as a special form of life story. This kind of historical texts have often been imitated in fiction like in Joseph Conrad's Marlow novels, where the narrator acts as witness to the actions of other characters. We can also mention Sudanese Tayeb Salih's novel *Season of Migration to the North* where an anonymous narrator tells a story of the voyage to Europe of Mustafa Sa'eed (see Fraser 2000, 81).[11] These narrating characters and witnesses, unlike the omniscient tellers of third-person

---

9  'Här proponerar jag att du injicerar några egna minnen från era årliga semestrar i Tunisien. Om du fruktar att behöva rivalisera med min metaforiska magnificens kan du variera ditt bokstavsformat. Memorerar du något från Jendouba? /**Såklart du minns Jendouba...**/ Staden i västra Tunisien där pappor är uppväxta. Staden där skrynkliga halmhattade bönder siter snett på hästryggar och röda traktorvagnar skramlar järnstänger.' (*M* 2006, 20–21.)

10 'Du minns hammamens mörbultning, det eviga framgnuggandet av svettsolk, pappors håriga kroppar och sen åka bilflak hem med förbisusande kaktusar och staplade vitlöksberg.' (*M* 2006, 21.)

11 Edward Said has interpreted Salih's novel as a *Heart of Darkness* in reverse (Said 1993, xx.)

The opening sentence in Jonas Hassen Khemiri's Montecore. The Silence of the Tiger *(2011/2006) aptly illustrates the problematic situation of hybrid identities: "They just think I'm a strange tiger who walks on two legs". Cover: Lotta Kühlhorn / Norstedts.*

novels, seem to simulate the natural (referential) discourses (e.g. Cohn 1999, 43). Khemiri's *Montecore* explores this kind of witness biography by its use of Kadir and Jonas as witnesses of Abbas's life story. Furthermore, *Montecore* also illuminates the problems that this kind of narrative mode induces in biographic writing.

Although Abbas's own voice is heard in a couple of his letters presented in the text, his life story is mainly presented from Kadir's and Jonas's perspectives since they discuss and plan the shape and content of Abbas's biography. The consequence is that they are trying to fill in the gaps in his biography in order to make the biographic narrative more coherent and reasonable. Kadir asserts, correspondingly, that he and Jonas should together formulate a clear motive for Abbas's recovery from his traumatic silence in Tunisia.

Furthermore, as both Jonas and Kadir act as biographers, we can emphasize that the idea of constructing the life story of Abbas is *culturally divided* since Jonas has been brought up in Sweden and Kadir in Tunisia. Thus the dialogues and journeys between Sweden and Tunisia, and Orient and Occident, in the novel are presented in the depiction of the psychological and geospatial voyages of the triadic protagonists of the book, Abbas, Jonas and Kadir.

Although the novel concentrates on the correspondence between Kadir and Jonas, as stated above, Abbas is also given some space to represent himself. This is enacted by the insertion of Abbas's letters to Kadir in the second part

*Jonas Hassen Khemiri.
Photo: Martin
Stenmark / Bonniers.*

of the book, which describes Abbas's settling in Sweden in the 1970s. In his letter, he confides to Kadir that he was told in Tunisia that his memory of his meeting with his father was wrong. Abbas's Tunisian relative Rachid claimed that Abbas's family had been infected with the infection 'where the forms of fantasy are given life in excess and in dangerous cases collide with reality' (*M* 2011, 100)[12]. These words shocked Abbas who started to rethink his life course. 'Suddenly all the details of my life seemed to be suspiciously slipping and uncertain. What else could I have fantasized? What else can be untrue that is reality in my thoughts?' (*M* 2011, 100)[13] Here Abbas's words clearly refer to the constructive nature of autobiography and biography where fact and fiction are easily blended.

Consequently, *Montecore* advocates the hypothetical construction of biography since it does not depict a coherent life story, although it tries to explain Abbas's life and character. We can notice that especially Kadir acts as an empathetic biographer. However, the constructing of Abbas's biography also illustrates the limitations of the biographic work planned by Kadir and

12 '[...] den där fantasins gestalter livges i excess och i farliga fall kolliderar med realiteten.' *M* 2006, 121
13 'Plötsligt tycktes alla mitt livs detaljer vara skumt glidande och osäkra. Vad mer kan jag ha fantiserat. Vad mer kan vara osant som i min tanke är realitet?' (*M* 2006, 121.)

Jonas, who are constrained and subjective in their presentation of their subject's life.

In fact, Abbas's speech is often quoted in the text but his thoughts are not rendered except in a couple of poignant passages, where Abbas ponders, what he is doing in Sweden. These passages resemble interior or narrated monologue. As follows, the information of Abbas is mainly unfolded in Kadir's and Jonas's descriptions of the life of Abbas, meanwhile Abbas's inner life is hardly depicted. On the other hand, the use of both Kadir's and Jonas's viewpoints in the presentation of Abbas's life story, creates an interesting perspective technique. This kind of plural mode for telling live stories serves as an intriguing postmodern and postcolonial stance. By telling and recounting Abbas's story in the incoherent, fragmented way in which it has been revealed to his son and to his friend, Khemiri shows how the construction of another person's life is always a subjective and interpretative process. Furthermore, the reader-addressing metafictional rhetoric highlights the difficulty of creating a coherent and truthful life story of Abbas.

As in biographies, Kadir and Jonas report the misery, oppression and delightful moments that Abbas has encountered and experienced, and they constantly evaluate, from their own point of view, the life course of Abbas and his place in Tunisia and Sweden. Moreover, Kadir wants them to use fictional techniques in the presentation of Abbas's life. Besides, Kadir even suggests some fictional techniques that would shape Abbas's life-story into something more coherent and dramatic. For instance, he advises that Abbas's recovery from his childhood trauma should be brought up to light by employing Joycean stream-of-consciousness technique in order to make the text more inspiring to the reader:

> In the book we will do our best to formulate an obvious motive for your father's cured tongue in order to avoid confusing the reader. [...] Or you could have him be afflicted by a magical dream sequence in which his future is depicted in a modern Joyce-esque stream of consciousness.' (*M* 2011, 13.)[14]

Kadir also suggests that they should add a bit more drama to the highlights of Abbas's life by using different kinds of literary strategies and orchestrate the text even with musical effects.

> Now comes the scene that we can call "Kadir's initiation to Sweden". Together your family and I delight everything that Stockholm's wintery spring has to offer in 1986.
>
> Let us here change the tone of the book and present this sequence in the musical form of the medley (with your father's photographing clicking sound as a steady beat-drum).

14 'I boken gör vi bäst att formulera ett tydligt motiv till din fars kurerade tunga för att undvika läsarnas förvirring. [...] Eller så kan du låta honom drabbas av en magisk drömsekvens där hans framtid tecknas i en modern joycisk medvetandeström.' (*M* 2006, 24.)

> Stockholm, oh Stockholm! CLICK! Show how we transport ourselves into the city and wander wharfs and superficially iced lakes. CLICK! (*M* 2011, 140.)[15]

Like many postmodern novels, *Montecore* contains numerous metafictional comments on the writing process.

> At the Museum of modern Art we inspect a gigantic and very popular retrospective exhibition of the celebrated Swedish photographer Christer Strömholm. Then write:
> My father notes Strömholm's photographs as standardized and unimpressive. Still, is it perhaps this visit which will influence so much of my father's future? Why? Read on and you will receive knowledge!!!
> (This is a so-called planting in order to feed the readers' curiosity.)
> Here we will die away the musical medley and normalize the form. (*M* 2011, 141–142.)[16]

## Multitopicality of the Epistolary Form

Letters have reduced the distances between people and connected them globally. Historically, the letters sent by migrants to their home countries, more than newspapers and books, for example, became the source of knowledge about life in the new location. Thus personal correspondence was a significant source for expanding knowledge of migration and migrants (Elliott, Gerber & Sinke 2006, 2, 3). Furthermore, e-mail form, especially, has made the connective, cognitive and communicative elements of a letter even faster and more easily in reach.

Moreover, letterform has also been employed as a literary device and genre of its own. It has been called, for example, as *epistolary genre* or *novel of letters*. Significantly, some postcolonial and migrant writers use epistolary address in their portrayal of cultural identities and transnational relations. In their works, letterform can be a device in bridging the cultural differences and distances. Conceived transnationally, the letter becomes a unique social space that exists neither in the homeland nor in the host country, but in a third place, which is in effect, in both places simultaneously (Elliot, Gerber & Sinke 2006, 12). Still the epistolary genre has not been studied much in postcolonial and migrant studies. Critics have not successfully related the issues of ethnicity to epistolarity, which can be a viable narrative method

---

15 'Ny följer den sken som vi kan kalla "Kadirs initiering till Sverige". Tillsammans njuter jag och din familj allt som Stockholms vintriga vår har att erbjuda 1986./ Låt oss här växla bokens ton och presentera sekvensen med medleyns musikaliska form (med din fars fotograferande klickljud som stadig takttrumma). /Stockholm, ack Stockholm! KLICK! Visa hur vi transporterar oss in till city och vandrar kajer och ytligt isade sjöar. KLICK!' (*M* 2006, 169–170.)

16 'Min far noterar Strömholms fotografier som standardiserade och oimponerande. Ändå är det kanske denna visit som kommer influera så mycket av min fars framtid? Varför? Läs vidare så får du vetskap!!! /Detta är en så kallad plantering för att mata läsarnas kuriositet.)/ Här tonar vi bort det musikaliska medleyt och normaliserar formen.' (*M* 2006, 170–171.)

for raising contemporary political questions about nationality, ethnicity, diaspority and migration (see also Sanae 2008, 277).

In the representation and voicing of migrant's experience the epistolary form plays a crucial role in *Montecore*. Abbas's biography in *Montecore* is mainly presented by e-mail-letters, which Kadir writes from Tunisia to Jonas in Sweden. Significantly, the epistolary genre usually involves a bifocality of perspectives, as the views of both the sender and the receiver are incorporated. As an epistolary novel, Montecore can be classified as *dialogic* (including the letters of two protagonists) or *polylogic* (with three or more letter-writing characters) since Abbas's biography is presented from three perspectives, Abbas's, Kadir's and Jonas's.

When Kadir's Tunisian views are introduced in the correspondence, this gives the novel a specific multicultural focus. Thus, letters present an intercultural dialogue that transcends and crosses cultural boundaries. Moreover, the embedded dialogic letter formula enlarges the more limited perspective of first-person narration. In fact, the striking feature of the letter genre is its dialogism. Thus it highlights the extent to which the self is defined by its relation with others as I mentioned earlier in connection to biographical writing.

Consequently, we can stress here that the letter genre serves as an emblem of changing cultural notions of textuality and generic modification in postcolonial and migrant novels. Moreover, it increases the dialogic elements in the novel. Epistolary genre embodies a postcolonial and multicultural situation in its way of describing a fragmented self in the midst of cultures and cultural differences. Significantly, several contemporary novelists have used the letter genre to express their characters' selves from the different angles and perspectives. This kind of mosaic and fragmentary writing also resembles a postmodern strategy by its emphasis on the significance of collage. Also in new postcolonial, minority, and migrant writing, the life stories are often presented as fragmented residues that the readers must reconstruct, as mentioned above. For instance, Elleke Boehmer (2005, 219) claims that a crucial feature of postcolonial women's writing is its mosaic or composite quality; the intermingling of forms derived from indigenous nationalist and European literary traditions. Coming from a very different cultural context themselves, writers emphasize the need for a lively heterogeneity of styles and speaking positions in their work. Boehmer (2005, 219) argues that they practice what Gayatri Spivak (1986) has described as a 'frontier style', favouring cross-hatched, fragmented, and choric forms. Thus this kind of fragmented form is more often used in women's, postcolonial and migration writing.

We can further emphasise the fact that the epistolary narrative is by definition a fragmented narrative. As Janet Gurkin Altman (1983, 169) notes, discontinuity is built into the blank spaces that makes each letter a footprint rather than a path. In constructing the mosaic of their narrative, epistolary novelists constantly choose between the discontinuity inherent in the letter form and the creation of a compensatory continuity.

We can underline the role of a specific voicing technique of characters in Khemiri's *Montecore*. In fact, in the history of epistolary writing, letters, like conversation, have increasingly been valued for their 'natural,' 'authentic' and purportedly inimitable qualities. Good letter writers were said to be those who could make their letters 'seem to speak,' in a plain and unpedantic style. Furthermore, the letter form may also provide the writer's non-authorial stance; thus, the illusion of an authentic text could be strengthened. Indeed, in the studies of epistolary form it has been emphasised that letters give an effect where the narrator's voice is rendered unmediated and truthful (Goldsmith 1986, 4, 47, 55). Thus, the conversational and personal tone in letters may also increase the effect of 'authentic' voicing of the characters. Therefore, the epistolary genre may be employed in order to give a voice to 'voiceless' people, for example, to such immigrants as Tunisian Abbas in Sweden. For example, in his letters to Kadir, Abbas describes his experiences in Sweden in the 1980s:

> [...] The frequency of immigrants is rising in step with the Swedes' suspiciousness. In this year's election commotion, the Conservatives' master, Ulf Adelson, expressed: "A Swede is a Swede and a Negro a Negro." He has also said that of course the Swedes' eyes sting when immigrant children take limousines from "upper-class Östermalm apartments" to sumptuous home language lessons, while Swedish children must hike. Even Sweden's socialists are starting to fly their kites in the same foreigner-antipathetic wind. Sometimes my soul is unsecured. What am I doing here? How will my three sons grow successfully in this country? How will their brown skin and black hair find success in a context where neo-Nazis have begun to manifest openly in the streets and refugee homes are attacked with firebombs? (*M* 2011, 135–136.)[17]

We can stress that epistolary address can add a greater realistic effect to the story, because it reproduces real speech. It is also able to demonstrate differing points of view without recourse to an omniscient narrator. Consequently, in letters we can hear the characters voices providing immediacy and 'authenticity'. Epistolary form also allows the authors to present the characters' thoughts without interference, and to convey events with dramatic immediacy.

Furthermore, we can stress the letter genre's communicative and intermediary nature. Thus, it can be employed intentionally as a literary strategy, which bridges the cultural differences and distances. For example, Janet Gurkin Altman (1983, 13) has emphasised the letter's function as a connector between two distant points, as a bridge between sender and

---

17 'Invandrarnas frekvens stiger i takt med svenskarnas misstänksamhet. I årets elektionsrörelse exprimerade dom konservativas patron Ulf Adelsohn: "En svensk är en svensk och en neger en neger". Han har också sagt att svenskars ögon såklart svider när invandrarbarn åker limousine från "överklassiska Östermalmslägenheter" till luxuösa hemspråkundervisningar, medan svenska barn måste fotvandra. Också svenska socialister börjar flyga sina drakar i samma främlingsantipatiska vind. Ibland osäkras min själ. Vad gör jag har? Hur ska mina tre söner växa lyckligt i detta land. Hur ska deras bruna hud och svarta hår finna succé i en kontext där nynazister börjat manifestera öppet på gator och flyktinghus attackeras med brandbomber?' (*M* 2006, 164.)

receiver, where the author can choose to emphasize either the distance or the bridge. Consequently, the power of the letter is to make the distant addressee present. In this it may also decrease the distance between the letter writer and the (internal and the external) reader. In the letter genre, the narratee is almost as important an agent as the narrator is. Moreover, the internal reader persona frequently loses his/her specificity to coincide with the external reader (Altman 1983, 91). In this way, especially in the epistolary genre, the role of the reader is central and in the foreground. Due to its interplay and dialogue between the text's internal reader (narratee) and 'real' reader, epistolary mode may convey increased affective response in the reader.

Moreover, *Montecore* also illuminates the reading act and experience of letters. When Jonas reads Kadir's reminiscences of his father, for instance, he starts to respond in his mind to Kadir's story and his childhood memories start to flow into his mind. The shift from the letter form into the presentation of Jonas's thoughts is presented here in the rarely used second-person form. The first sentence of Jonas's memories is printed in bold, which marks the shift of the narrator and focalizer from Kadir to Jonas:

> [Kadir] I remember that your father returned to this subject in 2001 in an e-mail he wrote me from a Palestinian family in the Ramallah of occupation. He wrote: "Oh Kadir. What modifies life more than the magical insight about the potential freezing of everything?" This is a very beautiful phrase, which should be injected later in the book. (But exclude your father's continuation: "Wait, there is one thing…fifty-three years of permanent oppression by a blood-thirsty occupying power! Fuck the potential freezing of everything!") Do you understand you father's words, or are they on the side of fuzziness? Perhaps this emotion refers to your discovery of writing? If so, inject a section where you write, "As usual, the genial Kadir is entirely correct…"
> **And Kadir actually has a** point, and when you read his letters you remember that day when you had just learned to read, and it has to be the year before Kadir comes to visit. (*M* 2011, 44–45.)[18]

As the narrative moves between Tunisia and Sweden, and the other character, the Tunisian Kadir, is located in a distant country; for the reader, the cross-cultural identification may be difficult at first. However, my claim is, that the letter form, with its speaking subject may help the reader to empathise with the interlocutor located in a different country such as Tunisia more than,

---

18 '[Kadir] Jag minns att din far returnerade till detta subjekt år 2001 i ett e-brev som han skrev mig från en palestinsk familj i ockupationens Ramallah. Han skrev: "Ack, Kadir. Vad modifierar liv mer in den magiska insikten om alltings potentiella infrysning?" Detta är en mycket vacker fras som borde injiceras senare i boken. (Men exkludera din fars fortsättning: "Jo, en sak 53 års permanent förtryck av en blodtörstig ockupantmakt' Knulla alltings potentiella infrysning!" Förstår du din fars ord eller spelar dom flummighetens överkant? Kanske refererar denna emotion till upptäckt av skrivandet? Om ja, injicera en section där du skriver "Precis som vanligt är den geniale Kadir helt korrekt…"/ **Och Kadir har faktisk en** poäng och när du läser hans bokstäver minns du den där dagen när du precis lärt dig läsa och det måste vara året innan Kadir kommer på besök.' (*M* 59–60.)

for example, the more conventional third person form often employed in novelistic discourse. Indeed, the letter genre emphasises the exchange and communicative I-you relationship, which shapes the language used, and in which 'I' becomes defined relative to 'you' whom he/she addresses (see Altman 1983, 118).

In this, the rhetorical employment of the epistolary genre may serve an intentional postcolonial strategy, which tries to give voice and space to marginalised people such as migrants. Significantly, the letter genre may also employ an implied 'double audience' (minority or dominant cultures) or multicultural readers and audiences. Thus by its cross-cultural presentation of different cultural voices and audiences, the letter form, with its intimate form of address, may bring together different cultural voices and audiences, and thus entice the sympathy of the reader. Although the presentation of Tunisian characters, Kadir and Abbas, may imply cultural distance or a cognitive gap for the Swedish reader and his/her response, the first person mode, typical of the letter genre, may be a form that conduces a dialogical response in the (external) reader. Accordingly, it may rhetorically retain the potential to pull the (external) reader easily into the addressee role, invite her/him to project him/herself into the narratee's subject position and so generate empathetic responses although the character-correspondent has a different cultural background.[19]

As letters accumulate, they create a story of Abbas. This intercultural dialogue, written in a letter formula, highlights the bicultural positions and living in-between-cultures. Through these intercontinental dialogues between Tunisia and Sweden, different versions and perspectives of Abbas's life story are presented. Both Kadir and Jonas try to explain the choices that Abbas was forced to make both in Sweden and in Tunisia. In his letters to Kadir, Abbas, for example, explains why he has not learned Swedish quickly enough. As his motive, he explains that the choice of language is significant. In Sweden, English or French will be attractive to Swedes, whereas to use an Arabic broken Swedish attracts only angry comments and a negative atmosphere (*M* 2011, 137; *M* 2006, 166).

The letters of Tunisians Abbas and Kadir, written in Swedish (it is explained to the reader that Kadir learned Swedish when he stayed a year in Stockholm), consist of a hybridised language, mixed with French and Arabic words and expressions. By these means, for example, the linguistic pressure of a former colonial country (France) to the colonial selves (Tunisians) is expressed. On the other hand, hybridised language also conceives the culturally hybrid identities typical for the formerly colonised countries as well as migrants in present day postcolonial and multicultural Europe.

We can stress here that migrant and postcolonial writing have renewed the ways in which the spatial issues have been presented in fiction. For example, Gerald Prince (2005, 375) has argued that 'postcolonial narratology should pay particular attention to multitopicality (e.g. "here" as opposed to

---

19 See also James Phelan's (1996, 135–153) discussion on narrative audiences. However, Phelan does not discuss culturally divided audiences.

"there") – as well as to the degrees of heterotopicality, to the kinds of mixtures and inconsistencies, of gaps and cracks within spaces or between them, and to spatial alignments along such semantic axes as natural, or artificial, familiar or strange, independent, or colonized'. Certainly, this multitopicality is intriguingly presented in *Montecore*, which is set both in Tunisia and Sweden. Moreover, past events and histories can be flexibly conveyed by the use of the epistolary mode. For instance, the novel includes different spatial and temporal levels and different historical chronologies. An example is the temporal polyvalence seen in Kadir's letters to Jonas; observations of the present-day Sweden are included, as well as descriptions of Tunisia and Sweden in the 1960s, 1970s, 1980s and 1990s.

Significantly, *Montecore* depicts two histories: the historical events of Tunisia and Algeria in the 50s, 60s and 70s and the history of Sweden in the 1980s and 1990s. Hence, it recounts French colonial oppression of Algerians and Tunisians, for example, by telling about the traumatic childhood of Abbas, who experienced a shock and became mute after his parents were killed in a bomb attack during the Algerian war in 1954–1962. Moreover, it depicts a story of a Tunisian protagonist as a victim of racism in Swedish society. On a thematic level, connected with migration and colonial history of Tunisia and Algeria, the novel can therefore be read as giving voice to formerly colonised subjects in Algeria and non-heard migrants in Swedish society. It also describes the migrant spaces such as Rinkeby's urban neighbourhood where the inhabitants are mainly migrants or immigrant descent.

We can emphasise here the role of epistolary form with its temporal and spatial hiatus that Janet Gurkin Altman (1983, 135) has emphasised. The word present in the letter is charged with both its temporal and its spatial meanings; it signifies 'now' as opposed to the 'then' of past and future events or contact, and it means 'here' as opposed to the 'there where the addressee always is'. The shifts of places (Tunisia, Sweden) are flexibly produced in *Montecore* by the use of the epistolary form, where the letters describe the life and happenings in different countries and continents. Thus I claim that the epistolary genre seems particularly suited to the presentation of characters of different cultural background and who act as a kind of transnational subjects, crossing and moving between cultures, places and states.

In the history of the epistolary genre, the theme of cultural exchange is often employed as in Montesquieu's *The Persian letters* (1721) that depicts Europe from the perspective of non-Europeans. This pioneering epistolary novel contains ironic comparisons of East and West, and it tries to serve dialogic or double perspective on both continents. By this kind of setting, Western perspective is rendered as relative. In the letters of Kadir and Jonas between 'Occident' and 'Orient', irony of the Western orientalist representations of East is used, for instance, in the depiction of 'imagined' Tunisia as an exotic East in the fantasies of tourists. Kadir especially describes European women tourists in humorous vein in his accounts when he and Abbas are busy seducing the tourist women in Tabarka in the 1970s. The tourist women are attracted by Tunisian exotic men as Kadir ironically explains; at that time, the word 'Arab' was not used as a provocation or virus but attracted 'sexual frequency'. The result was that Tunisian men took on the role of 'Oriental men', such as oriental poets with melancholy eyes, for the benefit of the western tourist women, when having erotic nights with them in the hotel rooms (*M* 2011, 42, 50; *M* 57–58, 62). The Orientalist discourse employed by Western people towards Tunisians is often noted by Kadir and Abbas in their correspondence. For example, in Tabarka, a Greek photographer staged Abbas in tourist photos as an Arab with a fez, fake moustache, gold platter, tea service, djellaba, veil, decorative hookah, and leather slippers (*M* 2011, 32; *M* 2006, 45).

The introduction of the point of view of Kadir and Abbas creates to this Swedish novel an intercultural and intercontinental perspective that transcends the cultural boundaries. Significantly, the embedded dialogic letter formula augments the more limited perspective of the first-person narrator or omniscient third-person narrator typical of novelistic discourse. For example, Robert Fraser (2000, 45), who has explored the grammatical use of persons in postcolonial narratives, maintains that a third-person narrator especially may signify 'omniscience', which often turns out to be a position with uncomfortable political consequences. Moreover, third person omniscient narration has even been denounced as inherently inauthentic, and the use of epistolary form with its different correspondents and subjects may increase the effect of dialogism (see e.g. Altman 1983, 139) since within a letter written by a single correspondent we may also hear several voices and different points of view. For example, Kadir's letters, for example, often cite and paraphrase Jonas and Abbas, who are represented through their own words. Thus, the use of multilingual narrators and the rejection of the third-person narrative seem to reform the conventional presentations of narrators in fiction. Also the use of epistolary form with its different correspondents and subjects may increase the effect of dialogism (see Altman 1983, 139).

Dialogism inherent in the letter genre may be increased even more with its paratextual elements when epistolary texts also include prefaces, prepefaces, and postfaces, which conduct a dialogue with each other and with the text proper, and which can be viewed as a continuation of the text's dialogical model (Altman 1983, 163). *Montecore* also includes a fictional preface with its metafictional dialogue with the reader addressed as 'dear reader' (hej, kära läsare!) in prologue.

*Montecore* interweaves shifting Swedish and Tunisian contexts, whereby the novel's metaphoric language is marked by elements signifying cultural differences. The ethnic and cultural differences are also ironised. Besides, we can note that the novel contains ironical remarks on the depiction of authentic migrant speech. In *Montecore*, there is a reference to the reception of Khemiri's first novel *Ett öga rött* where the language of the novel was misinterpreted as a depiction of 'authentic' migrant speech.

> Despite your protests you are celebrated because you have written a book in "Authentic Rinkeby Swedish." Apparently you have brought "the immigrant's story" to life in a language that sounds as though on has "Dropped a microphone" into an immigrant area of one's choice. Did you not write that your book was about

a Swedish-born man who breaks his language with intention? What happened to your asserted exploration of "the authenticity theme"? (*M* 2011, 27.)[20]

It is true that *Montecore* cannot straightforwardly be categorised as a 'realist' representation or voicing of migrants because of the many postmodern distancing techniques. However, the presentation of the multilingual language that the migrants in Sweden of Arabic descent use in *Montecore*, can be seen as a narrative device that approaches realistic representation and has rarely been presented in Swedish literature. The multicultural position is very clearly visible and audible in the language of *Montecore*, which is composed of hybridised Swedish including French and Arabic words and expressions that Kadir and Abbas employ in their letters. Moreover, Elleke Boehmer (1995/2005, 258–259) has asserted that a creolized or polyglot story or poem both recalls the way in which cultures are syncretically interlinked, and provides a gateway to feeling otherness, experiencing how it might be to be beside one's self. Significantly, postcolonial critical reading can thus put into play the invitation of the text to think as the other.

## *Is There an Ending in Life Stories or Correspondence?*

In the beginning of 1990s, a stolen poster is put up in front of Abbas's studio Silvia depicting a clown who asserts 'Keep Sweden CLEAN' (*M* 2011, 244).[21] The consequences of racism culminate, when Abbas's studio is burned down by the neo-Nazis. Due to these tragic events, Abbas's artistic dreams collapse and he becomes depressed. His tragic realisation is that his attempts to integrate in Swedish society did not succeed. Finally, Abbas leaves his family and returns to Tunisia and then disappears. However, the end of the story is open to many interpretations since the text includes two endings.

As a proponent for postcolonial narratology, Gerald Prince (2005, 375) has suggested that it could investigate, for instance, the themes and preoccupations of the old and the new, nostalgia and hope, authentic and fake beginnings and ends, or memory, amnesia, and anamnesis. It might also concentrate on the depiction of time such as datelessness, quasi- or pseudo-chronology, heterochronology, multichronology, simultaneities, continuities and inconsistencies.

We can recognise that in *Montecore* the chronological narration of the events presented in the letter form is broken especially by the end of the novel. Significantly, in a postmodern way, two endings of the story are presented. Indeed, the novel juxtaposes multiple realities, since the narrator

20 'Trots dina protester celebreras du för att ha skrivit en bok på "tvättäkta Rinkebysvenska". Tydligen har du gett liv åt "invandrarens historia" på ett språk som låter som om man "sänker ned en mikrofon" i valfritt invandrarområde. Skrev du inte att din bok handlade om svenskfödd man som bryter sitt språk med intention? Vad hände med din påstådda exploration av "autenticitetstemat"?' (*M* 2006, 39.)
21 'Håll Sverige RENT.' (*M* 2006, 286.)

Jonas suggests to the reader two alternative endings of the story. The first version provides a happy ending of a love story between Abbas and Pernilla. In this positive version, Jonas's father returns to Sweden, and the family lives together happily ever after. This imaginary ending is served as the son's romantic dream. However, in the novel's diegetic reality, emphasis is more on the pessimistic and 'realistic' version, in which the parents are divorced and the father cuts off all contact with his family and leaves Sweden altogether. The alternative scenarios, two endings, presented in the end of *Montecore* particularly underline the constructiveness of the biographic mode, which is emphasised in postmodern fiction. Finally, it refers to the idea of a life-story as open-ended. The uncertain ending also seems to imply the strong involvement of Jonas's imagination in the creation of Abbas's life story.

Similarly, the ending and the prologue refer to Abbas's new heroic life in New York, which seems to remain only as Kadir's boastful fabulation. In the depiction of Abbas's new life, a humorously declarative style is used, where Abbas shuttles between glamorous film stars, rock musicians and powerful politicians on the world stage.

> Via the global world net I have followed your father's goldish success. When he is not photographing, he is establishing close relations to political intellectuals all over the world. He drinks righteously pressed juice with Sting, he brunches with writers like Arundhati Roy, and once a month he playa traditional Scrabble with Noam Chomsky. (*M* 2011, 300–301.)[22]

The hyperbolic description of a world-wide great success of now glamorous Abbas forms an ironic contrast to Abbas's former pathetic everyday efforts to succeed in Swedish society that were deemed to failure. The imaginative portrayal of Abbas as a super hero is contrasted with Kadir's more 'realistic' tones in descriptions of melancholic Abbas as a pornographic photographer in Tunisia. In this light, Abbas's new successful career as an internationally famous art photographer hardly seems probable to the reader.

Why are two endings implemented in the novel? Firstly, it seems that these unsolvable endings can be traced to Khemiri's interest in postmodern literary strategies. Also the epistolary address itself evokes the question of openness and closure (Altman 1983, 144). For instance, Kadir's letters lend themselves to multiple interpretations and demand the interpreter's collaboration in order to be created and completed. As a literary form, the letter narrative imposes the ritual of closing upon the individual correspondents. On the other hand, a letter narrative may leave the end open: a new letter might be received after the closure. The lack of resolution in open-ended novels is often due to an enigmatic silence on the part of one of the letter writers (Altman 1983, 149).

---

22 'Via det globala världsnätet har jag följt din fars guldiska succé. När han inte fotograferar knyter han nära relationer till politiskt intellektuella världen över. Han dricker rättfärdigt pressade joser med Sting, han brunchar med skribenter som Arundhati Roy och en gång i månaden spelar han traditionsenlig alfapet med Noam Chomsky.' (*M* 350.)

Silence can also be conceived as a type of communication and it has been claimed to be one form of postcolonial resistance.[23] In fact, by the end of the novel, Abbas remains silent; he has stopped writing letters to Kadir and has not contacted Jonas either. On the other hand, this kind of ellipsis in the narration, Abbas's silence, may suggest the openness of the novel form; for instance, it may imply Abbas's possible later contact with Jonas or Kadir. The circuit of communication by device of the letters may be rendered as unending, a never closed text, typical in postmodern novels. Moreover, Elleke Boehmer (2006, 237) has claimed that multivoiced migrant novels have given vivid expression to theories of the 'open', indeterminate text, or of transgressive, non-authoritative reading.

To make the reading of *Montecore* more complicated, the identity play between Jonas, Kadir and Abbas becomes more enigmatic towards the end of the novel. Surprisingly, in the end it is suggested that Kadir might be a camouflaged identity of Abbas. At this point, his letters may have been an attempt to contact Jonas secretly. Although the 'real Kadir' also exists since Jonas remembers him working in his father's studio in Stockholm. Evidence for Abbas actually taking Kadir's disguise is confirmed, for example, by the use of language since it is difficult for Jonas to discern between the idiom of the speech patterns allotted to Abbas and to Kadir, whose voices echo each other. In any case, in his final letter, Kadir/Abbas disapproves of Jonas's version of the biography of Abbas and thus the interpretation of Abbas's real life-story is left open.

## *Conclusion*

In the novel, it is illustrated how Abbas must constantly struggle and negotiate his place in Swedish society, which has ignored his talents and finally has become hostile to him. Abbas's life story unfolds gradually and indirectly as a palimpsest persisting beneath Kadir's correspondence with Jonas and Abbas. It is also revealed by flashbacks in Jonas's and Kadir's memories.

The changes of chronology and the changes of places (Sweden, Tunisia) may at first perplex the reader. Similarly, it may be difficult for the reader to follow the hybridised language that the characters use. At any rate, *Montecore* merges in a postmodern and postcolonial way with the epistolary and biographical modes. Thus, this mock-biographic travesty works against the expected generic forms, and employs fragmented structure and episodic narrative typical of postmodern texts. *Montecore* converges postmodern writing, which rejects simple closures of realism. This is also evoked by its play with language and use of linguistic dislocation when presenting Abbas's and Kadir's speech (Swedish hybridised with Arab and French words). Ultimately, it shows how Abbas's life-story cannot easily be trapped and

---

23 See, for instance, Tuomas Huttunen's article 'The Calcutta Chromosome: The Ethics of Silence and Knowledge' in *Seeking the self – Encountering the Other. Diasporic narrative and the ethics of representation*. Ed. by Tuomas Huttunen et al. New Castle upon Tyne: Cambridge Scholars Publishing, 2008.

enclosed. Instead, it is rendered in alternate versions, shaped like a jigsaw puzzle, which the other narrators, Jonas and Kadir, as well as the reader, try to put together. This seems to illuminate that person's selves remain intangible; biographers, as well as writers and readers, can only reconstruct versions of selves.

In its complex form, *Montecore* uses multiple modes of narration as letters in first-person are juxtaposed with short second-person segments and first-person reminiscences. By its taking up three perspectives, Kadir's, Jonas's and Abbas's, *Montecore* can be called as multiperson texts, which moves back and forth between different narrative positions. Brian Richardson (2006, 61–62) has presumed that the use of multiple disparate voices generates a greater degree of dialogism than the application of more conventional literary techniques typically allows. Plural voicing of characters reflects the new innovative literary devices employed especially by postcolonial and ethnic minority writers.

Indeed, when different narrators are weaving the story, this creates a specific kind of pluralism in the narration. When the poignant events of Abbas's life are recounted from many perspectives, this will enlarge the reader's (interpreter's) point of view. Contending with only one perspective, would create a biased and partial biography, whereas many perspectives will create a many-faceted portrait of this unique Tunisian man. We can also note that the use of plural narrators in *Montecore* is not very common in fictional discourse. It is comparable with the new fictional and postcolonial modulations of autobiographic, biographic and epistolary genre.

*Montecore* also enlarges conventional epistolary form by its use of culturally divergent narrators. With its three talking subjects, Abbas, Kadir and Jonas, it could be called a Bakhtinian *polyphonic* novel, which highlights the presence of dialogue. When the Tunisian characters are permitted to speak for themselves, it engages, for example, Swedish or European reader's identification with their otherwise culturally distant position. Moreover, in the history of the epistolary genre, it has been claimed that the epistolary form was especially well suited for the sympathetic communication of feeling (Goldsmith 1986, 97). Indeed, as a narrative technique, epistolary form with its enunciation in the first person may shape a more close sympathetic identification for the Swedish reader, for example, with the Tunisian characters – sympathy that crosses the cultural boundaries.

Bill Ashcroft, Gareth Griffiths and Helen Tiffin (1989, 39; also Ball 2003, 22) claim that on a fundamental level 'all post-colonial literature are cross-cultural because they negotiate a gap between "worlds", a gap in which the simultaneous processes of abrogation and appropriation continually strive to determine their practice. There is a power gap between the majorities and minorities, dominant and dominated. There is a geographical gap, separating different landscapes and climates, and the different cultural and social traditions that arise out of and adapt to those different experiences of place. And there is a language gap, differences in the way of speaking and writing a common language.'

But postcolonial theoreticians and writers have also introduced many kinds of ways to bridge these gaps with their workings of such terms as hybridisation, ambiguity and 'thirdness'. For example, Françoise Lionnet (1989, 3–4) claimed, even as early as the end of 1980s, that the central questions of orality and literacy, speech and writing, truth and hyperbole, transparency and obscurity have become the cornerstone of the cultural aesthetics of many postcolonial writers. *Montecore*, with its versatile literary devices, can also be placed in this kind of postcolonial continuum. Clearly, *Montecore* illustrates that Khemiri is well aware of the dilemmas of contemporary migrant and postcolonial writing. At least, such a prominent theoretician of colonialism such as Frantz Fanon is mentioned in *Montecore*. In addition, some postcolonial writers such as Arundhati Roy, Salman Rushdie and Wole Soyinka are explicitly referred to in the novel. With its themes, use of language and direct references to postcolonial issues, Khemiri's *Montecore* can clearly be placed in the postcolonial frame. The introduction of the points of view of the Tunisian Kadir and Abbas creates in this Swedish novel a unique intercultural and intercontinental perspective that transcends and deconstructs the cultural and linguistic boundaries underlining the force of dialogue in cultural contacts.

# References

Altman, Janet Gurkin 1982: *Epistolarity. Approaches to a Form*. Columbus: Ohio State University Press.
Ashcroft, Bill, Griffiths, Gareth & Tiffin, Helen 1989: *The Empire Writes back. Theory and Practice in Post-Colonial Literature*. London and New York: Routledge.
Ball, John Clement 2003: *Satire & the Postcolonial Novel. V.S. Naipaul, Chinua Achebe, Salman Rushdie*. New York and London: Routledge.
Bhabha, Homi K. 1994: *Location of Culture*. London: Routledge.
Boehmer, Elleke 1995/2005: *Colonial & Postcolonial Literature*. Oxford, New York et al.: Oxford University Press.
Campbell-Hall, Devon 2009: Writing Second-Generation Migrant Identity in Meera Syal's Fiction. *Shared Waters: Soundings in Postcolonial Literatures*. Ed. by Stella Borg Barthet. Amsterdam: Rodopi. 284–300.
Cohn, Dorrit 1999: *The Distinction of Fiction*. Baltimore & London: The Johns Hopkins University Press.
Cortés-Conde, Florencia & Boxer, Diana 2002: Bilingual word-play in literary discourse: the creation of relational identity. *Language and Literature. Journal of the Poetics and Linguistics Association.* Vol 11, Number 2, May. 137–151.
Eakin, Paul John 1999: *How Our Lives Become Stories*. Ithaca and London: Cornell University Press.
Elliott, Bruce S, Gerber, David A. & Sinke, Suzanne M. 2006: Introduction. *Letters across Borders. The Epistolary Practices of International Migrants*. Ed. by Bruce S. Elliott, David A. Gerber & Suzanne M. Sinke. Gordonville, VA: Palgrave, Macmillan. 1–21.
Goldsmith, Elizabeth C. 1986: Authority, Authenticity, and the Publication of Letters by Women. *Writing the Female Voice. Essays on Epistolary Literature*. Ed. by Elizabeth C. Goldsmith. Boston: Northeastern University Press. 46–59.
Goldsmith, Elizabeth C. 1986: Introduction. *Writing the Female Voice. Essays on Epistolary Literature*. Ed. by Elizabeth C. Goldsmith. Boston: Northeastern University Press. vii–xiii.
Khemiri, Jonas 2003: *Ett öga rött*. Stockholm: Norstedts.

Khemiri, Jonas 2006: *Montecore. En unik tiger.* Stockholm: Månpocket.
Khemiri, Jonas 2011: *Montecore. The Silence of the Tiger.* Transl. Rachel Willson-Broyles. New York: Alfred A. Knopf.
Lionnet, Françoise 1989: *Autobiographical Voices. Race, Gender, Self-Portraiture.* Ithaca and London: Cornell University Press.
Lionnet, Françoise 1995: *Postcolonial Representations.* Ithaca, NY: Cornell University Press.
Phelan, James 1996: *Narrative as Rhetoric. Technique, Audiences, Ethics, Ideology.* Ohio: Ohio State University Press.
Prince, Gerald 2005: On Postcolonial Narratology. *A Companion to Narrative Theory.* Ed. by James Phelan. Malden: Blackwell.
Rantonen, Eila 2013: Cultural Hybridity and Humour in Jonas Hassen Khemiri's Montecore. *Le roman migrant au Québec et en Scandinavie. The Migrant Novel in Quebec and Scandinavia. Performativité, conflits signifians et créolisation. Performativity, Meaningful Conflicts and Creolization.* Ed. by Svante Lindberg. Frankfurt am Main et al.: Peter Lang. 141–160.
Richardson, Brian 2006: *Unnatural Voices: extreme narration in modern and contemporary fiction.* Columbus: Ohio State University Press.
Said, Edward 1994: *Culture and Imperialism.* London: Vintage.
Sanae, Tokizane 2008: Letters, Diaspora, and Home in The Color Purple. *Seeking the Self – Encountering the Other. Diasporic Narrative and the Ethics of Representations.* Ed. by Tuomas Huttunen, Kaisa Ilmonen, Janne Korkka & Elina Valovirta. Newcastle: Cambridge Scholars Publishing. 276–290.
Smith, Sidonie and Watson, Julia 2005: The Trouble with Autobiography. *A Companion to Narrative Theory.* Ed. by James Phelan. Malden: Blackwell. 356–371.
Spivak, Gayatri 1987: *In Other Worlds. Essays in Cultural Politics.* London: Routledge.

# List of Contributors

PIRJO AHOKAS (https://orcid.org/0000-0001-6638-4754)
PhD, Professor Emeritus, Comparative Literature, University of Turku, Finland.
Research Areas: African-American literature, Chinese-American literature, Jewish-American literature, gender studies.
Recent Publications: Migrating Multiculturalisms in Zadie Smith's *On Beauty* and Gish Jen's *Mona in the Promised Land*. *Moving Migration: Narrative Transformations in Asian American Literature*. Ed. by Johanna J. Kardux ja Doris Einsedel. Berlin: LIT Verlag, 2010. 161–177
Challenging the Color-Blind American Dream: Transnational Adoption. *A Gesture Life*, *Love Wife* and *Digging to America*. American Studies in Scandinavia 45(1–2) 2013. 109–133.
Värisokea amerikkalainen unelma Selasin *Ghana Must Go* ja Adichien *Americanah* -romaaneissa. *Nainen kulttuurissa, kulttuuri naisessa*. Ed. by Viola Parente-Capková, Heidi Grönstrand, Ritva Hapuli ja Kati Launis. k & h, kulttuurihistoria 13. Turku, 2015. 81–105.

JOHANNA DOMOKOS (https://orcid.org/0000-0001-7586-2463)
PhD, Associate Professor, Institute of Arts Studies and General Humanities. Károli Gáspár University of the Reformed Church, Hungary.
Research Areas: Minority and multilingual literature, Science performance studies.
Recent Publications: *Inger-Mari Aikio. Die Sonne leckt Sahne*. Ed. by Johanna Domokos. Hochroth Bielefeld, 2016. 38 p.
*Maailma kotona. Kohtaamisen opas*. Ed. by Johanna Domokos et al. Varna: Lecti Books Studio, 2016. 288 p.
Prohibiting Translations: Nils-Aslak Valkeapää and the Question of Text- Process-, and Agent-driven Untranslatability. *Critical Multilingualism Studies* 4/1, 2016. 44–55.

SATU GRÖNDAHL (  https://orcid.org/0000-0002-7471-6306)
PhD, Associate Professor, Senior Lecturer, Uppsala University. The Hugo Valentin Center, Sweden.
Research Areas: The cultural politics of minority and migrant literature, trans-national literature, nation building processes and literature, and gender studies.
Recent Publications: Från fångarnas kör till Svinalängorna: Kvinnliga erfarenheter i den interkulturella svenska litteraturen. *Genusvetenskapliga litteraturanalyser.* Red. Åsa Arping & Anna Nordenstam. 2 uppl. Studentlitteratur. Lund Studentlitteratur, 2011. 205–245.
Satu Gröndahl & Eila Rantonen. Romanikirjallisuus perinteiden ja modernin jatkumolla. *Suomen nykykirjallisuus 2: Kirjallinen elämä ja yhteiskunta.* Ed. Mika Hallila, Yrjö Hosiaisluoma, Sanna Karkulehto, Leena Kirstinä, Jussi Ojajärvi. Helsinki: Finnish Literature Society, 2013. 72–75.
Different Directions in Analyzing Migration and Minority Literatures in the Nordic Countries. *Globalization in Literature.* Ed. Per Thomas Andersen. Acta Nordica: Studier i språk- og litteraturvitenskap. Bergen: Fagbokforlaget, 2014. 93–110.

ANNE HEITH (  https://orcid.org/0000-0002-0682-2668)
PhD, Associate professor in Comparative Literature, Department of Culture and Media Studies, Umeå University, Sweden.
Research Areas: migration and literature, postcolonial studies, Sámi and Tornedalian literature, indigenous studies, critical race and whiteness studies, place-making.
Recent Publications: *Laestadius and Laestadianism in the Contested Field of Cultural Heritage: A study of Contemporary Sámi and Tornedalian Texts.* Northern studies monographs. Umeå: Umeå University and the Royal Skyttean Society, 2018. 249 p.
Indigeneity, Cultural Transformations and Rethinking the Nation: Performative Aspects of Sámi Elements in Umeå 2014. Lundgren, Britta & Matiu, Ovidiu (eds.), *Culture and Growth: Magical Companions or Mutually Exclusive Counterparts?* UNEECC Form Volume 7, 2015. Sibiu: Lucian Blaga University of Sibiu Press. 110–126.
Displacement and Regeneration: Minorities, Migration and Postcolonial Literature. Sharmilla Beezmohun (ed.), *Continental Shifts, Shifts in Perception: Black Cultures and Identities in Europe.* Newcastle upon Tyne: Cambridge Scholars Publishing, 2016. 49–71.

KUKKU MELKAS
PhD, Senior lecturer, Finnish Literature, University of Turku, Finland.
Research Areas: feminist theory, nationalism and transnationalism and literary history.
Recent Publications: Melkas, Kukku ja Löytty, Olli: Sekoittuneet äänet. Johanna Holmströmin Asfaltsänglar ja lomittuvat lukemiskontekstit. *Kansallisen katveesta – Suomen kirjallisuuden ylirajaisuudesta.* Toim. Heidi Grönstrand, Ralf Kauranen, Olli Löytty, Kukku Melkas, Hanna-Leena

Nissilä, Mikko Pollari. Helsinki: SKS, 2016. 118–138.
Pollari, Mikko, Nissilä-Hanna-Leena, Melkas, Kukku, Löytty Olli, Kauranen Ralf and Grönstrand, Heidi: National, Transnational and Entangled Literatures: Methodological Considerations Focusing on the Case of Finland. *Rethinking National Literatures and the Literary Canon in Scandinavia*. Ed. by Heidi Grönstrand, Dag Heede, Anne Heith and Ann-Sofie Lönngren. Cambridge: Cambridge Scholars Publishing, 2015. 2–29.
Melkas, Kukku ja Löytty, Olli (eds.): *Toistemme viholliset? Kirjallisuus kohtaa sisällissodan*. Tampere: Vastapaino, 2018. 150 p.

HANNA-LEENA NISSILÄ (https://orcid.org/0000-0003-1457-0277)
PhD, University of Oulu, Finland.
Research Areas: Transnational literature in Finland, Feminist studies.
Recent Publications: *Sanassa maahanmuuttaja on vähän kitkerä jälkimaku. Kirjallisen elämän ylirajaistuminen 2000-luvun alun Suomessa*. Acta Universitatis Ouluensis B Humaniora 136. Oulu: University of Oulu, 2016. 116 p.
Vuotoja kansallisessa säiliössä – muistiinpanoja tutkimusmatkaltani ylirajaiseen kirjallisuudentutkimukseen. *Kansallisen katveesta – Suomen kirjallisuuden ylirajaisuudesta*. Toim. Heidi Grönstrand; Ralf Kauranen, Olli Löytty, Kukku Melkas, Hanna-Leena Nissilä & Mikko Pollari. Helsinki: SKS, 2016. 139–171.
Pollari, Mikko; Nissilä, Hanna-Leena; Melkas, Kukku; Löytty, Olli; Kauranen, Ralf & Grönstrand, Heidi: National, transnational and entangled literatures. *Rethinking National Literatures and the Literary Canon in Scandinavia*. Ed. by Ann-Sofie Lönngren, Heidi Grönstrand, Dag Heede & Anne Heith. Cambridge: Cambridge Scholars Publishing, 2015. 2–29.

EILA RANTONEN (https://orcid.org/0000-0002-1807-4361)
PhLic, Researcher. Comparative Literature. University of Tampere, Finland.
Research Areas: Postcolonial theory, literature and ethics, migration and literature, Nordic minorities, gender studies.
Recent Publications: Cultural Hybridity and Humour in Jonas Hassen Khemiri's Montecore. *Le roman migrant au Québec et en Scandinavie. The Migrant Novel in Quebec and Scandinavia*. Ed. by Svante Lindberg. Frankfurt am Main et al.: Peter Lang, 2013. 141–160.
Rantonen, Eila and Nissilä, Hanna-Leena: Pelottavia muukalaisia ja arkisempia maahanmuuttajia. *Suomen nykykirjallisuus 2*. Toim. Mika Hallila, Yrjö Hosiaisluoma, Sanna Karkulehto, Leena Kirstinä ja Jussi Ojajärvi. Helsinki: Finnish Literature Society, 2013. 76–91.
Litteratur von Immigranten in Finnland. *Invasion Paradies. Lesebuch über die Möglichkeiten, Finne zu Sein*. Ed. Johanna Domokos. Übersetzt von der Gruppe B. Pluralica. 2014. 254–273.

MARTA RONNE (https://orcid.org/0000-0002-2587-0913)
PhD, Literary critic, lecturer and essayist, Uppsala, Sweden. Research Areas: The genre of university novels in Sweden and in Anglo-Saxon literature, women's 20th century Swedish literature, literary critique and migrant literatures.

Recent Publications: Petra Broomans and Marta Ronne (ed.): *In the Vanguard of Cultural Transfer: Cultural Transmitters and Authors in Peripheral Literary Fields* [Studies on Cultural Transfer and Transmission, 2]. Barkhuis: Groningen, 2010. 183 p.

Strangers to Their Mother Tongue. Zenta Mauriņa (1897–1978) and Konstantin Raudive (1909–1974) as German-Speaking Latvian Writers in Exile in Sweden. Broomans, P., Jiresch, E. (eds.), *The Invasion of Books in Peripheral Literary Fields. Transmitting Preferences and Images in Media, Networks and Translations* [Studies on Cultural Transfer and Transmission, 3]. Barkhuis: Groningen, 2011. 182–213.

Gendering Cultural Transfer and Transmission History (together with Petra Broomans). Broomans, P., van Voorst, S. (eds.), *Rethinking Cultural Transfer and Transmission. Reflections and New Perspectives* [Studies on Cultural Transfer and Transmission, 4]. Barkhuis: Groningen, 2012. 117–129.

MARJA SORVARI (https://orcid.org/0000-0002-3311-726X)
PhD, University Lecturer in Russian language, Culture and Translation, University of Eastern Finland (Joensuu).

Research Areas: Contemporary Russian women's writing; autobiographical writing and cultural memory in Russia; Russian women's cultural history; lay accounts of health and wellbeing in post-Soviet Russia; Russian migrant writing in Finland.

Recent Publications: On the Margins and Beyond: Girl Protagonists in Novels by Svetlana Vasilenko, Dina Rubina, and Elena Chizhova. *Russian Review* (2018) 77 2. 279–293.

'To Tell the Truth as I Understand It': Lived Religion, Post-Secularism and Gender in Liudmila Ulitskaia's *Daniel Stein, Interpreter. The Slavonic and East European Review.* Vol. 95, No. 2, April 2017. 252–270.

'On Both Sides': Translingualism, Translation and Border-Crossing in Zinaida Lindén's Takakirves-Tokyo. *Scando-Slavica*, 62, 2, 2016. 141–159.

# Abstract

## Migrants and Literature in Finland and Sweden

Edited by Satu Gröndahl and Eila Rantonen

*Migrants and Literature in Finland and Sweden* presents new comparative perspectives on transnational literary studies. This collection provides a contribution to the production of new narratives of the nation. The focus of the contributions is contemporary fiction relating to experiences of migration. The volume discusses multicultural writing, emerging modes of writing and generic innovations.

When people are in motion, it changes nations, cultures and peoples. The volume explores the ways in which transcultural connections have affected the national self-understanding in the Swedish and Finnish context. It also presents comparative aspects on the reception of literary works and explores the intersectional perspectives of identities including class, gender, ethnicity, 'race' and disability. Further, it also demonstrates the complexity of grouping literatures according to nation and ethnicity.

The case-studies are divided into three chapters: II 'Generational Shifts', III 'Reception and Multicultural Perspectives' and IV 'Writing Migrant Identities'. The migration of Finnish labourers to Sweden is reflected in Satu Gröndahl's and Kukku Melkas's contributions to this volume, the latter also discusses material related to the placing of Finnish war children ('krigsbarn') in Sweden during World War II. Migration between Russia and Finland is discussed by Marja Sorvari, while Johanna Domokos attempts at mapping the Finnish literary field and offering a model for literary analysis. Transformations of the Finnish literary field are also the focus of Hanna-Leena Nissilä's article discussing the reception of novels by a selection of women authors with an im/migrant background.

The African diaspora and the arrival of refugees to Europe from African countries due to wars and political conflicts in the 1970s is the backdrop of Anne Heith's analysis of migration and literature, while Pirjo Ahokas deals with literature related to the experiences of a Korean adoptee in Sweden. Migration from Africa to Sweden also forms the setting of Eila Rantonen's article about a novel by a successful, Swedish author with roots in Tunisia. Exile, gender and disability are central, intertwined themes of Marta Ronne's article, which discusses the work of a Swedish-Latvian author who arrived in Sweden in connection to World War II.

This collection is of particular interest to students and scholars in literary and Nordic studies as well as transnational and migration studies.

# Index of Names

Aase, Berg 84
Abu al Fawz, Yousif 123, 124, 128, 131
Abu-Hanna, Umayya 29, 113, 114, 116, 120–25, 128, 129, 130, 132–133
Aghaee, Mana 23, 24
Ahokas, Pirjo 12, 29
Ahrenberg, Jac 25
Aksionov, Vasili 61
Alakoski, Susanna 26, 28, 38, 41, 43, 48, 49, 50–53, 83–90, 92, 93, 104, 105
Alfonso, Carolin 158
Allwood, Martin 22, 23
Altman, Janet Gurkin 212–218, 220
Amelina, Anna 85, 114–116
Anderson, Benedict 115, 134
Andersson, Lena 49
Anokhina, Anna 59
Anyuru, Johannes 20, 29, 141–162
Appadurai, Arjun 115
Aronson, Asta 190
Arping, Åsa 51
Arwidsson, Adolf Ivar 100
Ashcroft, Bill 18–20, 146, 147, 148, 222
August, Pernilla 84, 87
Autio, Milla 118, 119
Axelsson, Majgull 88

Bachmann-Medick, Doris 109
Bakhtiari, Marjaneh 147
Ball, John 222, 223
Ballard, Roger 152, 162
Bartky, Sandra 192, 201
Baschmakoff, Natalia 63, 77
Beezmohun, Sharmilla 18, 20, 29, 30, 164
Behschnitt, Wolfgang 27, 40, 147
Berman, Gabrielle 148
Benstock, Shari 169

Bhabha, Homi K. 16–20, 30, 57, 58, 77, 98, 144, 153
Björklund, Krister 39
Björkman, Maria 175
Blasim, Hassam 131
Boehmer, Elleke 212, 213, 219, 221
Boije, Ronja 23
Bolay, Karl H. 23
Bourdieu, Pierre 13, 39, 54, 59, 77, 109
Boxer, Diana 205
Brah, Avtar 94
Braziel, Jana Evans 155, 156
Brodsky, Joseph 62
Bunin, Ivan 62
Bus, Heiner 57

Callahan, Cynthia 168
Campbell-Hall, Devon 205, 223
Cheng, Anne Anlin 169, 170, 178, 184
Cohn, Dorrit 208, 209, 223
Conrad, Joseph 208
Cortés-Conde, Florencia 206
Couser, Thomas 191
Crul, Maurice 150

Dausendschön-Gay, Ulrich 108
Davis, Lennard D. 191, 192
Davydova, Olga 61
Delanty, Gerard 149
Deleuze, Gilles 144
Devarenne, Nicole 68
Diehl, Barbro 27
Diktonius, Elmer 26, 119
Doggelito, Dogge 166
Domokos, Johanna 29, 98, 108
Dovlatov, Sergei 62
Duric, Dubranko 168

## Index of Names

Eakin, Paul 206, 207
Edie, James 203
Ekelöf, Maja 44
Ekman, Michel 114
Elliot, Bruce 212
ElRamly, Ranya 29, 99, 101, 105, 106, 113–116, 122–124, 126, 128–130, 132, 133
Eng, David L. 167, 170–174, 176, 178, 179, 181, 183, 184
Epple, Angelika 94
Eriksson, Anneli 23

Faist, Thomas 116
Fanon, Frantz 156, 177, 223
Fares, Josef 166
Felski, Rita 86
Fenton, Steve 142
Fethkes, Margot 190
Figes, Orlando 63
Fischer, Susan Alice 74, 76
Flygt, Torbjörn 50
Foucault, Michel 192
Frank, Søren 17, 18, 30, 94, 115
Franklin, Anna 25
Fraser, Robert 208, 218
Freud, Sigmund 170, 179
Fries, Jonna 84
Furuland, Lars 27, 44, 49

Gates, Henry Louis 175
Gebauer, Mirjam 16, 113, 133, 141, 163
Gentele, Jeanette 90
Gerber, David 212
Gilroy, Paul 29, 143, 147, 148, 158, 162
Gippius, Zinaida 62
Goldsmith, Elizabeth 214, 222, 223
Gondouin, Johanna 171, 172, 185
Gordon, Tuula 91, 96, 130, 134
Griffiths, Gareth 18, 19, 20, 30, 147, 148, 163, 222, 223
Grosz, Elisabeth 190, 191, 193, 194
Grundström, Elina 126
Gröndahl, Satu 12, 15, 25, 28, 40, 44, 50, 84, 88, 89, 90, 93, 107, 114, 121, 123, 166
Grönstrand, Heidi 26, 27, 102, 114, 116, 118, 119, 120
Guattari, Felix 144
Gurr, Andrew 190

Haavikko, Paavo 106
Hagström, Ahn-Za 182
Hakalahti, Nina 105, 123

Hall, Kim Q. 194
Hall, Stuart 18, 29, 49, 57, 58, 98, 143, 147, 149, 157, 158, 175
Hallila, Mika 102
Han, Shinhee 169
Hansen, Julie 57, 68, 71
Harel, Simon 16
Hassan, Mohamed 11, 12, 14
Hegel, G. W. F. 148, 153
Heinämäki-Sepponen, Riina 70
Heith, Anne 7, 12, 14, 15, 18, 19, 20, 29, 142, 147, 149, 153
Henke, Suzette 169
Hetekivi Olsson, Eija 27, 29, 37–39, 42, 43, 49, 50–52, 54, 83–85, 88–90, 93
Hietamies, Heikki 90
Hirvonen, Vuokko 102, 114
Hoggart, Richard 98
Homans, Margret 170, 174, 180
Homer 142
Hosiaisluoma, Yrjö 102
Hotakainen, Kari 104
van Houtum, Henk 143, 144
Huhtala, Liisi 102
Huss, Markus 26
Huttunen, Laura 89, 115
Huttunen, Tuomas 221
Hübinette, Tobias 155, 168, 171, 172, 180, 181
Hypén, Tarja-Liisa 132
Hämäläinen, Timo 15, 118
Härö, Klaus 29, 83, 85, 86, 89, 90, 93

Ierman, Elena 61, 62, 74
Immonen, Kari 61

Jalava, Antti 41, 42, 43, 47–49, 52, 54, 88
Jama, Olavi 114
Jasinskaja-Lahti, Inga 61
Jay, Paul 116, 133
Jensen, Lars 119
Jergn, Mark C. 170, 172, 180, 181
Johansson, Eva 84, 88
Johansson, Kjell 88
Johansson Rissén, Ann-Christine 39, 49
Jokinen, Maijaliisa 41
Juhila, Kirsi 128
Järnefelt, Arvid 104

Kajanto, Anneli 87
Kallifatides, Theodor 23
Kambourelli, Smaro 98
Kaminer, Wladimir 68, 70
Kangasharju, Johanna 53

Kangro, Bernard 24
Karemaa, Outi 61
Karkulehto, Sanna 102
Karlsson, Jimmy 90
Kauhanen, Anna-Liisa 166
Kavén, Pertti 91–92
Kellman, Steven G. 59
Kervinen, Anni 124
Keskinen, Suvi 19
Khemiri, Jonas Hassen 23, 30, 147, 166, 204–223
Kim, Eleana J. 171, 182
Kim, Hoo-ran 168, 169
Kingston, Maxine Hong 178, 207
Kirstinä, Leena 102
Kivimäki, Sanna 52, 85, 92
Klapuri, Tintti 102, 117, 118
Kleberg, Lars 106
Klein, Melanie 170, 173, 176, 183, 184
Kleinert, Inge 103
Knuuttila, Sirkka 94
Koivisto, Päivi 124
Koivunen, Anu 87
Kokot, Waltraud 159
Kol', Liudmila 28, 57, 60, 64, 66, 67, 68, 71
Kolomainen, Robert 71
Kolstø, Pål 64
Komulainen, Katri 91
Kongslien, Ingeborg 28, 122, 128
van Koningsveld, P. S. 154
Kopylova, Polina 60
Koskimies, Rafael 102
Koukoulis, Kostas 25
Kouros, Alexis 131
Kourouma, Ahmadou 157
Krafft, Ulrich 108
Kristeva, Julia 70
Kukkola, Liisa 71, 72
Kurki, Tuulikki 114
Kurkijärvi, Riitta 122
Kurkinen, Vesa 60
Kylänpää, Riitta 128
Könönen, Maija 57

Lacatus, Corinna 166, 167, 175, 176, 177
Lagus, Gabriel 102
Lardot, Raisa 104
Lassila, Pertti 102
Latysheva, Inna 28, 57, 73–76
Laukkonen, Taisija 64
Launis, Kati 69
Lehtimäki, Riitta 119, 121
Lehtola, Veli-Pekka 103

Lehtolainen, Leena 105
Lehtonen, Mikko 119, 132
Leinonen, Marja 60, 74
Leitzinger, Antero 101
Lempiäinen, Kirsti 91
Lennon, John 39, 40
Leppänen, Katarina 130
Leppäniemi, Henriikka 42, 43, 53
Leydesdorff, Selma 84, 89, 90
Lidman, Sara 44
Liebkind, Karmela 60, 61
Lindberg, Svante 16
Lindén, Zinaida 15, 16, 28, 29, 57, 68–71, 98, 113, 114, 116–119, 121–124, 127, 128, 130, 132, 133
Linder, Marie 68
Linderborg, Åsa 50, 92
Linders, F. J. 19
Lindholm, Arto 122, 126
Lindström, Sofia 168, 181
Lionnet, Françoise 223
Littorin, Jens 50
Loftsdóttir, Kristin 19
Lo-Johansson, Ivar 86
Lundberg, Svante 156
Lundborg, Herman 19
Lundqvist, Maria 90
Lundström, Stig 21
Lyytikäinen, Pirjo 126
Lång, Helmer 23
Löytty, Olli 26, 59, 89, 102, 115, 127, 129, 130

Magga-Kumpulainen, Rita 99
Magga-Miettunen, Siiri 104
Majander, Antti 127
Makine, Andreï 68
Maliniemi Lindbach, Kaisa 114
Malmio, Kristina 26, 114, 119, 120
Markusson Winkvist, Hanna 197
Martinson, Moa 86, 87
Massey, Doreen 57
Matinlompolo, Martta 42, 46–49
Matthis, Moa 15
Mauriņa, Zenta 23, 29, 30, 187–203
May, Stephen 142
McCall, Leslie 116
McEachrane, Michael 142
Melkas, Kukku 12, 29
Mercer, Kobena 141
Merleau-Ponty, Maurice 191, 193–194
Merolla, Daniella 16, 19, 153
Mikkonen, Kai 25, 102, 123
Moisio, Mikki 128, 129

233

Montesquieu 217
Moster, Stefan 101
Motturi, Aleksander 142
Månsson, Anna 153
Mäkelä, Matti 71
Mäkikalli, Aino 70
Mäkinen, Esa 127

Nabokov, Vladimir 62
Najmi, Samina 175
Nash, Jürgen 23
Neimala, Kaisa 86
Nevalainen, Pekka 60, 63
Niemi, Riitta 53
Nilsson, Magnus 15, 26, 37–39, 40, 51, 88, 100, 105
Nissilä, Hanna-Leena 12, 25, 26, 29, 89, 102, 105, 113, 122, 123, 124, 126
Ntibanyitesha, Sakina 157
Nuolijärvi, Pirkko 126
Nuotio, Eppu 105
Nõu, Helga 24, 25
Näslund, Mia 84

Ojajärvi, Jussi 102
Okpewho, Isidore 156, 157
Oksanen, Sofi 101
Olsson, Anders 16, 190
Olsson, Hagar 106
Omi, Michael 175
Onkeli, Kreetta 87
Orehovs, Ivars 187, 190, 201, 202
Ortiz, Ferdinand 98
Ouditt, Sharon 190, 195

Paavola, Elisa 122
Pachmuss, Temira 60, 62, 63
Palm, Göran 44, 161
Papadopoulos, Dimitris 144
Paradies, Yin 149
Parente-Čapková, Viola 102, 114
Parvikko, Tuija 125
Patrakova, Inna 28, 57, 73, 75, 76
Pelvo, Martti 114
Pere-Antikainen, Gyöngyi 129
Persman, Peter 182
Pertseva, Tatiana 60
Perttu, Arvi 11, 12, 13, 14, 28, 57, 71–73, 77, 128, 131
Petäjä, Jukka 125
Piety, M. G. 142
Polén, Fredrik 102
Pollari, Mikko 17, 114, 162
Ponzanesi, Sandra 16, 19, 153

Pratt, Mary Louise 17, 58
Pred, Allan 184
Prince, Gerald 216, 219
Protasova, Ekaterina 60
Pynnönen, Marja-Liisa 40, 41, 114
Pyykkönen, Miikka 58, 61, 101, 102

Radhakrishnan, R. 58
Rantonen, Eila 12, 18, 25, 26, 30, 52, 69, 73, 85, 89, 92, 102, 113, 114, 124
Rastas, Anna 26
Ratinen, Suvi 122, 123
Reckwitz, Andreas 107
Reinans, Sven Alur 20
Rezvan, Morteza 25
Rezvani, Reza 25
Richardson, Brian 222
Riekko, Iida 125
Riley, Joan 74
Rimmon-Kenan, Shlomith 146
Robinson, Douglas 58
Rojola, Lea 102, 124
Ronne, Marta 12, 29, 30, 189, 197, 198, 200, 201
Ropponen, Ville 128
Rosendahl Thomsen, Mats 133
Rossi, Oscar 83
Rossiello, Leonardo 25
Roth, Hans-Ingvar 175, 176
Roy, Arundhati 220, 223
Rumford, Chris 149
Runblom, Harald 15, 21
Rushdie, Salman 223
Rystad, Göran 156

Saber, Rafik 25
Sachs, Nelly 23
Sahlberg, Asko 104, 105
Said, Edward 61, 190, 195, 199, 201, 208
Said, Sami 14, 142
Saisio, Pirkko 125, 126
Salih, Tayeb 208
Salmela, Alexandra 29, 113–115, 117, 120–123, 125, 127–130, 132, 133
Samuelsson, Tony 50
Sanae, Tokizane 213
Santarelli, Christopher 142
Sapienza, Filipp 64
Saukkonen, Pasi 101, 102
Savolainen, Matti 8, 19, 114
Schatz, Roman 98, 101, 104, 107–109, 127, 131
Schepp, Otto 190
Schneider, Gertrude 198, 199

Schneider, Jens 150
Schramm, Moritz 129
Schulze-Engler, Frank 11
Schwartz Lausten, Pia 16
Seyhan, Azade 18, 94, 95, 115, 119, 120, 126
Shadid, W. A. R. 154
Shakely, Farhad 25
Sharma, Leena 123
Shenshin, Veronica 60, 64
Sigg, Isa 189
Sinke, Suzanne 212
Sinkkonen, Lassi 87
Smith, Zadie 124
Snellman, Anja 105
Sofronieva, Tzveta 103
Solzhenitsyn, Aleksandr 62
Sonnevi, Göran 142, 152, 161
Sorvari, Marja 12, 26, 28, 70, 71, 229
Soyinka, Wole 223
Spiegelman, Art 207
Spivak, Gayatri Chakravorty 19, 98, 155, 207, 213
Srikanth, Rajini 175
Strelka, Joseph P. 190
Struve, Gleb 62
Strömberg, Gabriella 27
Ståhlberg, Sabira 104
Suhonen, Daniel 89
Svanberg, Ingvar 15, 21
Svedjedal, Johan 27, 44, 46, 49
Szigeti, László 104, 105, 107
Södergran, Edith 106, 119

Tabori, Paul 190, 195
Tamm, Maare 190
Tarkiainen, Viljo 102
Tayfun, Mehmed 24
Tervo, Jari 104, 105
Thomas, Carol 192, 194
Tidigs, Julia 26, 27, 114
Tiffin, Helen 18, 20, 26, 147, 148, 222
Tikkanen, Henrik 119
Tikkanen Rósza, Anneli 38
Topelius, Zacharias 100, 104, 106
Trenka, Jane Jeong 182
Trotzig, Astrid 14, 16, 29, 166–186
Tsvetaeva, Marina 62
Tul'chinskii, Grigorii 66
Tölöyan, Kachig 159

Ullgren, Malin 37, 39

Valenius, Johanna 91, 130
Valkeapää, Nils-Aslak 98
Vallenius, Erkki 40, 41, 45, 84
Varpio, Yrjö 101, 102
Vänttinen, Pekka 126
Vesala, Tiina 61
Vest, Jovnna-Ande 98
Vickroy, Laurie 169
Vihavainen, Timo 60, 61
Viinikka-Kallinen, Anitta 114
Vikman, Kirsi 90
Vilhuinen, Kaisa 38
Virkkunen, Juha 71
Vironen Vääriskoski, Orvokki 103

Waarala, Hannu 71
Waern, Carina 169
Waltari, Mika 43
Walters, Wendy W. 150
Wanner, Adrian 68, 70, 74
Warfvinge, Katarina 24
Waugh, Patricia 113
Weiss, Alexander 23
Weiss, Peter 26
Welsapar, Ak 25
Wendelius, Lars 14, 44
Wendell, Susan 191, 192, 194
Wenger, Leiva 147
Whitehead, Anne 183
Widmalm, Sven 175
Wierlacher, Alois 98
Wilhelmsson, Putte 124
Winant, Howard 175
Wrede, Johan 114
Wright, Michelle M. 148, 149, 153, 162
Wright, Richard 150

Yegenoglu, Meyda 149
Yildiz, Yasemin 26, 119, 121, 128
Ylitalo, Hannu 41, 42, 43–50, 52, 54
Ylitalo, Silja 129
Yuval-Davies, Nira 91, 130, 151

Zagar, Monika 184
Zavialov, Sergei 60
Zilliacus, Clas 114
Zimmerman, Peter 98

Özdamar, Evine Sevgi 49

## Studia Fennica Ethnologica

**Memories of My Town**
*The Identities of Town Dwellers and Their Places in Three Finnish Towns*
Edited by Anna-Maria Åström, Pirjo Korkiakangas & Pia Olsson
Studia Fennica Ethnologica 8
2004

**Passages Westward**
Edited by Maria Lähteenmäki & Hanna Snellman
Studia Fennica Ethnologica 9
2006

**Defining Self**
*Essays on emergent identities in Russia Seventeenth to Nineteenth Centuries*
Edited by Michael Branch
Studia Fennica Ethnologica 10
2009

**Touching Things**
*Ethnological Aspects of Modern Material Culture*
Edited by Pirjo Korkiakangas, Tiina-Riitta Lappi & Heli Niskanen
Studia Fennica Ethnologica 11
2008

**Gendered Rural Spaces**
Edited by Pia Olsson & Helena Ruotsala
Studia Fennica Ethnologica 12
2009

Laura Stark
**The Limits of Patriarchy**
*How Female Networks of Pilfering and Gossip Sparked the First Debates on Rural Gender Rights in the 19th-century Finnish-Language Press*
Studia Fennica Ethnologica 13
2011

**Where is the Field?**
*The Experience of Migration Viewed through the Prism of Ethnographic Fieldwork*
Edited by Laura Hirvi & Hanna Snellman
Studia Fennica Ethnologica 14
2012

Laura Hirvi
**Identities in Practice**
*A Trans-Atlantic Ethnography of Sikh Immigrants in Finland and in California*
Studia Fennica Ethnologica 15
2013

Eerika Koskinen-Koivisto
**Her Own Worth**
*Negotiations of Subjectivity in the Life Narrative of a Female Labourer*
Studia Fennica Ethnologica 16
2014

## Studia Fennica Folkloristica

Venla Sykäri
**Words as Events**
*Cretan Mantinádes in Performance and Composition*
Studia Fennica Folkloristica 18
2011

**Hidden Rituals and Public Performances**
*Traditions and Belonging among the Post-Soviet Khanty, Komi and Udmurts*
Edited by Anna-Leena Siikala & Oleg Ulyashev
Studia Fennica Folkloristica 19
2011

**Mythic Discourses**
*Studies in Uralic Traditions*
Edited by Frog, Anna-Leena Siikala & Eila Stepanova
Studia Fennica Folkloristica 20
2012

Cornelius Hasselblatt
**Kalevipoeg Studies**
*The Creation and Reception of an Epic*
Studia Fennica Folkloristica 21
2016

**Genre – Text – Interpretation**
*Multidisciplinary Perspectives on Folklore and Beyond*
Edited by Kaarina Koski, Frog & Ulla Savolainen
Studia Fennica Folkloristica 22
2016

**Storied and Supernatural Places**
*Studies in Spatial and Social Dimensions of Folklore and Sagas*
Edited by Ülo Valk & Daniel Sävborg
Studia Fennica Folkloristica 23
2018

**Oral Tradition and Book Culture**
Edited by Pertti Anttonen, Cecilia af Forselles and Kirsti Salmi-Niklander
Studia Fennica Folkloristica 24
2018

## Studia Fennica Historica

**Modernisation in Russia since 1900**
Edited by Markku Kangaspuro & Jeremy Smith
Studia Fennica Historica 12
2006

Seija-Riitta Laakso
**Across the Oceans**
*Development of Overseas Business Information Transmission 1815–1875*
Studia Fennica Historica 13
2007

**Industry and Modernism**
*Companies, Architecture and Identity in the Nordic and Baltic Countries during the High-Industrial Period*
Edited by Anja Kervanto Nevanlinna
Studia Fennica Historica 14
2007

Charlotta Wolff
**Noble conceptions of politics in eighteenth-century Sweden (ca 1740–1790)**
Studia Fennica Historica 15
2008

**Sport, Recreation and Green Space in the European City**
Edited by Peter Clark, Marjaana Niemi & Jari Niemelä
Studia Fennica Historica 16
2009

**Rhetorics of Nordic Democracy**
Edited by Jussi Kurunmäki & Johan Strang
Studia Fennica Historica 17
2010

**Fibula, Fabula, Fact**
*The Viking Age in Finland*
Edited by Joonas Ahola & Frog with Clive Tolley
Studia Fennica Historica 18
2014

**Novels, Histories, Novel Nations**
*Historical Fiction and Cultural Memory in Finland and Estonia*
Edited by Linda Kaljundi, Eneken Laanes & Ilona Pikkanen
Studia Fennica Historica 19
2015

Jukka Gronow & Sergey Zhuravlev
**Fashion Meets Socialism**
*Fashion industry in the Soviet Union after the Second World War*
Studia Fennica Historica 20
2015

Sofia Kotilainen
**Literacy Skills as Local Intangible Capital**
*The History of a Rural Lending Library c. 1860–1920*
Studia Fennica Historica 21
2016

**Continued Violence and Troublesome Pasts**
*Post-war Europe between the Victors after the Second World War*
Edited by Ville Kivimäki and Petri Karonen
Studia Fennica Historica 22
2017

**Personal Agency at the Swedish Age of Greatness 1560-1720**
Edited by Petri Karonen & Marko Hakanen
Studia Fennica Historica 23
2017

Pasi Ihalainen
**The Springs of Democracy**
*National and Transnational Debates on Constitutional Reform in the British, German, Swedish and Finnish Parliaments, 1917–19*
Studia Fennica Historica 24
2017

## Studia Fennica Anthropologica

**On Foreign Ground**
*Moving between Countries and Categories*
Edited by Marie-Louise Karttunen & Minna Ruckenstein
Studia Fennica Anthropologica 1
2007

**Beyond the Horizon**
*Essays on Myth, History, Travel and Society*
Edited by Clifford Sather & Timo Kaartinen
Studia Fennica Anthropologica 2
2008

Timo Kallinen
**Divine Rulers in a Secular State**
Studia Fennica Anthropologica 3
2016

## Studia Fennica Linguistica

**Minimal reference**
*The use of pronouns in Finnish and Estonian discourse*
Edited by Ritva Laury
Studia Fennica Linguistica 12
2005

Antti Leino
**On Toponymic Constructions as an Alternative to Naming Patterns in Describing Finnish Lake Names**
Studia Fennica Linguistica 13
2007

**Talk in interaction**
*Comparative dimensions*
Edited by Markku Haakana, Minna Laakso & Jan Lindström
Studia Fennica Linguistica 14
2009

**Planning a new standard language**
*Finnic minority languages meet the new millennium*
Edited by Helena Sulkala & Harri Mantila
Studia Fennica Linguistica 15
2010

Lotta Weckström
**Representations of Finnishness in Sweden**
Studia Fennica Linguistica 16
2011

Terhi Ainiala, Minna Saarelma & Paula Sjöblom
**Names in Focus**
*An Introduction to Finnish Onomastics*
Studia Fennica Linguistica 17
2012

**Registers of Communication**
Edited by Asif Agha & Frog
Studia Fennica Linguistica 18
2015

Kaisa Häkkinen
**Spreading the Written Word**
*Mikael Agricola and the Birth of Literary Finnish*
Studia Fennica Linguistica 19
2015

**Linking Clauses and Actions in Social Interaction**
Edited by Ritva Laury, Marja Etelämäki, Elizabeth Couper-Kuhlen
Studia Fennica Linquistica 20
2017

**On the Border of Language and Dialect**
Edited by Marjatta Palander, Helka Riionheimo & Vesa Koivisto
Studia Fennica Linquistica 21
2018

## Studia Fennica Litteraria

**The Emergence of Finnish Book and Reading Culture in the 1700s**
Edited by Cecilia af Forselles & Tuija Laine
Studia Fennica Litteraria 5
2011

**Nodes of Contemporary Finnish Literature**
Edited by Leena Kirstinä
Studia Fennica Litteraria 6
2012

**White Field, Black Seeds**
*Nordic Literacy Practices in the Long Nineteenth Century*
Edited by Anna Kuismin & M. J. Driscoll
Studia Fennica Litteraria 7
2013

Lieven Ameel
**Helsinki in Early Twentieth-Century Literature**
*Urban Experiences in Finnish Prose Fiction 1890–1940*
Studia Fennica Litteraria 8
2014

**Novel Districts**
*Critical Readings of Monika Fagerholm*
Edited by Kristina Malmio & Mia Österlund
Studia Fennica Litteraria 9
2016

Elise Nykänen
**Mysterious Minds**
*The Making of Private and Collective Consciousness in Marja-Liisa Vartio's Novels*
Studia Fennica Litteraria 10
2017

**Migrants and Literature in Finland and Sweden**
Edited by Satu Gröndahl & Eila Rantonen
Studia Fennica Litteraria 11
2018

www.ingramcontent.com/pod-product-compliance
Lightning Source LLC
Chambersburg PA
CBHW080803300426
44114CB00020B/2816